COMPUTER SCIENCE with PYTHON
for CBSE Class XII

Reema Thareja
Assistant Professor
Department of Computer Science
Shyama Prasad Mukherji College
University of Delhi

All rights reserved. No part of this book may be modified, reproduced or utilised in any form, or by any means, electronic or mechanical, including photocopying, recording or by any information storage and retrieval system, in any form of binding or cover other than in which it is published, without permission in writing from the publisher.

COMPUTER SCIENCE WITH PYTHON FOR CBSE CLASS XII

UNIVERSITIES PRESS (INDIA) PRIVATE LIMITED

Registered Office
3-6-747/1/A & 3-6-754/1, Himayatnagar, Hyderabad 500 029, Telangana, India
info@universitiespress.com; www.universitiespress.com

Distributed by
Orient Blackswan Private Limited

Registered Office
3-6-752 Himayatnagar, Hyderabad 500 029 Telangana, India

Other Offices
Bengaluru, Chennai, Guwahati, Hyderabad, Kolkata,
Mumbai, New Delhi, Noida, Patna, Visakhapatnam

© Universities Press (India) Private Limited 2022

ISBN 978-93-89211-91-7

Cover and book design:
© Universities Press (India) Private Limited 2022

Typeset in Adobe Garamond Pro 10.5 points *by*
Cameo Corporate Services Limited, Coimbatore

Printed in India by
B.B. Press, Noida.

Published by
Universities Press (India) Private Limited
3-6-747/1/A & 3-6-754/1, Himayatnagar, Hyderabad 500 029, Telangana, India

Disclaimer
Care has been taken to confirm the accuracy of the information presented in this book. The author and the publisher, however, cannot accept any responsibility for errors or omissions or for consequences from the application of the information in this book, and make no warranty, express or implied, with respect to its contents. This textbook does not constitute a standard, specification or regulation. The trademarks or manufacturers' names appear/are used in this book only because they are considered essential to the object of subject discussion and do not necessarily constitute endorsement of the product/standard by the author or publisher. All products and company names are trademarks™ or registered® trademarks of their respective holders. Use of them does not imply any affiliation with or endorsement by them.

*I dedicate this book to my family and my uncle Mr B L Theraja,
who is a well-known author himself*

Contents

Preface   *xvii*
About the Author   *xix*

Chapter 1: Python Revisited — 1

1.1	Introduction	1
1.2	Python Tokens	2
1.3	Literal Constants	3
	1.3.1 Numbers	3
	1.3.2 Strings	5
1.4	Type Conversion	9
1.5	Variables and Indentifiers	11
1.6	Creating Variables	11
1.7	Data Types of Identifiers	12
	1.7.1 Assigning or Initializing Values to Variables	12
	1.7.2 Multiple Assignments	14
	1.7.3 Data Type Boolean	15
1.8	Input Operation	16
1.9	Comments	17
	1.9.1 Multi-line Comments	17
1.10	Reserved Words	18
1.11	Indentation	18
1.12	Operators and Expressions	18
	1.12.1 Arithmetic Operators	19
	1.12.2 Comparison Operators	20
	1.12.3 Assignment and In-place or Shortcut Operators	20
	1.12.4 Unary Operators	21
	1.12.5 Bitwise Operators	21
	1.12.6 Shift Operators	22
	1.12.7 Logical Operators	23
	1.12.8 Membership Operators	23
	1.12.9 Identity Operators	24
	1.12.10 Operators Precedence and Associativity	25

	1.13	Expressions in Python	26

Key Terms | Chapter Highlights | Review Questions | Programming Exercises | Fill in the Blanks | State True or False | Multiple Choice Questions | Give the Output | Find the Error | Answers

Chapter 2: Decision Control Statements — 41

2.1	Introduction	41
2.2	Selection/Conditional Branching Statements	42
	2.2.1 `if` Statement	42
	2.2.2 `if-else` Statement	43
	2.2.3 Nested `if` Statements	45
	2.2.4 `if-elif-else` Statement	45
2.3	Iterative Statements	47
	2.3.1 `While` Loop	47
	2.3.2 `for` Loop	48
2.4	The `range()` Function	49
2.5	Selecting an Appropriate Loop	50
2.6	Nested Loops	51
2.7	The `break` Statement	52
2.8	The `continue` Statement	52
2.9	The `pass` Statement	53
2.10	The `else` Statement Used with Loops	54

Key Terms | Chapter Highlights | Review Questions | Programming Exercises | Fill in the Blanks | State True or False | Multiple Choice Questions | Give the Output | Find the Error | Answers

Chapter 3: Strings and Lists in Python — 69

3.1	Introduction	69
3.2	String Indexing	69
3.3	Finding the Number of Characters in a String	69
3.4	Traversing a String	70
3.5	Concatenating, Appending and Multiplying Strings	72
3.6	The `str()` Function	73
3.7	Strings are Immutable	74
3.8	String Formatting Operator	74
3.9	The `format()` Function	76
3.10	Built-in String Methods and Functions	76
3.11	Comparing Strings	80
3.12	`ord()` and `chr()` Functions	80
3.13	`in` and `not in` Operators	81

3.14	Lists		81
3.15	Accessing Values in Lists		82
3.16	The `eval()` Function		83
3.17	Updating Values in Lists		83
3.18	Relational Operations on Lists		85
3.19	Nested Lists		85
3.20	List Aliasing and Cloning		86
3.21	Deleting Elements		87
3.22	Deep Copies and Shallow Copies in Python		87
3.23	Basic List Operations		88
3.24	List Methods		89

Key Terms | Chapter Highlights | Review Questions | Programming Exercises | Fill in the Blanks | State True or False | Multiple Choice Questions | Give the Output | Find the Error | Answers

Chapter 4: Tuple and Dictionary in Python — 109

4.1	Tuple		109
4.2	Creating Tuple		109
4.3	Utility of Tuples		111
4.4	Accessing Values in a Tuple		111
4.5	Updating Tuple		112
4.6	Deleting Elements in a Tuple		113
4.7	Joining Tuples		113
4.8	Unpacking Tuples		114
4.9	Basic Tuple Operations		114
4.10	Tuple Assignment		115
4.11	Accessing Using Index		116
4.12	Tuples for Returning Multiple Values		117
4.13	Nested Tuples		117
4.14	The `count()` Method		118
4.15	The `zip()` Function		118
4.16	Advantages of Tuple Over List		120
4.17	Dictionaries		120
4.18	Creating a Dictionary		121
	4.18.1	Creating a Dictionary Using `dict()` Method	121
4.19	Accessing Values in a Dictionary		122
4.20	Adding an Item in a Dictionary		123
4.21	Modifying an Item in a Dictionary		123
4.22	Deleting Items		123
	4.22.1	The `pop()` Method	124

	4.23	Traversing a Dictionary	125
	4.24	Nested Dictionaries	126
	4.25	The `copy()` Method	126
	4.26	Built-in Dictionary Functions and Methods	127
	4.27	Difference Between a List and a Dictionary	128

Key Terms | Chapter Highlights | Review Questions | Programming Exercises | Fill in the Blanks | State True or False | Multiple Choice Questions | Give the Output | Find the Error | Answers

Chapter 5: Functions and Modules — 141

5.1	Function		141
	5.1.1	Need for Functions	142
5.2	Function Declaration and Function Definition		142
5.3	Function Definition		143
5.4	Function Call		144
5.5	Function Parameters		144
5.6	Parameter Passing – Mutable/Immutable Properties		146
5.7	Variable Scope and Lifetime		147
	5.7.1	Local and Global Variables	147
	5.7.2	Using the Global Statement	148
	5.7.3	Resolution of Names	150
5.8	The `return` Statement		151
5.9	Types of Function Parameters		152
	5.9.1	Required Arguments	152
	5.9.2	Keyword Arguments	153
	5.9.3	Default Arguments	154
	5.9.4	Variable-length Arguments	155
5.10	Passing Strings, Lists, Tuples, Dictionaries to Functions		156
5.11	Documentation Strings		157
5.12	Good Programming Practices		158
5.13	Function Redefinition		158
5.14	Modules		159
	5.14.1	Module Loading and Execution	159
	5.14.2	The `from...import` Statement	160
	5.14.3	Name of Module	161
	5.14.4	Making Your Own Modules	161
	5.14.5	Python Math Module	162

Programmer's Zone — 164

Key Terms | Chapter Highlights | Review Questions | Programming Exercises | Fill in the Blanks | State True or False | Multiple Choice Questions | Give the Output | Find the Error | Answers

Chapter 6:	File Handling		181
6.1	Introduction		181
6.2	File Path		181
	6.2.1	Relative Path and Absolute Path	182
6.3	Types of Files		182
	6.3.1	ASCII Text Files	182
	6.3.2	Binary Files	183
6.4	Opening and Closing Files		183
	6.4.1	The `open()` Function	183
	6.4.2	The File Object Attributes	185
	6.4.3	The `close()` Method	185
6.5	Reading and Writing Files		185
	6.5.1	`write()` and `writelines()` Methods	186
	6.5.2	`append()` Method	186
	6.5.3	The `read()` and `readline()` Methods	186
	6.5.4	Opening Files Using `with` Keyword	188
	6.5.5	Splitting Words	189
	6.5.6	Some Other Useful File Methods	189
6.6	File Positions		190
Programmer's Zone			*190*
6.7	Renaming and Deleting Files		191
Programmer's Zone			*192*
6.8	Comma Separated Values (CSV)		194
	6.8.1	Difference Between Excel vs. CSV	194
6.9	Working with CSV Files		195
	6.9.1	Reading CSV Files with CSV	195
	6.9.2	Optional Python CSV Reader Parameters	195
	6.9.3	Reading CSV Files into a Dictionary with CSV	195
	6.9.4	Writing CSV Files with CSV	196
	6.9.5	Writing CSV File from a Dictionary with CSV	196
6.10	Pickle Module		197
	6.10.1	Pickle Exceptions	198
	6.10.2	Advantages of Picking	198
	6.10.3	Disadvantages of Pickling	198

Key Terms | Chapter Highlights | Review Questions | Programming Exercises | Fill in the Blanks | State True or False | Multiple Choice Questions | Fill in the Blanks and Identify the Usage of the Lines | Give the Output | Find the Error | Answers

Chapter 7: Rescursive Functions and Data Structures — 205

- 7.1 Recursive Functions — 205
  - 7.1.1 Greatest Common Divisor — 207
  - 7.1.2 Finding Exponents — 207
  - 7.1.3 The Fibonacci Series — 208
  - 7.1.4 Recursion vs. Iteration — 209
- 7.2 Algorithm Efficiency — 210
- 7.3 Big-O Notation — 211
  - 7.3.1 Categories of Algorithms — 212
- 7.4 Data Structures — 213
  - 7.4.1 Abstract Data Type and Data Structures — 213
- 7.5 Classification of Data Structures — 213
  - 7.5.1 Primitive and Non-primitive Data Structures — 213
  - 7.5.2 Linear and Non-linear Structures — 214
- 7.6 Using Lists as Stack — 214
- 7.7 Using Lists as Queues — 215

Key Terms | Chapter Highlights | Review Questions | Programming Exercises | Fill in the Blanks | State True or False | Multiple Choice Questions | Give the Output | Find the Error | Answers

Chapter 8: Computer Networks — 221

- 8.1 Introduction — 221
  - 8.1.1 Limitations of Computer Network — 222
- 8.2 History of Internet — 222
- 8.3 The Internet — 222
- 8.4 Data Switching — 223
  - 8.4.1 Circuit Switching — 223
  - 8.4.2 Packet Switching — 223
- 8.5 Concept of Channel — 225
- 8.6 Data Transmission Mode of Channels — 225
  - 8.6.1 Simplex, Half-duplex, and Full-duplex Connections — 225
- 8.7 Bandwidth — 226
- 8.8 Wired Communication Media — 227
  - 8.8.1 Twisted Pair Cable — 227
  - 8.8.2 Coaxial Cable — 228
  - 8.8.3 Fibre-optic Cable — 229
- 8.9 Wireless and Satellite Communication — 230
- 8.10 Wireless or Wi-Fi Network — 230
  - 8.10.1 Advantages — 231
  - 8.10.2 Disadvantages — 231

8.11	Network Devices		231
	8.11.1	MODEM (MOdulator DEModulator)	231
	8.11.2	RJ45 Connector	232
	8.11.3	Network Interface Card or the Ethernet Card	233
	8.11.4	Switch	233
	8.11.5	Hub	234
	8.11.6	Router	235
	8.11.7	Gateway	235
	8.11.8	Wi-Fi Card	236
8.12	Network Topology		237
	8.12.1	Bus Topology	237
	8.12.2	Star Topology	237
	8.12.3	Ring Topology	238
	8.12.4	Mesh Topology	238
	8.12.5	Tree Topology	239
	8.12.6	Hybrid Topology	239
8.13	Types of Network		239
	8.13.1	LAN – Local Area Network	240
	8.13.2	WAN – Wide Area Network	240
	8.13.3	MAN – Metropolitan Area Network	241
	8.13.4	CAN – Campus Area Network or Corporate Area Network	242
	8.13.5	PAN – Personal Area Network	242
8.14	Transmission Control Protocol		242
8.15	Re-transmission and Rate Modulation		243
8.16	Internet Protocol		244
8.17	File Transfer Protocol		245
	8.17.1	How to Use FTP	245
8.18	Point-to-Point Protocol (PPP)		246
	8.18.1	Components of PPP	246
8.19	HTTP (Hypertext Transfer Protocol)		247
8.20	Simple Mail Transfer Protocol (SMTP)		247
	8.20.1	Working of SMTP	248
8.21	Post Office Protocol 3 (POP3)		248
8.22	Terminal Emulation		249
	8.22.1	How to Use Telnet	250
8.23	Wireless Access Point (WAP)		250
8.24	Worldwide Interoperability for Microwave Access (WiMAX)		251
8.25	Voice Over Internet Protocol (VoIP)		251
	8.25.1	How VoIP / Internet Voice Works	251

8.26	Malware		253
	8.26.1	VIRUS (Vital Information Resources Under Seige)	253
	8.26.2	Worms	256
	8.26.3	Trojan Horse	256
	8.26.4	Adware	257
	8.26.5	Spyware	257
	8.26.6	Keyloggers	258
	8.26.7	Ransomware	258
	8.26.8	Sweeper Attacks	258
	8.26.9	Spamming	258
8.27	HTTP Cookie		259
	8.27.1	Security Concerns	260
	8.27.2	Removing Cookies	260
8.28	Firewall		260
	8.28.1	Types of Firewalls	261
8.29	HTTPs		262
	8.29.1	HTTP vs. HTTPs	263
8.30	Information Technology Act 2000		263
	8.30.1	Salient Features of IT Act	263
8.31	Cybercrime		264
	8.31.1	Common Examples of Cybercrime	264
8.32	Intellectual Property Rights (IPR)		267
8.33	Hacking		269
8.34	World Wide Web		271
8.35	Hypertext Markup Language		272
8.36	Extensible Markup Language		272
8.37	Domain Name System		274
8.38	Uniform Resource Locator or Universal Resource Locator		275
8.39	Web Page		276
8.40	Website		277
	8.40.1	Static and Dynamic Websites	277
8.41	Web Servers		278
8.42	Web Hosting		279
	8.42.1	Types of Web Hosting Services	279
8.43	Web Scripting		281
	8.43.1	Client Scripting	282
	8.43.2	Server Scripting	282
8.44	Web 2.0		283

8.45		Electronic Commerce	285
8.46		E-Payments	286
	8.46.1	Cards	286
	8.46.2	E-money	287
	8.46.3	Electronic Fund Transfer	287
	8.46.4	Online Banking	288
	8.46.5	Bank on Your Mobile	288
	8.46.6	Mobile Wallet	289
	8.46.7	Mobile Payments	291
	8.46.8	Mobile Money	291
	8.46.9	E-cheque	291
	8.46.10	When to Use Which Technique	292

Key Terms | Chapter Highlights | Review Questions | Fill in the Blanks | State True or False | Multiple Choice Questions | Answers

Chapter 9: Data Management — 301

9.1	File Management System		301
9.2	Database		302
	9.2.1	Advantages of Database	303
	9.2.2	Application of Database System	303
9.3	Acid Property		303
9.4	Components of a Database System		304
9.5	Relational Databases		305
	9.5.1	Advantages of Relational Databases	306
	9.5.2	Disadvantages of Relational Databases	306
9.6	Components of DBMS		306
	9.6.1	Other Important Modules of DBMS	307
9.7	Basic Terminology of Relational Database Systems		308
9.8	Database Keys		309
		Candidate Key	309
9.8	Relational Data Integrity Rules		311

Key Terms | Chapter Highlights | Review Questions | Fill in the Blanks | State True or False | Multiple Choice Questions | Answers

Chapter 10: Structured Query Language (SQL) — 317

10.1	Introduction to MySQL		317
10.2	Structured Query Language (SQL)		317
	10.2.1	How MySQL Works	318

10.3	Uses of SQL	318
10.4	SQL Data Types	318
	10.4.1 Date and Time Types	319
10.5	Operators in SQL	320
10.6	Performing Simple Calculations with Select Statement	321
10.7	SQL Numeric Functions	322
10.8	String Functions	324
10.9	Creating Database	326
10.10	Removing Database	327
10.11	Creating Tables	328
10.12	Deleting Table	329
10.13	Inserting Values in Table	329
10.14	Retrieving Data from Table	330
10.15	The WHERE Clause	331
10.16	SQL AND and OR Operators	331
10.17	The WHERE BETWEEN Clause	332
10.18	The SQL WHERE IN Clause	333
10.19	The SQL SELECT DISTINCT Statement	333
10.20	ORDER BY Clause	335
10.21	Updating the Table	336
10.22	Deleting Rows from a Table	336
10.23	The WHERE LIKE Clause in SQL	337
10.24	SQL SELECT MIN, MAX Statement	339
10.25	Select COUNT, SUM, AVG	340
10.26	Column Aliases	341
10.27	The SQL GROUP BY Statement	342
10.28	The HAVING Clause	342
10.29	Handling Null Values	343
10.30	SQL Primary Key Constraint	345
10.31	Drop a Primary Key Constraint	347
10.32	Adding Foreign Key Constraint	348
10.33	SQL JOIN	349
	10.33.1 INNER JOIN	349
	10.33.2 LEFT JOIN	350
	10.33.3 RIGHT JOIN	351
	10.33.4 FULL JOIN	351

Key Terms | Chapter Highlights | Review Questions | Programming Exercises | Fill in the Blanks | State True or False | Multiple Choice Questions | Give the Output | Answers

Chapter 11: Interfacing Python With MySQL — 361

11.1	Interfacing Python with MySQL	361
11.2	Creating Tables	363
11.3	Setting Primary Key	364
11.4	Dropping Primary Key	365
11.5	Inserting Data	365
	11.5.1 Inserting Multiple Rows	366
11.6	Retrieve or Select Data	366
	11.6.1 Getting Some Columns	367
	11.6.2 WHERE Clause	368
11.7	ORDER BY Clause	368
11.8	Updating the Table	370
11.9	Aggregate Functions	370

Key Terms | Chapter Highlights | Review Questions | Programming Exercises | Fill in the Blanks | State True or False | Multiple Choice Questions | Answers

Preface

We all know that Information Technology (IT) is the buzzword of the 21st century. We use computers to store, retrieve, transmit and manipulate data. Today, computers are used to perform every other task such as publishing a newspaper, designing a building, coaching sports players and training pilots in flight simulators. Computers have become so widespread that almost every electrical and electronic device (like washing machines, air conditioners, etc.) has a small embedded computer within it. Even the mobile phones that we use are smart phones (phones with computing technology) that are connected to the Internet. Information technology has revolutionized our lifestyle. Thus in today's scenario, learning about computers is mandatory not only for students pursuing a career in engineering and technology but also for those in other professions like journalism, nursing, archaeology, construction and management, to name a few.

Computing skills always help one to be more productive and self-sufficient. Therefore, a basic knowledge of computers and their underlying technology will pay rich dividends in the future. In this context, Python is an open-source, excellent, easy, high-level, interpreted, interactive, object-oriented and a reliable language that uses English-like words. It is also a versatile language that supports development of a wide range of applications ranging from simple text processing to WWW browsers to games. Moreover, programmers can embed Python within their C, C++, COM, ActiveX, CORBA, and Java programs to give 'scripting' capabilities for users.

Python has a huge user base that is constantly growing. The strength of Python can be understood from the fact that this programming language is the most preferred language of companies like Nokia, Google, YouTube and even NASA for its easy syntax. The support for multiple programming paradigms, including object-oriented programming, functional Python programming, and parallel programming models makes it an ideal choice for the programmers.

However, no student can learn to program just by reading a book; rather, it is a skill that must be developed by practice. So, after learning the rudiments of program writing, students will find in this book, a number of examples and exercises that would help them learn to design efficient programs. The book presents various programming examples that have already been implemented and tested using Python 3.8.3.

KEY FEATURES

This book is aimed at serving as a textbook for students enrolled in Class XII of CBSE. It explores the techniques of Python Programming further after providing a quick recap of the concepts of Python covered in Class XI. It also discusses the basics of computer networking to familiarize students with how computers are interconnected in the real world for data transfer and information exchange. The book includes several student-friendly features:

Comprehensive Coverage: The book provides comprehensive coverage of all important topics from the examination point-of-view.

Easy to Understand: The book uses very simple language to explain the concepts and breaks down technical jargons to simpler terms for the student's benefit.

Pictorial Approach: Numerous well-labelled diagrams are provided throughout the text for clear understanding of the concepts.

Practical Orientation: Replete with solved examples and chapter-end exercises in the form of objective type questions and review questions, the book's well-defined pedagogy enables students to check their understanding of the concepts.

Glossary: A list of key terms is provided at the end of each chapter to facilitate easy revision.

Informative Textboxes: Important concepts are highlighted throughout the text for a quick recap.

Programmer's Zone examples are used in context to help the students understand the technique of programming.

Complementary App for CUCET: Students can download the free mobile app Jruma from Google Play Store or Apple Store for additional learning resources. The app would help them to recapitulate and test their understanding of the concepts learnt in Classes XI and XII. The app will also be useful for the students to hone their Computer Science (CS) and Logical Reasoning (LR) skills. CS and LR is a mandatory section in the CUCET and all other entrance exams the students may take throughout their professional career.

ACKNOWLEDGMENTS

The writing of this text book was a mammoth task for which a lot of help was required from many people. Fortunately, I have had the fine support of my family, friends and fellow members of the teaching staff at the Shyama Prasad Mukherji College.

My special thanks would always go to my father Late Sh. Janak Raj Thareja, my mother Smt. Usha Thareja, my brother Pallav and sisters Kimi and Rashi who were a source of abiding inspiration and are a divine blessing for me. I am especially indebted to my son Goransh, who has been very patient and cooperative in letting me realize my dreams. I am obliged to my uncle Mr B L Theraja for his inspiration and guidance in writing this book.

Last but not the least, my acknowledgements will always be incomplete if I do not thank the editorial team at Universities Press (India) Private Limited that gave me this brilliant opportunity to utilize my writing skills.

Reema Thareja
reema_thareja@yahoo.com

About the Author

Reema Thareja is Assistant Professor at Shyama Prasad Mukherji College, University of Delhi. She has over 15 years of experience, teaching computer science for various courses including BA, BSc, MSc, BBA, MBA, BCA and MCA. She has authored several books, including those on Computer Fundamentals, C Programming, OOPS with C++, Data Structures, Data Warehousing and Python Programming, which are well-accepted across the globe. She has also written books on Data Science and Machine Learning in R for the current academic session.

Dr Thareja has published 17 research papers in journals of national and international repute. In addition, she has got the acceptance for four more papers. A recipient of 64 Google Scholar Citations, she has launched a Computer Science Learning and Quizzing mobile app, Jruma, for both Android and iOS devices.

A recipient of the Nobel Laureate Maria Goeppert–Mayer Inspiring Woman of the Year 2021 Award in the field of Computer Science by International Multi-disciplinary Research Foundation (IMRF), Dr Thareja was also among "India's Top 50 Women Leaders in the Education Industry" recognized by uLektz Wall of Fame for the year 2020. She has conducted several faculty development programs, student workshops and webinars in India and the US, and participated in the International Dialogue on Empowered Future – Women's Role on the eve of International Women's Day 2021.

A member of the Computer Society of India and Editorial Board and Keynote Speaker of the IMRF Conference Board, Dr Thareja is a skilled motivator who helps students utilize their untapped skills and reinvent themselves. She was recently conferred with the Knowledge Mobilization Award at the Seventh Annual Research Awards event organized by Shri Param Hans Education and Research Trust and has been invited as a speaker for the Global Virtual Summit to be held in New York this summer.

Python Revisited

Chapter Objectives

In Class XI, we started with programming language, Python. We have already read about important topics like Strings, Tuples, Lists, Dictionaries, Modules and Sorting techniques. Before we start with some advanced topics, let us quickly revisit these key topics:

- Features, tokens, literals, variables, identifiers, data types and reserved words in Python
- Formatting and performing operations on strings
- Operators and expressions

1.1 INTRODUCTION

Python is a powerful programming language with the right combination of performance and features that makes programming fun and easy. It is a high-level, interpreted, interactive, object-oriented and a reliable language that uses English-like words. It has a vast library of modules to support integration of complex solutions from pre-built components.

Python is an open-source project, supported by many individuals. It can be used on any operating system. Some features which make Python a complete programming language are given below.

Simple: Python is a small and simple language. Reading a program written in Python feels almost like reading English.

Easy to Learn: A Python program is easy to read and understand. It uses a few keywords and a clearly defined syntax. This makes it easy for just anyone to pick up the language quickly.

Versatile: Python supports development of a wide range of applications ranging from simple text processing to games.

> Python is being continuously improved by a community of users who strive hard to take the language to the next level.

Free and Open Source: Python is an example of an open-source software. Therefore, anyone can freely distribute it, read the source code, edit it and even use the code to write new (free) programs.

High-level Language: When writing programs in Python, the programmers do not have to worry about the hardware-related details. They just need to concentrate on writing solutions for the current problem at hand.

Interactive: Programs in Python work in interactive mode. Users can give input and get the results accordingly. In this way, users feel as if they are directly communicating with the program.

Portable: Python is a portable language. Hence, the programs behave similarly on a wide variety of hardware platforms. The programs work on a wide range of operating systems without requiring any change.

Object-oriented: Python supports object-oriented as well as procedure-oriented style of programming. While object-oriented technique encapsulates data and functionalities within objects, *procedure-oriented* technique, on the other hand, builds the program around procedures or functions which are nothing but reusable pieces of programs.

Interpreted: Python program is processed at runtime by the interpreter. The interpreter converts each line of Python program into its equivalent machine language code. In case of any error, the interpreter halts the program execution until the user rectifies it. To help users, the interpreter displays an appropriate error message. Interpreted program executes faster than compiled programs.

Dynamic: Python program executes dynamically. They can be copied and used for flexible development of applications. If there is any error, it is reported at run time to allow interactive program development.

Extensible: Since Python is open-source software, anyone can add modules to the Python interpreter. These modules enable programmers to add to or customize their tools to work more efficiently.

Embeddable: Programmers can embed Python programs within their C, C++, COM, ActiveX, CORBA, and Java programs for added functionality.

Extensive Libraries: Python has a huge library that allows programmers to perform a wide range of applications varying from text processing and maintaining databases to GUI programming.

Besides the above-stated features, Python has a big list of good advantages, such as

Easy Maintenance: Code written in Python is easy to maintain.

Secure: The Python language environment is secure from tampering.

Robust: Python programmers cannot manipulate memory directly. Moreover, errors can be easily handled by the program code itself through exception handling procedures. For every syntactical mistake, a simple and easy-to-interpret message is displayed. All these things make the language robust.

Multi-threaded: Python supports multi-threading, that is, executing more than one process (or copy) of a program simultaneously.

Garbage Collection: Python performs garbage collection of all objects that are no longer used.

1.2 PYTHON TOKENS

Tokens are small units of the programming language (Fig. 1.1). Python supports the following types of tokens. In this chapter, we will read about literals in detail.

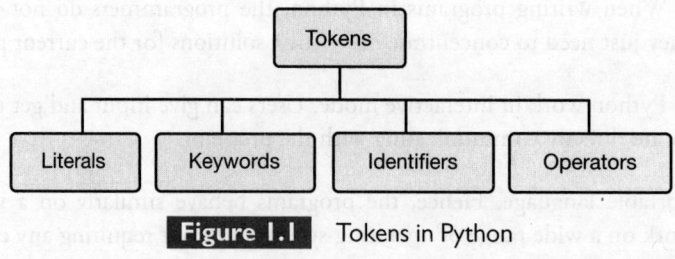

Figure 1.1 Tokens in Python

1.3 LITERAL CONSTANTS

The word "literal" has been derived from literally. The value of a literal constant can be used directly in programs. For example, 7, 3.9, 'A', and "Hello" are examples of literal constants. The number 7 always represents itself and nothing else. Moreover, it is a constant because its value cannot be changed. Hence, it is known as *literal constant*. In this section, we will read about number and string constants in Python.

> **Programming Tip:** You can specify integers in octal as well as hexadecimal number system.

1.3.1 Numbers

Number, as the name suggests, refers to a numeric value. You can use four types of numbers in Python programs. These include integers, long integers, floating-point and complex numbers.

- Numbers like 5 or other whole numbers are referred to as *integers*. Integers can be positive or negative or even equal to zero. They do not have any decimal point.
  Bigger whole numbers are called *long integers*. For example, 535633629843L is a long integer. Note that a long integer must have 'l' or 'L' as the suffix.
- Numbers like are 3.23 and 91.5E-2 are termed as *floating-point numbers*. They are real numbers with a decimal point dividing the integer and fractional parts. The real part of the number can be either negative or positive or even equal to zero.
- Numbers of $a + bi$ form (like $-3 + 7i$) are *complex numbers*, where a is the real part and b is the imaginary part of the number. Both a and b are floating-point numbers and i represents square root of -1.

> The 'E' notation indicates powers of 10. In this case, 91.5E-2 means $91.5 * 10^{-2}$.

Remember that commas are never used in numeric literals or numeric values. Therefore, numbers like 3,567, 123.89, –8,904 are not allowed in Python.

1.3.1.1 Types of Integer Literals

There are three types of integer literals – decimal, octal and hexadecimal integer literal.

Decimal Integer Literal: Any integer literal that does not start with a zero (0) is a decimal integer literal. Example, +17, –26, 1234, –89072.

Octal Integer Literal: Any integer literal that starts with digit zero followed by letter o is treated as an octal integer literal in Python. Example, 0o12, 0o7654. Type the following statements in IDLE and see the output.

```
>>>0o12    >>> -0o12    >>> 0o7654
10          -10          4012
Note that decimal equivalent of the octal value is displayed
```

OUTPUT
```
>>>0o1789
SyntaxError: invalid syntax
Digits 8 and 9 are not there in octal number system
```

Hexadecimal Integer Literal: Any integer literal that starts with digit zero followed by letter x is treated as a hexadecimal integer literal in Python. Example, 0x1234, 0xA7B6F. Type the following statements in IDLE and see the output.

```
>>>0x1234     >>>0xABCD     >>> 0x7B9CF1
4660           43981          8101105
Note that decimal equivalent of the hexadecimal value is displayed
```

OUTPUT
```
>>>0xTG1F
SyntaxError: invalid token
Digits T and G are not there in hexadecimal number system
```

1.3.1.2 Large Floating-point Numbers

Large floating-point numbers are efficiently represented in scientific notation. For example, $5.0012304*10^6$ (6 digits of precision) can be written as 5.0012304e+6 in scientific notation.

Do you remember that in a scientific notation, we have two parts – exponent and the mantissa? The mantissa appears before e and the exponent part follows e. While mantissa can be an integer or a floating-point number, the exponent is always an integer. Both mantissa and exponent can be either negative or positive.

1.3.1.3 Built-in `format()` Function

Any floating-point value may contain an arbitrary number of decimal places, so it is always recommended to use the built-in `format()` function to produce a string version of a number with specific number of decimal places. Observe the difference between the following outputs.

```
# Without using format()
>>> float(16/(float(3)))
5.333333333333333
```

```
# Using format()
>>> format(float(16/(float(3))), '.2f')
'5.33'
```

Here, .2f in the `format()` function rounds the result to two decimal places of accuracy in the string produced. For very large (or very small) values, 'e' can be used as a *format specifier*. The `format()` function can also be used to format floating-point numbers in scientific notation. Look at the result of the expression given below.

```
>>> format(3**50,'.5e')
'7.17898e+23'
```

The result is formatted in scientific notation with five decimal places of precision. This feature is especially useful when displaying results in which only a certain number of decimal places is needed. Finally, the `format()` function can also be used to insert a comma in the number as shown below.

```
>>> format(123456.8901,',.2f')
'123,456.89'
```

1.3.1.4 Simple Operations on Numbers

Python can carry out simple operations on numbers. To perform a calculation, simply enter numbers and the type of operations that needs to be performed on them directly into the Python console and it will print the answer, as shown below.

```
>>> 17 + 56
73
>>> 90 + 50 - 40
100
>>> 35 * 15
525
>>> 108 / 12
9.0
>>> -10 * 14
-140
```

The spaces around the plus and minus signs here are optional. They are just added to make the statement more readable. The code will execute even if you remove the spaces.

Dividing a number by zero in Python generates an error, and no output is produced, as shown below.

```
>>> 117 / 0
Traceback (most recent call last):
  File "<pyshell#7>", line 1, in <module>
    117 / 0
ZeroDivisionError: division by zero
```

When two numbers are divided, a floating-point number is always produced.

```
>>> 15 / 5
3.0
>>> 75 / 15.0
5.0
>>> 39.0 / 3
13.0
>>> 24.0 / 2.0
12.0
```

You can easily work with a floating-point number and an integer because Python automatically converts the integer to a float. This is known as **implicit conversion or type coercion**. An implicit conversion is performed by the compiler without programmer's intervention.

Quotient and Remainder: When dividing one number by another, if you want to know the quotient and remainder, use the floor division (//) and modulo operator (%), respectively. These operators can be used with both floats and integers. Observe the following statements and their output. When we divide 78 by 5, we get a quotient of 15 and a remainder of 3.

```
>>> 18 // 4
4
>>> 18 % 4
2
>>> 324.0 // 6.0
54.0
>>> 234.567 % 6.5
0.567000000000073
```

Exponentiation: Besides the conventional operators +, −, * and /, Python also supports ** operator. The ** operator is used for exponentiation, i.e., raising of one number to the power of another. Consider the given statements and observe the output.

```
>>> 11 ** 3
1331
>>> 5.25 ** 4
759.69140625
```

1.3.2 Strings

A *string* is a group of characters. In Python, there are three ways in which a string can be used.

Using Single Quotes ('): For example, a string can be written as 'HELLO'.

Using Double Quotes (""): Strings in double quotes are exactly same as those in single quotes. Therefore, 'HELLO' is same as "HELLO".

Using Triple Quotes (''' '''): A multi-line string is specified using triple quotes. We can use as many single quotes and double quotes as required in a string within triple quotes. An example of a multi-line string can be given as,

> All spaces and tabs within a string are preserved in quotes (single quote as well as double).

```
>>> ''' HELLO WORLD !!!
'GOOD MORNING'
"WELCOME TO THE WORLD OF 'PYTHON PROGRAMMING' "
HAPPY LEARNING....'''
' HELLO WORLD !!!\n\'GOOD MORNING\'\n"WELCOME TO THE WORLD OF \'PYTHON PROGRAMMING\' 
    "\nHAPPY LEARNING....'
```

Note that all the characters, spaces, tabs, new lines, and quotes (single as well as double) are preserved within triple quotes.

```
>>> 'Hello'
'Hello'
>>> "HELLO"
'HELLO'
>>> '''HELLO'''
'HELLO'
```

Irrespective of the way in which a string is specified, all strings are **immutable**. This means that once you have created a string, you cannot change it.

1.3.2.1 String Literal Concatenation

Python concatenates two string literals that are placed side by side. Consider the code below wherein Python has automatically concatenated three string literals.

```
>>> 'HELLO' 'WORLD'
'HELLOWORLD'
```

1.3.2.2 Unicode Strings

Unicode is a standard way of writing international text. That is, if you want to write some text in your native language like Hindi, then you need to have a Unicode-enabled text editor. Python allows you to specify Unicode text by prefixing the string with a u or U. For example,

```
>>> u"Shubh Prabhat"
'Shubh Prabhat'
```

> The 'U' prefix specifies that the file contains text written in language other than English.

1.3.2.3 Escape Sequences

Some characters (like ', ", \) cannot be directly included in a string. Such characters must be escaped by placing a backslash before them as given below.

```
>>> print('How's life?')
      SyntaxError: invalid syntax
>>> print('How\'s life?')
How's life?
```

> **Remember:** When a string is printed, the quotes around it are not displayed.

The reason for the error was that Python got confused as to where the string starts and ends. So, we need to clearly specify that this single quote does not indicate the end of the string. This indication can be given with the help of an *escape sequence* as specified in the second string – *a single quote preceded by a backslash.*

Similarly, to print a double quote in a string enclosed within double quotes, we must precede the double quotes with a backslash as given below.

```
>>> print("Sheena asked,"Will you come with me?"")
SyntaxError: invalid syntax
>>> print("Sheena asked,\"Will you come with me?\"")
Sheena asked,"Will you come with me?"
```

> An escape sequence is treated as a single character.

Other useful escape sequences are given in Table 1.1.

Table 1.1 Some of the escape sequences used in Python

Escape Sequence	Purpose	Example	Output
\\	Prints Backslash	print("\\")	\
\'	Prints single-quote	print("\'")	'
\"	Prints double-quote	print("\"")	"
\a	Rings bell	print("\a")	Bell rings
\f	Prints form feed character	print("Hello\fWorld")	Hello World
\n	Prints newline character	print("Hello\nWorld")	Hello World
\t	Prints a tab	print("Hello\tWorld")	Hello World
\o	Prints octal value	print("\o56")	.
\x	Prints hex value	print("\x65")	e

1.3.2.4 Multi-line Strings

When specifying a string, if a single backslash (\) at the end of the line is added then it indicates that the string is continued in the next line, but no new line is added otherwise. For example,

```
>>> print("Hello World,\
Good Morning !!!")
Hello World,Good Morning !!!
```

1.3.2.5 Raw Strings

If you want to specify a string that should not handle any escape sequences and display exactly as specified then you need to specify that string as a *raw string*. A raw string is specified by prefixing r or R to the string.

> Raw strings are not processed in any special way, not even the escape sequences.

```
>>> R"How\'s life at your end?"
"How\\'s life at your end?"
```

1.3.2.6 String Formatting

We have already used the built-in `format()` function to format floating-point numbers. The same function can also be used to control the display of strings. The syntax of `format()` function is given as,
`format(value, format_specifier)`

where, `value` is the value or the string to be displayed, and `format_specifier` can contain a combination of formatting options.

Example 1.1 Commands to display 'PYTHON' left-justified, right-justified and centre-aligned in a field width of 30 characters.

```
>>> format('PYTHON', '<30')      >>> format('PYTHON', '>30')      >>> format('PYTHON', '^30')
'PYTHON                        '   '                        PYTHON'   '            PYTHON            '
```

Here, the `'<'` symbol means to left justify. Similarly, to right justify the string use the `'>'` symbol and the `'^'` symbol to centrally align the string.

We have seen above that `format()` function uses blank spaces to fill the specified width. But you can also use the `format()` function to fill the width in the formatted string using any other character as shown below.

```
>>> print('PYTHON',format('-','-<10'),'PROGRAMMING')
PYTHON ---------- PROGRAMMING
```

1.3.2.7 String Concatenation

Like numbers, we can also add two strings in Python. The process of combining two strings is called **concatenation**. Two strings, whether created using single or double quotes, are concatenated in the same way.

Example 1.2

```
>>> 'HI... and ... '+ 'BYE'      >>> '"PYTHON"' + '"PROGRAMMING"'       >>> '"PYTHON"'+'"
    PROGRAMMING"'
'HI... and...BYE'                '"PYTHON""PROGRAMMING"'                '"PYTHON" "PROGRAMMING"'
```

1.3.2.8 Slice a String

A substring of a string is called a **slice**. You can extract subsets of strings by using the slice operator ([ ] and [:]). You need to specify index or the range of index of characters to be extracted. The index of the first character is 0 and the index of the last character is $n-1$, where n is the number of characters in the string (as shown in Fig. 1.2).

Index from the start	P	Y	T	H	O	N	Index from the end
	0	1	2	3	4	5	
	-6	-5	-4	-3	-2	-1	

Figure 1.2 String indexes

The syntax of slice operation is **s[start:end:stride]**, where start specifies the beginning index of the sub string and end is the index of the last character of the string s. *Omitting either start or end index by default takes start or end of the string. Omitting both means the entire string is taken.*

If you want *to extract characters starting from the end of the string, then you must specify the index as a negative number.* For example, the index of the last character is –1.

1.3.2.9 Specifying Stride While Slicing Strings

In the slice operation, you can specify a third argument as the ***stride.*** The stride specifies the number of characters to move forward after the first character is retrieved from the string. By default, the value of stride is 1, which means that every character between two index numbers is retrieved. If stride is 2, then every second character is accessed, if stride is 3 then every third character is accessed, and so on.

```
# Slice operation on string
>>> str = "Python Programming is Fun"
>>> str[0]         # prints the first character
P
>>> str[4:10]      # prints characters from 4 to 9
on Pro
>>> str[5:]        # prints all characters staring from fifth character
n Programming is Fun
>>> str[-1]        # prints the last character
n
>>>str[:-1]        # prints all except the last character
Python Programming is Fu
>>> str[-7:]       # prints last seven character
is Fun
>>> str[3:15:2]    # prints every 2nd character from 3rd - 15th character
'hnPorm'
```

*Did you notice that when we use the slice operator, e*lements are accessed from left towards right? For any index *n* (positive or negative), s[:n] + s[n:] = s. this means that the slice operation always partitions the string into two parts in such a way that all characters are conserved.

Even the whitespace characters are skipped as they are also a part of the string. ***If you omit the first two arguments and only specify the third one, then the entire string is used in steps.*** We can even have a negative value in the stride. For example, if the value of stride is –1 then the string is printed in reverse order.

Example 1.3

```
# print every third character
str = "Python programming is fun"
print(str[::3])
```

OUTPUT

Ph oai n

Example 1.4

```
# print string in reverse
str = "Python programming is fun"
print(str[::-1])
```

OUTPUT

nuf si gnimmargorp nohtyP

Example 1.5

```
# print every second character in the #reversed string
str = "Python programming is fun"
print(str[::-2])
```

OUTPUT

nfs nmagr otP

1.4 TYPE CONVERSION

In Python, it is not possible to complete certain operations that involves different types of data. For example, it is not possible to perform "4" + 7 since one operand is an integer and the other is of string type.

Example 1.6

```
>>> "7"+"4"      >>> int("7")+int("3")
'74'             10
```

Another situation in which type conversion is a must is when you want to accept a non-string value (integer or float) as an input. The `input()` function which accepts input(s) from the user takes it as a string. In case you want the user to enter a numeric value then the string value must be explicitly type-casted to numbers (integers or floats) so that calculations can be performed on them. In such situations, you must perform conversions between data types.

Example 1.7

```
x = input("Enter the first number: ")
y = input("Enter the second number: ")
print(x + y)
```

OUTPUT

```
Enter the first number: 7
Enter the second number: 4
74
```

Example 1.8

```
x = int(input("Enter the first number:"))
y = int(input("Enter the second number:"))
print(x + y)
```

OUTPUT

```
Enter the first number: 7
Enter the second number: 4
11
```

Python provides several built-in functions to convert a value from one data type to another. These functions return a new object representing the converted value. Some of them are given in Table 1.2.

Table 1.2 Functions for type conversions

Function	Description	Example
int(x)	Converts x to an integer	int(3.5) gives 3
float(x)	Converts x to a floating point number	float('123') gives 123.0
str(x)	Converts x to a string	str(123.45) gives '123.45'
tuple(x)	Converts list x to a tuple	tuple([1,2,3]) gives (1, 2,3)
list(x)	Converts tuple x to a list	list((1,2,3)) gives [1, 2, 3]
set(x)	Converts x to a set	set([1,2,3]) gives {1, 2, 3}
ord(x)	Converts a single character to its integer value.	ord('D') gives 68
oct(x)	Converts an integer to an octal string.	oct(9) gives '0o11'
hex(x)	Converts an integer to a hexadecimal string.	hex(1234) gives '0x4d2'
chr(x)	Converts an integer to a character.	chr(70) gives 'F'
complex(x)	Converts to a complex number	complex(3,-8) gives (3-8j)

However, before using type conversions to convert a floating-point number into an integer number, remember that `int()` converts a float to an integer by truncation (discarding the fractional part) and not by rounding to the nearest whole number. The `round()` works more appropriately by rounding a floating-point number to the nearest integer as shown below. The `round()` can even take a second, optional argument which is usually a number that indicates the number of places of precision to which the first argument should be rounded.

```
>>> int(3.7)
3
>>> round(3.7)
4
>>> round(1234.56789012,2)
1234.57
```

Note that each argument passed to a function has a specific data type. If you pass an argument of the wrong data type to a function, it will generate an error. For example, you cannot find the square root of a string. If you don't know what type of arguments a function accepts, you should use the `help()` before using the function.

1.5 VARIABLES AND INDENTIFIERS

Using just literal constants, nothing much can be done in programs. For developing complex programs, we must store information to manipulate it as and when required. This is where *variables* can help.

Variable, in simple terms, means something that may change. We can store any piece of information in a variable and this information may change. For example, a variable `today_temp` may have value = 30 today but tomorrow it may be 29 or 31.

Thus, we see that in Python, variable represents a named location that has a value which can be processed as and when required (as for calculating temperature).

To be identified easily, each variable is given an appropriate name. Variable names are examples of **identifiers**. *Identifiers* as the name suggests, are names given to identify something. This something can be a variable, function, class, module or any other object. For naming any identifier, there are some basic rules that you must follow. These rules are:

- The first character of an identifier must be an underscore ('_') or a letter (upper or lowercase).
- The rest of the identifier name can be underscores ('_'), letters (upper or lowercase), or digits (0–9).
- Identifier names are case-sensitive. For example, myvar and myVar are **not** the same.
- Punctuation characters such as @, $, and % are not allowed within identifiers.

> **Remember:** Python is a case-sensitive language.

Examples of valid identifier names are sum, __my_var, num1, r, var_20, First, etc.

Examples of invalid identifier names are 1num (starting with a digit), my-var (punctuation and special characters not allowed), %check (first character should be an alphabet or an underscore), Basic Sal (space not allowed), H#R&A (special characters not allowed), etc.

1.6 CREATING VARIABLES

To create a variable in Python, just assign a value to the identifier using the 'equal to sign' (also known as the assignment operator). For example, the following statements create variables with different values in Python.

Example 1.9

```
num = 7
float_num = 12.34
ch = 'A'
str = "ABC"
```

```
print(num)
print(float_num)
print(ch)
print(str)
```

OUTPUT

```
7
12.34
A
ABC
```

When we create a variable, Python creates labels referring to those values as shown in Fig. 1.3.

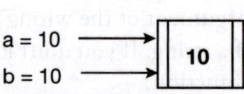 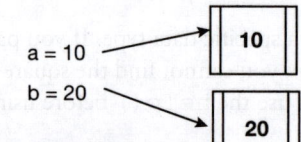 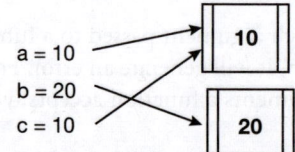

Here, both variables a and b have the same value. A label with value 10 is created and both variables point to the same label.

Here, the value of variable is changed. Both variables a and b have different values. A label with value 10 and another with label 20 are created and both variables point to their respective labels.

Here, both variables a and b have different values. A label with value 10 and another with label 20 are created and both variables point to their respective labels. When the variable c is created with same value as that of a, it points to the label to which a is pointing.

Figure 1.3 Creating labels

Do you know that Python IDLE remembers variables and their values? Just type the following lines in the command console of IDLE and observe the output.

```
>>> x = 10
>>> y = 20
>>> str1 = "HELLO"
>>> print(str1)
HELLO
>>> print(x * y)
200
```

1.7 DATA TYPES OF IDENTIFIERS

In any programming language, data type is a classification that specifies which type of value a variable has. It also specifies the type of mathematical, relational or logical operations that can be applied to it without causing an error. For example, a string data type is used to hold textual data. An integer is a data type that can store whole numbers.

Python has various standard data types that are used to define the operations possible on them and the storage method for each of them. Based on the data type of a variable, the interpreter reserves memory for it and also determines the type of data that can be stored in the reserved memory.

The five standard data types supported by Python include numbers, string, list, tuple, and dictionary. We can even create our own data types in Python (like classes). In this chapter, we will learn about numbers and strings. Other data types will be explored in subsequent chapters.

Remember: Python is a purely object-oriented language. It refers to everything as an object including numbers and strings.

1.7.1 Assigning or Initializing Values to Variables

In Python, programmers need not explicitly declare variables to reserve memory space. The declaration is done automatically when a value is assigned to the variable using the equal sign (=). The operand on the left side of equal sign is the name of the variable and the operand on its right side is the value to be stored in that variable.

Example 1.10

```
#Program to Display Data of Different Types Using Variables and Literal Constants
age = 27
salary = 1234567
gender = 'M'
name : "Siva"
print("NAME: " + name)
print("AGE : " + str(age))        ← To convert an integer to a string
print("SALARY:" +str(salary))

print("GENDER : " + gender)       ← To concatenate or to join two strings
```

OUTPUT

```
NAME = Siva
AGE : 27
SALARY : 1234567
GENDER = M
```

To run this program, type the code in IDLE. Save it with a suitable name with an extension .py. Press F5 or click on *Run* and then on *Run Module*.

In the code, the program assigns literal constant 27 to the variable age using the assignment operator (=). Similarly, we have assigned literal constants to other variables and then printed their values.

In Python, you can reassign variables as many times as you want to change the value stored in them. You may even store value of one data type in a statement and then a value of another data in a subsequent statement. This is possible because Python variables do not have specific types; so you can assign an integer to a variable, and later assign a string to the same variable.

Example 1.11

```
#Program to Reassign Values to a Variable
age = 27                ← age is an integer
print("AGE:", age)
age = 'TWELVE'          ← age is a string
print("AGE:", age)
age = 15.6              ← age is a floating-point number
print("AGE:", age)
```

OUTPUT

```
AGE:27
AGE : TWELVE
AGE : 15.6
```

While re-assigning values to variables, be cautious about ensuring that the right type of value is used in operations. This is very much evident from the code given below.

Example 1.12

```
a = 10
a = a*10
print(a)
a = "PYTHON"
a = a/10
print(a)
```

OUTPUT
```
100
Traceback (most recent call last):
    File "C:\Python37\try.py", line 5, in <module> a = a/10
TypeError:   unsupported operand type(s) for /:
    'str' and 'int'
```

```
num = 10
print(type(num))
val = 3.4
print(type(val))
ch = ' a '
print(type(ch))
str = "abc"
print(type(str))
```

OUTPUT
```
<class 'int'>
<class 'float'>
<class 'str'>
<class 'str'>
```

The type() Function

The `type()` function having the syntax type(object) is used to determine the data type of object. This function should be used to ensure that the right type of values is being used in the expressions.

lvalue and rvalue

As the name suggests, expressions that comes on the left side of the assignment operator is known as the lvalue. Correspondingly, expressions that come on the right side of the assignment operator is known as the rvalue.

This means that, lvalues are those objects to which values can be assigned. And, rvalues are the literals. That is, expressions that evaluate a value come on the right-hand side of the assignment operator.

Remember that,

- literals or expressions that evaluate a value cannot come on the left-hand side of the assignment operator
- variable names can come on the left-hand side of the assignment operator.

```
VALID LVALUE AND RVALUE
a = 10
B = a * 20
INVALID LVALUE AND RVALUE
10 = a
a * 20 = b
```

1.7.2 Multiple Assignments

Python allows programmers to assign a single value to more than one variable simultaneously. For example,

```
sum = flag = a= b = 0
```

In the above statement, all four integer variables are assigned a value 0. You can also assign different values to multiple variables simultaneously as shown below.

```
sum, a, b, mesg = 0, 3, 5, "RESULT"
```

Here, variable sum, a, and b are integers (numbers) and mesg is a string. sum is assigned a value 0, a is assigned 3, b is assigned 5 and mesg is assigned "RESULT".

Remember that *trying to reference a variable that has not been assigned any value causes an error*. This may happen if you have mistakenly used a variable without assigning it a value prior to its use or have deliberately deleted or removed a variable using the del statement and then tried to use it later in your code. The examples given below illustrate this concept.

Also remember that right-hand side expression is evaluated before assignment is done and if there are multiple expressions in a statement separated by commas then expressions on the RHS are evaluated from *left to right* and assigned in the same order.

Example 1.13

```
x,y = 10,20
y,y = y+5, y-20    # last value of y persists
print("x = ",x, " y = ",y)
```

OUTPUT

```
x =  10   y =  0
```

Programs to Assign and Access Variables

Example 1.14

```
>>> name = "Kartik"
>>> age = 15
>>> print(name)
Kartik
>>> print(grade)
Traceback (most recent call last):
    File "<pyshell#8>", line 1, in <module>
        print(grade)
NameError: name 'grade' is not defined
```

Variable not declared prior to use

Example 1.15

```
>>> name = "Kartik"
>>> age = 15
>>> grade = 'O'
>>> print(name)
Kartik
>>> del age
>>> print(age)
Traceback (most recent call last):
    File "<pyshell#14>", line 1, in <module>
        print(age)
NameError: name 'age' is not defined
```

Variable being used after it is deleted

1.7.3 Data Type Boolean

Boolean is another data type in Python. A variable of Boolean type can have one of the two values – *True* or *False*. Similar to other variables, the Boolean variables are also created while we assign a value to them or when we use a relational operator on them.

Remember: Boolean variables are also created by comparing values using the == operator.

Example 1.16

```
>>>Boolean_var = True
>>> Boolean_var
True
>>> 30 == 50
False
>>> "HELLO" == 'HELLO'
True
>>> 10 != 10
False
>>"Python3.7" != "Python3.4"
True
>>> 50 > 80
False
>>> 20 <= 20
True
>>> 13 == 13.0
False
>>> 13 >= 13.0
True
```

1.8 INPUT OPERATION

Real-world programs need to be interactive. By interactive, we mean that you need to take some sort of input or information from the user and work on that input to get the desired result.

To take input from the users, Python makes use of the `input()` function. The `input()` function prompts the user to provide some information on which the program can work and give the result. However, we must always remember that the *input function takes user's input as a string*. So, whether you input a number or a string, it is treated as a string only.

Program to Read Variables from the User

Example 1.17

```
name = input("What's your name? ")
age = input("Enter your age : ")
print(name + ", you are " + age + " years old")
```

OUTPUT

```
What's your name? Goransh
Enter your age : 13
Goransh, you are 13 years old
```

To read integers or floating-point numbers using the `input()` function, you must use the `int()` and the `float()` function respectively. The `int()` function is used to convert a non-integer value to integer. Similarly, the `float()` function is used to convert a non-floating-point value into a floating-point value. Hence, the output of the `input()` function which returns a string value can be passed to the `int()` or `float()` function to get a numeric value.

Example 1.18

```
a = int(input("Enter a number : "))
a = a + 10
print(a)
```

OUTPUT

```
Enter a number : 10
20
```

Example 1.19

```
marks = float(input("Enter your total marks : "))
avg = marks/5.0
print(avg)
```

OUTPUT

```
Enter your total marks : 495
99.0
```

1.9 COMMENTS

Comments are added in a program to describe the statements in the program code. They make the program easily readable and understandable by the programmer as well as other users who are seeing the code. In Python, a hash sign (#) that is not inside a string literal begins a comment. *All characters following the # and up to the end of the line are part of the comment.*

Program to Use Comments

Example 1.20

```
# Program to find the cost of a dozen pens
price_1 = int(input("Enter the price of 1 pen : "))
price_12 = price_1 * 12    # dozen means 12
print("Price of a dozen pens = ", price_12)
```

OUTPUT

```
Enter the price of 1 pen : 10
Price of a dozen pens =  120
```

Key points to remember

- Comments are the non-executable statements in a program.
- The interpreter simply ignores the comments.
- When the program is run, comments are not displayed.
- Comments can be either typed in a new line or on the same line after a statement or expression.
- A program can have any number of comments.

1.9.1 Multi-line Comments

In Python, multi-line comments are also known as docstrings. They can be specified in two ways. First, by using three single quotes (or apostrophe). Second, by using three double quotes. They are used when explanation of the statements cannot be sufficiently given in one line. The code given below demonstrates the use of multi-line comments.

Example 1.21

```
''' adding two
numbers'''
sum = 2 + 3
print(sum)
""" calculating average
of the two numbers
"""
avg = sum/2.0
print(avg)
```

OUTPUT
```
5
2.5
Did you notice that comments are not printed?
```

1.10 RESERVED WORDS

In every programming language, there are certain words which have a pre-defined meaning. These words, also known as reserved words or keywords, cannot be used for naming identifiers. Table 1.3 shows a list of Python keywords.

All the Python keywords contain lowercase letters only.

Table 1.3 Reserved words in Python

and	assert	break	class	continue	def	del	elif	else	except
exec	finally	for	from	global	if	import	in	is	lambda
not	or	pass	print	raise	return	try	while	with	yield

1.11 INDENTATION

Whitespace at the beginning of the line is called *indentation*. These whitespaces or indentations are very important in Python. In a Python program, the leading whitespace including spaces and tabs at the beginning of the logical line determines the indentation level of that logical line.

The level of indentation groups statements to form a block of statements. This means that statements in a block must have the same indentation level. Python very strictly checks the indentation level and gives an error if indentation is not correct.

In the code below, there is a tab at the beginning of the second line. The error indicated by Python tells us that there is an indentation error. Python does not allow you to arbitrarily start new blocks of statements.

Example 1.22
```
a = 10
    a = a + 1      # Indentation Error
print(a)
a = 10
a = a + 1
print(a)
```

Remember: Use a single tab for each indentation level.

OUTPUT
```
11
```

Like other programming languages, Python does not use curly braces ({...}). Therefore, to indicate blocks of code for class and function definitions or for flow control (discussed later in the book), it uses only indentation to form a block. *All statements inside a block should be at the same indentation level.*

1.12 OPERATORS AND EXPRESSIONS

Operators are the constructs that are used to manipulate the value of operands. Some basic operators include +, -, * and /. An expression in a programming language is any valid combination of tokens that represents a value. There are two types of expressions:

Simple expressions in which there are only values. For example, 29.

Complex expressions in which one or more operators are used on operand(s) to generate a value. For example, in the expression sum = 2 + 4. Here, 2 and 4 are operands and + is the operator. 10 * 8 / 2 is another example of a complex expression.

> Operands are values on which operators are applied to generate a value.

However, expressions can also be classified as arithmetic expressions, logical expressions, string expressions and relational expressions, where

- Arithmetic expressions consist of numbers and arithmetic operators.
- Logical expressions have literals or variables and logical operators.
- Relational expressions have literals or variables and relational operators.
- String expressions have string operands and string operators (like, * and +).

Different operators supported by Python include:

a. Arithmetic operators
b. Comparison (Relational) operators
c. Assignment operators
d. Logical operators
e. Unary operators
f. Bitwise operators
g. Membership operators
h. Identity operators

1.12.1 Arithmetic Operators

Some basic arithmetic operators are +, -, *, /, %, ** and //. You can apply these operators on numbers as well as on numeric variables to perform corresponding operations. For example, if a = 10 and b = 20, then the result of the operations can be shown as given in Table 1.4.

Table 1.4 Arithmetic operators

Operator	Description	Example	Output
+	Addition – Adds the operands	>>> print(a + b)	30
-	Subtraction – Subtracts operand on the right from the operand on the left of the operator	>>> print(a - b)	-10
*	Multiplication – Multiplies the operands	>>> print(a * b)	200
/	Division – Divides operand on the left side of the operator with the operand on its right. The division operator returns the quotient.	>>> print(b / a)	2.0
%	Modulus- Divides operand on the left side of the operator by the operand on its right. The modulus operator returns the remainder.	>>> print(b % a)	0

//	Floor Division – Divides the operands and returns the quotient. It also removes the digits after the decimal point. If one of the operands is negative, the result is floored (rounded away from zero towards negative infinity).	>>> print(24//5)
		>>> print(24.0//5.0)
		>>> print(-37//4)
		>>> print(-17.0//3)
			4
			4.0
			-10
			-5.0

**	Exponent – Performs exponential calculation. That is, it raises operand on the right side to the operand on the left of the operator.	>>> print(a**b)	1020

1.12.2 Comparison Operators

Comparison operators, also known as *relational operators*, are used to compare the values on its either side and determine the relation between them. For example, assuming $a = 10$ and $b = 20$, we can use the comparison operators on them as specified in Table 1.5.

Table 1.5 Comparison operators

Operator	Description	Example	Output
==	Returns True if the two values are exactly equal.	>>> print(a == b)	False
!=	Returns True if the two values are not equal.	>>> print(a != b)	True
>	Returns True if the value at the operand on the left side of the operator is greater than the value on its right side	>>> print(a > b)	False
<	Returns True if the value at the operand on the right side of the operator is greater than the value on its left side.	>>> print(a < b)	True
>=	Returns True if the value at the operand on the left side of the operator is either greater than or equal to the value on its right side.	>>> print (a >= b)	False
<=	Returns True if the value at the operand on the right side of the operator is either greater than or equal to the value on its left side.	>>> print (a <= b)	True

1.12.3 Assignment and In-place or Shortcut Operators

Assignment operator, as the name suggests, assigns value to the operand. In-place operators, also known as *shortcut operators* that include +=, -=, *=, /=, %=, //= and **=, allow you to write codes like num = num + 10 more concisely, as num += 3. Different types of assignment and in-place operators are given in Table 1.6.

> Remember that <, > operators can also be used to compare strings lexicographically.

Table 1.6 Assignment and in-place operator

Operator	Example
=	c = a, assigns value of a to c
+=	a += b is same as a = a + b
-=	a -= b is same as a = a - b
*=	a *= b is same as a = a * b
/=	a /= b is same as a = a / b
%=	a %= b is same as a = a % b
//=	a //= b is same as a = a // b
**=	a**= b is same as a = a** b

Example 1.23 Application of the += operator on strings.

```
>>> str1 = "PYTHON"
>>> str2 = "PROGRAMMING"
>>> str1 += str2
>>> print(str1)
PYTHONPROGRAMMING
```

1.12.4 Unary Operators

Unary operators act on single operands. Unary minus operator is strikingly different from the arithmetic operator that operates on two operands and subtracts the second operand from the first operand. When an operand is preceded by a unary minus sign, its value is negated.

For example, if a number is positive, it becomes negative when preceded with a unary minus operator. Similarly, if the number is negative, it becomes positive after applying the unary minus operator. Consider the given example.

Remember: Unlike other programming languages, Python does not support prefix and postfix increment or decrement operators.

Example 1.24

```
>>> a = -5
>>> b = -a
>>> print(b)
```

OUTPUT

5

```
>>> a = 5
>>> b = -a
>>> print(b)
```

OUTPUT

-5

1.12.5 Bitwise Operators

As the name suggests, bitwise operators perform operations at bit level. These operators include bitwise AND, bitwise OR, bitwise XOR, and shift operators. Bitwise operators expect their operands to be integers and treat them as a sequence of bits.

Bitwise AND (&): When we use the bitwise AND operator, the bit in the first operand is ANDed with the corresponding bit in the second operand. The bitwise AND operator compares each bit of its first operand with the corresponding bit of its second operand. If both bits are 1, the corresponding bit in the result is 1 and 0 otherwise.

Bitwise OR (|): When we use the bitwise OR operator, the bit in the first operand is ORed with the corresponding bit in the second operand. The bitwise OR operator compares each bit of its first operand with the corresponding bit of its second operand. If one or both bits are 1, the corresponding bit in the result is 1 and 0 otherwise.

Bitwise XOR (^): When we use the bitwise XOR operator, the bit in the first operand is XORed with the corresponding bit in the second operand. That is, the bitwise XOR operator compares each bit of its first operand with the corresponding bit of its second operand. If one of the bits is 1, the corresponding bit in the result is 1 and 0 otherwise.

Bitwise NOT (~): The bitwise NOT, or complement, is a unary operation that performs logical negation on each bit of the operand. By performing negation of each bit, it actually produces the ones' complement of the given binary value. Bitwise NOT operator sets the bit to 1, if it was initially 0 and sets it to 0, if it was initially 1.

The truth tables of these bitwise operators are summarized in Table 1.7.

Table 1.7 Truth tables for bitwise operators

A	B	A&B	A	B	A|B	A	B	A^B	A	!A
0	0	0	0	0	0	0	0	0	0	1
0	1	0	0	1	1	0	1	1	1	0
1	0	0	1	0	1	1	0	1		
1	1	1	1	1	1	1	1	0		

Example 1.25

```
>>> x = 6
>>> y = 8
>>> print(x&y)
```

OUTPUT
0

```
>>> x = 6
>>> y = 8
>>> print(x|y)
```

OUTPUT
14

Example 1.26

```
>>> x = 6
>>> y = 8
>>> print(x^y)
```

OUTPUT
14

```
>>> x = 6
>>> print(~x)
```

OUTPUT
-7

You can check the result of bitwise operator by converting a number into binary using the **bin() function**. For example, >>> bin(15) will give '0b1111'. >>> bin(7) gives '0b111'. >>> 15 & 7 gives 7, as 1 1 1 1 & 0 1 1 1 gives 0 1 1 1.

$$\begin{array}{r} 1111 \\ 0111 \\ \hline 0\ 111 \end{array}$$

1.12.6 Shift Operators

Python supports two bitwise shift operators. They are shift left (<<) and shift right (>>). These operations are used to shift bits to the left or to the right. The syntax for a shift operation can be given as:

operand op num,

where, the bits in operand are shifted left or right depending on the operator (left if the operator is << and right if the operator is>>) by the number of places denoted by num.

```
If we left shift 01011101, then after
first left shift we will get, 10111010.
After second left shift, we will get,
01110100.
If we right shift 01011101, then after first
right shift we will get, 00101110,
After second left shift, we will get,
00010111.
 >>> x = 5
>>>y= 4
>>>  x<< y
80
>>> x = 80
>>> y = 4
>>> x >> y
5
```

When we apply a left shift, every bit in x is shifted to the left by one place. Therefore, the MSB (most significant bit) of x is lost and the LSB of x is set to 0.

If you observe carefully, you will notice that *shifting once to the left multiplies the number by 2.* On the contrary, when we apply a right shift, every bit in x is

Remember: Bitwise operators cannot be applied to float or double variables.

shifted to the right by one place. Therefore, the LSB (least significant bit) of x is lost and the MSB of x is set to 0. **When we shift once to the right, it divides the number by 2.**

1.12.7 Logical Operators

Python supports three logical operators – logical AND, logical OR, and logical NOT. As in case of arithmetic expressions, the logical expressions are evaluated from left to right.

Logical AND: Logical AND operator is used to simultaneously evaluate two conditions or expressions with relational operators. If expressions on both sides (left and right side) of the logical operator are true, then the whole expression is true; else it is false. For example, (a > b) and (a > c), will return TRUE only is the value of a is greater than the values of b and c.

The AND operator tests the second operand only if the first operand is true.

Logical OR: Logical OR operator is used to simultaneously evaluate two conditions or expressions with relational operators. If one or both expressions of the logical operator are true, then the whole expression is true. This means that the expression is false only if both the expressions are false. For example, (a > b) or (a != b) will return TRUE if a is either greater than b or less than b. It will return FALSE if a is equal to b.

> **Remember:** The truth table of logical AND, OR and NOT is exactly same as that of Bitwise AND, OR and NOT operators.

Logical NOT: The logical NOT operator takes a single expression and negates the value of the expression. Logical NOT produces a zero if the expression evaluates to a non-zero value and produces a 1 if the expression produces a zero. In other words, it just reverses the value of the expression. For example,

```
>>> a = 10
>>> b = not a       # a is non-zero (or TRUE) so b is FALSE
>>> print(b)
False
>>> a = 0
>>> b =not a        # a is zero (or FALSE) so b is TRUE
>>> print(b)
True
```

It can be noted that the *logical expressions operate in a shortcut (or lazy) fashion and stop the evaluation when it knows the final outcome for sure.* For example, in a logical expression involving logical AND, if the first operand is false, then the second operand is not evaluated as it is certain that the result will be false. Similarly, for a *logical expression involving logical OR, if the first operand is true, then the second operand is not evaluated as it is certain that the result will be true.*

1.12.8 Membership Operators

Python supports two types of membership operators – **in** and **not in**. These operators, as the name suggests, test for membership in a sequence such as strings, lists, or tuples that will be discussed in later chapters and are listed below.

```
>>> str1="HELLO"
>>> 'L' in str1
True
>>> 'T' in str1
False
>>> str1 = "HELLO"
>>> 'e' not in str1
True
>>> 'E' not in str1
False
```

***in* Operator:** The operator returns true if a variable is found in the specified sequence and false otherwise.

***not in* Operator:** The operator returns true if a variable is not found in the specified sequence and false otherwise.

```
>>> a = "r"
>>> str = "Good Morning"
>>> a in str
True
>>> 'R' in str
False
```

1.12.9 Identity Operators

Python supports two types of identity operators. These operators compare the memory locations of two objects and are given as follows.

***is* Operator:** Returns true if operands or values on both sides of the operator point to the same object and false otherwise. For example, if a is b returns TRUE if id(a) is same as id(b).

***is not* Operator:** Returns true if operands or values on both sides of the operator do not point to the same object and false otherwise. For example, if a is not b returns TRUE if id(a) is not same as id(b).

We have learnt that Python creates labels when a variable is created. Two variables with the same value refer to the same label and thus have the same id. This concept can be understood by the following example.

> The id() function returns a unique id of the object. Every object in Python has its own unique id which is assigned to the object when it is created. This id is the object's memory address, and will be different for each time you run the program.

Example 1.27

```
>>> a = 10
>>> b = 10
>>> a is b
True
>>> a = 20
>>> b = 10
>>> a is b
False
```

When the is operator returns True, it also indicates that the equality operator will also return True. But this is not always applicable the other way. That is, two objects having the same value and returning True with equality operator may return False with the `is` operator. This generally happens in three cases.

- First, when input is taken from the user
- Second, with integer literals having several digits
- Third, with floating-point and complex numbers.

In all the cases, Python creates two different objects even if they have the same value. This is illustrated below.

Example 1.28

```
CASE 1:
>>> s1 = "HELLO"
>>> s2 = input("Enter a string: ")
Enter a string: HELLO
>>> s1 == s2
True
>>> s1 is s2
False
```

```
CASE 2:
>>>n1 = 1234567
>>> n2 = 1234567
>>> n1 == n2
True
>>> n1 is n2
False
CASE 3:
>>> n1 = 1.23
>>> n2 = 1.23
>>> n1 == n2
True
>>> n1 is n2
False
```

1.12.10 Operators Precedence and Associativity

Table 1.8 lists all operators from highest precedence to lowest. When an expression has more than one operator, then it is the relative priorities of the operators with respect to each other that determine the order in which the expression will be evaluated.

Remember: Operators are associated from left to right. This means that operators with same precedence are evaluated in a left-to-right manner.
Parentheses can change the order in which an operator is applied. The operator in parenthesis is applied first even if there is a higher priority operator in the expression.

Table 1.8 Operator precedence chart

Operator	Description
()	Parenthesis (for grouping)
**	Exponentiation
~,+,-	Complement, unary plus and minus
*,/,%,//	Multiply, divide, modulo and floor division
+,-	Addition and subtraction
>>,<<	Right and left bitwise shift
&	Bitwise 'AND'
^|	Bitwise exclusive 'OR' and regular 'OR'
<=,<,>,>=	Comparison operators
<>,==,!=	Equality operators
=,%=,/=,//=,-=,+=,*=,**=	Assignment operators
Is, is not	Identity operators
In, not in	Membership operators
Not, or, and	Logical operators

```
>>> 5 * 6 + 3
33
>>> 5 + 6*3
23
```

> * has higher precedence than +. Hence, first the operands will be multiplied and then addition will be performed.

Let us try some more codes to see how operator precedence works in our expressions.

Example 1.29

```
>>> (50 + 40) *10/20
45.0
>>> ((50 + 40) * 20) / 10
180.0
>>> (50 + 40) * (20 / 10)
180.0
>>> 50 + (40 * 10) / 20
70.0
>>> (False==False) or True
True
>>> False==(False or True)
False
>>> 50*100/5//4
250.0
>>> (((50* 100)/5)//4)
250.0
>>> 50*(100/(5//4))
5000.0
```

1.13 EXPRESSIONS IN PYTHON

In any programming language, an expression is any legal combination of symbols (like variables, constants and operators) that represents a value. Every language has its own set of rules that define whether an expression is valid or invalid in that language. *In Python, an expression must have at least one operand (variable or constant) and can have one or more operators. On evaluating an expression, we get a value.*

Operand is the value on which the operator is applied. These operators use constants and variables to form an expression. A * B + C – 5 is an example of an expression, where +, *, – are operators; A, B and C are variables and 5 is a constant. Some valid expressions in Python are: x = a / b, y = a * b, z = a^ b, x = a > b, etc. When an expression has more than one operator, then the expression is evaluated using the operator precedence chart.

An example of an illegal expression can be a+ –b or <y++. When the program is compiled, the validity of all expressions is checked. If an illegal expression is encountered, an error message is displayed.

In Python, we can categorize expressions based on the data type of the result obtained on evaluating an expression. These types of expressions include,

Constant Expressions that involves only constants. Example: 8 + 9 – 2

Integral Expressions that produces an integer result.

Example:
a = 10, b = 5
c = a * b

> **Remember:** Deleted variables can be used again in the code if and only if you reassign them some value.

Floating-point Expressions produce floating-point results. Example: a * b / 2

Relational Expressions return either true or false value. Example: c = a > b

Logical Expressions combine two or more relational expressions and returns a value as *true* or *false*. Example: a > b and y != 0.

Bitwise Expressions manipulate data at the bit level. Example: x = y & z.

Assignment Expressions assign a value to a variable. Example: c = 10.

Key Terms

String: A string is a group of characters.

String concatenation: The process of combining two strings.

Slice: A substring of a string is called a slice.

Variable: Variable means something that may change. In Python programs, any piece of information can be stored in a variable and this information may change.

Identifiers: Names given to identify a variable, function, class, module or any other object.

Lvalue: Expressions that comes on the left side of the assignment operator

Rvalue: Expressions that comes on the right side of the assignment operator.

Docstring: In Python, multi-line comments are also known as docstrings.

Keywords: Reserved words in a programming language that have a pre-defined meaning.

Operators: Constructs used to manipulate the value of operands.

Operands: Values on which the operator is applied.

Expression: An expression in a programming language is any valid combination of tokens that represents a value.

Unary operator: Operator applied on a single operand.

Chapter Highlights

- Python is a high-level, interpreted, interactive, object-oriented and reliable language.
- If you want to execute the program in Python shell, then press **F5** key or click on Run Menu and then select **Run Module**.
- The character set of a language is a set of valid characters that the language can recognize. Such characters may be digits, alphabets, or any other symbol.
- Tokens are the small units of the programming language. Python supports literals, keywords, identifiers and operators as tokens.
- Number, as the name suggests, refers to a numeric value. You can use four types of numbers in Python programs. These include integers, long integers, floating-point and complex numbers.
- When two very large floating-point numbers are multiplied, it may result in an *arithmetic overflow*. Arithmetic overflow is a condition that occurs when a calculated result is too large.
- Arithmetic underflow occurs when one floating-point number is divided by another. It is a condition that occurs when a calculated result is too small in magnitude to be represented.
- Any floating-point value may contain an arbitrary number of decimal places, so it is always recommended to use the built-in `format()` function to produce a string version of a number with specific number of decimal places. It can also be used to control the display of strings.
- A raw string does not handle any escape sequences. It is specified by prefixing r or R to the string.
- To create a variable in Python, assign a value to the identifier using the equal to sign.
- When we create a variable, Python creates labels referring to those values.
- Variables can hold values of different types called data types.
- Based on the data type of a variable, the interpreter reserves memory for it and also determines the type of data that can be stored in the reserved memory.

- The five standard data types supported by Python are numbers, string, list, tuple, and dictionary.
- In Python, you can reassign variables as many times as you want to change the value stored in them. You may even store value of one data type in a statement and then a value of another data in a subsequent statement.
- The `type()` function is used to determine data type of an object.
- Python allows programmers to assign a single value to more than one variable simultaneously.
- Trying to reference a variable that has not been assigned any value causes an error. This may happen if you have mistakenly used a variable without assigning it a value prior to its use or have deliberately deleted or removed a variable using the `del` statement and then tried to use it later in your code.
- A variable of Boolean type can have one of the two values – True or False.
- Comments are added in a program to describe the statements in the program code. They make the program easily readable and understandable by the programmer as well as other users who are seeing the code.
- To take input from the users, Python makes use of the `input()` function.
- Whitespace at the beginning of the line is called indentation. These whitespaces at the beginning of the logical line determines the indentation level of that logical line.
- Comparison operator, also known as relational operator, is used to compare the values on its either side and determine the relation between them.
- Unary operators act on single operands. When an operand is preceded by a unary minus sign, its value is negated.
- Python supports two bitwise shift operators. They are shift left (<<) and shift right (>>). These operations are used to shift bits to the left or to the right. The syntax for a shift operation can be given as: operand op num
- Python supports two types of membership operators – in and not in. These operators test for membership in a sequence such as strings, lists, or tuples.

Review Questions

1. Explain the features of Python.
2. Write a short note on literals in Python.
3. What are the problems that can arise while dealing with floating-point numbers?
4. With the help of an example, explain the use of `format()` function.
5. What is a string in Python? Explain the different ways in which you can define a string.
6. Differentiate between implicit conversion and type conversion.
7. What is an escape sequence? Give examples. Why are they called so?
8. Write the commands to display the text "I love programming" in a width of 50 characters when the text is left-justified, right-justified and centre-aligned.
9. Write a command to print a string in reverse.
10. Justify the statement: "Python is a free and open-source programming language".
11. Which of the following expressions would result in overflow or underflow error? Justify your answer.
    a. `1.23e+150*4.56e+100` b. `6.78e-100/4.67e+200`
12. Identify the expressions which will involve coercion and the ones which will involve explicit type conversion
    a. `5.0+2` b. `6.5*3.0`
    c. `7.0+float(8)` d. `6.2*5.0`
    e. `5.7+int(9.0)`
13. Find and correct the error (if any).
    a. `>>> print('It is Teacher's Daty today ')`
    b. `>>> print("Rohan knows "Hindi","English","Punjabi"")`
14. What are identifiers? List some rules that must be kept in mind while naming an identifier.
15. With the help of a diagram, explain what happens when a variable is created in Python.

16. With the help of an example, explain how variables can be re-assigned values in Python.
17. Can we re-assign a value of another data type to a variable? If yes, why?
18. Differentiate between lvalue and rvalue.
19. What do you understand by the term 'multiple assignment'?
20. What are Boolean variables? How are they created?
21. What are comments? How are they written in Python?
22. What is a docstring? How is it defined in a Python program?
23. Why is indentation necessary in Python?
24. Logical expressions operate in a shortcut (or lazy) fashion. Justify this statement.
25. Consider the statement: print "Python # Programming". Will it be executed or not? If yes, justify its output.
    Hint: The # is inside a string, so it is just considered as a character and not as comment.
26. Differentiate between = and ==.
    Hint: The = is used to assign value but the == is used to test if two things have the same value.
27. Which data type will you use to represent the following data values?
    a. Number of days in a week.
    b. The circumference of a circle
    c. You school fees
    d. Distance between moon and the earth
    e. Your favorite book
    f. Whether you will give the entrance exam of not
28. Which type of value will you use for storing the following information?
    a. Employee ID
    b. Employee name
    c. Employee salary
    d. Phone number
29. Which of the following are correct type conversions?
    a. `int (8.2+6.3)`   b. `str (5.6 * 6.7)`
    c. `float ("12"+"3.4")`   d. `str ( 6/4 )`
30. Express the following floating-point numbers in scientific notation:
    a. `123.456789`
    b. `0.000123456`
    c. `1.234567`
31. Evaluate the following arithmetic expressions using the rules of operator precedence in Python.
    a. `4+5*10`
    b. `6+7*2+5`
    c. `20//4*2`
    d. `5*6**3`
    e. `24//6//3`
    f. `4**2**3`
    g. `100-(15*3)`
    h. `50%7`
    i. `-(100/6)+5`
32. Write the following values in exponential notation.
    a. `1230.4567`
    b. `0.00000056009`
    c. `7000809.000000000003`
33. Evaluate the following expressions:
    a. `True and False`
    b. `(100<10) and (100>50)`
    c. `True or False`   d. `(100<10) or (100>200)`
    e. `not(True) and False`
    f. `not (100<10) or (100>50)`
    g. `not(True and False)`
    h. `not (100<10 or 100>50)`
    i. `not True and False`
    j. `100<10 and not 100>50`
    k. `not True and False or True`
    l. `not (100<10 or 50<200)`
35. Which of the following results is True?
    a. `>>>90 == 90 and 11==11`
    b. `>>>31==51 and 71==31`
    c. `>>>72!=12 and 25==25`
    d. `>>>54<51 and 61>86`
    e. `15<20 or 20`
36. Identify the correct arithmetic expression in Python.
    a. `10 (13+76)`
    b. `(15*16) (47+18)`
    c. `14*(33-52)`
    d. `15***2`

37. Give an appropriate Boolean expression for each of the following.
    a. Check if variable var is greater than or equal to 10, and less than 100.
    b. Check if variable var is less than 100 and greater than or equal to 10, or it is equal to 50.
    c. Check if either the name 'Kalam' or 'Azad' appears in a list of names assigned to variable names.
    d. Check if the name 'Abdul' appears and the name 'Maulana' does not appear in a list of names assigned to variable names.
38. Write the data types of the following:
    a. type(5+4)
    b. (20*345)
    c. type(987/45)
    d. type(2345//12)
    e. type(123%34)
39. Identify the data types of the following literals: 9, 29.4, 5j, 3+7i
40. Write the following expressions in Python:

    $$\frac{-b \pm \sqrt{b^2 - 4ac}}{2a} \qquad \sqrt{a^2 + b^2} \qquad \frac{\pi}{2}rh \qquad x^2yz \qquad (a-b)^2 = a^2 - 2ab + b^2$$

    $$d = a^{mn}/a^{-3} \qquad (e^m)^n = e^{mn}$$

41. Differentiate between a. bool('0') and bool('') b. bool(0k) and bool('0k')

Programming Exercises

1. Write a program to calculate the Body Mass Index (BMI) of a person. (BMI = kg/m², where kg is the person's weight and m is his/her height in metres)
2. Write a program to perform string concatenation.
3. Write a program to demonstrate the printing of a string within single quotes, double quotes and triple quote.
4. Write a program to print the ASCII value of a character.
5. Write a program to read a character in upper case and then print it in lower case.
6. Write a program to swap two numbers using a temporary variable.
7. Write a program to read the address of a user. Display the result by breaking it in multiple lines.
8. Write a program to calculate simple interest and compound interest.
9. Write a program that prompts users to enter two integers x and y. The program then calculates and displays xy
10. Write a program that prompts the user to enter his first name and last name and then displays a message "Greetings!!! First name Last name"
11. Write a program to calculate the salary of an employee, given his basic pay (to be entered by the user), HRA = 10 per cent of basic pay, TA = five per cent of basic pay. Define HRA and TA as constants and use them to calculate the salary of the employee.
12. Write a program to prepare a grocery bill. As input, enter the name of the items purchased, quantity in which it is purchased and its price per unit. Then display the bill in the following format.
    ```
    *************** B I L L ****************
    Item Quantity     Price Amount
    *****************************************
    Total Amount to be paid
    *****************************************
    ```
13. Energy is calculated as, $e = mc^2$, where m is the mass of the object and c is its velocity. Write a program that accepts an object's mass (in kilograms) and velocity (in metres per second) and displays its energy.
14. Write a program that calculates the number of seconds in a day.
15. Write a program to read and display the details of a student. While printing use '-' to separate two values.
16. Write a program that prompts the user to enter the first name and the last name. Then display the following message.
    Hello *firstname lastname*
    Welcome to Python!

Fill in the Blanks

1. Python files are stored with a _____ extension.
2. The _____ function prints one or more literals (or values) followed by a newline.
3. To execute Python script file, _____ key is pressed.
4. _____ are the small units of the programming language.
5. Large floating-point numbers are efficiently represented in _____ notation.
6. _____ denotes that an arithmetic overflow has occurred.
7. _____ function is used to produce a string version of a number with specific number of decimal places.
8. The _____ prefix specifies that the file contains text written in language other than English.
9. A _____ is specified by prefixing r or R to the string.
10. The process of combining two strings is called _____.
11. The _____ specifies the number of characters to move forward after the first character is retrieved from the string.
12. A line in Python can have maximum _____ characters.
13. _____ are used to store values.
14. Names given to identify a variable, function, class, module or any other object are generally known as _____.
15. >>>not 10 ==10 gives the answer _____.
16. >>>not 100>700 gives _____.
17. A variable in Python is assigned a value by using the _____ operator.
18. When we create variables, Python creates _____ referring to these values.
19. Variables can hold values of different types called _____.
20. _____ are those objects to which values can be assigned.
21. To take input from the users, Python uses the _____ function.
22. The _____ function is used to convert a non-integer value to integer.
23. In Python, multi-line comments are also known as _____.
24. The level of _____ groups statements to form a block of statements.
25. Values on which the operator is applied is called _____.
26. _____ operator is used to negate the value of the operand on which it is applied.
27. _____ expressions operate in a shortcut (or lazy) fashion and stop the evaluation when it knows the final outcome for sure.
28. If a is b returns TRUE, then _____.
29. _____ can change the order in which an operator is applied.
30. Literals of the form a + bi are called _____.
31. 123.45E-9 is equal to _____.
32. _____ converts an integer to a floating-point number.
33. The _____ operator returns the quotient after division.
34. To find x^y, you will use _____ operator.
35. _____ is a group of characters.
36. Variable names can contain only _____, _____ and _____.
37. >>>90 != 70 gives output _____.

38. 29%0 = _____.
39. int("10"+"20") will give _____.
40. _____ operator treats operand as a sequence of bits.
41. >>> print (format(12356.265901, '.3f')) will result in the value _____.

State True or False

1. Integers can be specified as octal and hexadecimal numbers also.
2. Arithmetic underflow is a condition that occurs when a calculated result is too large.
3. Strings are mutable in Python.
4. When specifying a string, if a single backslash (\) at the end of the line is added then it indicates that the string is continued in the next line, but no new line is added otherwise.
5. A Unicode string does not handle any escape sequence. It is specified by prefixing r or R to the string.
6. format() function can be used to control the display of strings.
7. The default value of stride is 0.
8. Whitespace characters are also counted as a character in a string.
9. Computational thinking means thinking like a computer or to give instructions to a computer.
10. Coding is not a part of computational thinking.
11. Computational thinking involves considering different options carefully before deciding upon he best one.
12. \r represents a new line.
13. An escape sequence is treated as a single character.
14. In Python, a semicolon is used to terminate every statement.
15. Python allows writing multiple statements in a single line.
16. The first character of an identifier must be a dollar sign ($).
17. Python is a case-sensitive language.
18. Based on the data type of a variable, the interpreter reserves memory.
19. While re-assigning values to a variable, the data type must not change.
20. Python variables do not have specific data types.
21. Comments are written to make the program easily readable and understandable.
22. Comments are the executable statements in a program.
23. When the program is run, comments are not displayed.
24. All keywords are written in uppercase characters.
25. Statements in a block must have the same indentation level.
26. Arithmetic operators also known as relational operators.
27. Relational operators can be used to compare strings.
28. Python does not support prefix and postfix increment/decrement operators.
29. Bitwise OR operator produces the ones' complement of the given binary value.
30. Shifting once to the right multiplies the number by 2.
31. The is operator returns true if operands or values on both sides of the operator do not point to the same object and false otherwise.
32. INT = 2; print(INT) will give an error.
33. The id() function can be used to print the address of the variable.

Multiple Choice Questions

1. Python is a _____ language.
   a. high-level   b. interpreted   c. object-oriented   d. All of these.
2. Python programs work on any of the operating systems without requiring any change. This means that Python is _____.
   a. Interactive   b. simple   c. portable   d. dynamic
3. Which of the following is not a valid token in Python?
   a. Character set   b. Literals   c. Identifiers   d. Keywords
4. Which of the following is not a valid literal constant in Python?
   a. 1.2   b. 5   c. H5   d. "H5"
5. Which of the following is not a valid number in Python?
   a. 50000000000L   b. 5E10
   c. 5000000000.123455D   d. 3 – 8i
6. The value _____ indicates that an arithmetic underflow has occurred.
   a. -inf   b. inf   c. 0.0   d. All of these
7. Which of the following is known as the exponentiation operator?
   a. %   b. //   c. **   d. ^
8. By default, the format() function uses _____ character to fill the specified width.
   a. blank space   b. >   c. <   d. ^
9. A string can be sliced using which of the following operators?
   a. []   b. [:]   c. Both a and b.   c. None of these.
10. The index of the first character is _____ and the index of the last character is _____, where n is the number of characters in the string.
    a. 0, n b. 0, $n-1$ c. 1, n d. 1, $n-1$
11. The index of the last character is _____.
    a. –1   b. 0   c. $n-1$ d. n
12. Which of the following statements is syntactically not correct?
    a. a = input ()   b. a = input ("enter a number")
    c. a = input (enter a number)   d. a = INPUT ("enter a number")
13. Which of the following statements is correct?
    a. a = 10 * 5   b. 50 = 10 * 5   c. 15 + 60 = y   d. print 3 * 4
14. Identify the invalid string literal.
    a. 'PYTHON'   b. "PYTHON"   c. '"PYTHON"'   d. ""PYTHON""
15. Identify the valid floating-point value.
    a. 9   b. 23/4   c. 123,456.67   d. 1.2
16. Which of the following is a valid long floating-point value?
    a. 1.2e   b. 1.2e2.3   c. 1.2e01   d. 1,234e9
17. Which of the following is not a valid integer literal in Python?
    a. 0o123   b. 0x123   c. 0X123   d. 0123
18. Which of the following is a valid identifier in Python?
    a. _AaBb   b. 1A_Bb   c. @AaBB   d. Aa-Bb
19. Which of the following can be the first character of a valid identifier in Python?
    a. #   b. @   c. _   d. -
20. Which of the following is known as the string concatenation symbol?
    a. +   b. *   c. ,   d. -
21. Which function is used to determine the data type of an object?
    a. data()   b. type()   c. val()   d. str()

22. A variable can be removed by using the _____ statement.
    a. Remove   b. Erase   c. Del   d. Delete
23. Boolean variables are created using which of the following operator(s)?
    a. Equality   b. Assignment   c. Both a and b.   d. None of these.
24. The input function takes user's input as a/an _____.
    a. integer   b. floating-point   c. string   d. None of these.
25. All characters following the _____ symbol and up to the end of the line are part of the comment.
    a. #   b. _____   c. %   d. @
26. Which operator is used for integer division?
    a. /   b. %   c. //   d. \
27. If both bits are 1, the corresponding bit in the result is 1 and 0 otherwise. This is a feature of which bitwise operator?
    a. AND   b. NOT   c. OR   d. XOR
28. Which operator returns True if a variable is found in the specified sequence and False otherwise?
    a. is   b. not is   c. in   d. not in
29. Identify valid assignment statements
    a. x = y + 2   b. a = a++   c. x + y = 10   d. x + 10 = y
30. Which line of code produces an error?
    a. "one" + "2"   b. 'one' + 2   c. 1 + 2   d. "1" + "two"
31. abc ="AABBCC"; print(abc*3)
    a. abcabcabc   b. "abcabcabc" c. ABCABCABC   d. AABBCCAABBCCAABBCC
32. Identify the correct variable creation statement.
    a. my_var =7   b. 123my_var =10   c. my var = 12   d. 10 = myvar
33. Bitwise operator can be applied on which data type?
    a. Integer   b. Float   c. String   d. Complex number
34. Which operator is also known as string repetition operator?
    a. +   b. *   c. &   d. ^
35. The following statement will produce _____ lines of output.
    `print('Python \n Programming \n is\n ---Fun')`
    a. 1   b. 2   c. 3   d. 4
36. Identify the expression that may result in arithmetic overflow.
    a. a*b   b. a**b   c. a/b   d. a+b
37. Which operations do not result in 9?
    a. 95 // 10   b. 130 % 11   c. 3 **3   d. 81 ** 0.5

Give the Output

1. ```
   print("Hello")
   print("My Dear Students", end = ' ')
   print("Let us learn Python")
   print("Programming")
   ```
2. `>>> format(10**25,'.2e')`
3. `>>> format(987654321.315978,',.3f')`
4. `>>> 'PYTHON'`
5. `>>> "PROGRAMMING IN PYTHON"`
   ```

6. ```
   >>> ''' I ENJOY PROGRAMMING
   IN
   PYTHON'''
   ```
7. `>>> 'PYTHON' "PROGRAMMING"`
8. ```
   >>> print("Python Programming \
   is FUN !!!!")
   ```
9. `>>> print(R'It is Teacher's Day today ')`
10. `>>> "I" + 'LOVE' + '''PROGRAMMING'''`
11. ```
    str = "I Love Programming in Python"
    print(str[0])
    print(str[7])
    print(str[-5])
    print(str[7:10])
    print(str[::2])
    print(str[3:11:3])
    print(str[:-7])
    print(str[-6:])
    ```
12. `>>> print(type(int('10')))`
13. `>>> str(print())+"abc"`
14. `>>> print(print("abc"))`
15. `>>> str(print("abc"))+"xyz"`
16. `>>> print(print("abc",end=" "))`
17. `(10<20) and (20 < 10) or (5 < 30) and not (15 < 40)`
18. ```
    x,y,z = 10,20,30
    y,z,x = x+5, y+7, z-3
    print("x = ",x, " y = ",y, "z = ",z)
    ```
19. ```
    x,y = 10,20
    y,z = x+5, y-20
    print("x = ",x, " y = ",y," z = ",z)
    ```
20. `>>> 350 + 230 - 170`
21. `>>> (51 + 9.7 - 4) * 100`
22. `>>> 110%(95//3)`
23. `>>> 'Python Programming is fun… '`
24. `>>>"Python Programming is fun…"`
25. ```
    >>>'''Python… \n
       Programming?'''
    ```
26. `>>> print("Python \n Programming")`
27. `>>> print("PYTHON !!!!"*3)`

28. ```
>>>x = 100 ; x *= 3; print(x)
```
29. ```
>>> s1 = "HELLO"   ;    s1 += "WORLD"   ;    print(s1)
```
30. ```
days = "Mon Tue Wed Thu Fri Sat Sun"
months = "Jan\nFeb\nMar\nApr\nMay\nJun\nJul\nAug"
print("Days are : "+ days)
print("Months are: "+ months)
print(""" There's a new dream today.
I'll tell you some other day.
Come on, let's enjoy. """)
```
31. ```
# print(ABCD)
```
32. ```
>>> num1 = "7"
>>> num1 += "10"
>>> num2 = int(num1) + 3
>>> print (float(num2))
```
33. ```
name = input("Enter a word :")
print ('HELLO' + name)
```
34. ```
>>> abs(100-200) * 3
```
35. ```
>>>float("5678" * int(input("Enter a number:")))
```
36. ```
>>> int = 2; print(int)
```
37. ```
a,b = 10,20
b,a = a *5, b /2
print("a = ",a, " and b = ", b)
```
38. ```
a,b = 10,20
a,b,a = a*10, b*5,a*20
print("a = ",a, " and b = ", b)
```
39. ```
x =10
print(id(x))
x = x + 10
print(id(x))
x = x - 10
print(id(x))
```
40. 0 or 10
41. 10 or 0
42. 0 or 0
43. "abc" or ""
44. '' or ''
45. 'k' or 'r'
46. 10 ** 3 ** 2
47. 7 -5 -12 > -5 *3 +8

48. `len(str(7 -5 -12 > -5 *3 +8)) == len('true')`
49. `bool('0') and (10 < 20)`
50. `23%5 is 23%5`
51. `20 or len(20)`
52. `10 == 10.0`
53. `10 == int(10)`
54. `str(10)==str('10.0')`
55. `'R' == 'R'`
56. `70/(7-(2+4))or 4<5`
57. `5 < 9 or 60/(10-(6+4))`
58. `len("abcd") == 30/6 or 30/10`
59. `2 * (5 *(len("007")))`
60. `30 < 70 and 40 > 50`
61. `N = 1 + 1 + 1 == 0.3; print(N)`
62. `a = True;      b = 0<5`
    `a==b    ;     a is b`
63. `print(bool(int('0')))`
    `print(bool(str(0)))`
    `print(bool(float('0.0')))`
    `print(bool(str(0.0)))`
64. `a,b,c = 12,13,16`
    `d = a + b *c/b`
    `print(d)`

Find the Error

1. `>>>10+'20'+30+'40'`
2. `>>>'10'*'20'`
3. `x = 10`
      `print(x)`
4. `x = 123.456`
   `print('%'+x)`
5. `x = 1; y = 2;`
   `print(x+y+z)`
6. `if = 5; print(if)`
7. `a = 10; b = 20; print(a;b)`
8. `x =10`
   `y = x * 30`

```
x = "PYTHON"
z = x/10
```
9. ```
name = int(input("Enter your name : "))
print("HELLO", name)
```
10. `print(len(bool(0)))`
11. `>>> print("HELLO"/2)`
12. `>>> print(type(int("HELLO")))`
13. ```
n1 = 20
n2 = 30
del num1
n2 = 40
n1 = 50
print(num1 - num2)
```
14. ```
n1 = 90
n2 = n1 + 50
n2 = int(str(n2) + "40")
print(num2)
```

## Answers

### Fill in the Blanks

1. py
2. `print()`
3. F5
4. Tokens
5. scientific
6. Infinity (inf)
7. `format()`
8. 'U'
9. raw string
10. string concatenation
11. stride
12. 79
13. Variables
14. identifiers
15. False
16. True
17. assignment
18. labels
19. data types
20. Lvalues
21. `input()`
22. `int()`
23. docstrings
24. indentation
25. operand
26. Unary minus
27. Logical
28. id(a) is same as id(b).
29. Parentheses
30. complex numbers
31. 0.00000012345
32. `float()`
33. / or //
34. **
35. String
36. underscore, upper case, lower case character
37. True
38. ZeroDivisionError
39. 1020
40. Bitwise
41. 12356.266

### State True or False

1. True
2. False
3. True
4. True
5. False
6. True
7. False
8. True
9. False
10. True
11. True
12. False
13. True
14. False
15. True
16. False
17. True
18. True
19. False
20. True
21. True
22. False
23. True
24. False
25. True
26. False
27. True
28. True
29. False
30. False
31. False
32. False
33. True
```

Multiple Choice Questions

1. d
2. c
3. a
4. c
5. c
6. c
7. c
8. a
9. c
10. b
11. a
12. c
13. a
14. d
15. d
16. c
17. d
18. a
19. c
20. a
21. b
22. c
23. c
24. c
25. a
26. c
27. a
28. c
29. a
30. b
31. d
32. a
33. a
34. b
35. d
36. b
37. c

Give the Output

1. Hello
   My Dear Students Let us learn
   Python
   Programming
2. '1.00e+25'
3. '987,654,321.316'
4. 'PYTHON'
5. 'PROGRAMMING IN PYTHON'
6. ' I ENJOY PROGRAMMING\nIN\nPYTHON'
7. 'PYTHONPROGRAMMING'
8. Python Programming is FUN !!!!
9. It is Teacher's Day today
10. 'ILOVEPROGRAMMING'
11. I
    P
    y
    Pro
    ILv rgamn nPto
    o o
    I Love Programming in
    Python
12. <class 'int'>
13. 'Noneabc'
14. abc
    None
15. abc
    'Nonexyz'
16. abc None
17. False
18. x =   27 y =   15 z =   27
19. x =   10 y =   15 z =   0
20. 410
21. 5670.0
22. 17
23. 'Python Programming is fun… '
24. 'Python Programming is fun… '
25. 'Python… \n\n   Programming?'
26. Python
      Programming
27. PYTHON !!!!PYTHON !!!!PYTHON !!!!
28. 300
29. HELLOWORLD
30. Days are : Mon Tue Wed Thu Fri Sat
    Sun
    Months are: Jan
    Feb
    Mar
    Apr
    May
    Jun
    Jul
    Aug
      There's a new dream today.
    I'll tell you some other day.
    Come on, let's enjoy.
31. Nothing
32. 713.0
33. Enter a word :abcd
    HELLOabcd
34. 300

35. ```
    Enter a number:6
    5.6785678567856787e+23
    ```
36. 2
37. a = 10.0 and b = 50
38. a = 200 and b = 100
39. 140705644503984
    140705644504304
    140705644503984
40. 10
41. 10
42. 0
43. 'abc'
44. ''
45. 'k'
46. 1000000000
47. False
48. False
49. True
50. True
51. True
52. True
53. True
54. False
55. True
56. 70.0
57. True
58. 3.0
59. 30
60. False
61. False
62. True True
63. False True False True
64. 28.0

Find the Error

1. TypeError: unsupported operand type(s) for +: 'int' and 'str'
2. TypeError: can't multiply sequence by non-int of type 'float'
3. Error! Tab at the start of the line
4. TypeError: cannot concatenate 'str' and 'float' objects
5. NameError: name 'z' is not defined
6. SyntaxError: invalid syntax
7. SyntaxError: invalid syntax
8. TypeError: unsupported operand type(s) for /: 'str' and 'int'
9. ValueError: invalid literal for int() with base 10: 'ABC'
10. TypeError: object of type 'bool' has no len()
11. TypeError: unsupported operand type(s) for /: 'str' and 'int'
12. ValueError: invalid literal for int() with base 10: 'HELLO'
13. NameError: name 'num1' is not defined
14. NameError: name 'num2' is not defined
    ```

Decision Control Statements

Chapter Objectives

Until now, we have executed simple statements in Python. Such statements are executed sequentially from the first line of the program to the last. That is, the second statement is executed after the first; the third statement is executed after the second, and so on. This way of execution is known as sequential control flow.

However, in some cases we may want to either execute only a selected set of statements (i.e., selection control) or execute a set of statements repeatedly (i.e., iterative control). In such cases, decision control system comes into picture. In this chapter, we will therefore read about the following topics in Python.

- `If` statement
- `If-else` statement
- Nested `if` statement
- `If-elif-else` statement
- Iterative statements like the `while` loop and `for` loop
- `Else` statement with loop
- Special statements like `pass`, `break` and `continue`

2.1 INTRODUCTION

A ***decision control statement*** is a statement that determines the flow of control in a program. Flow of control means the flow of instructions in the order in which they have to be executed, that is, depending on which instruction should be executed next. A decision control statement can skip either one or more instructions. The three fundamental methods of control flow in a programming language are *sequential, selection, and iterative control*.

Selection and iterative control are a part of decision control system. Thus, a decision control statement can alter (change) the flow of a sequence of instructions. And this type of conditional processing helps users to extend the usefulness of programs.

Programmers can make programs that determine which statements of the code should be executed and which should be ignored in certain circumstances. Figure 2.1 shows the categorization of decision control statements.

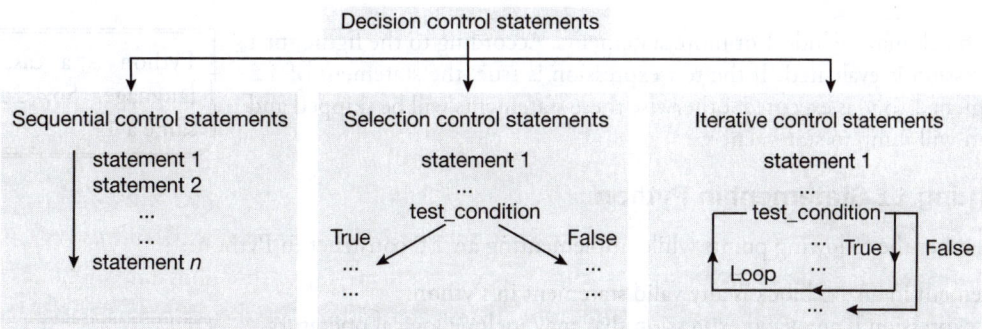

Figure 2.1 Categorization of decision control statements

2.2 SELECTION/CONDITIONAL BRANCHING STATEMENTS

The decision control statements usually jump from one part of the code to another depending on whether a particular condition is satisfied or not. That is, they execute statements selectively based on certain decisions. Such type of decision control statements is known as **selection control statements** or *conditional branching statements*. The Python language supports the following types of conditional branching statements:

- If statement
- If-else statement
- Nested if statement
- If-elif-else statement

2.2.1 if Statement

If statement is the simplest form of decision control statements that is frequently used in decision making. It is a selection control statement based on the value of a given Boolean expression. The general form of a simple if statement is shown in Fig. 2.2.

Syntax of if Statement

```
if test_expression:
     statement1
..........
     Statement n
statement x;
```

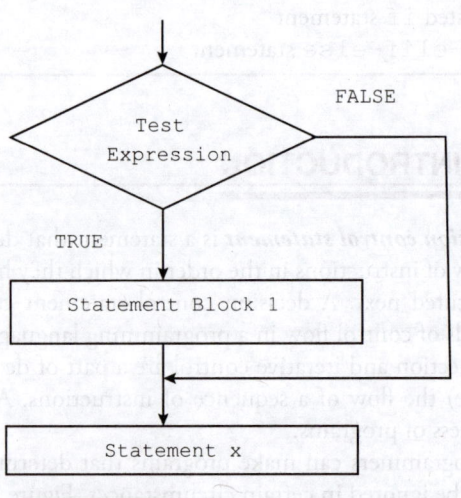

Figure 2.2 if statement construct

The if block may include 1 or more statements. According to the figure, first the test expression is evaluated. If the test expression is true, the statement of if block (statement 1 to *n*) is executed; otherwise these statements will be skipped and the execution will jump to statement *x*.

> Python is a case-sensitive language. So, if is not same a IF.

Implementing if Statement in Python

Always remember the following points while implementing an if construct in Python.

- The statement in an if block is any valid statement in Python.
- The test expression is any valid expression that may include logical operators.
- **A header in Python is a specific keyword followed by a colon.** In Fig.2.2, the if statement has a header, "**if text_expression:**" having keyword if.

> Header and its suite are together known as a clause.

- The group of statements following a header is called a **suite**. After the header, all instructions that are indented at the same level forms a suite.
- While four spaces are commonly used for each level of indentation, any number of spaces may be used.

Example 2.1 Program to increment a number if it is positive.

```
x = 10 #Initialize the value of x
if(x>0): #test the value of x
    x = x+1 #Increment the value of x if it is > 0
print(x) #Print the value of x
```

> Remember to properly indent the statements that are dependent on the previous statements.

OUTPUT:

x = 11

In the above code, we take a variable *x* and initialize it to 10. In the test expression, we check if the value of *x* is greater than 0 or not. If the test expression evaluates to true, then the value of *x* is incremented and is printed on the screen. Note that the print statement will be executed even if the test expression is false.

Python uses indentation to form a block of code. Other languages such as C and C++, use curly braces to accomplish this.

Example 2.2 Write a program to determine whether a person is eligible to vote.

```
age = int(input("Enter the age : "))
if(age>=18):
    print("You are eligible to vote")
```

OUTPUT

```
Enter the age : 35
You are eligible to vote
```

Example 2.3 Write a program to determine the character entered by the user.

```
char = input("Press any key : ")
if(char.isalpha()):
    print("The user has entered a character")
if(char.isdigit()):
    print("The user has entered a digit")
if(char.isspace()):
    print("The user entered a white space character")
```

OUTPUT

```
Press any key: 7
The user has entered a digit
```

2.2.2 `if-else` Statement

Although `if` statement plays a vital role in conditional branching, its usage is very limited. Its simplicity is also its drawback. In the `if` statement, the test expression is evaluated; if the result is true, the statement(s) followed by the expression is/are executed. But if the expression is false, nothing useful happens. So, using an `if-else` statement solves our problem. The general form of a simple `if-else` statement is shown in Fig. 2.3.

Syntax of `if-else` Statement

```
if (test expression):
        statement block 1
else:
        statement block 2
statement x;
```

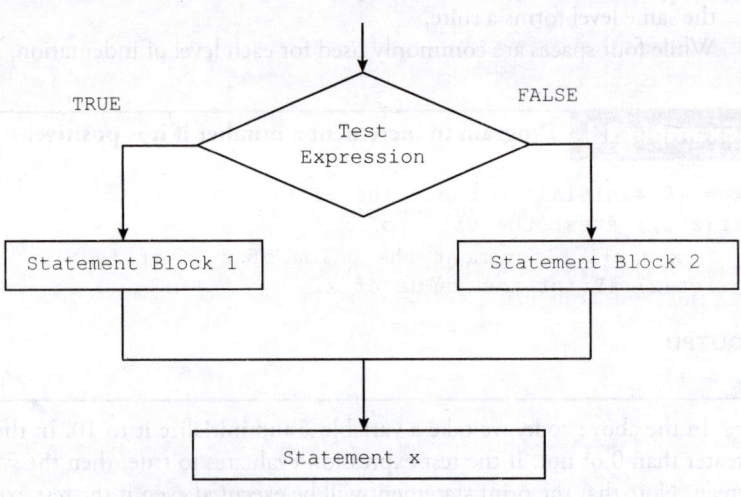

Figure 2.3 `if-else` statement construct

In the above syntax, we have written the statement block. A statement block may include one or more statements. According to the `if-else` construct, first the test expression is evaluated. If the expression is true, statement Block 1 is executed and statement Block 2 is skipped. Otherwise, if the expression is false, statement Block 2 is executed and statement Block 1 is ignored. In any case, after the statement Block 1 or 2 gets executed, the control will pass to statement x. Therefore, statement x is executed in every case.

Example 2.4 Write a program to determine whether a person is eligible to vote or not. If he is not eligible display how many years are left to be eligible.

```
age = int(input("Enter the age : "))
if(age>=18):
print("You are eligible to vote")
else:
yrs = 18 - age
print("You have to wait for " + str(yrs) +" years")
```

OUTPUT
```
Enter the age : 10
You have to wait for 8 years
```

Example 2.5 Write a program to find larger of two numbers.

```
a = int(input("Enter the value of a : "))
b = int(input("Enter the value of b : "))
if(a>b):
large = a
else:
large = b
print("Large= ",large)
```

OUTPUT
```
Enter the value of a : 50
Enter the value of b : 30
Large = 50
```

2.2.3 Nested `if` Statements

A statement that contains other statements is called a ***compound statement***. To perform more complex checks, `if` statements can be nested, that is, one statement can be placed one inside the other. In such a case, the inner `if` statement is the statement part of the outer one. Nested if statements are used to check if more than one conditions are satisfied. Consider the code given below to understand this concept.

Example 2.6 **Program that prompts the user to enter a number and then print its interval.**

```
num = int(input("Enter any number from 0-30: "))
if(num>=0 and num<10):
print("It is in the range 0-10")
elif(num>=10 and num<20):
print("lt is in the range 10-20")
elif(num>=20 and num<30):
print("lt is in the range 20-30")
```

> `if` statements can be nested resulting in multi-way selection. You can do the same program using `if-else` and `if-elif-else` statements.

OUTPUT
```
Enter any number from 0-30: 25
It is in the range 20-30
```

2.2.4 `if-elif-else` Statement

Python supports `if-elif-else` statements to test additional conditions apart from the initial test expression. The `if-elif-else` construct works in the same way as a usual `if-else` statement. If-elif-else construct is also known as **nested if construct**. The `elif` (short for else if) statement is a shortcut to `if` and `else` statements. *A series of if and elif statements have a final else block, which is executed if none of the if or elif expressions is True.* Its syntax is given in Fig. 2.4.

Comparing Floating-point Numbers

Never test floating-point numbers for exact equality. This is because floating-point numbers are just approximations, so it is always better to test floating-point numbers for 'approximately equal' rather than testing for exactly equal.

We can test for approximate equality by finding the difference between the two floating point numbers (that are to be tested) and comparing their absolute value of the difference against a very small number, epsilon.

Syntax of `if-elif-else` Statement

```
if ( test expression 1)
    statement block 1
elif ( test expression 2)
    statement block 2
..........................
elif (test expression N)
    statement block N
else
    Statement Block X
Statement Y
```

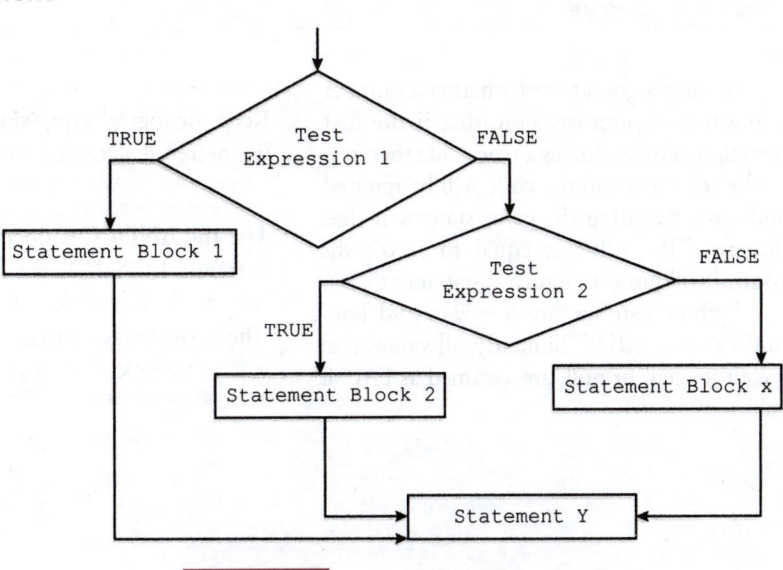

Figure 2.4 `if-elif-else` syntax

Note that it is not necessary that every `if` statement should have an else block as Python supports simple `if` statements also. After the first test expression or the first `if` branch, the programmer can have as many `elif` branches as he wants depending on the expressions that have to be tested. The final else block is called if none of the `if` or `elif` expressions is True.

> **Remember:** The `elif` and `else` parts are optional.

Example 2.7 — To test whether a number entered by the user is negative, positive or equal to zero.

```
num = int(input("Enter any number: "))
if(num==0):
    print("The value is equal to zero")
elif(num>0):
    print("The number is positive")
else:
    print("The number is negative")
```

OUTPUT

```
Enter any number: -10
The number is negative
```

Example 2.8 — Write a program to determine whether the character entered is a vowel or not.

```
ch = input("Enter any character: ")
if(ch=="A" or ch=="E" or ch=="I" or ch=="O" or ch=="U"):
    print ch,"is a vowel")
elif(ch=="a" or ch=="e" or ch=="i" or ch=="o" or ch=="u"):
    print(ch,"is a vowel")
else:
    print(ch,"is not a vowel")
```

OUTPUT

```
Enter any character: h
h is not a vowel
```

In the program to test whether a number is positive or negative, note that if the first test expression evaluates a true value then rest of the statements in the code will be ignored and after executing the print statement that displays "The value is equal to zero", the control will jump to return 0 statement.

Python assumes any non-zero and non-null value as TRUE. Similarly, all values that are either zero or null, are assumed as FALSE value.

> Keep the logical expressions simple and short. For this, you may use nested if statements.

> Use the AND/ OR operators to form a compound relation expression. In Python, the following expression is invalid.
> `if (60 ≤ marks ≤ 75):`
> The correct way to write is,
> `if ((marks ≥ 60) and (marks ≤ 75):`

2.3 ITERATIVE STATEMENTS

Python supports basic loop structures. Iterative statements are used to repeat the execution of one or more statements. In Python, iterative statements are implemented through `while` loop and `for` loop.

2.3.1 While Loop

The `while` loop provides a mechanism to repeat one or more statements when a particular condition is true. Figure 2.5 shows the syntax and general form of representation of a `while` loop.

Syntax of `while` Loop

```
statement x
while (condition):
     statement block
statement y
```

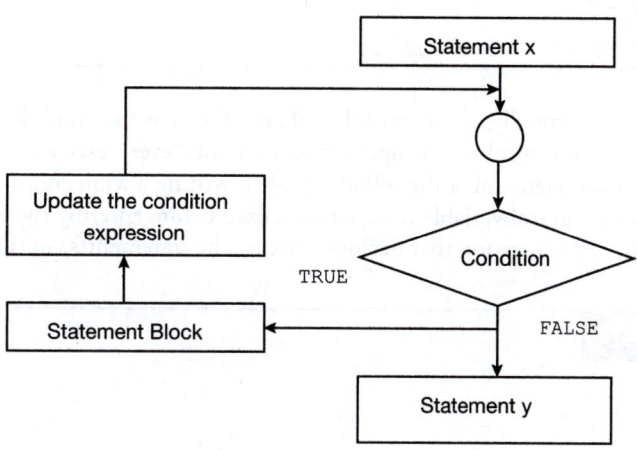

Figure 2.5 The `while` loop construct

Note that in the `while` loop, the condition is tested before any of the statements in the statement block is executed. The statements will be executed only when the condition is true; otherwise, if the condition is false, the control will jump to statement y, which is the immediate statement outside the `while` loop block.

We must update the condition with every iteration of the loop. This is necessary because it is this condition which determines when the loop will end. If we do not update the condition, then it will never become false. This will result in an infinite loop, which is never desirable.

A `while` loop is also referred to as a top-checking loop since control condition is placed as the first line of the code. If the control condition evaluates to false, then the statements enclosed in the loop are never executed. Look at the following example code.

> Iterative statements are used to repeat the execution of a list of statements, depending on the value of an integer expression.

Example 2.9 To print first 10 numbers using a `while` loop.

```
i = 0
while(i<=10):
    print(i,end='')
    i = i+1
```

OUTPUT

0 1 2 3 4 5 6 7 8 9 10

Example 2.10 Write a program to calculate the sum and average of first 10 numbers.

```
i = 0
s = 0
while(i<=10):
    s = s+i
    i=i+1
avg = float(s)/10
print("The sum of first 10 numbers is :",s)
print("The average of first 10 numbers is :",avg)
```

OUTPUT
```
The sum of first 10 numbers is : 55
```

In the program initially, *i* = 0 and is less than 10, that is the condition is true, so in the `while` loop, the value of *i* is printed and the condition is updated so that with every execution of the loop, the condition becomes more approachable. Always remember the following when writing a while loop:

First, the loop control variable must be initialized before entering the loop.

Second, the test expression that decides whether the statement(s) in the loop will be executed or not is evaluated.

Example 2.11

```
i = 0
sum = 0
avg = 0.0
while(i<=10):
    sum = sum + i
avg = sum/10
print("\n The sum of first 10 numbers = ", sum)
print("\n The average of first 10 numbers = ", avg)
```

> The infinite loop is a loop which never stops running. Its condition always True.

Third, the statement(s) inside the loop are executed if the test expression is True.

Fourth, the loop control variable is updated.

While loop is very useful for designing interactive programs in which the number of times the statements in loop has to be executed may or may not be known in advance. Let us look at a program which results in an infinite loop. Though the program is supposed to calculate the average of first 10 numbers, the condition never becomes False, and the desired output is *not* generated. If you clearly observe the code, you will see that the statement updating the value of loop control variable (*i*) is missing here. So, every time the loop executes, the value of *i* is zero. In no way, will the value of *i* become equal to or greater than 10. Hence, an infinite loop – a loop that never ends is entered.

Once you have entered the infinite loop, either press Ctrl + C keys on the keyboard or press the close button of the Python shell window.

2.3.2 `for` Loop

Like the `while` loop, the `for` loop provides a mechanism to repeat a task until a particular condition is true. For loop is usually known as a determinate or definite loop because the programmer knows exactly how many times the loop will repeat. The number of times the loop has to be executed can be determined mathematically by checking the logic of the loop.

The `for..in` statement is a looping statement used in Python to iterate over a sequence of objects, i.e., go through each item in a sequence. Here, by sequence we mean just an ordered collection of items. The flow of statements in a `for` loop can be given as in Fig. 2.6.

Syntax of for Loop

```
for loop_contol_var in
    sequence:
statement block
```

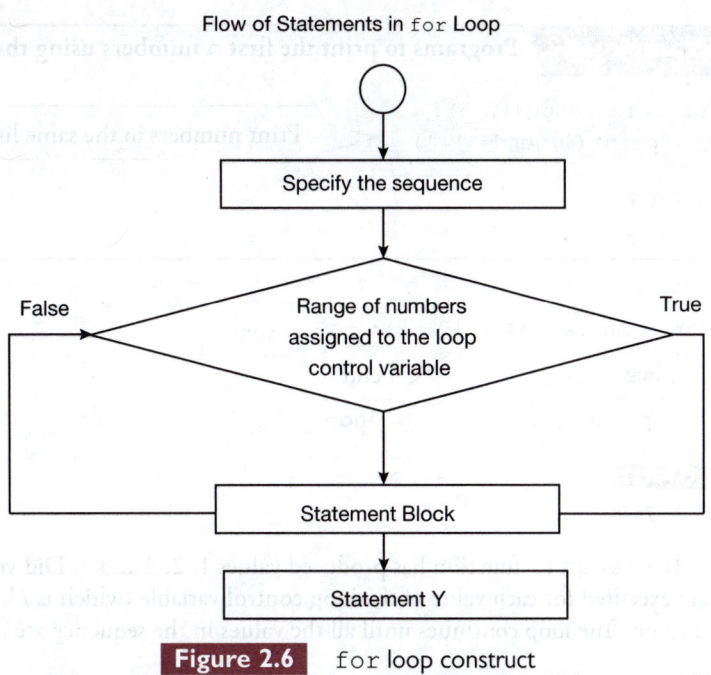

Figure 2.6 for loop construct

When a `for` loop is used, a range of sequence is specified (only once). The items of the sequence are assigned to the loop control variable one after the other. The `for` loop is executed for each item in the sequence. With every iteration of the loop, a check is made to ensure if the loop control variable has been assigned all the values in the sequence. If all the values have not been assigned, the statement block of the loop is executed; else, the statements comprising the statement block of the `for` loop are skipped and the control jumps to the immediate statement following the `for` loop body. Note that every iteration of the loop must make the loop control variable closer to the end of the sequence.

Let us print all the characters in a string using the `for` loop. We know that a string is a sequence of characters. So, the `for` loop statement(s) will be executed for each character in the string.

Example 2.12

```
for i in "PYTHON":
    print(i, end = ' ')
```

OUTPUT

```
P Y T H O N
```

2.4 THE RANGE() FUNCTION

The `range()` is a built-in function in Python that is used to iterate over a sequence of numbers. The syntax of `range()` is **range(beg, end, [step])**.

The **range()** generates a sequence of numbers starting with **beg** (inclusive) and ending with one less than the number **end**. The **step** argument is optional (hence, written in brackets). By default, every number in the range is incremented by 1 but we can specify a different increment using step. It can be both negative

> Step can be either positive or negative but cannot be zero.

and positive, but not zero.

Example 2.13 Programs to print the first n numbers using the `range()` in a `for` loop:

```
for i in range(1, 5):
    print(i, end= ' ')
```
← Print numbers in the same line

OUTPUT

```
1 2 3 4
```

```
for i in range(1, 10, 2):
    print(i, end= ' ')
```
beg / end / step

OUTPUT

```
1 3 7 9
```

The `range()` function has produced values 1, 2, 3 and 4. Did you notice that the statement(s) of the `for` loop is/are executed for each value of the loop control variable (which is *i* here). Initially, i is 1, in the next iteration it is 2, and so on. The loop continues until all the values in the sequence are processed.

2.5 SELECTING AN APPROPRIATE LOOP

Loops can be either counter-controlled or condition controlled (or sentinel-controlled). When we know in advance the number of times the loop should be executed, we use a counter-controlled loop. Counter is a variable that must be initialized, tested, and updated for performing the loop operations. Such a counter-controlled loop in which the counter is assigned a constant or a value is also known as a ***definite repetition loop***.

When we do not know in advance the number of times the loop will be executed, we use a condition-controlled (or sentinel-controlled or indefinite) loop. In such a loop, a special value called the *sentinel value* is used to change the loop control expression from true to false. For example, when the user is supposed to enter as many values as he likes then the programmer may specify that to stop the loop, – 1 (or any other value) should be entered. This special value is called a ***sentinel value***. A condition-controlled loop is often useful for indefinite repetition loops as they use a true/false condition to control the number of times the loop is executed.

If your requirement is to have a *counter-controlled loop, then choose for loop; else if you need to have a sentinel-controlled loop then go for a while loop*. Table 2.1 shows the comparison between the counter-controlled and condition-controlled loops.

Counter-controlled

```
i = 0
while(i<=10):
    print(i,end ='')
    i+=1
```

Condition-controlled

```
i = 0
while(1):
    print(i,end ='')
    i+=1
    if(i==11):
        break
```

Counter-controlled

```
for i in range(11):
    print(i, end = '')
```

Table 2.1 Comparison between condition-controlled and counter-controlled loops

Attribute	Counter-controlled loop	Condition-controlled loop
Number of execution	Used when number of times the loop has to be executed is known in advance.	Used when number of times the loop has to be executed is not known in advance.
Condition variable	In counter controlled loops, we have a counter variable.	In Condition controlled loops, we use a sentinel variable.
Value and limitation of variable	The value of the counter variable and the condition for loop execution, both are strict.	The condition for loop execution is strict but the value of the sentinel variable may vary

2.6 NESTED LOOPS

Nested loop means that a loop is placed inside another loop. Although both `for` and `while` loops can be nested, we usually use nested `for` loops as they are easiest to control. In such a case, the inner `for` loop can be used to control the number of times a particular set of statements will be executed and the outer `for` loop can be used to control the number of times the inner loop is repeated. In Python, loops can be nested to any desired level.

Example 2.14 Write a program to print the following pattern.

Pass 1-1 2 3 4 5
Pass 2-1 2 3 4 5
Pass 3-1 2 3 4 5
Pass 4-1 2 3 4 5
Pass 5-1 2 3 4 5

```
for i in range(1,6):
    print("PASS",i,"- ",end="")
    for j in range(1,6):
        print(j, end='')
    print()
```

Example 2.15 Write a program to print the following pattern.

```
**********
**********
**********
**********
**********
```

```
for i in range(5):
    print()
    for j in range(5):
        print "*",end=''
```

2.7 THE break STATEMENT

The break statement is used to terminate the execution of the nearest enclosing loop in which it appears. The break statement is widely used with for loop and while loop. When the compiler encounters a break statement, the control passes to the statement that follows the loop in which the break statement appears. Its syntax is quite simple, just type keyword break.

Example 2.16 **Program to demonstrate the break statement.**

```
i = 1
while i <= 10:
    print(i,end='')
    if i==5:
        break
    i = i+1
print("\n Done")
```

OUTPUT

```
1 2 3 4 5
Done
```

Note that the code is meant to print first 10 numbers using a while loop, but it will actually print only numbers from 0 to 4. As soon as i becomes equal to 5, the break statement is executed and the control jumps to the statement following the while loop.

Hence, the break statement is used to exit a loop from any point within its body, bypassing its normal termination expression. When the break statement is encountered inside a loop, the loop is immediately terminated, and program control is passed to the next statement following the loop. Figure 2.7 shows the transfer of control when the break statement is encountered.

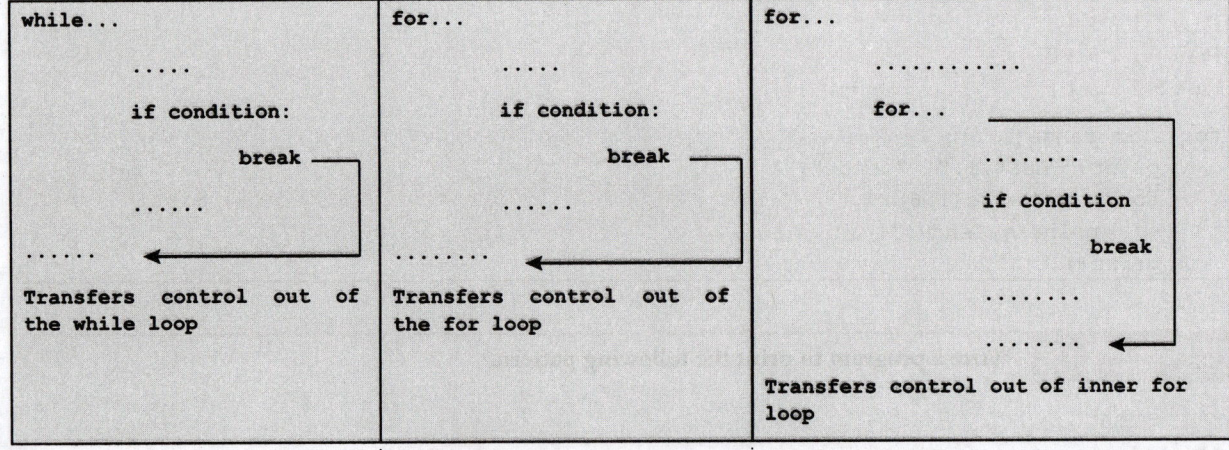

Figure 2.7 The break statement

2.8 THE continue STATEMENT

Like the break statement, the continue statement can only appear in the body of a loop. When the compiler encounters a continue statement then the rest of the statements in the loop are skipped and the control is unconditionally transferred to the loop-continuation portion of the nearest enclosing loop. Its syntax is quite simple, just type keyword **continue** as shown below.

When the `continue` statement is encountered in the `while` and `for` loop, the control is transferred to the statement that tests the controlling expression. However, if placed with a for loop, the continue statement causes a branch to the code that updates the loop variable.

Example 2.17   **Program to demonstrate the continue statement.**

```
for i in range(1,11):
    if(i==5):
        continue
    print(i, end='')
print("\n Done")
```

OUTPUT

```
1 2 3 4 6 7 8 9 10
Done
```

Note that the code is meant to print numbers from 0 to 10. But as soon as i becomes equal to 5, the `continue` statement is encountered, so the rest of the statement(s) in the `for` loop are skipped. In the output, there is no 5 (5 could not be printed as `continue` caused early increment of i and skipping of statement that printed the value of i on screen). Figure 2.8 illustrates the use of `continue` statement in loops.

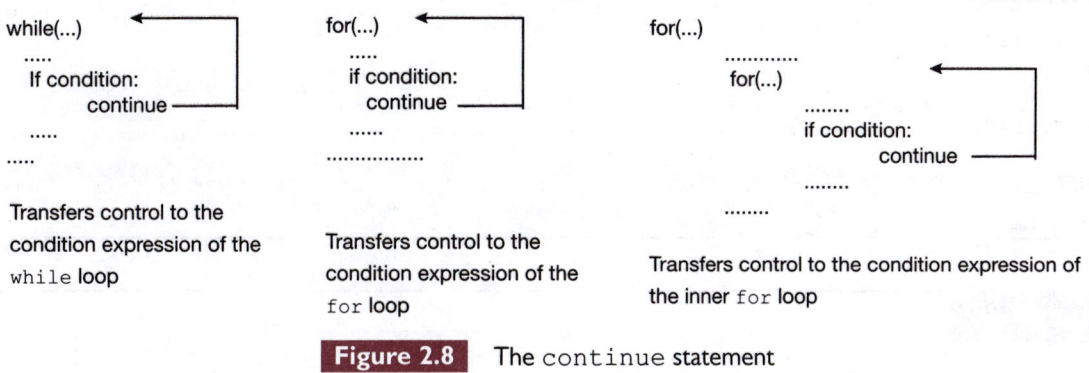

Figure 2.8   The `continue` statement

Hence, the **continue** statement is the opposite of the **break** statement. It forces the next iteration of the loop, thereby skipping any statements that were a part of the loop. The `continue` statement is usually used to restart a statement sequence when an error occurs.

2.9   THE pass STATEMENT

`pass` statement is used when a statement is required syntactically but no instruction has to be executed. It specifies a *null* operation or simply **No Op**eration (NOP) statement. Nothing happens when the `pass` statement is executed. Syntax of pass statement is simple, just type the keyword **pass**.

The `pass` statement is used as a placeholder for future statements. For example, if we have a loop that is not implemented yet, in which we may wish to write some code in it in the future. Then, we can use the pass statement instead of an empty body of the loop. Though the pass statement will not do anything, it will make the program syntactically correct. This is shown in the code.

Example 2.18   Program to demonstrate `pass` statement.

```
for i in range(5):
pass  #The statement is doing nothing
print(i,end ='')
print("Done")
```

OUTPUT

```
012 3 4 Done
```

Difference between `comment` and `pass` statements In Python programming, *pass* is a null statement. While the interpreter ignores a comment entirely, *pass* is not ignored. `comment` *is not executed but* `pass` *statement is executed but nothing happens.*

2.10 THE `else` STATEMENT USED WITH LOOPS

We have studied `if-else` block in the previous chapter. We can also have an *else* statement associated with loop statements. *If the else statement is used with a for loop, the else statement is executed when the loop has completed iterating. But when used with the while loop, the else statement is executed when the condition becomes false.*

Example 2.19

```
for i in range(3):
print(i, end='')
else:
print("Done")
```

OUTPUT

```
012 3 Done
```

Example 2.20

```
i = 10
while(i<0):
print(i)
i = i + 1
else:
print(i, "is not negative so loop did not execute")
```

OUTPUT

```
i is not negative so loop did not execute
```

Key Terms

Sequential control flow: A programming style in which the statements in a program are executed one after the other

Flow control: Flow control means the flow of instructions in the order in which they have to be executed, that is, depending on which statement should be executed next.

Decision control flow: A type of flow control in which either a selected set of statements are executed or a particular set of statements is executed repeatedly.

Selection control statements: Decision control statements that allow the flow control to jump from one part of the code to another depending on whether a particular condition is satisfied or not. Since they execute statements selectively based on certain decisions, such type of decision control statements is known as selection control statements or *conditional branching statements*.

Clause: Combination of header and its suite

Suite: Group of statements following the header

Nested (or compound) statement: A statement that contains other statements is called a compound statement.

Iterative statement: Statements that repeat the execution of a block of statements depending on the value of an integer expression.

Definite repetition loop: A counter-controlled loop in which the counter is assigned a constant or a value is also known as a definite repetition loop.

Nested loop: A loop that is placed inside another loop.

Chapter Highlights

- The test expression is any valid expression that may include logical operators.
- After the header, all instructions that are indented at the same level form a suite.
- Python uses indentation to form a block of code.
- An `if-else` statement specifies what has to be done if the statement is True as well as when it is False.
- Nested `if` statements are used to check if more than one conditions are satisfied.
- A series of `if` and `elif` statements have a final `else` block, which is executed if none of the `if` or `elif` expressions is True.
- In Python, iterative statements are implemented through `while` loop and `for` loop.
- The `while` loop provides a mechanism to repeat one or more statements while a particular condition is True.
- The value of the loop control variable is updated with every iteration of the loop.
- The `for` loop provides a mechanism to repeat a task until a particular condition is True.
- The `for..in` statement is a looping statement used in Python to iterate over a sequence of objects.
- The `range()` is a built-in function in Python that is used to iterate over a sequence of numbers.
- Loops can be either counter-controlled or condition controlled (or sentinel-controlled) loops.
- When we do not know in advance the number of times the loop will be executed, we use a condition-controlled loop.
- The `break` statement is used to terminate the execution of the nearest enclosing loop in which it appears.
- When the compiler encounters a `continue` statement then the rest of the statements in the loop are skipped and the control is unconditionally transferred to the loop-continuation portion of the nearest enclosing loop.
- `pass` statement is used when a statement is required syntactically but no instruction has to be executed. It specifies a null operation or simply No Operation (NOP) statement.
- If the `else` statement is used with a `for` loop, the `else` statement is executed when the loop has completed iterating. But when used with the `while` loop, the `else` statement is executed when the condition becomes false.

Review Questions

1. What is flow control?
2. Differentiate between sequential control flow and selection control flow.
3. Why do we need decision control statements?
4. With the help of a flowchart, explain the syntax of the following statements:
   a. If   b. if-else   c. if-el-if   d. nested if

5. What are conditional branching statements? How does Python support such statements?
6. How will you identify the suite of an `if` statement?
7. With the help of an example, explain why `if-else` statement is better than a simple `if` statement.
8. What do you mean by a nested `if` statement? How is it implemented in Python?
9. Why should we not use floating-point numbers to test for exact equality?
10. Change the indentation to make the code syntactically correct.
    ```
    if condition1:
    statement1
    elif condition2:
      statement2
    elif condition3:
       statement3
    elif condition4:
     statement4
    ```
11. Under what conditions, Programming will be printed?
    ```
    if a < 10:
       print("Python")
    elif a < 20:
       print("Programming")
    else:
       print("is fun..")
    ```
12. With the help of a flowchart, explain the construct of a `while` loop.
13. Why is the value of the loop control variable updated with every iteration of the loop?
14. With the help of a flowchart, explain the construct of a `for` loop.
15. With the help of an example explain the use of `range()` function.
16. Differentiate between a condition-controlled and a counter-controlled loop.
17. With the help of an example, explain the use of `break` statement.
18. What happens when the `pass` statement executes?
19. Differentiate between the `comment` and the `pass` statements.
20. When is the `else` statement with loops executed?
21. What will happen if we replace the `break` statement in the code with a `continue` statement?
22. Fill in the blanks to complete the code:
    a. Create a loop that increments the value of x by 3 and prints the odd values from 0-100.
    ```
    x = 0
    _____ x <= _____
        _____(x)
    x += 2
    ```
    b. Create a `for` loop that prints only the even values in the range 0-50:
    ```
    _____ i in range(_____):
        print(_____)
    ```
23. Identify the definite and indefinite loop.
    a.
    ```
    n = input('Enter a number: ')
    while n != -1:
        n = input('Enter a number: ')
    ```
    b.
    ```
    x = 0
    ```

```
            while x<10:
                print 10**num
        n = n+1
```
24. Correct the code to produce the desired output.
    a.
    ```
    for i in range(10,0):
        print(i)
    ```
    b.
    ```
    i=10
    while(i>0):
        print(i)
        i-1
    ```
    c.
    ```
    i=10 ;  result = 1
    while(i>0):
        result = result + i**2
        i = i+1
    print(result)
    ```
25. The following for loops are written to print numbers from 1 to 10. Are these loops correct? Justify your answer.
    a.
    ```
    for i in range(10):
        print(i)
    ```
    b.
    ```
    for i in range(10):
        num = i+1
        print(num)
    ```
    c.
    ```
    for i in range(10):
        print(i)
        i = i+1
    ```
26. Write the following piece of code using `for` loop.
    ```
    i = 20
    while i>0:
        print(i)
        i = i-2
    ```

Programming Exercises

1. Write a program to check whether a number is divisible by 10 or not. If the number is not divisible, then print how much should be added to it to make it completely divisible by 10.
2. Write a program to verify whether a candidate is eligible to appear for an exam or not. The minimum and maximum age of a person to appear for the exam is 21 and 35 respectively.
3. Write a program that prompts the user to enter an angle and then prints its quadrant.
4. Write a program that prompts the user to enter a number between 1–12 and then display the corresponding month of the year.
5. Write a menu driven program that prompts the user to enter the two sides of a rectangle. The user can then choose from a given set of options, if he/she needs to calculate perimeter, area or diagonal of the rectangle.
6. Write a program that prompts users to enter a character (A, B, C, D, E). Then using `if-elif-else` construct a display showing Outstanding, Very Good, Good, Average and Fail respectively.

7. Write a program that determines whether a student is eligible for PG course or not. To be eligible, the student must have obtained more than 80% in X and XII examination, and 70% plus marks in graduation course. If the student changes his stream (Science, Commerce, Arts), then deduct 5% from his Graduation score.

8. Write a program to read a floating-point number and an integer. If the value of the floating-point number is greater than 3.14 then multiply the value of the integer with 100.

9. Write a program that prompts the user to enter two integers. Divide the greater number with the smaller one and print the remainder and quotient thus obtained.

10. What output will be generated when the expression 5 or 100/0 is evaluated? What change can you do so that Python reports a Divide-by-Zero error?

11. Write a program that accepts the current date and the date of birth of the user. Then calculate the age of the user and display it on the screen. Note that the date should be displayed in the format specified as dd/mm/yy.

12. Write a code to calculate the amount to be paid by a customer by considering the following points:
    If the amount_to_be_paid >=30000, then discount = 30%.
    If the amount_to_be_paid >=20000, then discount = 20%.
    If the amount_to_be_paid >=10000, then discount = 10%.
    Otherwise, discount = 5%

13. Write a program that prompts user to enter his/her age (15–18 years) and then display the perfect height and weight for that age.

Age	Height (kgs)	Weight (cms)
15	56	170
16	60	173
17	64	175
18	66	176

14. Write a program that prompts the user to enter his/her body temperature. Check and display whether the user has normal body temperature, high fever or low fever.

15. Write a program that prompts the user to enter a number. Display the square root of the number. Remember that square root of negative numbers is not defined.

16. Write a program that prompts the user to enter lengths of three sides. Check whether these are the sides of a triangle.
    Hint: Sides of a triangle follow the rule, a + b > c. Similarly, b + c > a and a + c > b.

17. Write a program that prompts the user to enter the angles of a triangle. Check whether the triangle is acute-, obtuse- or right-angled.

18. Write a program to check whether a number entered by user is positive, negative or equal to zero.

19. Write a program that prompts users to enter status code 'S', 'M', 'D', or 'U' and returns the string `Separated`, `Married`, `Divorced`, or `Unmarried`, respectively. In case an inappropriate letter is passed, print an appropriate message.

20. An employee's total weekly pay is calculated by multiplying the hourly wage and number of regular hours plus overtime pay, if any, which in turn is calculated as total overtime hours multiplied by 1.5 times the hourly wage. Write a program that takes as inputs the hourly wage, total regular hours, and total overtime hours and prints an employee's total weekly pay.

21. Write a program to calculate electricity bill based on the following information.

Consumption Unit	Rate of Charge
0–150	Rs 3 per unit
151–350	Rs 100 plus Rs 3.75 per unit exceeding 150 units
301–450	Rs 250 plus Rs 4 per unit exceeding 350 units
451–600	Rs 300 plus Rs 4.25 per unit exceeding 450 units
Above 600	Rs 400 plus Rs 5 per unit exceeding 600 units

22. Write a program that converts a decimal number into its equivalent octal value.
23. Write a program that converts an octal number into its equivalent decimal value.
24. Write a function that accepts two positive numbers n and m where m <=n, and returns numbers between 1 and n that are divisible by m.
25. Write a program to convert time in hours into minutes and vice-versa.
26. Write a program to calculate conveyance charges to be paid by the users. Enter the type of car as a character (like s for sedan, p for prime, m for mini) and distance in kms. Calculate charges as given below: sedan – 17 Rs per km, prime – 12 Rs per km, mini – 10 Rs per km.
27. Modify the above program to calculate the conveyance charges. Read the km between when the user sits in the car and the time of his/her exit. Calculate the difference between the two readings and calculate the charges based on following rules.

Car Type	Rate up to First 5 km (Rs)	Rate after First 5 km (Rs)
Mini	10	10
Prime	20	12
Sedan	30	17

28. Write a program to sum the series $1^2/1 + 2^2/2 + 3^2/3 +.....+ n^2/n$.
29. Write a program that prints the cube of numbers in the range (1,n).
30. Write a program that prompts the user to enter the distance between his/her home and school. If the distance is in kilometers, display it in meters and vice versa.
31. Write a program that displays Python Programming as
    a. python programming   b. PYTHON PROGRAMMING
    c. pYTHON pROGRAMMING
32. Write a program that prompts users to enter numbers. Once the user enters -1, it displays the count, sum and average of even numbers and that of odd numbers.
33. Write a program to display the sin(x) value where x ranges from 0 to 360 in steps of 45.
34. Write a program that displays all the numbers from 1-100 that are not divisible 7 as well as by 11.
35. Write a program that accepts any number and prints the number of digits in that number.
36. Write a program that prints numbers from 100 to 1 in steps of 4.
37. Write a program to generate the following pattern:
    ```
    * * * * *
    *       *
    *       *
    *       *
    * * * * *
    ```
38. Write a program to generate the following pattern:
    ```
    $ * * * *
    * $     *
    *   $   *
    *     $ *
    * * * * $
    ```
39. Write a program to generate the following pattern:
    ```
    $ * * * $
    * $   $ *
    *   $   *
    * $   $ *
    $ * * * $
    ```

40. Write a program that reads integers until the user wants to stop. When the user stops entering numbers, display the largest of all the numbers entered.
41. Write a program to generate the Fibonacci series.
42. Write s program to print first 20 even numbers in descending order.
43. Write a program to print the sum of the following series:
    a. -x + x2 - x3 + x4 + ...
    b. 1 - x + x2/2! - x3/3! + ...
44. Write a program to print the following patterns:

a.
```
    *
   * *
  * * *
   * *
    *
```

b.
```
*
* *
* * *
* *
*
```

c.
```
    *
   * *
  *   *
   * *
    *
```

d.
```
    *
   * *
  *   *
   * *
    *
```

e.
```
A
A B A
A B C B A
A B C D C B A
```

f.
```
    1
   2 1 2
  3 2 1 2 3
```

g.
```
12345
2345
345
45
5
```

h.
```
1
12
123
1234
12345
```

Fill in the Blanks

1. _____ means the flow of instructions in the order in which they have to be executed, that is, depending on which statement should be executed next.
2. _____ is the simplest form of decision control statements.
3. Header and its suite together forms a _____.
4. Python uses _____ to form a block of code.
5. A _____ statement contains other statements.
6. A series of `if` and `elif` statements have a final _____ block.
7. _____ and _____ operators are used to form a compound relational expression.
8. _____ is a short form of "else if" statement.
9. Python uses _____ to form a block of code.
10. A series of `if`, `elif` statements have a final _____ block, which is executed if none of the `if` or `elif` expressions is True.
11. Python assumes any non-zero and non-null values as _____.
12. _____ begin with a keyword and end with a colon.
13.
```
x = 10
y = 20
_____x>y_____
print print("In if")
_____
    print ("In else")
```
14. Fill the blanks to print *Python* on the screen.
```
x = 10
y = 50
if x>10 _____ y<100:
    _____ ("Python")
```

15. _____ statements are used to repeatedly execute one or more statements in a block.
16. In Python, iterative statements are implemented through _____ and _____ loops.
17. An _____ loop will occur if the condition of while loop never becomes false.
18. The `for` loop provides a mechanism to repeat a task until a particular condition is _____.
19. The _____ function in Python that is used to iterate over a sequence of numbers.
20. When we know in advance the number of times the loop should be executed, we use a _____ controlled loop.
21. When we do not know in advance the number of times the loop will be executed, we use a _____ controlled loop.
22. When _____ statement is encountered, rest of the statements in the loop are skipped and the control is unconditionally transferred to the loop-continuation portion of the nearest enclosing loop.
23. _____ statement specifies a null operation.
24. The _____ statement is executed when the for loop has completed iterating.

State True or False

1. A sequential control program can skip one or more statements.
2. In selection control statements, all the statements are executed from the first one to the last.
3. Group of statements following the header is known as a clause.
4. After the header, all instructions that are indented at the same level forms a suite.
5. It is mandatory to use four spaces to define each level of indentation.
6. The final `else` block in an `if-elif-else` statement is executed when none of the `if` or `elif` expressions is True.
7. You can use floating-point numbers for checking for equality in the test expression.
8. Indentation identifies a statement block.
9. Statements within a suite can be indented at different levels.
10. `elif` and `else` blocks are optional.
11. The `while` loop repeats one or more statements while a particular condition is False.
12. Iterative statement repeats the execution of a block of statements depending on the value of an expression that evaluates to an integer value only.
13. In the `while` loop, the condition is tested after the statement block is executed at least once.
14. The value of the loop control variable is updated with every alternate iteration of the loop.
15. An infinite loop will occur if the condition of while loop is always False.
16. The `for` loop is executed for each item in the sequence.
17. Every iteration of the loop must make the loop control variable farther from the end of the sequence.
18. The step argument in the `range()` function is optional.
19. Sentinel value is used in counter-controlled loop.
20. Both `for` and `while` loop can be nested.
21. The `break` and `continue` statements can only appear in the body of a loop.
22. In a `for` loop, the `continue` statement causes a branch to the code that updates the loop variable.
23. The `pass` statement is a non-executable statement that is ignored by the compiler.
24. The number of times the loop control variable is updated is equal to the number of times the loop iterates.
25. In a `while` loop, the loop control variable is initialized in the body of the loop.

Multiple Choice Questions

1. Which part of if statement should be indented?
   a. The first statement
   b. All the statements
   c. Statements within the if block
   d. None of these.

2. A programming style in which the statements in a program are executed one after the other.
   a. Sequential
   b. Decision control
   c. Iterative control
   d. None of these

3. A test expression must have a/an _____ operator.
   a. arithmetic
   b. logical
   c. unary
   d. assignment

4. In an if statement, which of the following headers are optional?
   a. If
   b. elif
   c. else
   d. Both b and c.

5. Logical expression should not be _____.
   a. simple
   b. long
   c. positive
   d. Both b and c.

6. Which of the following is placed after the if condition?
   a. ;
   b. .
   c. :
   d. ,

7. Which keys are not pressed to exit from the infinite loop?
   a. Alt + C
   b. Ctrl + C
   c. Alt + F4
   d. Ctrl + Q

8. The step argument in the range() function cannot be _____.
   a. Less than zero
   b. greater than zero
   c. zero
   d. None of these.

9. range(1,5) will generate numbers _____.
   a. 0,1,2,3,4,5
   b. 0,1,2,3,4
   c. 1,2,3,4
   d. 1,2,3,4,5

10. By default, every number in the range is incremented by _____.
    a. 0
    b. 1
    c. 2
    d. 3

11. In a counter-controlled loop, the counter must be _____.
    a. Initialized
    b. tested
    c. updated
    d. All of these.

12. A loop within another loop is also known as a _____ loop.
    a. sentinel-controlled
    b. condition-controlled
    c. counter-controlled
    d. nested

13. Which statement is used to terminate the execution of the nearest enclosing loop in which it appears?
    a. break
    b. continue
    c. pass
    d. else

14. In a while loop, if the body is executed *n* times, then the test expression is executed _____ times.
    a. *n* – 1
    b. *n*
    c. *n* + 1
    d. 2*n*

15. ```
    i = 1
    while i > 0:
    print("loop")
    ```
    The above loop is best example of _____ loop.
    a. nested
    b. infinite
    c. counter-controlled
    d. condition-controlled

16. How many numbers will be printed?
    ```
    i = 5
    while i>=0:
    print(i)
    i=i-1
    ```
    a. 5
    b. 6
    c. 4
    d. 0

17. How many numbers will be printed?
    ```
    i = 10
    while True:
    print(i)
    i = i - 1
    ```
    ```

```
if i<=7:
break
```
a. 1   b. 2   c. 3   d. 4

18. How many lines will be printed by this code?
```
while False:
print("Hello")
```
a. 1   b. 0   c. 10   d. Countless

Give the Output

1. ```
   for i in range(1,20):
       if i%5==0:
           break
       else:
           print(i)
   ```

2. ```
   for i in range(1,20):
       if i%5==0:
           continue
       else:
           print(i)
   ```

3. ```
   while(4>5):
       print("DONE")
   else:
       print("NOT DONE")
   ```

4. ```
   for i in range(1,5):
       for j in range(1,i):
           print('#',end = ' ')
       print()
   ```

5. ```
   while(5*2 > 10):
       print("JUST DO IT")
   else:
       print("DONE")
   ```

6. ```
   a = 10; b = 0
   while(a>b):
       print(a,b)
       a=a-1
       b=b+1
   ```

18.
```
run = True
a = 100
while run == True:
    print(a)
    a = a - 10
```

```
        if a < 40:
            run = False
 7. for i in range(100,50,-10):
        print(i)
 8. for i in range(100,50,-10):
        print(i)
 9. x = 10; y = 5
    for i in range(x-y*2):
        print("%")
10. if(5.0 < 9.0):
        print("DONE")
11. years = 99
    if(years == 100):
        print("Century")
    elif(years == 75):
        print("Platinum Jublee")
    elif(years == 50):
        print("Half Century")
    elif(years == 25):
        print("Silver Jublee")
    elif(years == 10):
        print("Decade")
    else:
        print("Long way to go….")
12. years = 99
    if years > 30:
        print("30")
    if years < 50:
        print("50")
    if years == 7:
        print("70")
13. num = int((10*6 + 10 - 20) > 0)
    if num == 50:
        print("You win...")
    else:
        print("Try Again")
14. num = 3
    if (num ** 3) > (5%2 - 3 * 4 /2):
        if (num // 4) >= 2:
            print("You win")
```

```
        else:
            print("Try Again")
```

15. ```
    num = 3
    if num == 2:
        print("Yes")
    elif num == 4:
        print("Yes")
    elif num == 8:
        print("Yes")
    else:
        print("Number is not an even number")
    ```

16. ```
    if(10 == 100) and (100 + 200 > 300):
        print("Win Win..")
    else:
        print("Oh No !!!")
    ```

17. ```
    if not True:
        print("WRONG")
    elif not((10+10 - 20 * 3) == 30):
        print("Really !")
    else:
        print("May Be")
    ```

18. ```
    if (10 << ((41 - 40 // 2 + 1)%2)) == 60:
        print("WoW")
    else:
        print("Gosh")
    ```

19. ```
    a = 5
    b = 70
    if not 10 + 10 == b or a == 40 and 70== 80:
        print("Yeah")
    elif a != b:
        print("Nope")
    ```

20. ```
    num = 10
    if num > 30:
        if num > 40:
            print("Python")
        else:
            print("Programming")
    elif num < 20:
        if(num!=0):
            print("is fun..")
            print("Isnt it !!!")
    ```

21. ```
    weather = 'foggy'
    if weather == 'sunny':
        print("Take your shades")
    elif weather == 'raining':
        print("Take your umbrella")
    else:
        print("Stay at home")
    ```

22. ```
    for letter in "HELLO":
            pass
    ```

23. ```
    i=1
    while i<=6:
        print(i),
        i=i+1
    print("Done")
    ```

24. ```
    i=0
    while i<10:
        i = i + 1
        if(i == 5):
            print("\n Continue")
            continue
        if(i==7):
            print("\n Breaking")
            break
        print(i, end = '   ')
    print("\n Done")
    ```

25. ```
    for i in range(5):
        print("hello!", end= " ")
    ```

26. ```
    for i in range(10):
        if not i%2==0:
            print(i+1, end = ' ')
    ```

27. ```
    for i in range(10,0,-1):
        print(i, end = ' ')
    ```

28. ```
    for i in range(5,25,3):
        print(i, end = ' ')
    ```

29. ```
    for i in "PYTHON":
        print(i,'-',end='')
    ```

30. ```
    for i in range(10):
        pass
    print(i)
    ```

31.
```
while True:
    str = input("Enter a string (Bye to exit) : ")
    if str == "bye":
        break
    print(str)
else:
    print("Exiting......")
```

Find the Error

1.
```
while(i<10):
    print(i)
```

Answers

Fill in the Blanks

1. Flow control
2. If statement
3. clause
4. indentation.
5. compound/ nested
6. else
7. and, or
8. elif
9. indentation
10. else
11. True
12. Header
13. if, :, else:
14. or, print
15. For
16. while, for.
17. infinite
18. true
19. `range()`
20. counter
21. condition
22. `continue`
23. Pass
24. else

State True or False

1. False
2. False
3. False
4. True
5. False
6. True
7. True
8. True
9. False
10. True
11. False
12. True
13. False
14. False
15. False
16. True
17. False
18. True
19. False
20. True
21. True
22. True
23. False
24. True
25. False

Multiple Choice Questions

1. b
2. a
3. b
4. d
5. b
6. C
7. a
8. c
9. c
10. b
11. d
12. d
13. a
14. c
15. b
16. b
17. c
18. b

Give the Output

1.
2. 1 2 3 4 6 7 8 9 11 12 13 14 16 17 18 19
3. NOT DONE

4.
```
#
# #
# # #
```

5. DONE
6. The output for 6. is
   10   0
   9   1
   8   2
   7   3
   6   4
7. 100 90 80 70 60
8. No output
9. No output
10. Done
11. Long way to go….
12. 30
13. Try Again
14. Try Again
15. Number is not an even number
16. Oh No !!!
17. Really !
18. Gosh
19. Yeah
20. is fun..
    Isnt it !!!
21. Stay at home
22. no output on the screen.
23. 1
    2
    3
    4
    5
    6
    Done
24. 1 2 3 4
    Continue
    6
    Breaking
    Done
25. hello! hello! hello! hello! hello!
26. 2 4 6 8 10
27. 10 9 8 7 6 5 4 3 2 1
28. 5 8 11 14 17 20 23
29. P -Y -T -H -O -N -
30. 9
31. no output when bye is entered.

Find the Error

1. NameError: name 'i' is not defined

Strings and Lists in Python

3

Chapter Objectives

In this chapter, we will quickly revise Python strings and lists. We will read about the different operations, functions and methods that can be applied on these non-primitive data structure in Python. Let us quickly have a look at the topics discussed in this chapter:

- Traversing, comparing, and determining the length of strings
- String built-in functions and methods
- Using the `str()`, `format()`, `eval()`, `ord()`, `char()` functions
- Applying relational operators on list elements
- Nested lists
- Inserting and deleting elements from a list
- Updating, aliasing and cloning list objects
- List built-in functions and methods

3.1 INTRODUCTION

The Python string data type is a sequence made up of one or more individual characters, where a character could be a letter, digit, whitespace, or any other symbol enclosed within single, double or even triple quotes. Python has a built-in string class named "str" that has many useful features. We can create a variable of string type in many ways. For example,

```
lang = "Python"    gender= 'F'    choice = lang    message = str("How are you?")
```

We have already seen that escape sequences work with each type of string literal. A multiple-line text within quotes must have a backslash \ at the end of each line to escape the newline.

3.2 STRING INDEXING

Individual characters in a string are accessed using the subscript ([ ]) operator. The expression in brackets is called an *index*. The index specifies the character to be accessed from the given set of characters in the string.

The index of the first character is 0 and that of the last character is $n - 1$ where n is the number of characters in the string. *If you try to exceed the bounds (below 0 or above n – 1) then an error is raised.*

3.3 FINDING THE NUMBER OF CHARACTERS IN A STRING

Python determines the size of the length of a string by counting the number of characters in it. For example, len("abcd") is 4 since there are four characters. Although this calculation is simple, some points must be considered while counting.

a. An escape sequence is counted as a single character.
b. In a multi-line string created with triple quotes, the **EOL** (End-of-Line) character at the end of the line is also counted. Usually, the EOL is the carriage return character when the Enter key is pressed.
c. In a multi-line string, backslash character at the end of the line is not counted.

```
>> len("\n")
1
>>> str1= '''A
B
C
D'''
>>> len("HELLO \t WORLD")
13
>>> len(str1)
7
>>> len("Neeru\'s Pen")
11
>>> str2 = '''A\
B\
C\
D'''
>>> len("Neeru\'s Pen")
11
```

3.4 TRAVERSING A STRING

String is a sequence type (sequence of characters). It can be traversed in two ways. First, by accessing each character in the string and second, by accessing the element at each index. The `len()` function returns the length of the string. That is, number of characters in the string. We can then use `for` loop in which the loop control variable varies from 0 to $n-1$, where n is the number of characters in the string.

Whichever method you use, always remember that if you try to access a character *with index less than 0 and/or greater than n – 1 then an IndexError:* string index out of range error will be generated.

Example 3.1

```
# traversing string
lang ="PYTHON"
for i in lang:
    print(i, end = '') #print each character
```

OUTPUT
```
PYTH O N
```

Example 3.2

```
# traverse string using index
lang = "PYTHON"
for i in range(len(lang)):
    print(lang[i], end = '')
```

OUTPUT
```
P YT H O N
```

In the first code, the `for` loop executes for every character in str. The loop starts with the first character and automatically ends when the last character is accessed. In the second code, the string is traversed using the index of each character (rather than the character itself). We can also iterate through the string using the `while` loop.

Example 3.3

```
# traversing string using while loop
lang = "PYTHON"
index = 0
l = len (lang)
while index < l:
    ch = lang[index]
    print(ch, end = ")
    index += 1
```

OUTPUT

```
PYTHON
```

Example 3.4

```
# access string out of index
lang = "PYTHON"
l = len(lang)
    print(lang[l+1]) #not a part of string
```

OUTPUT

```
Traceback (most recent call last):
File "C:\Users\Python37\try.py", line 3, in <module>
    print(lang[l+1])
IndexError: string index out of range
```

In the above program, the `while` loop traverses the string and displays each character. The loop condition is index < len(lang), so the moment index becomes equal to the length of the string, the condition evaluates to false, and the body of the loop is not executed. As we said earlier, the index of the last character is len(message) – 1.

Key points to remember

- Even the whitespace characters, exclamation mark and any other symbols (like ?, <,>,*, @, #, $, %, etc.) that form a part of the string would be assigned their own index number.
- Index can either be an integer or an expression that evaluates to an integer.
- A character cannot be used for string indexing.

Example 3.5

```
# indexing string in different ways
msg ="PYTHON PROGRAMMING IS FUN"
i = 2
print(msg[i]) # index is an integer
print(msg[i*3+ 2]) # index is an expression that evaluates to an integer
print(msg['N']) # character as an index
```

OUTPUT

```
T
R
Traceback (most recent call last):
File "C:\Users\Python37\try.py", line 5, in <module>
    print(msg['N']) # character as an index
TypeError: string indices must be integers
```

3.5 CONCATENATING, APPENDING AND MULTIPLYING STRINGS

The word **concatenate** means to join together. Python allows you to concatenate two strings using the + operator as shown below.

Append means to add something at the end. In Python, one string can be added at the end of another string using the += operator.

Example 3.6

```
# String Concatenation
str1 = "Python"
str2 = "Programming"
str3 = str1 + str2   # string concatenation
print("The concatenated string is : ", str3)
```

OUTPUT

```
The concatenated string is: Python Programming
```

Example 3.7

```
# Appending and concatenating strings
str1 = "Good morning, "
name = input("\n Enter your name: ")
str1 += name  # appending strings
str2 = str1 + ''. Welcome to Python Programming."
print(str2)
```

OUTPUT

```
Enter your name: Priya
Good morning, Priya. Welcome to PythonProgramming.
```

We can **multiply** a string using the * operator. When a string is multiplied with an integer number *n*, then the string is repeated *n* number of times. The order of string and integer is not important. Therefore, 5*"HI" is same as "HI" * 5.

However, remember that you cannot multiply two strings. Also, you cannot multiply a string with a floating-point number.

Example 3.8

```
# multiplying string
str = "I WILL DO IT"
print(str * 3) # multiplying string
```

OUTPUT

```
I WILL DO IT I WILL DO IT I WILL DO IT
```

Example 3.9

```
# multiplying string
str = "PYTHON" * '3'
print(str)
```

OUTPUT

```
Traceback (most recent call last):
File "C:\Users\Python37\try.py", line 2, in
```

```
    <module>
        str = "PYTHON" * '3'
TypeError: can't multiply sequence by non-int of type 'str'
```

Example 3.10

```
# multiplying string
str  = "HELLO" * 3.0
print(str)
```

OUTPUT

```
Traceback (most recent call last):
File "C:\Users\Python37\try.py",line 2,
in <module>
    str = "HELLO" * 3.0
TypeError: can't multiply sequence by non-int of type 'float'
```

Example 3.11

```
# Checking object's ID
str1= "Python"
str2 = "Python"
str3 = "Programming"
# ID of str1 and str2 will be same
print("ID OF STR1 = ",id(str1))
print("ID OF STR2 = ",id(str2))
print("ID OF STR3 = ",id(str3))
# changing the value of str2
str2 = "Programming"
# ID of str2 and str3 will be same
print("\n\n ID OF STR1 = ",id(str1))
print("ID OF STR2 = ",id(str2))
print("ID OF STR3 = ",id(str3))
# changing the value of str3
str2 = "Programming is fun"
# All IDs will be different
print("\n\n ID OF STR1 = ",id(str1))
print("ID OF STR2 = ",id(str2))
print("ID OF STR3 = ",id(str3))
```

OUTPUT

```
ID OF STR1 = 3091055531600
ID OF STR2 = 3091055531600
ID OF STR3 = 3091069698480

ID OF STR1 = 3091055531600
ID OF STR2 = 3091069698480
ID OF STR3 = 3091069698480

ID OF STR1 = 3091055531600
ID OF STR2 = 3091070019384
ID OF STR3 = 3091069698480
```

3.6 THE str() FUNCTION

The str() function is used to convert values of any other type into string type. This helps the programmer to concatenate a string with any other data which is otherwise not allowed.

Example 3.12

```
# concatenating string and a number
roll_no = 9
name = "Aditi"
print(name + " is roll number" + roll_no)
```

OUTPUT
```
Traceback (most recent call last):
File "C:\Users\
TypeError: can only concatenate str (not "int") to str
```

Example 3.13

```
# concatenating string and a number
roll_no = 9
name = "Aditi"
print(name + " is roll number" + str(roll_no))
```

OUTPUT
```
Aditi is roll number 9
```

3.7 STRINGS ARE IMMUTABLE

Python strings are immutable. This means that once a string is created, it cannot be changed. If you try to modify an existing string variable, a new string is created.

Every object in Python is stored in memory. You can find out whether two variables are referring to the same object or not by using the id(). The **id()** returns the memory address of that object. Since both str1 and str2 points to the same memory location, they both actually point to the same object.

In Python, every two objects having the same value have the same id. The moment the value of one object is changed, a new object is created with a different id.

From the output, it is very clear that when values of str1 and str2 were same, their IDs were same as they were pointing to the same object. When we changed the value of str2 and later of str3, the ids of the object changed.

Now can you guess the output of the following code?

```
str = "PYTHON"
str[3] = 'A'
print(str)
```

Yes, the code will result in an error – TypeError: 'str' object does not support item assignment simply because strings are immutable. It does now allow any changes. If you want to make any kind of changes you must create a new string as shown below.

Always remember that we cannot delete or remove characters from a string. But we can delete the entire string using the keyword del.

3.8 STRING FORMATTING OPERATOR

This string formatting operator (%) takes a format string on the left (that has %d, %s, etc) and the corresponding values in a tuple (to be discussed in a subsequent chapter) on the right. The format operator % allows users to construct strings, replacing parts of the strings with the data stored in variables. The syntax for the string formatting operation is:

```
"<FORMAT>" % (<VALUES>)
```

Strings and Lists in Python

The statement begins with a *format* string consisting of a sequence of characters and *conversion specifications*. Conversion specifications start with a % operator and can appear anywhere within the string. Following the format string is a % sign and then a set of values, one per conversion specification, separated by commas and enclosed in parentheses. If there is a single value, then parentheses are optional.

> A tuple is made of values separated by commas inside parentheses.

Example 3.14

```
# Formatting strings
roll_no = 23
name = "Aarish"
print("ROll NO. = %d Name = %s" %(roll_no, name))
print("ROll NO. = %d Name = %s" %(39, "Anika"))
```

OUTPUT

```
ROll NO. = 23 Name = Aarish
ROll NO. = 39 Name = Anika
```

In the output we can see that %s has been replaced by a string and %d has been replaced by an integer value. You can either supply these values directly or by using variables. Table 3.1 lists other string formatting characters.

Note that the number and type of values in the tuple should match the number and type of format sequences or conversion specifications in the string; otherwise an error is returned.

Example 3.15

```
# number of arguments don't match
>>> '%d %f %s' % (15, 92.75)
Traceback (most recent call last):
File "<pyshell#0>", line 1, in <module>
    '%d %f %s' %(15,92.75)
TypeError: not enough arguments for format string
```

Example 3.16

```
# type of argument don't match
>>> '%d %f %s' % (92, "Myra", "Sood")
Traceback (most recent call last):
File "<pyshell#1>", line 1, in <module>
'%d %f %s' %(92, "Myra", "Sood")
TypeError: must be real number, not str
```

Table 3.1 Formatting symbols

Format Symbol	Purpose
%c	Character
%d or %i	Signed decimal integer
%s	String
%u	Unsigned decimal integer
%o	Octal integer
%x or %X	Hexadecimal integer (x for lower case characters a-f and X for upper case characters A-F)
%e or %E	Exponential notation
%f	Floating point number
%g or %G	Short numbers in floating-point or exponential notation

In the code, we have set the width of each column independently using the string formatting feature of Python. The - after each % in the conversion string indicates left justification. The numerical values specify the minimum length. Therefore, %-15d means it is a left justified number that is at least 15 characters wide.

Example 3.17

```
# String Formatting for printing power of number
i =1
print("%-4s%-5s%-6s%-8s%-13s" % ('i', 'i**2', 'i**3', 'i**4', 'i**5'))
while(i <= 5):
    print("%-4d%-5d%-6d%-8d%-13d" % (i, i**2, i**3, i**4, i**5))
    i += 1
```

OUTPUT

```
i    i**2 i**3  i**4    i**5
1    1    1     1       1
2    4    8     16      32
3    9    27    81      243
4    16   64    256     1024
5    25   125   625     3125
```

3.9 THE format() FUNCTION

The format() function is also used for formatting strings. Format strings have curly braces {} as placeholders or replacement fields which gets replaced. We can even use positional arguments or keyword arguments to specify the order of fields that have to be replaced. Consider the code given below and carefully observe the sequence of fields in the output and then compare the sequence as given in the arguments of format() function.

Example 3.18

```
# format() function with strings
str1 = "{}, {} {}" .format('Python','is','Easy')
print("\n The default sequence of arguments is : " + str1)
str2 = "{1} {0} {2}?" .format('Python','Is', 'Easy')
print("\n The positional sequence of arguments (1, 0 and 2) is : " + str2)
str3 = "{c}, {b} very {a}" .format(a='Python',b='Is',c='Easy')
print("\n The keyword sequence of arguments is : " + str3)
```

OUTPUT

```
The default sequence of arguments is : Python, is Easy
The positional sequence of arguments (1,0 and 2) is : Is Python Easy?
The keyword sequence of arguments is : Easy, Is very Python
```

3.10 BUILT-IN STRING METHODS AND FUNCTIONS

Strings are an example of Python **objects**. An object is an entity that contains both data (the actual string itself) as well as functions to manipulate that data. These functions are available to any **instance** (variable) of the object.

Python supports many built-in methods to manipulate strings. A method is just like a function. The only difference between a function and a method is that method is invoked or called on an object. For example, If the variable str is a string, then you can call the upper() method as str.upper() to convert all the characters of str in upper case. Table 3.2 discusses some of the most commonly used string methods.

Table 3.2 Commonly used string functions and methods

Function	Usage	Example

`capitalize()`	This function is used to capitalize the first letter of the string.	`str = "python"`
		`print(str.capitalize())`
		OUTPUT
		`Python`

`center(width, fillchar)`	Returns a string with the original string centered to a total of width columns and filled with fillchar in columns that do not have characters	`str = "python"`
		`print(str.center(15, '*'))`
		OUTPUT
		`*****python****`

`count(str, beg, end)`	Counts the number of times `str` occurs in string. You can specify beg and end to specify as 0 to len of string to search the entire length of the string or with any other value to just search a part of the string.	`str = "se"`
		`message = "He sells sea shells on the sea shore"`
		`print(message.count(str,0,len(message)))`
		OUTPUT
		`3`

`endswith(suffix, beg, end)`	Checks if string ends with suffix; returns True if so and False, otherwise. You can either set beg = 0 and end to length of the message to search the entire string or use any other value to search a part of it.	`message = "He sells sea shells on the sea shore"`
		`print(message.endswith("ore", 0,len(message)))`
		OUTPUT
		`True`

`startswith(prefix, beg, end)`	Checks if string starts with prefix; returns True if so and False, otherwise. You can either set beg = 0 and end to length of the message to search the entire string or use any other value to search a part of it.	`message = "He sells sea shells on the sea shore"`
		`print(message.startswith("sea", 0,len(message)))`
		OUTPUT
		`False`

`find(str, beg, end)`	Checks if `str` is present in string. If found, it returns the position at which `str` occurs in string; otherwise, it returns −1. You can either set beg = 0 and end to the length of the message to search the entire string or use any other value to search a part of it.	`message = "He sells sea shells on the sea shore"`
		`print(message.find("sea",0,len(message)))`
		OUTPUT
		`9`

`index(str, beg, end)`	Same as `find` but raises an exception if `str` is not found	`message = "He sells sea shells on the sea shore"`
		`print(message.index("in", 0, len(message)))`
		ValueError: substring not found

`rfind(str, beg, end)`	Same as `find` but starts searching from the end. So it will return index of the last occurrence of `str` in the main string.	`message = "He sells sea shells on the sea shore"`
		`print(message.rfind("sea", 0, len(message)))`
		OUTPUT
		`27`

Table 3.2 (*Continued*)

Table 3.2 Continued

Function	Usage	Example

`rindex(str, beg, end)`	Same as rindex but start searching from the end and raises an exception if str is not found	`message = "He sells sea shells on the sea shore"`
		`print(message.rindex("gg", 0, len(message)))`
		OUTPUT
		`ValueError: substring not found`

`isalnum()`	Returns True if string has at least 1 character and every character is either a number or an alphabet and False otherwise.	`message = "JamesBond007"`
		`print(message.isalnum())`
		OUTPUT
		`True`

`isalpha()`	Returns True if string has at least 1 character and every character is an alphabet and False otherwise.	`message = "JamesBond007"`
		`print(message.isalpha())`
		OUTPUT
		`False`

`isdigit()`	Returns True if string contains only digits and False otherwise.	`message = "108"`
		`print(message.isdigit())`
		OUTPUT
		`True`

`islower()`	Returns True if string has at least 1 character and every character is a lower case alphabet and False otherwise.	`message = "Python"`
		`print(message.islower())`
		OUTPUT
		`False`

`isspace()`	Returns True if string contains only whitespace characters and False otherwise.	`message = "   "`
		`print(message.isspace())`
		OUTPUT
		`True`

`isupper()`	Returns True if string has at least 1 character and every character is an uppercase alphabet and False otherwise.	`message = "PYTHON"`
		`print(message.isupper())`
		OUTPUT
		`True`

`len(string)`	Returns the length of the string	`str = "PYTHON"`
		`print(len(str))`
		OUTPUT
		`6`

`ljust(width[, fillchar])`	Returns a string left-justified to a total of width columns. Columns without characters are padded with the character specified in the `fillchar` argument	`str = " PYTHON"`
		`print(str.ljust(10, '*'))`
		OUTPUT
		`PYTHON****`
		`23351823`

`rjust(width[, fillchar])`	Returns a string right-justified to a total of width columns. Columns without characters are padded with the character specified in the `fillchar` argument	`str = "PYTHON"`
		`print(str.rjust(10, '&'))`
		OUTPUT
		`&&&&PYTHON`

Table 3.2 (*Continued*)

Table 3.2 Continued

Function	Usage	Example

`zfill (width)`	Returns string left-padded with zeros to a total of width characters. It is used with numbers and also retains its sign (+ or –).	`str = "5678"`
		`print(str.zfill(10))`
		OUTPUT
		`0000005678`

`lower()`	Converts all characters in the string into lowercase.	`str = "PYTHON"`
		`print(str.lower())`
		OUTPUT
		`python`

`upper()`	Converts all characters in the string into upper case.	`str = "python"`
		`print(str.upper())`
		OUTPUT
		`PYTHON`

`lstrip()`	Removes all leading whitespace in string.	`str = "   PYTHON"`
		`print(str.lstrip())`
		OUTPUT
		`PYTHON`

`rstrip()`	Removes all trailing whitespace in the string.	`str = "PYTHON     "`
		`print(str.lstrip())`
		OUTPUT
		`PYTHON`

`strip()`	Removes all leading and trailing whitespace in the string. The `strip()` function when used with a `string` argument will strip (from both ends) any combination of the specified characters in the string	`str = "   PYTHON    "`
		`print(str.strip())`
		`str = "abcPYabcTHONabc"`
		`print(str.strip("abc"))`
		OUTPUT
		`PYTHON`
		`PYabcTHON`

`max(str)`	Returns the highest alphabetical character (having highest ASCII value) from the string str.	`str = "PyThoN pRoGrAmMiNg"`
		`print(max(str))`
		OUTPUT
		`y`

`min(str)`	Returns the lowest alphabetical character (lowest ASCII value) from the string str.	`str = "PyThoNpRoGrAmMiNg"`
		`print(min(str))`
		OUTPUT
		`A`

`replace(old, new [, max])`	Replaces all or max (if given) occurrences of old in string with new	`str = "She sells sea shells on the sea shore"`
		`print(str.replace("se", "SE"))`
		OUTPUT
		`She SElls SEa shells on the SEa shore`

`title()`	Returns string in title case	`str = "she sells sea shells on the sea shore"`
		`print(str.title())`
		OUTPUT
		`She Sells Sea Shells On The Sea Shore`

Table 3.2 (*Continued*)

Table 3.2 Continued

Function	Usage	Example

`swapcase()`	Toggles the case of every character (upper case character becomes lower case and vice versa)	`str = "PyThoNpRoGrAmMiNg"`
		`print(str.swapcase())`
		OUTPUT
		`pYtHOnPrOgRaMmInG`

`split(delim)`	Returns a list of substrings separated by the specified delimiter. If no delimiter is specified, then by default, it splits strings at all whitespace characters	`str = "She, sells, sea shells, on the, sea shore"`
		`print(str.split(','))`
		OUTPUT
		`['She', ' sells', ' sea shells', ' on the', ' sea shore']`

`join(list)`	It is the opposite of split. The function joins a list of strings using the delimiter with which the function is invoked.	`str = ['Power','of','the','Universe','HE-MAN']`
		`print('#'.join(str))`
		OUTPUT
		`Power#of#the#Universe#HE-MAN`

`str.splitlines()`	Returns a list of the lines in the string. This method uses the newline characters like \r, \n to split lines.	`print('Python is \n\n a very \r simple language\r\n'.splitlines())`
		OUTPUT
		`['Python is ', '', ' a very ', ' simple language']`

3.11 COMPARING STRINGS

In Python, a string can be compared using relational operators like >, <, <=, <=, ==, !=. The comparison is done lexicographically, i.e., using ASCII value of the characters. The ASCII values of A–Z are 65–90, the ASCII codes for a–z are 97–122 and for 0–9, the codes are 48–57. This means that bread is greater than Bread because the ASCII value of 'b' is 98 and 'B' is 66.

```
>>> "PYTHON" == "python"
False
>>> "PYTHON" >= "python"
False
>>> "SMILE" < "laughter"
True
>>> "GIVE" != "EXPECT"
True
```

Did you notice that String values are ordered using lexicographical (dictionary) ordering? For this, the comparison is done internally.

3.12 ord() AND chr() FUNCTIONS

ord() function returns the ASCII code of the character and chr() function returns the character represented by an ASCII number.

Example 3.19

```
ch ='P'
print(ord(ch))
```

OUTPUT

80

```
ch ='y'
print(ord(ch))
```

OUTPUT

121

Example 3.20

```
print(chr(79))
```

OUTPUT

O

```
print(chr(117))
```

OUTPUT

u

3.13 in AND not in OPERATORS

`in` and `not in` operators can be used with strings to determine whether a character or a string is present in another string. Therefore, the `in` and `not in` operators are also known as membership operators.

Example 3.21

```
# using in operator
str1 = "Python programming is fun"
str2 = "is"
if str2 in str1:
    print("Found")
else:
    print("Not Found")
```

OUTPUT

Found

```
# using not in operator
str1 = "Arav is a very naughty boy"
str2 ="good"
if str2 not in str1:
    print("Arav is not a good boy.")
else:
    print("Arav is a very good boy.")
```

OUTPUT

Arav is not a good boy.

You can also use the `in` and `not in` operators to check whether a character is present is in a word. Also remember that a string is a substring of itself.

Example 3.22

```
>>> 'y' in "PYTHON"
False
>>> 'N' in "PYTHON"
True
>>> 'PYTHON' in 'PYTHON'
True
>>> 'V' in 'V'
True
```

3.14 LISTS

List is a versatile data type available in Python, in which elements are written as a list of comma-separated values (items) between square brackets. Lists in Python are mutable as we can change the value of their elements. This is in striking contrast with strings which are immutable.

The key feature of list is that it can have elements that belong to different data types. The syntax of defining a list can be given as, **List_variable = [val1, val2,.....]**

```
list_A = [1,2,3,4,5]
print(list_A)
[1, 2, 3, 4, 5]
list_B = ['A', 1, 'C', 2, 'E']
print(list_B)
['A', 1, 'C', 2, 'E']
list_C = ["HELLO","WORLD"]
print(list_C)
['HELLO', 'WORLD']
list_D = [1, 'a', 'HELLO']
print(list_D)
[1, 'a', 'HELLO']
```

We can even create an empty list by writing **list_variable = []**. An empty list is equivalent to False when use with logical operators.

```
>>> list = []
>>> list == True
False
```

3.15 ACCESSING VALUES IN LISTS

Like strings, lists can also be sliced and concatenated. To access values in a list, square brackets are used to slice along with the index or indices to get the value stored at that index. As discussed earlier, the syntax for the slice operation is, **seq = List[start:stop:step]**

For example, seq = List[::2] # *gets every other element, starting with index 0*
seq = List[10::3] # *gets every third element, starting with index 10*
seq = List[–3] # *gets third element from the end*
seq = list_A[–3]   # *3rd element from the end*
seq = List[3:] # *get all elements starting from the third index from the beginning*

Example 3.23

```
num_list = [2,4,6,8,10,12,14,16,18,20]
print(" num_list is: ", num_list)
print("First element in the list is ", num_list[0])
print("num_list[2:5] = ", num_list[4:7])
print(" num_list[::2] = ", num_list[::3])
print(" num_list[1::3] = ", num_list[1::2])
```

OUTPUT
```
num_list is: [2, 4, 6, 8, 10, 12, 14, 16, 18, 20]
First element in the list is 2
num_list[2:5] = [10, 12, 14]
num_list[::2] = [2,8, 14, 20]
num_list[1::3] = [4,8, 12, 16,20]
```

If the `start` and `end` values of the slice operation are beyond the size of the list, then all the elements within the specified range are returned. For example, consider the given example in which the `start` and `end` values are out of range of the size of the list.

Note that the valid index range of the list is 0–4. Values –9 and 9 are beyond the size of the list, so the entire list is returned. But in the second case, when start = –3 and end = 9, –3 lies in the valid range which is the third element from the end, hence the result.

Example 3.24

```
l = [1,2,3,4,5]
print(I[-9:9])
```

OUTPUT

[1, 2, 3, 4, 5]

```
l = [1,2,3,4,5]
print(I[-3:9])
```

OUTPUT

[3, 4, 5]

3.16 THE EVAL() FUNCTION

Example 3.25

```
>>> eval("10 == 10")
True
>>> eval("20 <= 10")
False
>>> eval("30 - 5 * 4 + 20")
30
>>> eval(" 'HELLO' * 3")
'HELLOHELLOHELLO'
```

The eval() function is used to evaluate and return the result of an expression as string.

We can use the eval() function to read value(s) of any type. However, its use is discouraged as we may get unforeseen problems as a result of using this function.

3.17 UPDATING VALUES IN LISTS

Once created, one or more elements of a list can be easily updated by giving the slice on the left-hand side of the assignment operator. You can also append new values in the list and remove existing value(s) from the list using the append() method and del statement respectively.

Example 3.26 Using the eval() function to accept input of different types.

```
a = eval (input ("Enter an integer : "))
print (type (a) )
b = eval(input("Enter a float:"))
print (type (b) )
c = eval (input ("Enter a tuple : "))
print(type(c))
d = eval (input ("Enter a list : "))
print (type (d))
```

OUTPUT

```
Enter an integer : 1
<class 'int'>
Enter a float: 2.3
<class 'float'>
Enter a tuple: (4,5,6)
<class 'tuple'>
Enter a list : [7,8,9]
<class 'list'>
```

Example 3.27

Let us write a program that uses the `eval()` function to accept a list of numbers and print the sum of the elements.

```
list = eval (input ("Enter values : "))
print (list)
sum(list)
print("SUM = ",sum(list))
```

OUTPUT

```
Enter values: [1,2,3,4,5,6,7,8,9,10]
[1,2,3,4,5, 6,7,8, 9, 10]
SUM = 55
```

Example 3.28

```
num_list = [2,4,6,8,10,12,14,16,18,20]
print("List is: ", num_list)
num_list[5] = 100
print("List after udpation is : ", num_list)
num_list.append(200)
print("List after appending a value is ", num_list)
del num_list[3]
print("List after deleting a value is ", num_list)
```

OUTPUT

```
List is: [2,4, 6, 8, 10, 12, 14, 16, 18, 20]
List after udpation is: [2, 4, 6, 8, 10, 100, 14, 16, 18, 20]
List after appending a value is [2,4, 6, 8, 10, 100, 14, 16, 18, 20, 200]
List after deleting a value is [2, 4, 6, 10, 100, 14, 16, 18, 20, 200
```

If you know exactly which element(s) to delete, use the `del` statement; otherwise, use the `remove()` method to delete the unknown elements.

Example 3.29

```
num_list = [2,4,6,8,10,12,14,16,18,20]
del num_list[3:6]   # deletes numbers at index 3,4,5
print(num_list)
del num_list[:]   #deletes all the numbers from the list
print(num_list) # an empty list is printed
```

OUTPUT

```
[2, 4, 6, 14, 16, 18, 20]
[]
```

```
del(num_list)
print(num_list)   # the list no longer exists
```

OUTPUT

```
Traceback (most recent call last):
File "C:\Users\Reema\Python\Python37\try.py",
line 5, in <module>
    print(num_list) # the list no loger exists
NameError: name 'num_list' is not defined
```

Note that when we write del num_list, the entire variable is deleted. If you make any attempt to use this variable after the `del` statement, then an error will be generated.

3.18 RELATIONAL OPERATIONS ON LISTS

We can compare two list objects using relational operators like ==, >,<,>=,<=!=, etc. Python compares elements of a list in lexicographical order. Each element of the list is compared with the corresponding element in the other list. However, to use operators like >=,<=,>,< the two values must be of compatible type; otherwise, an error will be generated.

Example 3.30

```
l1 = [1,2,3]
l2 = [1,2,3]
l3 = [1,[2,3]]
print(l1==l2)
print(l1==l3)
```

OUTPUT
True
False

```
l1 = [1,2,3]
l2 = [1,3,3]
print(l1>=l2)
print(l1<=l2)
```

OUTPUT
False
True

Example 3.31

```
l1 = [1,2,3,4]
l2 = [1,2,3]
print(l1>=l2)
```

OUTPUT
True

```
l1 = [1,2,3,4]
l2 = ['a','b','c']
l3 = [1.0,2.0,3.0]
print(l1>=l3)
print(l2>=l3)
```

OUTPUT
True
Traceback (most recent call last):
File "C:\Python37\try.py", line 5, in
    <module>
print(l2>=l3) TypeError: '>=' not
    supported
between instances of 'str' and 'float'

3.19 NESTED LISTS

Nested list means a list within another list. We have already said that a list has elements of different data types. So besides other elements, a list can also have another list as its element. For example, **list1 = [1,2,'a',[5.0,6,"ABCD"],"BYE"]**. Here, `list1` is a list that has another list at index 3.

To *insert items from another list* at a particular location, we can use the slice operation. This would create a nested list, i.e., a list within another list.

Remember that you can specify an element in the nested list by using a set of indices. For example, assuming that the inner list starts at index 3 in the main list, to print the second element of the nested (or the inner) list, we will write `print list[3][1]`. The first index specifies the starting location of the nested list in the main list and the second index specifies the index of the element within the nested list. The code given below clarifies this concept.

Example 3.32

```
# Creating a Nested List
list1 = [1,2,'a',[5.0,6,"ABCD"],"BYE"]
i=0
while i<len(list1)):
    print("List1[",i,"] = ",list1[i])
    i+=1
```

OUTPUT

```
List1[ 0 ] = 1
List1[ 1 ] = 2
List1[ 2 ] = a
List1[ 3 ] = [5.0,6, 'ABCD']
List1[ 4 ] = BYE
```

Example 3.33

```
# Inserting a list within another list- creating a nested list
num_list = [2,4,12,14]
print("Original List: ", num_list)
num_list[2] = [6,8,10]
print("After inserting another list, the updated list is : ", num_list)
print("Second element of nested list is : ",num_list[2][1])
```

OUTPUT

```
Original List: [2,4, 12, 14]
After inserting another list, the updated list is: [2,4, [6,8, 10], 14]
Second element of nested list is : 8
```

3.20 LIST ALIASING AND CLONING

When one list is assigned to another list using the assignment operator (=), then a new copy of list is not made. Instead, assignment operation makes the two variables point to the one list in memory. This is also known as *aliasing*.

Cloning lists: If you want to modify a list and also keep a copy of the original list, then you should create a separate copy of the list (not just the reference). This process is called *cloning*. The slice operation is used to clone a list.

Example 3.34

```
list1 = [1,2,3,4,5,6,7,8,9,10]
print("List1 =", list1)
list2 = list1   #list aliasing
print("List2 =", list2)
list3 = list1[2:5] #list cloning
print("List3 =", list3)
```

OUTPUT

```
List1 = [1,2,3,4, 5, 6, 7, 8, 9, 10]
List2 =[1,2,3,4, 5, 6, 7, 8, 9, 10]
List3 = [3, 4, 5]
```

3.21 DELETING ELEMENTS

We can delete one or more elements from the list by using the **del** statement. The syntax to remove a single element from the list is del **list_variable[index]**. And to remove more than one element from the list, we use the syntax, **del[start:stop]**. Finally, to remove the entire list, we need to write **del list_variable.**

Example 3.35

```
l =[1,2,3,4,5,6,7,8,9,10]
print(l)
# deleting third element
del l[2]
print(l)
# deleting fourth, fifth, sixth and seventh elements from the list
del l[2:6]
print(l)
#deleting the entire list
print("Deleting List ........")
del l
print(l)
```

OUTPUT
```
[1,2,3,4,5,6, 7, 8, 9, 10]
[1,2,4,5,6, 7, 8, 9, 10]
[1, 2, 8, 9, 10]
Deleting List ........
Traceback (most recent call last): File "C:\Python37\try.py", line
12, in <module> print(l)
NameError: name 'l' is not defined
```

3.22 DEEP COPIES AND SHALLOW COPIES IN PYTHON

When copying lists or any other object in Python, we can make a deep copy of the original object or a shallow copy. *A deep copy makes a new and separate copy* of an *entire* object or list with its own unique memory address. Therefore, any changes made in the new copy of the object/list will not be reflected in the original one.

A deep copy creates a new list or object by recursively copying the elements from the original object to the new one. So, both the objects are completely independent of each other. This is similar to the concept of passing by value in languages like C++, Java, and C#.

A shallow copy also makes a separate new object or list. However in this case, instead of copying the elements to the new object, *it simply copies the references to their memory addresses.* Hence, changes made in the original object would also be reflected in the copied object, and vice versa. Therefore, both the copies are dependent on each other. This is similar to the concept of passing by reference in programming languages like C++, C#, and Java.

Talking in terms of lists, *the assignment operator is used to create a shallow copy of the* `list` *and the* `list()` *creates a deep copy* as illustrated below.

Example 3.36

```
# Creating a shallow copy of a list
l1  =    [1,2,3,4,5]
l2 = l1
print("L1 = ", l1)
print("L2 = ",l2)
```

```
l1[2] = 10
print("L1 =", l1)
print("L2 =", l2)
```

OUTPUT
```
L1 = [1, 2, 3, 4, 5]
L2 =[1, 2, 3, 4, 5]
L1 =[1, 2, 10, 4, 5]
L2 = [1,2, 10,4,5]
```

Example 3.37

```
# Creating a deep copy of a list
l1 = [1,2,3,4,5]
l2 = list(l1)
print("L1 =", l1)
print("L2 =", l2)
l1[2] =10
print("L1 =", l1)
print(" L2 =", l2)
```

OUTPUT
```
L1 = [1,2, 3,4,5]
L2 = [1, 2, 3, 4, 5]
L1 = [1,2, 10,4,5]
L2 = [1, 2, 3, 4, 5]
```

3.23 BASIC LIST OPERATIONS

Lists behave in the similar way as strings when operators like + (concatenation) and * (repetition) are used. It works similar in case of operations discussed in Table 3.3.

Table 3.3 Operations on lists

Operation	Description	Example	Output
`len`	Returns length of list	`len([1,2,3,4,5,6,7,8,9,10])`	`10`
`concatenation`	Joins two lists	`[1,2,3,4,5] + [6,7,8,9,10]`	`[1, 2, 3, 4, 5, 6, 7, 8, 9, 10]`
`repetition`	Repeats elements in the list	`"Love", "Python"*2`	`['Love', 'Python', 'Love', 'Python']`
`in`	Checks if the value is present in the list	`'a' in ['a','e','i','o','u']`	`True`
`not in`	Checks if the value is not present in the list	`9 not in [0,2,4,6,8]`	`True`
`max`	Returns maximum value in the list	`>>> num_list = [1,0,3,7,4,2,4,9]` `>>> print(max(num_list))`	`9`

Table 3.3 (*Continued*)

Table 3.3 Continued

Operation	Description	Example	Output
`min`	Returns minimum value in the list	`>>> num_list = [1,0,3,7,4,2,4,9]` `>>> print(min(num_list))`	`0`
`sum`	Adds the values in the list that has numbers	`num_list = [1,2,3,4,5,6,7,8,9,10]` `print("SUM = ", sum(num_list))`	`SUM = 55`
`all`	Returns True if all elements of the list are true (or if the list is empty)	`>>> num_list = [8,9,0,10]` `>>> print(all(num_list))`	`False`
`any`	Returns True if any element of the list is true. If the list is empty, returns False	`>>> num_list = [,0,1,2,4,9]` `>>> print(any(num_list))`	`True`
`List`	Converts tuple or string to a list	`>>> list1 = list("PYTHON")` `>>> print(list1)`	`['P', 'Y', 'T', 'H', 'O', 'N']`

`Sorted`	Returns a new sorted list. The original list is not sorted.	`>>> list1 = [1,0,3,7,4,2,9]`
		`>>> list2 = sorted(list1)`
		`>>> print(list2)`
			`[0,1,2,3,4,7,9]`

3.24 LIST METHODS

Python has various methods to help programmers work efficiently with lists. Some of these methods are summarized in Table 3.4.

Table 3.4 List methods

Method	Description	Syntax	Example	Output

`append()`	Appends an element to the list. In insert(), if the index is 0, then element is inserted as the first element and if we write, list.insert(len(list), obj), then it inserts obj as the last element in the list. That is, if index= len(list) then insert() method behaves exactly same as append() method.	`list.append(obj)`	`num_list = [1,2,3,4]`
			`num_list.append(5)`
			`print(num_list)`
				`[1,2,3,4,5]`

`count()`	Counts the number of times an element appears in the list	`list.count(obj)`	`num_list = [1,2,3,4,3,2,4,6]` `print( num_list.count(4))`	`1`

Table 3.4 (*Continued*)

Table 3.4 Continued

Method	Description	Syntax	Example	Output
`index()`	Returns the lowest index of obj in the list. Gives a ValueError if obj is not present in the list	`list.index(obj)`	`num_list = [1,2,3,4,3,2,4,6]` `print(num_list.index(3))`	2

`insert()`	Inserts obj at the specified index in the list.	`list.insert(index, obj)`	`num_list = [1,2,3,4,5]`
			`num_list.insert(3, 0)`
			`print(num_list)`
				[1,2,3,0,4,5]

`pop()`	Removes the element at the specified index from the list. Index is an optional parameter. If no index is specified, then it removes the last object (or element) from the list.	`list.pop([index])`	`num_list = [1,2,3,4,5]`
			`print(num_list.pop())`
			`print(num_list)`
				5
				[1,2,3,4]

`remove()`	Removes or deletes obj from the list. ValueError is generated if obj is not present in the list. If multiple copies of obj exist in the list then the first value is deleted.	`list.remove(obj)`	`num_list = [0,1,2,3,4,5]`
			`num_list.remove(0)`
			`print(num_list)`
				[1, 2, 3, 4, 5]

`reverse()`	Reverses the elements in the list.	`list.reverse()`	`num_list = [1,2,3,4]`
			`num_list.reverse()`
			`print num_list`
				[4,3,2,1]

`sort()`	Sorts the elements in the list	`list.sort()`	`num_list = [3,5,0,4,1]`
			`num_list.sort()`
			`print(num_list)`
				[0,1,3,4,5]

`extend()`	Adds the elements in a list to the end of another list. Using + or += on a list is similar to using extend().	`list1.extend(list2)`	`num_list1 = [1,2,3]`
			`num_list2 = [4,5,6]`
			`num_list1.extend(num_list2)`
			`print(num_list1)`
				[1, 2, 3, 4, 5, 6]

Recall the difference between a function and a method. A **function** is a piece of code that is directly called by name. It may or may not accept parameters and may or may not return data. All data that is to be used by a function is explicitly passed (or made global). Example, *len(list1)*.

However, a **method** is a piece of code that is called by name of the object followed by a dot operator and name of the method. Example, *list1.sort()*.

Key points to remember

- The `sort()` method uses ASCII values to sort the values in the list. Since lower case characters' ASCII value starts from 97and upper case characters starts from 65, upper case characters appear before lower case characters when sorting is done.

- Items in a list can also be deleted by assigning an empty list to a slice of elements as shown in the codes below.
- The `range()` function can be used to print index as shown in the code given below.

Example 3.38

```
list1 = ['1', 'a', "Abc", '2', 'B', "def"]
list1.sort()
print(list1)
```

OUTPUT

```
['1', '2', "Abc", 'B', 'a', 'def']
```

Example 3.39

```
list = ['P', 'r', 'o', 'g', 'r', 'a', 'm', 'm', 'i', 'n', 'g']
list[3:6] = []
print(list)
```

OUTPUT

```
['P', 'r', 'o', 'm', 'm', 'i', 'n', 'g']
```

Example 3.40

```
list = ['B','Y','E']
for i in range(len(list)):
    print("index: ", i)
```

OUTPUT

```
index:  0
index:  1
index:  2
```

- If you give an index out of range or the legal indices, then an **IndexError** will be generated. For a list, the legal indices include index from 0 to length of the list – 1. Consider the example, given below.

Example 3.41

```
list = [1,'a',3.4,"PYTHON"]
print(len(list))
# error because length is 4 and we are accessing access an index out of range
print(list[4])
```

OUTPUT

```
4
Traceback (most recent call last):
  File "C:\Python37\try.py", line 4, in <module>
    print(list[4])
IndexError: list index out of range
```

- The + operator can also be used to join two lists. But if you try to join a number or string or any other data with a list using the + operator, **TypeError** will be generated.

Example 3.42

```
l1 =[1,2,3,4,5]
l2 =l1 + 6
print(l2)
```

OUTPUT
```
Traceback (most recent call last):
File "C:\Python37\try.py", line 2, in <module>
l2 =l1 + 6
TypeError: can only concatenate list (not "int") to list
```

Example 3.43

```
# Correct Way
l1 =[1,2,3,4,5]
l2 =l1 + [6]
print(l2)
```

OUTPUT
```
[1, 2, 3, 4, 5, 6]
```

- Like strings, lists can also be repeated using the * operator.
- While the append() method adds a single element to a list, the extend() method is used to add multiple elements from one list to another list.

Example 3.44

```
# Repeating a list
l1 = ['B','Y','E']
l2 =l1 * 3
print(l2)
```

OUTPUT
```
['B' 'Y' 'E' 'B' 'Y' 'E' 'B' 'Y' 'E']
```

Example 3.45

```
# Difference between append() and extend()
l1 = [1,2,3,4,5]
l1.append(6)
l1.extend([7,8])
print(l1)
```

OUTPUT
```
[1, 2, 3, 4, 5, 6, 7, 8]
```

In the insert() method, if we specify a negative index that is not in the set of valid indices, the element is added at the beginning of the list.

Example 3.46

```
l1 = [1,2,3,4,5]
l1.insert(-10,123)
print(l1)
```

OUTPUT

```
[123, 1, 2, 3, 4, 5]
```

If the pop() method is called on an empty list, then and IndexError will be generated.

Example 3.47

```
l1 = []
l1.pop()
```

OUTPUT

```
Traceback (most recent call last):
  File "C:\ Python37\try.py", line 2, in <module>    l1.pop()
IndexError: pop from empty list
```

Key Terms

Traversing a string: Accessing each character in the string, one at a time.

Dot notation: Use of the dot operator (.) to access functions inside a module.

Index: A variable or value used to access a member of an ordered set.

Slice: A part of a string obtained by specifying a range of indices.

Whitespace: Characters that move the cursor without printing visible characters.

Method: A function that is called on an object using dot notation.

Sequence: An ordered set of values in which each value is identified by an integer index.

Empty string: A string that has no characters and has a length = 0.

Format operator: % operator that takes a format string and a tuple to generate a string that includes values of the tuple formatted as specified by the format string.

Format sequence: Sequence of characters in a format string, like %d, which specifies how a value should be formatted.

Format string: String used with the % or format operator that contains format sequences.

Invocation: A statement that calls a method.

Immutable: The property of a sequence whose items cannot be assigned.

Immutable data: Data that cannot be modified. Assigning values to elements or slices of immutable data results in a runtime error.

Mutable data value: Data that can be modified.

List: A mutable data structure that can have elements that belong to different data types.

Nested list: Nested list means a list within another list.

List aliasing: When one list is assigned to another list using the assignment operator (=), then a new copy of the list is not made. Instead, assignment makes the two variables point to the one list in memory. This is also known as aliasing.

List cloning: The process of creating a separate copy of the list (not just the reference) is known as list cloning. The slice operation is used to clone a list.

Chapter Highlights

- The Python string data type is a sequence made up of one or more individual characters, where a character could be a letter, digit, whitespace, or any other symbol.

- The `in` operator checks if one character or string is contained in another string.
- The whitespace characters, exclamation mark and any other symbol (like ?, <,>,*, @, #, $, %, etc) that forms a part of the string would be assigned their own index number.
- Concatenate means to join together and append means to add something at the end.
- A raw string literal which is prefixed by an 'r' passes all the characters as it.
- Python strings are immutable, which means that once the strings are created they cannot be changed.
- The number and type of values in the tuple should match the number and type of format sequences or conversion specifications in the string; otherwise, an error is returned.
- Strings are an example of Python objects.
- `in` and `not in` operators can be used with strings to determine whether a string is present in another string. Therefore, the `in` and `not in` operators are also known as membership operators.
- The string module consists of a number of useful constants, classes and functions. These functions are used to manipulate strings.
- List is a versatile data type available in Python, in which elements are written as a list of comma-separated values (items) between square brackets.
- Like strings, lists can also be sliced and concatenated.
- Once created, one or more elements of a list can be easily updated by giving the slice on the left-hand side of the assignment operator.
- We can append new values in the list and remove existing value(s) from the list using the `append()` method and `del` statement respectively.
- To insert items from another list at a particular location, we can use the slice operation. This would create a nested list, that is, a list within another list.
- Lists behave in a similar way as strings when operators like + (concatenation) and * (repetition) are used.

Review Questions

1. With the help of an example, explain how we can create string variables in Python.
2. With the help of an example, explain how we can concatenate a string and a floating-point data.
3. Python strings are immutable. Comment on this statement.
4. Write a short note on format operator.
5. What will happen when the `strip()` is used with a string argument?
6. Explain the use of `format()` with the help of an example.
7. What is slice operation? Explain with an example.
8. With the help of an example, explain the significance of membership operators.
9. Differentiate between the following:
   a. A method and a function
   b. `find()` and `index()`
   c. `find()` and `rfind()`
   d. `captalize()` and `upper()`
10. Name the function to do the following operations:
    a. Return a string with the original string centered to a total of width columns.
    b. Check if a string ends with suffix; return True if so and False otherwise
    c. Return True if a string has at least 1 character and every character is either a number or an alphabet and False otherwise.
    d. Return True if a string has at least 1 character and every character is a lower case alphabet and False otherwise.
    e. Remove all trailing whitespace in string.
    f. Return the highest alphabetical character (having highest ASCII value) from the string str.
    g. Toggle the case of every character
    h. Return a list of substrings separated by the specified delimiter.
    i. The function joins a list of strings using the delimiter with which the function is invoked.
11. Return a list of the lines in the string.

12. If str = 'Welcome to the world of Python Programming', answer the following:
    a. Write an instruction to print the tenth character of the string.
    b. Write an instruction that prints the index of the first occurrence of the letter 'o' in the string.
13. What is a list?
14. How can we define a list in Python?
15. With the help of an example, demonstrate how lists can be sliced to access its values.
16. Explain the syntax of the `slice` operation.
17. What is the role of `del` statement with list variables?
18. Differentiate between shallow copy and deep copy of an object in Python.
19. Differentiate the use of `del` statement and `remove()` function.
20. What is a nested list? How can we make one in Python?
21. Differentiate between list cloning and list aliasing.
22. Differentiate between `pop()` and `remove()` methods of list objects.
23. Explain the purpose of the following functions:
    a. `sorted()`   b. `list()`   c. `any()`   d. `sum()`   e. `min()`
24. Name the function or the operator that can be used for the following tasks:
    a. Return length of list
    b. Repeat elements in the list
    c. Join two lists
    d. Check if the value is present in the list
    e. Returns maximum value in the list.
25. Name the methods that can be used in the following situations:
    a. Append an element to the list
    b. Count the number of times an element appears in the list
    c. Returns the lowest index of obj in the list.
26. Explain the purpose of the following methods in Python:
    a. `insert()`   b. `reverse()`   c. `extend()`
27. Given a list, l = [1,2,3,4,5], write instructions for the following tasks:
    a. Set the third element to 100
    b. Insert 200 at the second index
    c. Append 300 to the list
    d. Remove the fourth element from the list
    e. Sort the list
    f. Reverse the list.
28. Given a list L = [1,2,3,4,[5,6,7,8],9,10], write expressions that will print the values:
    a. [5,6,7,8]   b. [6,7]   c. [2,3,4]   d. [1,3,[5,6,7,8], 10]

Programming Exercises

1. Modify the `find_ch` function so that it starts finding the character from the specified position in the string.
2. Write a program to calculate the length of a string.
3. Write a program to count the number of vowels and consonants present in a user-inputted string.
4. Write a program to count the number of lower case and uppercase characters present in a user-inputted string.
5. Write a program to count the number digits, spaces and alphabets present in a user-inputted string.
6. Write a Python program to get a string made of the first 2 and the last 2 chars from a given string. If the string length is less than 2, return instead the empty string.
7. Write a Python program to get a string from a given string where all occurrences of its first char have been changed to '$', except the first char itself.
8. Write a Python program to get a single string from two given strings, separated by a space and swap the first two characters of each string.

9. Program to copy a string.
10. Write a Python program to add `'ing'` at the end of a given string (length should be at least 3). If the given string already ends with `'ing'` then add `'ly'` instead. If the length of the given string is less than 3, leave it unchanged.
11. Write a program to find the first appearance of the substring 'not' and 'poor' in a given string. If 'bad' follows 'poor', replace the whole 'not'…'poor' substring with 'good'. Return the resulting string.
12. Write a function that takes a list of words and returns the length of the longest one.
13. Write a program to remove the *n*th index character from a non-empty string.
14. Write a program to change a given string to a new string where the first and last chars have been exchanged.
15. Write a program to remove the characters which have odd index values of a given string.
16. Write a program to count the occurrences of each word in a given sentence.
17. Write a program that accepts a comma-separated sequence of words as input and prints the unique words in a sorted form (alphanumerically).
18. Write a function to insert a string in the middle of a string.
19. Write a function to get a string made of 4 copies of the last two characters of a specified string (length must be at least 2).
20. Write a function to get a string made of the first three characters of a specified string. If the length of the string is less than 3, then return the original string.
21. Write a function to get the first half of a specified string of even length.
22. Write a function to reverse a string if its length is a multiple of 4.
23. Write a function to convert a given string to all uppercase if it contains at least 2 uppercase characters in the first 4 characters.
24. Write a program to sort a string lexicographically.
25. Write a program to remove newline characters from text.
26. Write a program to check whether a string starts with specified characters.
27. Write a program to remove existing indentation from all of the lines in a given text.
28. Write a program to add a prefix text to all of the lines in a string.
29. Write a program to set the indentation of the first line.
30. Write a program to print floating numbers up to 2 decimal places.
31. Write a program to print floating numbers up to 2 decimal places with sign.
32. Write a program to print floating numbers with no decimal places.
33. Write a program to print integers with zeros on the left of specified width.
34. Write a program to print integers with '*' on the right of specified width.
35. Write a program to display a number with comma separator.
36. Write a program to format a number with percentage.
37. Write a program to display a number in left, right and center aligned format of width 10.
38. Write a program to reverse words in a string.
39. Write a program to strip a set of characters from a string.
40. Write a program to create a mirror of the given string. For example, `"abc"` = `"abccba"`.
41. Write a program that removes all the occurrences of a specified character from a given string.
42. Write a program to check whether a string is a palindrome or not.
43. Write a program to remove all the occurrences of a given word from the string.
44. Write a program to concatenate two strings in a third string. Do not use + operator.
45. Write a program to append a string to another string. Do not use += operator.
46. Write a program to swap two strings.

47. Write a program to insert a string in another string.
48. Write a program to delete a string from another string.
49. Write a program to replace a string with another string. Do not use the `replace()`
50. Write a program that removes leading and trailing spaces from a string.
51. Write a program to read a name and then display it in abbreviated form. For example, Janak Raj Thareja should be displayed as JRT.
52. Write a program to read a name and then display it in abbreviated form, For example, Janak Raj Thareja should be displayed as J.R. Thareja.
53. Write a program to count the number of characters, words, and lines in a given text.
54. Write a program to count the number of digits, upper case characters, lower case characters and special characters in a given string.
55. Write a program to extract the first n characters of a string.
56. Write a program to copy n characters of a string from the mth position in another string. Do not use the slice operation.
57. Write a program to delete the last character of a string.
58. Write a program to delete the first character of a string.
59. Write a program to encrypt a string using substitution cipher.
60. Write a program that encrypts a string using multiplicative cipher. Generate the key randomly.
61. Write the command to print "hello world" as "Hello world".
62. Write the command to print "hello world" as "Hello World".
63. Write the command to print "hElLo WoRlD" as "HeLlO wOrLd".
64. Write the command to print "hello world" as "Hello Friends".
65. Write a program that prompts the user to enter a 10-digit mobile number. Display the number by putting a '-' after area code and next three digits. (like `123-456-7890`).
66. Write a program that prompts the user to enter five words. If the length of any word is less than 8 or if the word does not contain any digit then prompt the user to enter that word again.
67. Write a program that creates a list of numbers in the series $2^n - 1$. Display only the even indexed values in this list.
68. Write a program that prints the elements along with their indices from the start and end of the list.
69. Write a program that reads two lists. Make another list of all those elements in the first list that are also present in the second list.
70. Write a program that creates a list ['a','bb','ccc','dddd',....].
71. Write a program that forms a list of numbers in the series
    a. 2/9, −5/13, 8/17, ...　　　　b. $x, -x^2/2!, x^3/3!, -x^4/4!, x^5/5!, \ldots$
72. Make a list of five random numbers. Write instructions to sum the elements and find mean of the elements.
73. Write a program that adds the corresponding elements of two lists.
74. Make a list of the first ten letters of the alphabet; then using the slice operation do the following operations
    a. Print the first three letters from the list
    b. Print any three letters from the middle
    c. Print the letters from any particular index to the end of the list.
75. Write a program that prints the maximum value of the second half of the list.
76. Write a program that finds the sum of all the numbers using a `while` loop.
77. Write a program that finds sum of all even numbers in a list.
78. Write a program that reverses a list using a loop.
79. Write a program to find whether a particular element is present in the list using a loop.
80. Write a program that prompts the user to enter an alphabet. Print all the words in the list that starts with that alphabet.

81. Write a program that prompts a number from the user and adds it in a list. If the value entered by the user is greater than 100, then add "EXCESS" in the list.
82. Write a program that counts the number of times a value appears in the list. Use a loop to do the same.
83. Write a program to insert a value in a list at the specified location using `while` loop.
84. Write a program that creates a list of numbers from 1-50, that are either divisible by 3 or divisible by 6.
85. Write a program to create a list of numbers in the range 1 to 20. Then delete all the numbers from the list that are divisible by 3.
86. Write a program to randomly select an item from a list.
87. Write a program to print the string "HELLOWORLD" as

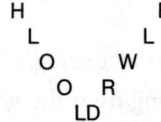

Fill in the Blanks

1. String is a sequence made up of one or more _____.
2. A multiple-line text within quotes must have a _____ at the end of each line.
3. Individual characters in a string are accessed using the _____ operator.
4. _____ error is generated when index out of bounds is accessed.
5. _____ means to join together.
6. The _____ function is used to convert values of any other type into string type.
7. The _____ returns the memory address of that object.
8. Conversion specifications start with a _____ operator.
9. A method is invoked or called on an _____.
10. _____ function checks if string ends with suffix.
11. _____ function toggles the case of every character.
12. The _____ returns a list of the lines in the string.
13. Omitting both ends in the slice operation means selecting the _____.
14. If we access the string from the first character then we use a _____ based index but when doing it backward, the index starts with _____.
15. _____ function returns the ASCII code of the character
16. _____ and _____ operators are known as membership operators.
17. _____ function is used to know the details of a particular item.
18. _____ function displays the methods in a module.
19. _____ defines a particular way of storing and organizing data in a computer.
20. When using slice operation, _____ is generated if the index is outside the list.
21. [10,20] < [20,10] will return _____.
22. `insert()`, `remove()` and `sort()` returns _____.
23. _____ is used to print both index as well as an item in the list.
24. Fill in the blanks to create a list and print its second element.
    List = _____ 10, 20, 30, 40]
    print(list[_____])
25. Fill in the blanks to create a list, reassign its third element and print the list.
    List = [1,2,3,4,5_____

```
    List[_____] = 30
    print(_____)
```
26. Fill in the blanks to print "Hello" if the list contains 'H':
```
    Letters = ['W', 'G', 'H']
    _____ 'H' _____ Letters:
        print("_____")
```
27. Fill in the blanks to add 'G' to the end of the list and print the list's length.
```
    Letters._____('G')
    print(_____  _____)
```
28. Fill in the blanks to print the letters in the list.
```
    Letters = ['H', 'E', 'L', 'L','O']
    _____ i _____ Letters_____
        print(i)
```
29. Fill in the banks to print the first two elements of the list:
```
    List = [1,2,3,4,5,6]
    print(list[0_])
```
30. The range of index values for a list of 10 elements will be _____.

State True or False

1. Character in a string could be a letter, digit, whitespace, or any other symbol.
2. Python treats strings as continuous series of characters delimited by single or double quotes but not triple quotes.
3. Python has a built-in string class as well as a string module that has many methods.
4. Index can either be an integer or an expression that evaluates to a floating-point number.
5. In a string, all whitespace characters are also assigned an index value.
6. Raw strings do not process escape sequences.
7. 'r' is used as a prefix for Unicode strings.
8. We cannot delete or remove characters from a string.
9. The % operator takes a format string on the right and the corresponding values in a tuple on the left.
10. Conversion specifications start with a % operator and can appear anywhere within the string.
11. The number and type of values in the tuple should match the number and type of format sequences or conversion specifications in the string
12. The - after each % in the conversion string indicates right justification.
13. You can access a string using negative indexes
14. odr() function returns character represented by a ASCII number.
15. A string is a substring of itself.
16. Strings are compared based on ASCII values of their characters.
17. The index value starts from zero.
18. List is an immutable data structure.
19. Once created, one or more elements of a list can be easily updated.
20. It is possible to edit, add and delete elements from a list.
21. Slice operation can be used to insert items from another list or sequence at a particular location.
22. The slice operation is used to clone a list.
23. We cannot insert a list into another list.
24. When a list is assigned to another using the assignment operator, then a new copy of list is made.
25. Items in a list can be deleted by assigning an empty list to a slice of elements.

26. If you specify a non-integer number as the index, then `IndexError` will be generated.
27. Python sorts the original list with the help of `sorted()` function.

Multiple Choice Questions

1. The index of the first character in the string is _____.
   a. 0   b. 1   c. n-1   d. n
2. The index of the last character in the string is _____.
   a. 0   b. 1   c. n-1   d. n
3. Which error is generated when the index is not integer?
   a. `IndexError`   b. `NameError`   c. `TypeError`   d. `BoundError`
4. Which of the following words best means to add something at the end?
   a. Concatenate   b. Append   c. Join   d. Add
5. In Python a string is appended to another string by using which operator?
   a. +   b. *   c. []   d. +=
6. Which operator is used to repeat a string *n* number of times?
   a. +   b. *   c. []   d. +=
7. The `print` statement prints one or more literals or values followed by a _____.
   a. Newline   b. Tab   c. Whitespace d. Exclamation
8. Which error is generated when a character in a string variable is modified?
   a. `IndexError`   b. `NameError`   c. `TypeError`   d. `BoundError`
9. You can delete the entire string using which keyword?
   a. del   b. erase   c. remove   d. delete
10. Which operator takes a format string on the left and the corresponding values in a tuple on the right?
    a. +   b. *   c. []   d. %
11. Which character is used for hexadecimal integers in the format string?
    a. u   b. x   c. d   d. s
12. When using `find()`, if str is not present in the string then what is returned?
    a. 0   b. -1   c. n-1   d. `ValueError`
13. "   Cool   " becomes "COOL", which two functions must have been applied?
    a. `strip()` and `upper()`   b. `strip()` and `lower()`
    c. `strip()` and `capitalize()`   d. `lstrip()` and `rstrip()`
14. In the `split()`, if no delimiter is specified then, by default, it splits strings on which characters?
    a. Whitespace b. Comma   c. Newline   d. Colon
15. The `splitlines()`, splits lines in strings on which characters?
    a. Whitespace b. Comma   c. Newline   d. Colon
16. By default, the value of stride is _____.
    a. 0   b. -1   c. 1   d. n-1
17. To print the original string in reverse order, you can set the stride as _____.
    a. 0   b. -1   c. 1   d. n-1
18. Identify the correct result from the following.
    a. ord('10') = 50   b. chr(72) = 'H'   c. chr(55) = 9   d. ord('z') = 123
19. Which of these patterns would not match the string "Good Morning" when used with `match()`?
    a. Good   b. Morning   c. Go   d. Good Morn
20. If `List = [1,2,3,4,5]` then `List[5]` will result in _____.
    a. 4   b. 3   c. 2   d. Error
21. If `List = [1,2,3,4,5]` and we write `List[3] = List[1]`, then what will be `List[3]`?
    a. 1   b. 3   c. 2   d. 4

22. `type(x)` will print _____.
    a. `<class 'list'>`
    b. `<class 'tuple'>`
    c. `<class 'int'>`
    d. `Error`
23. If `List = [1,2,3,4,5,6,7,8,9,10]`, then print `List[8:4:-1]` will give _____.
    a. `[2,3,4,5]`   b. `[9,8,7,6]`   c. `[6,7,8,9]`   d. `[5,4,3,2]`
24. If `List = min([sum([10,20]),max(abs(-30),4)])`, then `List =` _____
    a. 10   b. 20   c. 30   d. 4
25. Which slice operation will reverse the list?
    a. `Lists[-1::]`   b. `numbers[::-1]`   c. `numbers[:-1:]`   d. `List[9:8:1]`
26. If `List = (12,8,7,5)`, then `print(max(min(List[:2]),abs(-6)))` will print _____.
    a. 12   b. 8   c. 7   d. 5
27. Which operator is used for list aliasing?
    a. `=`   b. `+`   c. `*`   d. `&`
28. Which operation is used for list cloning?
    a. assignment   b. slice   c. comparison   d. repetition

Give the Output

1. ```
   s = "Welcome"
   print s[1:3]
   ```
2. ```
   s = "Welcome"
   print s[ : 6]
   ```
3. ```
   s = "Welcome"
   print s[4 : ]
   ```
4. ```
   s = "Welcome"
   print s[1:-1]
   ```
5. ```
   str = "Welcome"
   print "come" in str
   ```
6. ```
   str = "Welcome"
   print "come" not in str
   ```
7. `"free" == "freedom"`
8. `print("12" + "34")`
9. `"man" != "men"`
10. `>>> 3*"PYTHON"`
11. ```
    str = "Welcome to Python"
    print(str.isalnum())
    ```
12. `"Hello".isalpha()`
13. `"14-10-2106".isdigit()`
14. `print "hello".islower()`
15. `"\t".isspace()`
16. ```
    str = "Hello"
    print str.startswith("he")
    ```
17. ```
    str = "Hello, welcome to the world of Python"
    print str.find("o")
    ```
18. ```
    str = "Hello, welcome to the world of Python"
    print str.find("if")
    ```
19. `str = "Hello, welcome to the world of Python"`

```
       print str.rfind("of")
20. str = "Hello, welcome to the world of Python"
    print str.count("o")
21. "us" not in "success"
22. "mi" in "ours"
23. for i in 'Python':
        print 2 * i,
24. string.find("abcdabcdabcd", "cd", 3)
25. string.find("abcdabcdabcdabcdabcd", "cd", 7, 13)
26. a = 10
    b = 20
    print "3**4 = %d and %d * %d = %f" % (3**4, a, b, a * b)
27. print "%d %f %s" % (7, 15, 28)
    print "%-.2f" % 369
    print "%-10.2f%-10.2f" % (91, 23.456)
    print "%5.2f %5.2f $%5.2f" % (9, 1.2, 55.78)
28. str1 = 'Welcome!'
    str2 = 'to Python'
    str3 = str1[:2] + str2[len(str2) - 2:]
    print str3
29. print("She sells sea shells on the sea shore.".find("sea", 3, -6))
30. len("She sells sea shells on the sea shore.")
31. str = "Welcome to the world of Python"
    print(str[:10].find("t"))
32. str = "Welcome to the world of Python"
    start = 3
    end = 10
    print(str[start:end])
33. str = "Hello"
    print str.startswith('h')
    print str.lower().startswith('h')
34. 'In %d years I have saved %g %s.' % (3, 4.5, 'lakh rupees')
35. ', '.join(['Sun', 'Stars', 'Planets'])
36. ' '.join(['Welcome', 'to', 'the', 'world', 'of', 'Python!'])
37. 'Hello'.join(['Welcome', 'to', 'the', 'world', 'of', 'Python!'])
38. "Good morning students".split()
39. 'WelcomeHellotoHellotheHelloworldHelloofHelloPython!'.split('Hello')
40. >>> s = 'abcdefghijkl'
    >>> print(s[-100:-5],s[-100:5])
41. s1 = "HELLO"
    s2 = s1 + s1[-1]
    print(s2)
42. str = "xyz"
    while(len(str)<=4):
        if(str[-1] == 'z'):
            str = str[0:3]+'c'
        elif 'a' in str:
            str = str[0] + 'bb'
```

```
               elif 'x' not in str:
                   str = '1'+str[1:]+'z'
               else:
                   str = str+'*'
       print(str)
```
43. ```
    str = "helloworldofpython"
    print(str[10],str[11:30])
    ```
44. ```
    str1 = '''PYTHON
    PRO'''
    str2 = '''PYTHON\
    PRO'''
    print(len(str1)>len(str2))
    ```
45. ```
    str1= 'PYTHON'; str1[-4]
    ```
46. ```
    colors = ['red', 'blue', 'green']
    print(colors[2])
    print(len(colors))
    ```
47. ```
    list = ['abc', 'def', 'ghi', 'jkl']
    print(list[1:-1])
    list[0:2] = 'xyz'
    print(list)
    ```
48. ```
    list = ['abc', 'def', 'ghi', 'jkl', [1,2,3,4,5]]
    print(list[4][2])
    ```
49. ```
    list = ['p','r','o','g','r','a','m','m','i','n','g']
    print(list[2:5])
    print(list[:-5])
    print(list[5:])
    print(list[:])
    ```
50. ```
    even = [2,4,6]
    print(even + [10, 12, 14])
    print(even*2)
    even.insert(1,0)
    print(even)
    del even[2]
    print(even)
    ```
51. ```
    list = ['p','r','o','g','r','a','m']
    list.remove('p')
    print(list)
    print(list.pop(1))
    print(list)
    print(list.pop())
    print(list)
    ```
52. ```
    list = [9,4,3,8,0,2,3,6]
    print(list.index(3))
    print(list.count(8))
    list.sort()
    print(list)
    list.reverse()
    print(list)
    print(0 in list)
    ```
53. ```
    list = [(1, 2), [3, 4], '56', 78, 9.0]
    print(list[0], type(list[0]))
    ```
    ```

```
    print(list[2:3], type(list[0:1]))
    print(list[2], type(list[2]))
```
54. ```
    list =[ [1,2]*3 ] *4
    print(list)
    ```
55. ```
    list = [10, 20, 30, 40, 50, 60, 70, 80, 90]
    print(list[-4:-1])
    print(list[-1:-4])
    print(list[-5:])
    print(list[-6:-2:2])
    print(list[::-1])
    ```
56. ```
    list = [[10, 20, [30, 40, [50, 60]]]]
    print(list[0])
    print(list[0][2])
    print(list[0][2][2])
    print(list[0][0])
    print(list[0][2][1])
    print(list[0][2][2][0])
    ```
57. ```
    List = [100, 90, 80, 70, 60, 50]
    List[2] = List[1] - 20
    if 30 in List:
        print(List[3])
    else:
        print(List[4])
    ```
58. ```
    List = list(range(2, 20, 3))
    print(List[5])
    ```
59. ```
    def add_two(x):
        return x+2
    List = [10,20,30,40,50]
    result = list(map(add_two,List))
    print(result)
    ```
60. ```
    str = "abcdefghijklmno"
    for i in range(0, len(str), 2):
        print(str[i], end = ' ')
    ```
61. ```
    print [ord(ch) for ch in 'PYTHON']
    >>> eval("10 ** 2")
    ```
62. ```
    eval("'hello' + 'py'")
    ```
63. ```
    l1 = [1,2,3]
    l2 = ['a','b','c']
    l3 = [1.2,3.4,5.6]
    l4 = l1 + l2 + l3
    print(l4)
    ```
64. ```
    print([1,2,8,9] < [1,2,8,9,10])
    ```
65. ```
    l = [1,2,3,4,5,6,7,8,9,10]
    print(l[-1])
    print(l[l[0]])
    print(l[l[-8]])
    print(l[l[l[0]+1]]+2)
    ```
66. ```
    msg = ["PYTHON","is","a",["simple","iterpreted","OOP"],"language"]
    print(msg[2:4])
    print(msg[2:4][1][2])
    print(msg[2:4][1][2][1])
    print("im" in msg[2:4][1][2][1])
    ```
    ```

```
print(msg[2:4][1][1][3:])
print(msg[1]+msg[4])
```
67. `>>> [1,2,3] +[1,2,3] == [1,2,3]*2`
68. ```
    l = [1,2,3]
    l * 3 == [l,l,l]
    ```
69. ```
    msg = ["PYTHON","is","a",["simple","interpreted","OOP"],"language"]
    print(msg[::2])
    print('n' in msg[4])
    print(msg[2] in msg[4])
    ```
70. ```
    l = [1,2,3]
    print((l + [4,5,6])[3])
    ```
71. `[1,2] == [1,2]`
72. `[1,2] is [1,2]`
73. ```
    L = [1,2,3,4,5,6,7,8,9,10,11,12,13,14]
    print(L[::-1])
    print(L[-1:-2:-3])
    ```
74. ```
    for i in [1,2,3]:
        for j in [4,5,6]:
            print(i,j, end = "    ")
    ```
75. ```
    count = 0
    for i in range(5):
        for j in range(10):
            count = count + 1
    print(count)
    ```
76. ```
    list = [55, 66, 77, 88, 99]
    print("random.choice to select a random element from a list - ",
    random.choice(list))
    ```
77. ```
    import random
    city_list = ['New York', 'Los Angeles', 'Chicago', 'Houston',
    'Philadelphia']
    print("Select random element from list - ", random.choice(city_list))
    ```

Find the Error

1. ```
   str = "Hello world"
   str[6] = 'W'
   print(str)
   ```
2. `"%s %s %s %s" % ('Welcome', 'to', 'Python')`
3. `"%s %s %s" % ('East', 'West', 'North', 'South')`
4. `"%d %f %f" % (10, 20, 'Hello')`
5. ```
   str = 'abcdefgh'
   str[5] = 'a'
   print(str)
   str = 'Python'
   print(str)
   ```
6. ```
   str = "Hello World"
   del str[2]
   print(str)
   ```
7. `print("Hello World" + 10)`
   ```

8. `print("Hello" * "World")`
9. `list = ['abc', 'def', 'ghi', 'jkl']`
   `print list[2.0]`
10. `even = [2,4,6]`
    `del even`
    `print(even)`
11. `list = [(1, 2), [3, 4], '56', 78, 9.0]`
    `list.remove('abc')`
12. `msg = "Hello"`
    `msg.append("World")`
    `print(msg)`
13. `[1,2,3] + 2`
14. `L = [1,2,3,4]`
    `L.remove(7)`
15. `[1,2,3] * 3.0`

Answers

Fill in the Blanks

1. characters
2. backslash (\)
3. subscript ([ ])
4. IndexError
5. concatenate
6. str()
7. id()
8. %
9. object
10. endswith()
11. swapcase()
12. splitlines()
13. entire string
14. zero, –1
15. ord()
16. in and not in
17. type()
18. dir()
19. Data structure
20. IndexError
21. True
22. ASCII
23. enumerate() function
24. [, 1
25.], 2, List
26. if, in, Hello
27. append, len, (, Letters,)
28. for, in, :
29. :2
30. 0–10

State True or False

1. True
2. False
3. True
4. False
5. True
6. True
7. False
8. True
9. False
10. True
11. True
12. False
13. True
14. False
15. True
16. True
17. True
18. False
19. True
20. True
21. True
22. False
23. False
24. False
25. True
26. False
27. True

Multiple Choice Questions

1. a
2. c
3. c
4. b
5. d
6. b
7. a
8. c
9. a
10. d
11. b
12. b
13. a
14. a
15. c
16. c
17. b
18. b
19. b
20. d
21. c
22. d
23. b
24. c
25. b
26. b
27. a
28. b

Give the Output

1. el
2. Welcom
3. ome
4. elcom
5. True
6. False
7. False
8. 1234
9. True
10. 'PYTHONPYTHONPYTHON'
11. False
12. True
13. False
14. True
15. True
16. False
17. 4
18. -1
19. 28
20. 6
21. True
22. False
23. PP yy tt hh oo nn
24. 6
25. 10
26. 3**4 = 81 and 10 * 20 = 200.000000
27. 7 15.000000 28
    369.00
    91.00   23.46
    9.00   1.20 $55.78
28. Weon
29. 10
30. 38
31. 8
32. come to
33. False
    True
34. 'In 3 years I have saved 4.5 lakh rupees.'
35. 'Sun, Stars, Planets'
36. 'Welcome to the world of Python!'
37. 'WelcomeHellotoHellothe HelloworldHelloofHelloPython!'
38. ['Good', 'morning', 'students']
39. ['Welcome', 'to', 'the', 'world', 'of', 'Python!']
40. abcdefg abcde
41. HELLOO
    HELL
    O
42. xvzc*
43. o fpython
44. True
45. 'T'
46. green, 3
47. ['def', 'ghi']
    ['xyz', 'ghi', 'jkl']
48. 3
49. ['o', 'g', 'r']
    ['p', 'r', 'o', 'g', 'r', 'a']
    ['a', 'm', 'm', 'i', 'n', 'g']
    ['p', 'r', 'o', 'g', 'r', 'a', 'm', 'm', 'i', 'n', 'g']
50. [2, 4, 6, 10, 12, 14]
    [2, 4, 6, 2, 4, 6]
    [2, 0, 4, 6]
    [2, 0, 6]
51. ['r', 'o', 'g', 'r', 'a', 'm']
    o
    ['r', 'g', 'r', 'a', 'm']
    m
    ['r', 'g', 'r', 'a']
52. 2
    1
    [0, 2, 3, 3, 4, 6, 8, 9]
    [9, 8, 6, 4, 3, 3, 2, 0]
    True
53. ((1, 2), <type 'tuple'>)
    (['56'], <type 'list'>)
    ('56', <type 'str'>)
54. [[1, 2, 1, 2, 1, 2], [1, 2, 1, 2, 1, 2], [1, 2, 1, 2, 1, 2], [1, 2, 1, 2, 1, 2]]

55. [60, 70, 80]
    []
    [50, 60, 70, 80, 90]
    [40, 60]
    [90, 80, 70, 60, 50, 40, 30, 20, 10]
56. [10, 20, [30, 40, [50, 60]]]
    [30, 40, [50, 60]]
    [50, 60]
    10
    40
    50
57. 60
58. 17
59. [12, 22, 32, 42, 52]
60. a c e g i k m o
61. 100
62. 'hellopy'
63. [1, 2, 3, 'a', 'b', 'c', 1.2, 3.4, 5.6]
64. True
65. 10   2   4   6
66. ['a', ['simple', 'iterpreted', 'OOP']]
    OOP   O   False   rpreted islanguage
67. True
68. False
69. ['PYTHON', 'a', 'language']
    True
    True
70. ['PYTHON', 'a', 'language']
    True   True
71. True
72. False
73. [14, 13, 12, 11, 10, 9, 8, 7, 6, 5, 4, 3, 2, 1]
    [14]
74. 1 4   1 5   1 6   2 4   2 5
    2 6   3 4   3 5   3 6
75. 50
76. random.choice to select a random element from a list - 77
    (Note that the output may vary)
77. Select random element from list - Chicago

Find the Error

1. TypeError: 'str' object does not support item assignment
2. TypeError: not enough arguments for format string
3. TypeError: not all arguments converted during string formatting
4. TypeError: float argument required, not str
5. TypeError: 'str' object does not support item assignment
6. TypeError: 'str' object does not support item deletion
7. TypeError: can only concatenate str (not "int") to str
8. TypeError: can't multiply sequence by non-int of type 'str'
9. TypeError: list indices must be integers, not float
10. NameError: name 'even' is not defined
11. ValueError: list.remove(x): x not in list
12. AttributeError: 'str' object has no attribute 'append'
13. TypeError: can only concatenate list (not "int") to list
14. ValueError: list.remove(x): x not in list
15. TypeError: can't multiply sequence by non-int of type 'float'

Tuple and Dictionary in Python

Chapter Objectives

In this chapter, we will revise two more very important non-primitive data structure in Python – Tuple and Dictionary. We will discuss the operations, functions and methods that can be performed on their objects. All these concepts that we have been revising till now act as the building blocks using which our programs will be written. In this chapter, we will therefore cover topics like:

- Creating, accessing, updating, joining, unpacking and indexing tuples
- Assigning, inserting and deleting values from a tuple
- Built-in string functions and methods
- Nested tuples
- Returning values using tuple
- Creating, accessing and traversing dictionaries
- Inserting and deleting keys and values
- Built-in dictionary functions and methods

4.1 TUPLE

A tuple is very similar to lists but it differs in two things.

- First, a tuple is an immutable object. This means that while you can change the value of one or more elements in a list, you cannot change the values in a tuple.
- Second, tuples use parentheses to define its elements whereas lists use square brackets.

> You cannot add elements to a tuple. Methods like append or extend do not work with tuple

4.2 CREATING TUPLE

Creating a tuple is very simple and almost similar to creating a list. You need to just put the different comma-separated values within a parenthesis.

Example 4.1

```
# Creates an empty tuple
Tup1 =()
print(Tup1)
```

OUTPUT

```
()
```

```
# Creates a tuple with a single element
Tup1 =(5,)
print(Tup1)
```

OUTPUT

```
5
```

```
# A tuple of characters
Tup1 =('a','b','c','d')
print(Tup1)
```

OUTPUT

```
('a', 'b', 'c', 'd')
```

```
# Creates a tuple of strings
Tup1 = ("abc","def","ghi")
print(Tup1)
```

OUTPUT

```
('abc', 'def', 'ghi')
```

```
# Tuple of integers
Tup1 =(1,2,3,4,5)
print(Tup1)
```

OUTPUT

(1, 2, 3, 4, 5)

```
#Tuple of floating point numbers
Tup1 =(1.2,2.3,3.4,4.5)
print(Tup1)
```

OUTPUT

(1.2, 2.3, 3.4, 4.5)

```
#Creates a tuple of mixed values
Tup5 =(1, "abc",2.3,'d')
print(Tup5)
```

OUTPUT

(1, 'abc', 2.3, 'd')

Key points to remember

- Any set of comma-separated values written without an identifying symbol like brackets or parentheses, etc., is treated as a tuple by default.

```
print('A', "bcd", 5, 6.7}
```

OUTPUT

A bcd 5 6.7

```
a,b,c =10, 20, 30
print(a,b,c)
```

OUTPUT

10 20 30

- If you want to create a tuple with a single element, you must add a comma after the element. In the absence of a comma, Python treats the element as an ordinary data type.

```
# comma after first element
Tup = (15,)
print type(Tup)
```

OUTPUT

<type 'tuple'>

```
# comma missing
Tup = (10)
print type(Tup)
```

OUTPUT

<type 'int'>

- We can use the `eval()` function to input a tuple. But while specifying the input elements, enclose them within parentheses as shown in the code.

```
#eval() Function to read Tuple
Tup = eval(input("Enter values of the tuple: "))
print(Tup)
print(type(Tup))
```

OUTPUT

Enter values of the tuple: (1,2,'a','bcd',7.8)
(1,2, 'a', 'bcd', 7.8)
<class 'tuple'>

- We can also use the `tuple()` function to create a tuple with the specified sequence.

```
# Using the tuple() Function
Tup = tuple("abc")
print(tup)
tup = tuple([1,2,3])
print(tup)
```

OUTPUT
```
('a', 'b', 'c')
(1, 2, 3)
```

4.3 UTILITY OF TUPLES

In real-world applications, tuples are extremely useful for representing *records* or structures as we call in other programming languages. These structures store related information about a subject together. The information belongs to different data types. For example, a tuple that stores information about a student will have roll_no, name, course, total_marks, avg, etc. If you carefully observe these individual elements, you will see that they belong to different data types. For example, roll_no can be an integer or an alphanumeric value, name and course will be string, total_marks and avg can be floating-point numbers.

Example 4.2

```
Tup1 = (1,20,3,40,5,60,7,80,9,100,11,120)
print("Tup[4:8] = ", Tup1[4:8])
print("Tup[:5] =", Tup1[:5])
print("Tup[3:] =", Tup1[3:])
print("Tup[:]=", Tup1[:])
print("Tup[:-4] =", Tup1[:-4])
print("Tup[-1:5] =", Tup1[-1:5])
print("Tup[::-2] =", Tup1[::-2])
```

OUTPUT
```
Tup[4:8] = (5,60,7,80)
Tup[:5] =(1, 20, 3, 40, 5)
Tup[3:] = (40, 5, 60, 7, 80, 9, 100, 11, 120)
Tup[:] = (1,20,3,40, 5,60, 7, 80, 9, 100, 11, 120)
Tup[:-4] =(1, 20, 3,40,5,60, 7, 80)
Tup[ -1:5] =()
Tup[::-2] =(120, 100, 80, 60, 40, 20)
```

Some built-in functions return a tuple. For example, the `divmod()` function returns two values – quotient as well as the remainder after performing the divide operation.

Example 4.3 Program to illustrate `divmod()` function.

```
quo, rem = divmod(157,4)
print("Quotient = ",quo)
print("Remainder= ", rem)
```

OUTPUT
```
Quotient = 39
Remainder = 1
```

4.4 ACCESSING VALUES IN A TUPLE

Again, like other sequences (like strings and lists), indices in a tuple start at 0. Slice operation, concatenation and other operations possible with other sequences can also be applied on tuples.

Example 4.4

```
#Slice operation on a tuple
Tup = (1,'a',2,'bcd',3.4,5, 'e',6.7,'efg')
print(tup[3])
print(tup[10 - 4*2 + 5])
print(tup[-5])
print(tup[3:6])
print(tup[2:7:2])
print(tup[-10: 10])
```

OUTPUT

```
bcd
6.7
3.4
('bcd', 3.4,5)
(2, 3.4, 'e')
(1, 'a', 2, 'bcd', 3.4,5, 'e', 6.7, 'efg')
```

In the slice operation, we can also use negative indices, strides and even expressions.

When accessing a tuple, if the index is out of the range of legal indices of the tuple, then Python raises an IndexError.

The start and stop parameters of the slice operation specify the boundaries of elements to be accessed. All elements falling within the boundary are returned.

> You can't delete elements from a tuple. Methods like remove or pop do not work with tuple.

4.5 UPDATING TUPLE

We have already said that *tuple is immutable*. So, you cannot change the value(s) in the tuple. You can only extract values from a tuple to form another tuple.

Example 4.5

```
tup = (1,2,3)
print(tup[10])
```

OUTPUT

```
Traceback (most recent call last):
File "C:\Python37\try.py", line 2, in
<module> print(tup[10])
IndexError: tuple index out of range
```

```
tup = (1,2,3)
print(tup[-10:10])
```

OUTPUT

```
(1, 2, 3)
```

Example 4.6

```
#Updating tuple
tup = (1,'a',2,'bcd',3.4,5,'e')
tup[3] = 'Not Possible'
print(tup)
```

OUTPUT

```
Traceback (most recent call last):
File "C:\Python37\try.py", line 2, in <module>
    tup[3] = 'Not Possible'
TypeError: 'tuple' object does not support item assignment
```

4.6 DELETING ELEMENTS IN A TUPLE

Since tuple is an immutable data structure, you cannot delete value(s) from it. Of course, you can create a new tuple that has all elements in your tuple except the ones you do not want (those you wanted to be deleted). However, the entire tuple can be deleted by using the `del` statement.

Example 4.7

```
Tup1 = (1,2,3,4,5)
Tup2 = (6,7,8,9,10)
Tup3 = Tup1 + Tup2
print(Tup3)
```

OUTPUT

```
(1,2,3,4, 5, 6, 7, 8, 9, 10)
```

Example 4.8

```
Tup1 = (1,2,3,4,5)
del Tup1[3] # delete an element
print(Tup1)
```

OUTPUT

```
Traceback (most recent call last):
File "C:\Users\Python37\try.py",line 2, in
   <module>
    del Tup1[3]
TypeError: 'tuple' object doesn't support
    item
deletion
```

```
Tup1 = (1,2,3,4,5)
# delete tuple
del Tup1
print(Tup1)
```

OUTPUT

```
Traceback (most recent call last):
File "C:\Users\Python37\try.py", line 4,
   in
<module>
    print(Tup1)
NameError: name 'Tup1' is not defined
```

4.7 JOINING TUPLES

Like lists, two or more tuples can be joined using the + operator. The + operator requires that both the operands must be of tuple types. Numbers or any other type values cannot be added to a tuple. To add a single element to a tuple, we must use comma after the value.

Example 4.9

```
# Joining tuples
tup1 = (1,2,3)
tup2 = (4,5,6)
tup3 =tup1 + tup2
print(tup3)
```

OUTPUT

```
(1,2,3,4, 5, 6)
```

```
# Joining tuples with a
# non-number value
tup1 = (1,2,3)
tup2 = tup1 + 'a'
print(tup2)
```

OUTPUT

```
Traceback (most recent call last):
File "C:\Python37\try.py",line 2, in
    <module>
    tup2 = tup1 + 'a'
TypeError: can only concatenate tuple (not
    "str") to tuple
```

Example 4.10

```
# Joining single
# value to a tuple
tup1 = (1,2,3)
tup2 = tup1 + (4,)
print(tup2)
```

OUTPUT

(1,2,3,4)

4.8 UNPACKING TUPLES

Creating a tuple from a set of values is called packing. Correspondingly, creating individual values from a tuple is known as unpacking. The syntax of unpacking can be given as,

var1, var2, var3, ..., varn = tuple_variable

While unpacking a tuple, remember that the number of elements in the tuple must match with the number of variables on the left side of the assignment operator.

Example 4.11

```
# Unpacking tuple                          # Packing tuple
tup = (1,'a',2.0,'bcd',3)                  a =1; b='a';c=2.0; d='bcd'
(a,b,c,d,e) = tup                          tup = (a,b,c,d)
print("a = ",a, end = ' ')                 print("tup = ",tup)
print("b = ",b, end = ' ')
print("c = ",c, end = ' ')                 OUTPUT
print("d = ",d, end = ' ')                 tup =  (1, 'a', 2.0, 'bcd')
print("e = ",e, end = ' ')
```

OUTPUT

a = 1 b = a c = 2.0 d = bcd e = 3

Tuple packing and unpacking are very useful to change the values in a tuple. We know that tuples are immutable objects in Python, so their values cannot be changed. In case we need to change values, there are three ways – unpacking and packing tuple is just one of them.

The first way is to create a new tuple with modified values.

The second way is to first unpack the tuples into variables. Modify the value of the variables and then pack those variables to form a tuple.

The third way is to convert a tuple into a list using the `list()` function. Modify the list values and then use the `tuple()` function to convert the list into a tuple.

4.9 BASIC TUPLE OPERATIONS

Like strings and lists, you can also perform operations like concatenation, repetition, etc. on tuples. The only difference is that a new tuple should be created when a change is required in an existing tuple. Table 4.1 summarizes some operations on tuples.

Table 4.1 Operations on tuples

Operation	Expression	Output
Length	len((1,2,3,4,5,6))	6
Concatenation	(1,2,3) + (4,5,6)	(1, 2, 3, 4, 5, 6)
Repetition	('Python..')*3	Python.. Python.. Python..'
Membership	5 in (1,2,3,4,5,6,7,8,9)	True
Iteration	for i in (1,2,3,4,5,6,7,8,9,10): print(i,end=' ')	1,2,3,4,5,6,7,8,9,10
Comparison (Use >, <, ==)	Tup1 = (1,2,3,4,5) Tup2 = (1,2,3,4,5) print(Tup1>Tup2)	False
Maximum	max(1,9,3,6,4,0)	9
Minimum	min(1,9,3,6,4,0)	0
Convert to Tuple (converts a sequence into a tuple)	tuple("PYTHON") tuple([1,2,3,4,5])	('P', 'Y', 'T', 'H', 'O', 'N') (1, 2, 3, 4, 5)

While using the **max()** and **min()** functions, remember that the values in the tuple must be of same type. If the values are not of the same type, then **TypeError** will be returned.

Example 4.12

```
# Finding largest and smallest value
tup = (23,75,12,90,82)
print("LargestValue =",max(tup))
print("SmallestValue = ",min(tup))
```

OUTPUT

```
Largest Value = 90
Smallest Value = 12
```

Example 4.13

```
# Finding largest and smallest value in a tuple
tup  = (23,'a',12.56,90,'bcd')
print("Largest Value = ",max(tup))
print("Smallest Value = ",min(tup))
```

OUTPUT

```
Traceback (most recent call last):
    File "C:\Python37\try.py", line 3, in <module>
        print("Largest Value = ",max(tup))
TypeError: '>' not supported between instances of 'str' and 'int'
```

4.10 TUPLE ASSIGNMENT

Tuple assignment is a very powerful feature in Python. It allows a tuple of variables on the left side of the assignment operator to be assigned values from a tuple given on the right side of the assignment operator. Each value is assigned to its respective variable.

In case an expression is specified on the right side of the assignment operator, first that expression is evaluated and then assignment is done. This feature makes tuple assignment quite versatile. The codes given below show different ways of tuple assignment.

Example 4.14

```
# an unnamed tuple of values assigned to
# values of another unnamed tuple
(val1, val2, val3) = (10,20,30)
print(val1, val2, val3)
Tup1 = (10, 20, 30)
(val1, val2, val3) = Tup1 # tuple
    assigned to another
tuple
print(val1, val2, val3)
```

OUTPUT

```
10  20  30
10  20  30
```

```
# expressions are evaluated before assignment
(val1, val2, val3, val4)= (1+2, 4/3 -
    5,6%7,8 **
2)
print(val1, val2, val3, val4)
```

OUTPUT

```
3 -3.666666666666667 6 64
```

Note that **when assigning values to a tuple, you must make sure that the number of values on both the sides of the assignment operator must be same.** Otherwise, an error will be generated as shown here.

Example 4.15

```
(val1, val2, val3, val4)= (1+2, 6%7, 8 ** 2)
print(val1, val2, val3, val4)
Traceback (most recent call last):
    File "C:\Users\Python37\try.py", line 1, in <module>
        (val1, val2, val3, val4)= (1+2, 6%7, 8 ** 2)
ValueError: not enough values to unpack (expected 4, got 3)
```

4.11 ACCESSING USING INDEX

Like other sequences, we can access an individual element of a tuple by using its index. Correspondingly, we can also get the index of an element by specifying the element in the index method. The `index()` method is used to get the index of an element in the tuple. If the element being searched is not present in the list, then error is generated. The syntax of `index()` is given as, **list.index(obj),** where obj is the object whose index has to looked.

> Tuples are faster than lists, but they cannot be changed.

Example 4.16

```
Tup = (11, 67, 642,'AB', "Good Morning",
    4.5)
print(Tup.index('AB'))
```

OUTPUT

```
3
```

```
Tup = (11, 67, 642,'AB', "Good Morning",
    4.5)
print(Tup.index(5.4))
Traceback (most recent call last):
    File "C:\Users\Python37\try.py", line
    2, in <module>
        print(Tup.index(5.4))
ValueError: tuple.index(x): x not in tuple
```

4.12 TUPLES FOR RETURNING MULTIPLE VALUES

We have learnt that a function can return only a single value. But at times, we need to return more than one value from a function. In such situations, it is preferable to group together multiple values and return them together.

Example 4.17

```
Program returning the highest as well as the lowest score.
def max_min_score(vals):
    x = max(vals)
    y= min(vals)
    return (x,y)
score = (99, 98, 90, 97, 89, 86, 93, 82)
(max_score, min_score) =max_min_score(score)
print("Highest Score =", max_score)
print("Highest Score =", min_score)
```

OUTPUT

```
Highest Score =99
Highest Score =82
```

4.13 NESTED TUPLES

In Python, users can easily define a tuple inside another tuple. Such a tuple is called a nested tuple. Consider the nested table in the code given below that stores and prints the details of employees.

Example 4.18

```
#Nested Tuple
Emps =(("Arav", "Back Office", 35000), ("Chaitanya", "Technical Assistant", 50000),
    ("Dhruvika", "Programmer", 100000))
for i in Emps:
    print(i)
```

OUTPUT

```
('Arav', 'Back Office', 35000)
('Chaitanya', 'Technical Assistant', 50000)
('Dhruvika', 'Programmer', 100000)
```

You can even specify a list within a tuple. The code given below prints the name of the topper and her marks in four subjects. These marks are specified as list in the tuple Topper.

> Slicing can be done on tuples.

Example 4.19

```
# List within a nested tuple
Toppers = (("Janvi",[94, 95,96, 97]),("Khushi",[99, 95,90,93]), ("Myra",[91,
    95,93,94]))
print("Second Topper is: ''. Toppers[1])
```

OUTPUT

```
Second Topper is: ('Khushi', [99, 95, 90, 93])
```

4.14 THE count() METHOD

The count() method returns the number of elements with a specific value in a tuple.

Example 4.20

```
# count() method on tuple
tup =(10,7,8,10,9,7,3,8,5,8,1,8)
print(tup.count(8))
tup =("abc","def","abc","efg")
print(tup.count("abc"))
```

OUTPUT

```
4
2
```

4.15 THE zip() FUNCTION

Zip is a built-in function that takes two or more sequences and "zips" them into a list of tuples. The tuple thus formed has one element from each sequence. The code given below illustrates this concept.

> Reassigning a value in a tuple causes a TypeError.

Example 4.21

```
# Count number of y using count()
tup ="xyyyyzyyyzxzzedbgsyyy"
print("Number of y =", tup.count('y'))
```

OUTPUT

```
Number of y =10
```

```
# zip() method
Tup =(2,4,6,8,10)
List1 =['A','E','I','O','U']
print(list((zip(Tup, List1))))
```

OUTPUT

```
[(2, 'A'), (4, 'E'), (6, 'I'), (8, 'O'),
    (10, 'U')]
```

From the output, we see that the **result of zip() function is a list of tuples** where each tuple contains a character from the list and an integer from the tuple. The example we have seen had an equal number of values in list and tuple but *if the two sequences have different lengths then the result has the length of the shorter one* as illustrated in the code given below. We can even print the elements in a tuple using the for statement as shown below.

> If the index specified in the Tuple slice is too big, then an IndexError exception is raised.

Example 4.22

```
# zip() method with unequal parameters
Tup = (2,4,6)
List1 = ['A', 'E', 'I', 'O', 'U']
print(list((zip(Tup, List1))))
```

OUTPUT

```
[(2, 'A'), (4, 'E'), (6, 'I')]
```

```
# printing tuple with for loop
Tup = (2,4,6)
List1 = ['A','E','I','O','U']
Tup =list((zip(Tup, List1)))
for i, char in Tup:
print(i, char)
```

OUTPUT

```
2 A
4 E
6 I
```

Key points to remember

- Tuples can be converted into lists, and vice-versa using the built-in `tuple()` function that takes a list and returns a tuple with the same elements. Similarly, the `list()` function takes a tuple and returns a list.
- You cannot divide or subtract tuples. If you try to do so, you will get a TypeError with "unsupported operand type."
- Since tuples are immutable, they do not support methods like `sort` and `reverse`, as these methods modify the existing sequence.

> Unlike lists, tuples do not support `remove()`, `pop()`, `append()`, `sort()`, `reverse()`, and `insert()` methods.

Example 4.23

```
# list from tuple and vice-versa
Tup =(2,4,6)
List1 =list(Tup)
print("LIST=", List1)
List1 =List1 + [8,10,12]
Tup1 =tuple(List1)
print("TUPLE =", Tup1)
```

OUTPUT

```
LIST = [2, 4, 6]
TUPLE =(2, 4, 6, 8, 10, 12)
```

Example 4.24

```
# subtracting two tuples
Tup1 =(2,4,6)
Tup2 =(1,3,5)
Tup3 =Tup1- Tup2
print(Tup3)
```

OUTPUT

```
Traceback (most recent call last):
File "C:\Users\Python37\try.py", line
3, in <module>
    Tup3 =Tup1- Tup2
TypeError: unsupported operand
type(s) for -: 'tuple' and 'tuple'
```

Example 4.25

```
# reverse method on tuple
Tup1 =(2,1,4,8,6)
Tup1.reverse()
print(Tup1)
```

OUTPUT

```
Traceback (most recent call last):
    File "C:\Users\try.py", line 2, in <module>
    Tup1.reverse()
AttributeError: 'tuple' object has no
attribute 'reverse'
```

- However, Python has a built-in function `sorted()` which takes any sequence as a parameter and returns a new list with the same elements but in a different order. Example 4.26 given below illustrates this concept.
- You can use string formatting feature to print values in the Tuple. This is shown in Example 4.27.

Example 4.26

```
Program to sort a tuple of values
Tup =(5,1,0,2,8,3,9)
print(sorted(Tup))
```

OUTPUT

```
[0, 1, 2, 3, 5, 8, 9]
```

Example 4.27

```
#Program to illustrate string formatting with tuple
Tup =("Mira", 12, 94.534)
print("%s studying in class %d scored %.2f aggregate" %(Tup[0], Tup[1], Tup[2]))
```

OUTPUT

```
Mira studying in class 12 scored 94.53 aggregate
```

4.16 ADVANTAGES OF TUPLE OVER LIST

Although tuples are similar to lists, there are some advantages of implementing a tuple over a list. Some of these advantages are listed below.

- Since tuples are immutable, iterating through tuple is faster than iterating over a list. This means that tuple performs better than a list.
- Tuples can be used as key for a dictionary but lists cannot be used as keys.
- Tuples are best suited for storing data that is write protected (you can read the data but cannot write to it).
- Tuples can be used in place of lists where the number of values is known and small.
- If you are passing a tuple as an argument to a function, then the potential for unexpected behavior due to aliasing gets reduced.
- Multiple values from a function can be returned using a tuple.

> If a negative value is used for the step, the slice is done backwards.

4.17 DICTIONARIES

Dictionary is a data structure in which we store values as a **pair of key and value.** Each key is separated from its value by a colon (:), and consecutive items are separated by commas. The entire set of items in a dictionary are enclosed in curly braces ({}). The syntax for defining a dictionary is

dictionary_name = {key_1: value_1, key_2: value_2, key_3: value_3}

If there are many keys and values in dictionaries, then we can also write just one key-value pair on a line to make the code easier to read and understand. This is shown below.

```
dictionary_name = {key_1: value_1,
                   key_2: value_2,
                   key_3: value_3,
                   }
```

> Using a mutable object as a dictionary key causes a TypeError.

While keys in the *dictionary must be unique and be of any immutable data type (like strings, numbers, or tuples), there is no stringent requirement for uniqueness and type of values.* That is, value of a key can be of any type. Remember that dictionaries are not sequences, rather they are **mappings**. Mappings are collections of objects in which the objects are stored by key instead of by relative position.

Dictionary is like an associative array (also known as hashes) in which any key of the dictionary can be associated or mapped to a value.

4.18 CREATING A DICTIONARY

The syntax to create an empty dictionary can be given as **dictionary_variable = []**, and the syntax to create a dictionary with key-value pairs is: dictionary_variable = {key1 : val1, key2 : val2, …}. In this syntax, we can specify key-value pairs separated by a colon in curly brackets as shown below.

Example 4.28

```
# To create an empty dictionary
Dict ={}
print Dict
```

OUTPUT

```
{}
```

Example 4.29

```
# Create a dictionary with key-value pairs
Dict ={'EMP_NO' : '123', 'Name' : 'Aaditya', 'Department' : 'SALES'}
print(Dict)
```

OUTPUT

```
{'EMP_NO': '123', 'Name': 'Aaditya', 'Department': 'SALES'}
```

4.18.1 Creating a Dictionary Using `dict()` Method

To create a dictionary with one or more key-value pairs you can also use the `dict()` function. The `dict()` creates a dictionary directly from a sequence of key-value pairs. For example, the line of code given below creates a dictionary using a list of key-value pairs.

Example 4.30

```
# Creating a dictionary using dict() function
Dict =dict([('EMP_NO','123'),('Name','Aaditya'),('Department','SALES')])
print(Dict)
```

OUTPUT

```
{EMP_NO': '123', 'Name': 'Aaditya', 'Department': 'SALES'}
```

We can enclose the keys and values in a separate tuple and then use them as argument in the `zip()` function. The output of the zip function can then be passed as an argument to the `dict()` function so that the dictionary can be created using the two tuples.

Example 4.31

```python
# Creating dictionary using keys and values that are stored as tuples
heads =('Roll No','Name','Marks')
vals =('101','Mishti',99)
Student =dict(zip(heads,vals))
print(Student)
```

OUTPUT

```
{'Roll No': '101', 'Name': 'Mishti', 'Marks': 99}
```

Note that in the program, the `zip()` function clubs the first value from the `heads` tuple with the first value in the `vals` tuple, then the second value from both the tuples are clubbed, and finally the third value is clubbed.

4.19 ACCESSING VALUES IN A DICTIONARY

To access values in a dictionary, square brackets are used along with the key to obtain its value. Note that if you try to access an item with a key, which is not specified in the dictionary, a KeyError is generated.

Example 4.32

```python
# Accessing dictionary values
Dict ={'EMP_NO' : '123', 'Name' : 'Aaditya', 'Department' : 'SALES'}
print("Dict[EMP_NO] =", Dict['EMP_NO'])
print("Dict[Name] =", Dict['Name'])
print("Dict[Department] =", Dict['Department'])
```

OUTPUT

```
Dict[EMP_NO] = 123
Dict[Name] =Aaditya
Dict[Department] =SALES
```

Example 4.33

```python
# Accessing key which is not present in dictionary
Dict ={'EMP_NO' : '123', 'Name' : 'Aaditya'}
print("Dict[EMP_NO] =", Dict['EMP_NO'])
print("Dict[Name] =", Dict['Name'])
print("Dict[Department] =", Dict['Department'])
```

OUTPUT

```
Dict[EMP_NO] =123
Dict[Name] =Aaditya
Traceback (most recent call last):
File "C:\Users\Python37\try.py", line 4, in <module>
    print("Dict[Department] =", Dict['Department'])
KeyError: 'Department'
```

4.20 ADDING AN ITEM IN A DICTIONARY

To add a new entry or a key-value pair in a dictionary, just specify the key-value pair as you had done for the existing pairs. the syntax to add an item in a dictionary is, **dictionary_variable[key] = val.**

4.21 MODIFYING AN ITEM IN A DICTIONARY

To modify an entry, just overwrite the existing value with the new value.

Example 4.34

```
# Adding and modifying values in a dictionary
Dict ={'EMP_NO' : '123', 'Name' : 'Aaditya'}
print("Original dictionary", Dict)
Dict['Department'] ='Sales'  # new key-value pair added
Dict['Name'] ='Aadi' # existing value modified
print("Updated Dictionary ",Dict)
```

OUTPUT

```
Original dictionary {'EMP_NO': '123', 'Name': 'Aaditya'}
Updated Dictionary {'EMP_NO': '123', 'Name': 'Aadi', 'Department': 'Sales'}
```

4.22 DELETING ITEMS

One or more items in a dictionary can be deleted using the **del** keyword. To delete or remove all the items in just one statement, use the `clear()` function. Note that the `clear()` method does not delete the dictionary, it just deletes all the elements inside the dictionary. To remove an entire dictionary from the memory, we can again use the `del` statement **as del Dict_name.** The syntax to use the `del` statement can be given as, **del dictionary_variable[key].**

Example 4.35

```
# deleting entries and the entire dictionary
Dict ={'EMP_NO' : '123', 'Name' : 'Aaditya','Department': 'Sales'}
print("Original Dictionary ", Dict)
del Dict['EMP_NO']   #a particular key-value pair deleted
print("After deleting EMP_NO ". Dict)
Dict.clear() # all entries deleted
print("After deleteing all entries ", Dict)
del Dict # delete dictionary
print("Printing Dictionary after deleting it ", Dict)
```
OUTPUT
```
Original Dictionary {'EMP_NO': '123', 'Name': 'Aaditya', 'Department': 'Sales'}
After deleteing EMP_NO {'Name': 'Aaditya', 'Department': 'Sales'}
After deleteing all entries {}
Traceback (most recent call last):
File "C:\Users\Python37\try.py", line 8, in <module>
    print("Printing Dictionary after deleting it ", Dict)
NameError: name 'Dict' is not defined
```

4.22.1 The pop() Method

The pop() method can be used to delete a particular key from the dictionary. The syntax of the pop() method is, **dict.pop(key [, default])**.

The pop() method removes an item from the dictionary and returns its value. *If the specified key is not present in the dictionary, then the default value is returned.* Since default value is optional, if you do not specify the default value and the key is also not present in the dictionary, then a KeyError is generated.

Another method **popitem()** randomly pops and returns an item from the dictionary. The use of these methods is illustrated in the program given below.

Example 4.36

```
#Program to randomly pop an element from a dictionary
Dict ={'EMP_NO' : '123', 'Name' : 'Aaditya','Department': 'Sales'}
print("Original Dictionary ", Dict)
print("Name is : ", Dict.pop('Name')) # returns Name
print("Dictionary after popping Name is : ", Dict)
print("Salary is :", Dict.pop('Salary', -1)) # returns default value
print("Randomly popping any item: ",Dict.popitem())
print("Dictionary after random popping is: ", Dict)
print("Designation is :", Dict.pop('Designation')) # generates error
print("Dictionary after popping Designation is: ", Dict)
```

OUTPUT

```
Original Dictionary {'EMP_NO': '123', 'Name': 'Aaditya', 'Department': 'Sales'}
Name is: Aaditya
Dictionary after popping Name is: {'EMP_NO': '123', 'Department': 'Sales'}
Salary is : -1
Randomly popping any item: ('Department', 'Sales')
Dictionary after random popping is: {'EMP_NO': '123'}
Traceback (most recent call last):
File "C:\Users\Python37\try.py", line 9, in <module>
    print("Designation is :", Dict.pop('Designation')) # generates error
KeyError: 'Designation'
```

Key points to remember

- Keys must have unique values. *Keys should not be duplicated in a dictionary.* If you try to add a duplicate key then the last assignment is retained.
- In a dictionary, *keys should be strictly of a type that is immutable.* This means that a key can be of strings, number or tuple type but it cannot be a list which is mutable. In case you try to make your key of a mutable type, then a **TypeError** will be generated.
- The keys() method of dictionary returns a list of all the keys used in the dictionary, in an arbitrary order. Use the sorted() function to sort the keys.

Example 4.37

```
# Dictionary with duplicate keys
Dict ={'EMP_NO' : '123', 'Name' : 'Aaditya','Department': 'Sales','EMP_NO' : '456'}
print(Dict)
```

OUTPUT

```
{'EMP_NO': '456', 'Name': 'Aaditya', 'Department': 'Sales'}
```

Example 4.38

```
# Program to use tuple as keys
Dict ={(1,2),([3,4])}
print(Dict)
```

OUTPUT

```
Traceback (most recent call last):
File "C:\Users\Python37\try.py", line 5, in
<module>
    Dict ={(1,2),([3,4])}
TypeError: unhashable type: 'list'
```

Example 4.39

```
# Dictionary with sorted keys
Dict ={'EMP_NO' : '123', 'Name' : 'Aaditya','Department': 'Sales','EMP_NO' : '456'}
print(sorted (Dict.keys()))
```

OUTPUT

```
['Department', 'EMP_NO', 'Name']
```

Example 4.40

```
# Program to check single key in a dictionary
Dict ={'EMP_NO' : '123', 'Name' : 'Aaditya','Department' : 'Sales','EMP_NO' : '456'}
if 'Department' in Dict:
    print(Dict['Department'])
```

OUTPUT

```
Sales
```

- The **in keyword** can be used to check whether a single key is in the dictionary.

The key-value pairs can be specified as a list or as a tuple. To create a dictionary out of this list or tuple, it must be passed as an argument to the `dict()` function.

Example 4.41

```
# Dictionary using a tuple of lists having key- value pairs
Student=dict((['RollNp','101'],['Name','Krish'],['Marks',90]))
print(Student)
```

OUTPUT

```
{'Roll Np': '101', 'Name': 'Krish', 'Marks': 90}
```

In the program, we have used a tuple having list of keys and values as its elements. In the same way, we could have even used nested tuples.

4.23 TRAVERSING A DICTIONARY

Looping over a Dictionary can be done to access only values, only keys or both using the `for` loop. We can use the `items()` method that returns a list of tuples (key-value pair). The `keys()` method returns a list of keys in the dictionary. The `values()` method returns a list of values in the dictionary.

Example 4.42

```
# Program to access items in a dictionary
Dict ={'EMP_NO' : '123', 'Name' : 'Aaditya','Department': 'Sales','EMP_NO' : '456'}
print("KEYS: ", end =' ')
for key in Dict:
    print(key, end ='') # accessing only keys
print("\nVALUES: ", end = '')
for val in Dict.values():
    print(val, end ='') # accessing only values
print("\nDICTIONARY: ", end = ' ')
for key, val in Dict.items():
    print(key, val, "\t", end ='') # accessing keys and values
```

OUTPUT

```
KEYS: EMP_NO Name Department
VALUES: 456 Aaditya Sales
DICTIONARY: EMP_NO 456 Name Aaditya Department Sales
```

4.24 NESTED DICTIONARIES

Like any other sequence, we can also have nested dictionary in Python. A nested dictionary has a dictionary defined inside another dictionary.

Example 4.43

```
# Program to illustrate nested dictionary
Employees ={'Aman' : {'EMP_NO':90, 'Sal':89, 'Desig': 'Analyst'},
    'Sadhvi' : {'EMP_NO':91, 'Sal':87, 'Desig': 'Programmer'},
    'Kiyan' : {'EMP_NO':92, 'Sal':92, 'Desig':'Testing Professional'}}
for key, val in Employees.items():
    print(key, val)
```

OUTPUT

```
Aman {'EMP_NO': 90, 'Sal': 89, 'Desig': 'Analyst'}
Sadhvi {'EMP_NO': 91, 'Sal': 87, 'Desig': 'Programmer'}
Kiyan {'EMP_NO': 92, 'Sal': 92, 'Desig': 'Testing Professional'}
```

4.25 THE COPY() METHOD

The `copy()` method of dictionary returns a shallow copy of the dictionary, i.e., the dictionary returned will not have a duplicate copy of the original dictionary but will have the same reference. This means that both the copies of dictionaries will point to the same object (or address) in the computer's memory.

Example 4.44

```
# Program using copy() method
Emp ={'EMP_NO':90, 'Sal':89, 'Desig': 'Analyst'}
print("Original Emp : ",Emp)
Emp_Copy =Emp.copy()
print("Copied Emp : ", Emp_Copy)
Emp_Copy['Sal'] =99
print("Emp after modification: ", Emp)
print("Copy of Emp after modification: ", Emp_Copy)
```

OUTPUT

```
Original Emp: {'EMP_NO': 90, 'Sal': 89, 'Desig': 'Analyst'}
Copied Emp: {'EMP_NO': 90, 'Sal': 89, 'Desig': 'Analyst'}
Emp after modification: {'EMP_NO': 90, 'Sal': 89, 'Desig':
'Analyst'}
Copy of Emp after modification: {'EMP_NO': 90, 'Sal': 99,
'Desig': 'Analyst'}
```

4.26 BUILT-IN DICTIONARY FUNCTIONS AND METHODS

Table 4.2 discusses some methods and functions that can be used on dictionaries in Python.

Table 4.2 Methods and functions of dictionaries

Operation	Description	Example	Output
`len(Dict)`	Returns the length of dictionary. That is, the number of items (key-value pairs)	`Emp = {'EMP_NO':90, 'Sal':89, 'Desig': 'Analyst'}` `print(len(Emp))`	3
`str(Dict)`	Returns a string representation of the dictionary	`Emp = {'EMP_NO':90, 'Sal':89, 'Desig': 'Analyst'}` `print(str(Emp))`	{'EMP_NO': 90, 'Sal': 89, 'Desig': 'Analyst'}
`Dict.get(key)`	Returns the value for the key passed as argument. If the key is not present in the dictionary, it will return the default value. If no default value is specified then it will return None	`Emp = {'EMP_NO':90, 'Sal':89, 'Desig': 'Analyst'}` `print(Emp.get('Desig'))`	Analyst
`Dict.setdefault(key, value)`	Sets a default value for a key that is not present in the dictionary	`Emp = {'EMP_NO':90, 'Desig': 'Analyst'}` `Emp.setdefault('Sal',0)` `print("Emp gets a salary = ", Emp.get('Sal'))`	Emp gets a salary = 0
`Dict1.update(Dict2)`	Adds the key-value pairs of Dict2 to the key-value pairs of Dict1	`Emp1 = {'EMP_NO':90, 'Desig': 'Analyst'}` `Emp2 = {'Name' : 'Krish', 'Sal' : 89}` `Emp1.update(Emp2)` `print(Emp1)`	{'EMP_NO': 90, 'Desig': 'Analyst', 'Name': 'Krish', 'Sal': 89}
`in and not in`	Checks whether a given key is present in the dictionary or not.	`Emp = {'EMP_NO':90, 'Sal':89, 'Desig': 'Analyst'}` `print('Name' in Emp)` `print('Name' not in Emp)`	False True

4.27 DIFFERENCE BETWEEN A LIST AND A DICTIONARY

There are two main differences between a list and a dictionary.

- First, a list is an ordered set of items. But a dictionary is a data structure that is used for matching one item (key) with another (value).
- Second, in lists, you can use indexing to access a particular item. But these indexes should be a number. In dictionaries, you can use any type (immutable) of value as an index. For example, when we write Dict['Name'], Name acts as an index but it is not a number but a string.
- Third, lists are used to look up a value whereas a dictionary is used to take one value and lookup another value. For this reason, dictionary is also known as a *lookup table*.
  In fact, the main advantage of a dictionary is that you don't need to search for a value one by one in the entire set of values; you can find a value instantly.
- Fourth, the key-value pair may not be displayed in the order in which it was specified while defining the dictionary. This is because Python uses complex algorithms (called hashing) to provide fast access to the items stored in the dictionary. This also makes the dictionary preferable to use over a list of tuples.

Key Terms

Tuple: An immutable data structure that stores related items together.

Packing a tuple: Creating a tuple from a set of values is called packing.

Unpacking a tuple: Creating individual values from a tuple is known as unpacking.

Nested tuple: Tuple inside another tuple.

Dictionary: A collection of key-value pairs that maps from keys to values. While keys can be of any immutable type, there is no such restriction on its associated value which can be of any type.

Key: Data that is *mapped to* a value in a dictionary. Keys are unique data items that are used to look up values in a dictionary.

Key-value pair: A pair of items in a dictionary. Key is used to lookup for a value stored in the dictionary.

Hash function: A function used to compute the location for a key.

Lookup: A dictionary operation that takes a key and finds the corresponding value.

Nested dictionary: A dictionary inside another dictionary.

Mappings: A collections of objects that store objects by key instead of by relative position

Chapter Highlights

- A tuple is an immutable object. This means that while you can change the value of one or more elements in a list, you cannot change the values in a tuple.
- Tuples use parentheses to define their elements whereas lists use square brackets.
- Any set of comma-separated values written without an identifying symbol like brackets or parentheses, etc., is treated as a tuple by default.
- We can use the `eval()` function to input a tuple.
- The `tuple()` function is used to create a tuple with the specified sequence.
- When accessing a tuple, if the index is out of the range of legal indices of the tuple, then Python raises an IndexError.
- Since tuple is an immutable data structure, you cannot delete value(s) from it.
- Two or more tuples can be joined using the + operator. The + operator requires that both the operands must be of tuple types.
- Zip is a built-in function that takes two or more sequences and "zips" them into a list of tuples.
- Python has a built-in function `sorted()` which takes any sequence as a parameter and returns a new list with the same elements but in a different order.

- While keys in the dictionary must be unique and be of any immutable data type (like strings, numbers, or tuples), there is no stringent requirement for uniqueness and type of values.
- Dictionaries are not sequences, rather they are mappings.
- To create a dictionary with one or more key-value pairs, the `dict()` function is used.
- To access values in a dictionary, square brackets are used along with the key to obtain its value.
- If an item with a key that is not specified in the dictionary is accessed, a KeyError is generated.
- One or more items in a dictionary can be deleted using the `del` keyword.
- The `clear()` method does not delete the dictionary, it just deletes all the elements inside the dictionary.
- The `pop()` method removes an item from the dictionary and returns its value. If the specified key is not present in the dictionary, then the default value is returned.
- Keys must have unique values. Keys should not be duplicated in a dictionary.
- The `keys()` method of dictionary returns a list of all the keys used in the dictionary, in an arbitrary order. Use the `sorted()` function to sort the keys.
- The key-value pairs can be specified as a list or as a tuple.
- The `copy()` method of dictionary returns a shallow copy of the dictionary, i.e., the dictionary returned will not be a duplicate copy of the original dictionary but will have the same reference.

Review Questions

1. With the help of an example, explain the significance of + and * operators when used with tuples.
2. Can we change the value of one or more elements in a tuple? Justify your answer.
3. How is a tuple different from a list?
4. Can we add or delete values from a tuple?
5. What are nested tuples?
6. Explain the different ways of defining a tuple.
7. How will you join two tuples?
8. With the help of an example, differentiate between packing and unpacking a tuple.
9. Why do we use the `index()` function?
10. Demonstrate the use of membership operators on a tuple.
11. Explain the use of `zip()` function.
12. Differentiate between `sort()` and `sorted()`.
13. List some advantages of using tuple over lists.
14. What is a dictionary?
15. How is a dictionary different from a list?
16. Discuss at least two ways in which you can create a dictionary.
17. Can lists be used as keys? Justify your answer.
18. How is the `zip()` function used to create a dictionary?
19. How will you add key-value pairs in a dictionary?
20. How will you modify key-value pairs in a dictionary?
21. Differentiate between the `del` statement and `clear()` method.
22. When will we use the `pop()` method?
23. List some restrictions which you will keep in mind when creating a dictionary.
24. Draw a comparison between a list and a dictionary.

Programming Exercises

1. Write a program that creates a list ['a', 'b', 'c'], then create a tuple from that list. Now, do the opposite. That is, create the tuple ('a', 'b', 'c'), and then create a list from it.
2. Create a tuple that has just one element which, in turn, may have three elements 'a', 'b', and 'c'. Print the length of this tuple.
3. Write a program that has a predefined list. Create a copy of this list in such a way that only those values that are in valid_tuple are added in the new list.
4. Create a nested tuple that has the marks of at least 5 students obtained in three subjects. Now, perform the following operations on it:
   a. Display the marks of the fourth student.
   b. Display the marks obtained by the second student in the first subject.
   c. Display the total marks obtained by each student.
   d. Display the average (or mean) marks obtained by each student.
   e. Using the average marks obtained by each student, calculate the average marks obtained by all the students (finding the mean of means).
   f. For each student, display the maximum and minimum marks obtained.
5. Write a program that concatenates the first tuple at the end of the second tuple.
6. Write a program that creates the following tuples:
   a. Squares of first 10 natural numbers
   b. Cube of first 10 odd numbers
   c. First 10 multiples of 7
   d. −5, −3, −1, 1, 3
7. Write a program that creates a tuple of at least 10 pair of values. Count the number of pairs having both values odd.
8. Write a program that has two tuples. Check if the first tuple is a super-set of the second tuple.
9. Create a dictionary of products purchased and their MRPs. Calculate the bill and display to the customer.
10. Find fib(n) using dictionaries.
11. Write a program that prompts the user to enter a string and returns in alphabetical order, a letter and its frequency of occurrence in the string. (Ignore case).
12. Write a program to implement sparse matrix using a dictionary.
13. Write a program that has a dictionary of your friend's name (as keys) and their birthdays. Print the items in the dictionary in a sorted order. Prompt the user to enter a name and check if it is present in the dictionary. If the name does not exist, then ask the user to enter DOB. Add the details in the dictionary.
14. Write a program that displays a menu and its price. Take the order from the customer. Check if the ordered product is in the menu. In case it is not there, the customer should be asked to reorder; if it is present then the product should be added in the bill.
15. Write a program that prints the maximum and minimum value in a dictionary.
16. Write a program to remove duplicates from a dictionary.
17. Write a program to check whether a dictionary has some key-value pairs stored in it or not.
18. Write a program that displays information about an employee. Use nested dictionary to do the task.
19. Write a program that prints keys with same values in the dictionary.
20. Write a program that prints keys with different values in the dictionary.
21. Write a program that accepts two dictionaries. Print all the keys that are present in both the dictionaries.
22. Create a dictionary which has name of the student as key and his total marks as value. Now, perform the following operations on this dictionary.
    a. Display the marks obtained by a particular student.
    b. Display the names of all the students who scored 90 and above.
    c. Display all key-value pairs sorted by keys.
    d. Display all key-value pairs sorted by marks.

e. Create a list of all students.
   f. Create another list having marks obtained by the students.
23. Create a dictionary storing names of months as keys and the number of days as values.
24. Create a dictionary using nested tuple.

Fill in the Blanks

1. _____ use parentheses to define its elements.
2. _____ function takes two or more sequences and "zips" them into a list of tuples.
3. To add a single element in the set, use the _____ method and to add multiple elements in the set, use the _____ method.
4. The _____ function to create a tuple with the specified sequence.
5. The entire tuple can be deleted by using the _____ statement.
6. If tup = ("abc", "def", "ghi", "jkl"), tup[–1] will print _____.
7. print(len((((('a',1,'bcd',3.0),'e',4.5),'fgh',(99,1.0)))) will give output _____.
8. We can access an individual element of a tuple by using its _____.
9. _____ are used to return more than one value from a function.
10. The _____ method returns the number of elements with a specific value in a tuple.
11. Fill in the blanks to print "Hi", if the key 90 is present in the dictionary named "Dict".
    if _____ _____ _____
    print("Hi")
12. Fill in the blanks to create a list, dictionary, and tuple.
    List=_____"abc", "def"_
    Dict=_____1:"abc", 2:"def"_____
    Tup=_____"abc","def"_____
13. _____ is a collection of objects that stores objects by key instead of by relative position.
14. The _____ function can be used to create a dictionary with one or more key-value pairs.
15. One or more items in a dictionary can be deleted using the _____ keyword.
16. The _____ method of dictionary returns a list of all the keys used in the dictionary in an arbitrary order.
17. The _____ method of dictionary returns a shallow copy of the dictionary.
18. The _____ function returns a string representation of the dictionary.
19. The _____ function returns the value for the key passed as argument.
20. Dictionary is also known as a _____ table.

State True or False

1. You cannot perform operations like concatenation, repetition, etc., on tuples.
2. It is possible to specify a list within a tuple.
3. If a sequence is specified without parenthesis, it is to be treated as a list by default.
4. Lists are faster than tuples.
5. A tuple can be sliced.
6. Once created, one or more elements of a tuple can be easily updated.
7. It is possible to edit, add and delete elements in a tuple.
8. Tuples can store information that belongs to different data types.
9. Numbers or any other type values cannot be added to a tuple.
10. `max()` and `min()` functions can be used on a tuple iff the values in it are of different data types.

11. In the `zip()` function, if the two sequences have different lengths, then the result has the length of the longer one.
12. Tuples cannot be divided or subtracted.
13. Keys in the dictionary must be of any mutable data type.
14. Tuples can be used as key for a dictionary but lists cannot be used as keys.
15. Values in a dictionary must be unique.
16. Slicing and concatenation operations are not possible on dictionaries.
17. Dictionary keys are case insensitive.
18. Dictionaries are sequences.
19. To remove an entire dictionary from the memory, we can use the `clear()` method.
20. `pop()` method randomly pops and returns an item from the dictionary.
21. Keys of a dictionary can be sorted using the `sorted()` method.
22. The key-value pairs can be specified as a list or as a tuple.

Multiple Choice Questions

1. If tup = ("abc", "def", "ghi", "jkl"), then tup("def") will return
   a. 1   b. 2   c. 0   d. Error
2. print((0, 10, 20) < (0, 30, 40)) will print
   a. True   b. False   c. Equal   d. Error
3. Which data structure allows you to return multiple values from a function?
   a. List   b. Tuple   c. Dictionary   d. Set
4. Which of the following will not create a tuple?
   a. T = ()   b. t= (10)   c. t = ([1,2],)   d. t = ((1,2),3)
5. Which of the following functions can be used to input a tuple?
   a. `input()`   b. `eval()`   c. `tuple()`   d. `raw_input()`
6. Which function returns a tuple of two values?
   a. `divmod()`   b. `input()`   c. `eval()`   d. `tuple()`
7. Indices in a tuple start at _____.
   a. −1   b. 0   c. 1   d. 10
8. Which error is returned when index is out of the range of legal indices of the tuple?
   a. ValueError   b. TypeError   c. IndexError   d. SliceError
9. Which error is returned when we try to modify the value of an element in a tuple?
   a. ValueError   b. TypeError   c. IndexError   d. NameError
10. The result of `zip()` function is a list of _____.
    a. tuples   b. lists   c. values   d. strings
11. Which error is returned if we divide two tuples?
    a. ValueError   b. TypeError   c. IndexError   d. NameError
12. Identify the function or method which is not supported on tuples?
    a. `sorted()`   b. `reverse()`   c. `count()`   d. `index()`
13. Identify the function or method which is supported on tuples?
    a. `append()`   b. `extend()`   c. `sort()`   d. `list()`
14. If Dict = {1:2, 3:4, 4:11, 5:6, 7:8}, then print(Dict[Dict[3]]) will print
    a. 2   b. 8   c. 11   d. 6
15. Which data structure does not allow duplicate values?
    a. List   b. Tuple   c. Dictionary   d. Set
16. Which data structure does not support indexing?
    a. List   b. Tuple   c. Dictionary   d. Set

17. Using a mutable object as dictionary will result in which error?
    a. TypeError   b. KeyError   c. NameError   d. IndexError
18. Which error is returned if an item with a key, which is not specified in the dictionary, is accessed?
    a. TypeError   b. KeyError   c. NameError   d. IndexError
19. _____ method can be used to delete a particular key from the dictionary.
    a. `clear()`   b. `del`   c. `pop()`   d. `delete()`
20. Which error will the `pop()` method generate if the default value is not specified and the key is also not present in the dictionary?
    a. TypeError   b. KeyError   c. NameError   d. IndexError
21. A _____ cannot be used as a key in the dictionary.
    a. strings   b. number   c. tuple   d. list
22. Which error will be generated if the key of the dictionary is a list?
    a. TypeError   b. KeyError   c. NameError   d. IndexError

Give the Output

1. ```
   tup1 = (1,2,3)
   tup2 = (1.0,2.0,3.0)
   print(tup1 == tup2)
   ```

2. ```
   Tup = ("abc", "def")
   (key, value) = Tup
   print(key, value)
   ```

3. ```
   Tup = (1,2,3)
   Add_Tup = Tup + Tup
   print(Add_Tup)
   Mul_Tup = Tup * 3
   print(Mul_Tup)
   ```

4. ```
   msg = "HelloWorld"
   pairs = []
   for i in range(1, len(msg), 2):
       first = msg[i - 1]
       second = msg[i]
       pairs.append((first, second))
   for item in pairs:
       print(item)
   ```

5. ```
   Tup  = (1, 'abc')
   List = [1, 'abc']
   print(Tup == List)
   print(Tup == tuple(List))
   print(list(Tup) == List)
   print((1, 2) + (3, 4))
   ```

6. ```
   list = ['Good', 'Morning']
   y, x = list
   print(x, y)
   ```

7. ```
   A = ('Chinu', 30, 'Female')
   B = ('Varun', 32, 'Male')
   for i in [A, B]:
       print('%s is a %d year old %s' %i)
   ```

8. ```
   Tup = ('Good',)
   for i in range(4):
   ```

```
        Tup = (Tup,)
        print(Tup)
 9. Tup1='a','bcd',12.34
    Tup2=Tup1,(5,6,7,8)
    print(Tup2)
10. Tup = (1, 2, [3, 4])
    Tup[2][0] = 5
    print(Tup)
11. Tup = ("Good Morning")
    print(Tup.index('M'), end = ' ')
    print(Tup.index('n', 5))
    print(Tup.index('r',4,8))
12. t = (1,2,3,'a')
    l = list(t)
    l
13. tup = (1,2,3,4,5,6,7,8,9)
    print(tup[3:5]*3)
14. tup = (10,7,8,9,6,3,4,5,0,1,2)
    print(tup[0])
    print(tup[tup[3]])
    print(tup[-4])
    print(tup[tup[-2]])
    print(tup[tup[tup[7]]-4])
    print(tup[10*2-15+3])
15. t = (1,2,3)
    a,b,c = (x,y,z) = t
    print(a,b,c)
    print(x,y,z)
16. t=('a')
    print(type(t))
    t=('a',)
    print(type(t))
17. t = (1,2,3)
    tup = ('GO',) + t
    print(tup)
18. t1 = (1,2,3)
    t2 = (4,5)
    print(t1 + t2)
19. t1 = (1,2,3)
    t2 = t1 * (3)
    print(t2)
20. t1 = (1,2,3)
    t2 = ('1','2')
    print(t1 + t2)
21. t = (78,98,80,76,53,54,78,98,87,74)
    print(t[3:])
    print(t[:6])
    print(t[-4:])
    print(t[-4:4])
    print(t[:])
```

22. ```
    t =("Python","Programming","is","fun")
    (a,b,c,d) = t
    print(t[0][0] + t[1][1]+t[1])
    ```
23. ```
    t1 = 'a','b'
    t2 = ("a","b")
    print(t1==t2)
    ```
24. ```
    t = ('a',('b',('c',('d',))))
    print(len(t))
    print(t[1][0])
    print('c' in t)
    ```
25. ```
    t = (1,2,(3,4),5,(6,(7,8),9))
    print(len(t))
    print(t[3]+10)
    print(t[t[1]])
    print(t[t[1]][1]*10)
    ```
26. ```
    t = ((1,2),)*7
    print(t)
    print(len(t[3:8]))
    ```
27. ```
    tup = ("abc","def")
    x,y = tup
    print x, y
    ```
28. ```
    Dict = {"India":"New Delhi", "Nepal":"Kathmandu", "USA":"Washington DC"}
    del Dict["Nepal"]
    for key,val in Dict.items():
        print(key,val)
    ```
29. ```
    Dict = {"India":"New Delhi", "Nepal":"Kathmandu", "USA":"Washington DC"}
    print(Dict.get("Russia"))
    print(Dict.get("Pakistan", "No Idea"))
    ```
30. ```
    Studs = {'Mitanshi', 'Harshita', 'Pritika'}
    Toppers = {}.fromkeys(Studs, 0)
    print(Toppers)
    Toppers['Mitanshi'] = 97
    Toppers['Harshita'] = 92
    Toppers['Pritika'] = 89
    Toppers.setdefault('Nisha', -1)
    print(Toppers)
    ```
31. ```
    Toppers = {}
    Toppers['Mitanshi'] = 97
    Toppers['Harshita'] = 92
    Toppers['Pritika'] = 89
    print('Harshita got ' + str(Toppers.get('Harshita')) + ' marks.')
    ```
32. ```
    rec = {'Name': {'First': 'Chaitanya', 'Last': 'Raj'},
                    'Marks': [80, 76, 84],
                    'Course': 'BTech'}
    print(rec['Name'])
    print(rec['Name']['Last'])
    print(rec['Marks'])
    rec['Marks'].append(72)
    print(rec)
    ```
33. ```
    Dict = {"Amna":4,"Brij":2,"Chaitanya":5,"Divyanka":3}
    s = 0
    ```

```
       for v in Dict.values():
           s = s + v
       print(s)
34.    Dict = {"Amna":4,"Brij":2,"Chaitanya":5,"Divyanka":3}
       n = ''
       for i in Dict:
           if n < i:
               n = i
       print(n)
35.    Dict = {"Amna":4,"Brij":2,"Chaitanya":5,"Divyanka":3}
       n = 'Chaitanya'
       v = 10
       if n in Dict:
           Dict[n] = v
       print(Dict)
36.    Dict = {'a':1, 'b':2, ('c','d'):3}
       print(Dict)
37.    Dict = {'a':1, 'b':2, 'c':3,'d':4}
       v = Dict['c']
       if v in Dict:
             print("FOUND")
       else:
             print("NOT FOUND")
38.    Dict = {'a':1, 'b':2, 'c':3,'d':4}
       k = ''
       for i in Dict:
          if i > k:
             k = i
             v = Dict[i]
       print(k,v)
       List = list(Dict.items())
       List.sort()
       print(List)
39.    Dict = {'a':1, 'b':2, 'c':3,'d':4, 'e':[5,6,7,8]}
       print(Dict)
40.    Dict = {10:"TEN","HUNDRED":100,(1,2):("ONE","TWO")}
       print(Dict)
41.    List = [10,10,10,20,30,30,20,40,40,40]
       counts= {}
       L= []
       for i in List:
           if i not in L:
               L.append(i)
               counts[i] = 1
           else:
               counts[i] += counts[i]
       print(counts)
42.    List = [10,10,10,20,30,30,20,40,40,40]
       counts = {}
       for i in List:
           if i in counts:
               counts[i] += 1
```

```
        else:
            counts[i] = 1
    print(counts)
```
43. ```
    Dict = {}
    Dict[1] = 1
    Dict['1'] = 2
    Dict[1] += 1
    sum = 0
    for i in Dict:
        sum += Dict[i]
    print(sum)
    ```

Find the Error

1. ```
   tup = ("abc", "def", "ghi", "jkl")
   tup.append("mno")
   ```
2. ```
   Tup1 = (9,8,7,6,5)
   Tup2 = (1,2,3,4,5)
   print(Tup1 - Tup2)
   ```
3. ```
   tup.remove("abc")
   ```
4. ```
   Tup = ('abc', 'def', 'ghi','jkl')
   Tup[2] = 'xyz'
   ```
5. ```
   x, y = 10, 20, 30
   ```
6. ```
   x = {1, 2, 3, 4, 5}
   x.add([6,7,8])
   print(x)
   ```
7. ```
   tup1 = (1,2,3)
   tup2 = tup1 + (2)
   print(tup2)
   ```
8. ```
   tup = (23,12.56,90,[34,56])
   print("Largest Value = ",max(tup))
   ```
9. ```
   (a,b,c,d) = (10,20,30)
   ```
10. ```
    t = (1,2,3,4,5)
    print(t[10])
    ```
11. ```
    t1 = (1,2,3)
    t2 = (1,2)
    print(t2-t1)
    ```
12. ```
    t1 = (1,2,3)
    t2 = t1 *(4,)
    print(t2)
    ```
13. ```
    t = (1,)*3
    t[0] = 2
    print(t)
    ```
14. ```
    Tup = (1,2,3,4.0,"abc")
    print(min(Tup))
    ```
15. ```
    students = ("Bhavya", "Era", "Falguni","Huma")
    index = students.index("Falguni")
    print("Falguni is present at location : ", index)
    index = students.index("Isha")
    ```

```
    print("Isha is present at location : ", index)
16. Dict = {"India":"New Delhi", "Nepal":"Kathmandu"}
    print(Dict["USA"])
17. Dict = {}
    print(Dict[0])
18. Dict = {'a':1, 'b':2, ['c','d']:[3,4]}
    print(Dict)
19. msg = "How are you doing?"
    counts = {}
    for c in msg:
        counts[c] = counts[c] + 1
    print(counts)
20. Dict = {}
    Dict[(1,2,3)] = 10
    Dict[[3,2,1]] = 20
    print(DIct)
21. Dict = {'a':1,'b':2,'c':3,'d':4}
    print(Dict['a','b'])
22. students = ("Bhavya", "Era", "Falguni","Huma")
    index = students.index("Falguni")
    print("Falguni is present at location : ", index)
    index = students.index("Isha")
    print("Isha is present at location : ", index)
```

Answers

Fill in the Blanks

1. Tuples
2. zip()
3. add(), update()
4. tuple()
5. Del
6. jkl
7. 3
8. index
9. Tuples
10. count()
11. 90, in, Dict
12. [], {}, ()
13. Mappings
14. dict()
15. del
16. keys()
17. copy()
18. str()
19. get()
20. lookup

State True or False

1. False
2. True
3. False
4. False
5. True
6. False
7. False
8. True
9. True
10. False
11. true
12. True
13. False
14. True
15. False
16. True
17. False
18. False
19. False
20. False
21. True
22. True

Multiple Choice Questions

1. a
2. a
3. b
4. b
5. b
6. a
7. b
8. c
9. b
10. a

11. b	14. c	17. a	20. b
12. b	15. b	18. b	21. d
13. d	16. d	19. c	22. a

Give the Output

1. True
2. abc def
3. (1, 2, 3, 1, 2, 3)
   (1, 2, 3, 1, 2, 3, 1, 2, 3)
4. ('H', 'e')
   ('l', 'l')
   ('o', 'W')
   ('o', 'r')
   ('l', 'd')
5. False
   True
   True
   (1, 2, 3, 4)
6. Morning Good
7. Chinu is a 30 year old Female
   Varun is a 32 year old Male
8. (('Good',),)
   ((('Good',),),)
   (((('Good',),),),)
   ((((('Good',),),),),)
9. (('a', 'bcd', 12.34), (5, 6, 7, 8))
10. (1, 2, [5, 4])
11. 5, 8, 7
12. [1, 2, 3, 'a']
13. (4, 5, 4, 5, 4, 5)
14. 10   1   5   7   2   0
15. 1 2 3
    1 2 3
16. <class 'str'> <class 'tuple'>
17. ('GO', 1, 2, 3)
18. (1, 2, 3, 4, 5
19. (1, 2, 3, 1, 2, 3, 1, 2, 3)
20. (1, 2, 3, '1', '2')
21. (76, 53, 54, 78, 98, 87, 74)
    (78, 98, 80, 76, 53, 54)
    (78, 98, 87, 74)
    ()
    (78, 98, 80, 76, 53, 54, 78, 98, 87, 74)
    ['programming', 'is']
    False
    ('but', 'fun')
    False
22. PrProgramming
23. True
24. 2   b   False
25. 5   15   (3, 4)   40
26. ((1, 2), (1, 2), (1, 2), (1, 2), (1, 2), (1, 2), (1, 2)) 4
27. abc def
28. India New Delhi
29. None
    No Idea
30. {'Pritika': 0, 'Harshita': 0, 'Mitanshi': 0}
    {'Pritika': 89, 'Harshita': 92, 'Nisha': -1, 'Mitanshi': 97}
31. Harshita got 92 marks.
32. {'Last': 'Raj', 'First': 'Chaitanya'}
    Raj
    [80, 76, 84]
    {'Course': 'BTech', 'Name': {'Last': 'Raj', 'First': 'Chaitanya'}, 'Marks': [80, 76, 84, 72]}
33. 14
34. Divyanka
35. {'Amna': 4, 'Brij': 2, 'Chaitanya': 10, 'Divyanka': 3}
36. {'a': 1, 'b': 2, ('c', 'd'): 3}
37. NOT FOUND
38. d 4
    [('a', 1), ('b', 2), ('c', 3), ('d', 4)]
39. {'a': 1, 'b': 2, 'c': 3, 'd': 4, 'e': [5, 6, 7, 8]}
40. {10: 'TEN', 'HUNDRED': 100, (1, 2): ('ONE', 'TWO')}
41. {10: 4, 20: 2, 30: 2, 40: 4}
42. {10: 3, 20: 2, 30: 2, 40: 3}
43. 4

Find the Error

1. AttributeError: 'tuple' object has no attribute 'append'
2. TypeError: unsupported operand type(s) for -: 'tuple' and 'tuple'
3. NameError: name 'tup' is not defined
4. TypeError: 'tuple' object does not support item assignment
5. ValueError: too many values to unpack (expected 2)
6. TypeError: unhashable type: 'list'
7. TypeError: can only concatenate tuple (not "int") to tuple
8. TypeError: '>' not supported between instances of 'list' and 'int'
9. ValueError: not enough values to unpack (expected 4, got 3)
10. IndexError: tuple index out of range
11. TypeError: unsupported operand type(s) for -: 'tuple' and 'tuple'
12. TypeError: can't multiply sequence by non-int of type 'tuple'
13. TypeError: 'tuple' object does not support item assignment
14. TypeError
15. Falguni is present at location : 2
    Traceback (most recent call last):
      File "C:\Python27\Try.py", line 4, in <module>
        index = students.index("Isha")
    ValueError: tuple.index(x): x not in tuple
16. KeyError: 'USA'
17. KeyError
18. TypeError: unhashable type: 'list'
19. KeyError: 'H'
20. TypeError: unhashable type: 'list'
21. KeyError: ('a', 'b')
22. Falguni is present at location : 2
    Traceback (most recent call last):
      File "C:\Python27\Try.py", line 4, in <module>
        index = students.index("Isha")
    ValueError: tuple.index(x): x not in tuple

Functions and Modules

Chapter Objectives

We have written many useful programs so far. To further extend the usability of our programs, we must learn about the concept of functions. In this chapter, we will discuss some very important concepts of functions including:

- Need for functions
- Defining and calling functions
- Passing parameter to functions
- Local and global variables
- Using the global statement
- Resolution of names
- The `return` statement
- Required arguments
- Keyword arguments
- Default arguments
- Variable-length arguments
- Passing lists, tuples, dictionaries and strings to function
- Documentation strings
- Redefining functions
- Importing modules
- Making your own module
- Built-in functions in math module

To understand functions, consider a scenario. If you are a project manager working on a very big project, then will you give the entire project to a single person or divide the project into *n* pieces and allocate each piece to a different person?

Of course, you will divide and allocate. Same is the case with programs. Instead of writing the entire code in one place, we must break the program into different functions or modules. Each module should then be coded individually. Whenever their functionality is required, they can just be called. In a program, you can call a function any number of times depending on the requirements.

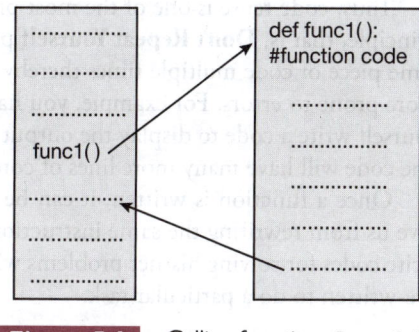

Figure 5.1 Calling function `func1()`

5.1 FUNCTION

A function is a block of organized and reusable program code that performs a single, specific and well-defined task. Consider Fig. 5.1, which explains how a function `func1()` is called to perform a well-defined task. As soon as `func1()` is called, the program control is passed to the first statement in the function. All the statements in the function are executed and then the program control is passed to the statement following the one that called the function.

In Fig. 5.2, we see that `func1()` calls another function named `func2()`. Therefore, `func1()` is known as the *calling function* and `func2()` is known as the **called function**. The moment the compiler encounters a function call, instead of executing the next statement in the calling function, the control jumps to the statements that are a part of the called function. After the called function is executed, the control is returned to the calling program.

It is not necessary that the `func1()` can call only one function; it can call as many functions as it wants and as many times as it wants. For example, a function call placed within `for` loop or `while` loop may call the same function multiple times until the condition holds true.

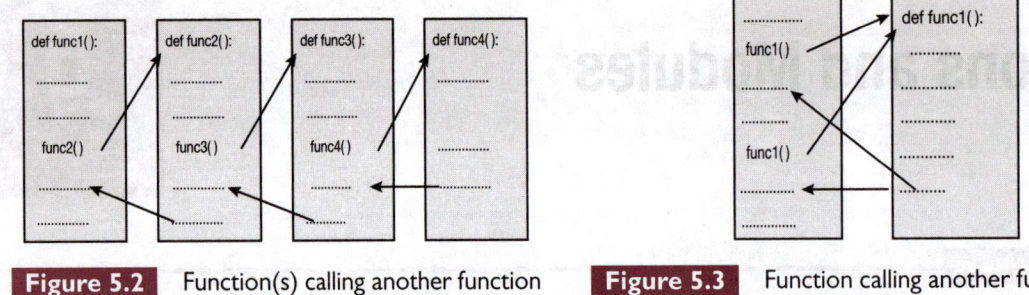

Figure 5.2 Function(s) calling another function   **Figure 5.3** Function calling another function twice

5.1.1 Need for Functions

Functions are needed to facilitate *each part of a program to be written and tested separately*. This simplifies the process of getting the total program to work.

Moreover, if a big program has to be developed without the use of any function, then there will be countless lines in the code and maintaining such a program will be quite messy.

In fact, *all the libraries in Python* contain a set of functions that the programmers can use in their programs. These functions have been prewritten and pre-tested, so the programmers use them without worrying about their code details. In this chapter, we will be using some libraries in our programs.

Functions or modules *speed up program development* as the programmer just needs to concentrate only on the code that he has to write. Also, when a big program is broken into multiple functions and then written by different programmers, the workload gets divided and program development gets speeded up.

Besides Python libraries, programmers can themselves *make their own functions* and modules to be used in other programs as well.

Thus, code reuse is one of the most prominent reasons to use functions. Large programs usually follow the DRY principle, that is, **Don't Repeat Yourself** principle. In the absence DRY principle, the programmer has to re-write the same piece of code multiple times thereby not only increasing the size and complexity of the code but also making it more prone to errors. For example, you have been using the `print()` function so often. Just imagine if you had to yourself write a code to display the output of a variable without using the `print()` function, then even a small 2–3 line code will have many more lines of complex instructions.

Once a function is written, it can be called multiple times wherever its functionality is required. This not only save us from rewriting the same instructions but also reduces the complexity of programs. Even a beginner can easily write codes for solving his/her problems without getting bogged down by unnecessarily writing instructions which are pre-written to do a particular task.

5.2 FUNCTION DECLARATION AND FUNCTION DEFINITION

We may declare a function that does not take any inputs at all, or a function that does not return any value at all. Before using a function, we must declare the function and also define it. Let us learn some important terminology that we will be using while using functions.

- A function *f*, that uses another function *g*, is known as the *calling function* and *g* is known as the *called function*.
- The inputs that the function takes are known as *arguments/ parameters*.
- When a called function returns some result back to the calling function, it is said to *return* that result.
- The calling function may or may not pass *parameters* to the called function. If the called function accepts arguments, the calling function will pass parameters, else it does not.
- *Function declaration* is a declaration statement that identifies a function with its name, a list of arguments that it accepts and the type of data it returns.
- *Function definition* consists of a function header that identifies the function, followed by the body of the function containing the executable code for that function.

5.3 FUNCTION DEFINITION

Users can write their own functions. Such functions are called user-defined functions and are created by users in their programs using the `def` keyword.

As a Python programmer, you can write any number of functions in your program. However, to define a function, you must keep the following points in mind.

> Function naming follows the same rules as for writing identifiers in Python.

- Function blocks starts with the keyword **def.**
- The keyword is followed by the function name and parentheses (( )). The function name is used to uniquely identify the function.
- After the parentheses, a colon (:) is placed.
- Parameters or arguments that the function accepts are placed within parentheses. Through these parameters, values are passed to the function. They are optional. In case no values are to be passed, nothing is placed within the parentheses.
- The first statement of a function can be an optional statement – the documentation string of the function or *docstring* describes what the function does.
- The code block within the function is properly indented to form the block code.
- A function may have a return [expression] statement. That is, the `return` statement is optional. If it exits, it passes back an expression to the caller. A `return` statement with no arguments is the same as return None.

Example 5.1 Program that adds two numbers using function.

```
def add(x,y):     # function to add two numbers
        return x+y
a = 20
b = 10
print(add(a,b))
```

> The words before parentheses specify the function name, and the comma-separated values inside the parentheses are function arguments.

OUTPUT
```
10
```

When a function is defined, space is allocated for that function in the memory. A function definition comprises of two parts:

- Function header
- Function body

The syntax of a function definition can be given as:

```
def function_name(variable1, variable2,..)    ← Function Header
    documentation string
    statement block
    return [expression]                        ← Function Body
```

Example 5.2 To write a function that displays a string repeatedly.

```
def func():
        for i in range(4):
                print("Hello World")
func()   #function call
```

OUTPUT
```
Hello World
Hello World
Hello World
Hello World
```

In the above code, name of the function is `func`. It takes no arguments, and prints "Hello World" four times. The function is first defined before being called. The statements in the function are executed only when the function is called.

5.4 FUNCTION CALL

Defining a function means specifying its name, parameters that are expected and the set of instructions. Once the basic structure is finalized, the function can be executed by calling it.

The function call statement invokes the function. When a function is invoked, the program control jumps to the called function to execute the statements that are a part of that function. Once the called function is executed, the program control passes back to the calling function.

> The parameter list in the function definition as well as function declaration must match with each other.

The syntax of calling a function that does not accept parameter is simply the name of the function followed by parentheses, which is given as,

`function_name()`

Function call statement has the following syntax when it accepts parameters.

`function_name(variable1, variable2, …)`

When the function is called, the interpreter checks that the correct number and type of arguments are used in the function call. It also checks the type of the returned value (if it returns a value to the calling function).

5.5 FUNCTION PARAMETERS

A function can take parameters which are nothing but some values that are passed to it so that the function can manipulate them to produce the desired result. These parameters are normal variables with a small difference that the values of these variables are defined (initialized) when we call the function and are then passed to the function.

Parameters are specified within a pair of parentheses in the function definition and are separated by commas.

Key points to remember

- Function name and the number and type of arguments in the function call must be same as that given in the function definition.
- If, by mistake, the parameters passed to a function are more than that it is specified to accept, then an error would be returned.

Example 5.3 Program to demonstrate the mismatch between function parameters and arguments.

```
def func(i, j):
        print("Hello World", i, j)
func(5)
```

OUTPUT

`TypeError: func() takes exactly 2 arguments (1 given)`

> The indented statements form the body of the function.

- If, by mistake, the parameters passed to a function are less than that it is specified to accept, then an error would be returned.

Example 5.4 Program to demonstrate the mismatch between function parameters and arguments.

```
def func(i):
        print("Hello World", i)
func(5, 5)
```

OUTPUT

```
TypeError: func() takes exactly 1 argument (2 given)
```

- Names of variables in function call and header of function definition may vary.

Example 5.5 Program to demonstrate mismatch of name of function parameters and arguments.

```
def func(i):    # function definition header accepts a variable with name i
print("Hello World", i)
j = 10
func(j)         # Function is called using variable j
```

OUTPUT

```
Hello World 10
```

- If the data type of the argument passed does not matches with that expected in function then an error is generated.

Example 5.6 Program to demonstrate mismatch between data types of function parameters and arguments.

```
def func(i):
    print("Hello World" + i)
  func(5)
```

OUTPUT

```
TypeError: cannot concatenate 'str' and 'int' objects
```

- Arguments may be passed in the form of expressions to the called function. In such a case, arguments are first evaluated and converted to the type of formal parameter and then the body of the function gets executed.

Example 5.7 Program to demonstrate that the arguments may be passed in the form of expressions to the called function.

```
def func(i):
        print("Hello World", i)
func(5+2*3)
```

> Before calling a function, you must define it.

OUTPUT

```
Hello World 11
```

- The parameter list must be separated with commas.
- If the function returns a value, then it may be assigned to some variable in the calling program. For example,

variable_name = function_name(variable1, variable2, …);

Let us now try a program using function.

Example 5.8 Program to add two integers using function that accepts two arguments.

```
def total(a,b):       # function accepting parameters
    result = a+b
    print("Sum of ", a, " and ", b, " = ", result)
a = int(input("Enter the first number : "))
b = int(input("Enter the second number : "))
total(a,b) #function call with two arguments
```

> It is a logic error if the arguments in the function call are placed in a wrong order.

OUTPUT

```
Enter the first number : 10
Enter the second number : 20
Sum of 10 and 20 = 30
```

In the `total()`, we have declared a variable result just like any other variable. Variables declared within a function are called local variables. We will read more about it in the next section.

5.6 PARAMETER PASSING – MUTABLE/IMMUTABLE PROPERTIES

Python uses a mechanism known as "Call-by-Object", or "Call-by-Object Reference" or "Call-by-Sharing".

When immutable arguments like integers, strings or tuples are passed to a function, the parameters are passed using call-by-value technique. The object reference is passed to the function parameters. Since they are immutable, their value(s) cannot be changed in the function.

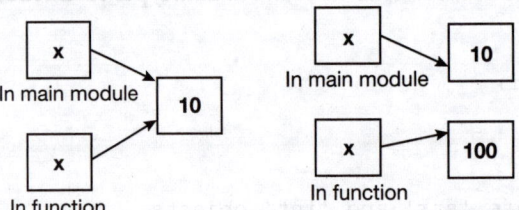

The same object is referenced as long as the value of x is not changed.

A new variable is created when the value of x is modified. The variable for the caller function remains unaffected.

Figure 5.4 Function parameters

When we pass mutable objects as arguments to the function, they are passed by object reference. However, their value(s) can be changed within the function. For example, when a list is passed to a function, its individual elements can be changed. Moreover, if we assign a new list to same name of the list, the old list will not be affected at all. The list remains unchanged in caller function's scope.

In Fig. 5.4, we have an integer variable *x*. When this parameter is passed to a function, a reference to *x* is used as long as the parameter is not changed. The moment an attempt is made to change the value of *x*, Python creates a separate local variable so that the caller function's variable is not changed.

Example 5.9

```
def func(x):
    print(" In Func, before modification, ID of x = ",id(x), " and value of x = ",x)
    x = 100
    print(" In Func, after modification, ID of x = ",id(x), " and value of x = ",x)
x = 10
```

```
print(" In main module, before calling function, ID of x = ",id(x), " and value of x
    = ",x)
func(x)
print(" In main module, after calling function, ID of x = ",id(x), " and value of x =
    ",x)
```

OUTPUT
```
In main module, before calling function, ID of x =
    1687091264   and value of x =   10
In Func, before modification, ID of x =   1687091264   and
    value of x =   10
In Func, after modification, ID of x =   1687092704   and
    value of x =   100
In main module, after calling function, ID of x =
    1687091264   and value of x =   10
```

> List of variables used in function call is known as actual parameter list. The actual parameter list may be variable names, expressions or constants.

In the above example, `id()` function is used. It takes an object as a parameter and returns the "identity" of the object. This identity is a unique integer which remains constant for this object during its lifetime.

The value and identity of x is printed at different locations to verify whether x is pointing to the same object or a different object. In the main module, the value and identity of x remains same before as well as after calling the function.

In the called function, the value and identity of x remains same as long as the value of x is not changed. When the value of x is modified, a new variable with name x but a different id is created. This new variable is local to the function and a copy of it in the main module is not affected by this change.

In programming languages like C, C++ and Java, we have call-by-value and call-by-reference techniques of passing arguments to a function. But in Python, we still have the same techniques but they are applicable in a different way. Python initially behaves like call-by-reference, but as soon as we change the value of a variable, Python "switches" to call-by-value.

5.7 VARIABLE SCOPE AND LIFETIME

In Python, you cannot just access any variable from any part of your program. Some of the variables may not even exist for the entire duration of the program. The part of the program where you can access a variable and the parts of the program where a variable exists depend on how the variable has been declared. Therefore, we need to understand two things:

> You can call a function from another function or directly from the Python prompt.

Scope of the variable: Part of the program in which a variable is accessible is called its *scope*

Lifetime of the variable: Duration for which the variable exists is called its *lifetime*.

5.7.1 Local and Global Variables

Global variables are those variables which are defined in the main body of the program file. They are visible throughout the program file. As a good programming habit, you must try to avoid the use of global variables because they may get altered by mistake and then result in erroneous output. But this does not mean that you should not use them at all. As a golden rule, use only those variables or objects that are meant to be used globally. For example, functions and classes should be put in the global section of the program (i.e., above any other function or line of code).

Correspondingly, a variable which is defined within a function is *local* to that function. A local variable can be accessed from the point of its definition until the end of the function in which it is defined. It exists as long as the function is executing. Function parameters behave like local variables in the function. Moreover, whenever we use the assignment operator (=) inside a function, a new local variable is created (provided a variable with the same name is not defined in the local scope).

Example 5.10 Program to understand the difference between local and global variables.

```
num1 = 10          # global variable
print("Global variable num1 = ", num1)
def func(num2):         # num2 is function parameter
       print("In Function - Local Variable num2 = ",num2)
       num3 = 30     #num3 is a local variable
       print("In Function - Local Variable num3 = ",num3)
func(20) #20 is passed as an argument to the function
print("num1 again = ", num1)       #global variable is being accessed
#Error- local variable can't be used outside the function in which it is defined
print("num3 outside function = ", num3)
```

> Trying to access local variable outside the function produces an error.

OUTPUT

```
Global variable num1 = 10
In Function - Local Variable num2 = 20
In Function - Local Variable num3 = 30
num1 again =  10
num3 outside function =
Traceback (most recent call last):
  File "C:\Python27\Try.py", line 12, in <module>
    print("num3 outside function = ", num3)
NameError: name 'num3' is not defined
```

Table 5.1 lists the differences between global and local variables.

Table 5.1 Comparison between global and local variables

Global Variables	Local Variables
They are defined in the main body of the program file.	They are defined within a function and are local to that function.
They can be accessed throughout the program file.	They can be accessed from the point of their definition until the end of the block in which they are defined.
Global variables are accessible to all functions in the program.	They are not related in any way to other variables with the same names used outside the function.

5.7.2 Using the Global Statement

To define a variable defined inside a function as global, you must use the global statement. This declares the local or the inner variable of the function to have module scope. Look at the code given below and observe its output to understand this concept.

Example 5.11 Program to demonstrate the use of global statement.

```
var = "Good"
def show():
       global var1
       var1 = "Morning"
       print("In Function var is - ", var)
```

> Variables can only be used after the point of their declaration.

```
        show()
print("Outside function, var1 is - ", var1)      #accessible as it is global variable
print("var is - ", var)
```

OUTPUT

```
In Function var is -  Good
Outside function, var1 is -  Morning
var is -  Good
```

Key points to remember

- You can have a variable with the same name as that of a global variable in the program. In such a case a new local variable of that name is created, which is different from the global variable. For example, look at the code below and observe its output.

Example 5.12 Program to demonstrate name clash of local and global variable.

```
var = "Good"
def show():
        var = "Morning"
        print("In Function var is - ", var)
show()
print("Outside function, var is - ", var)
```

> All variables have the scope of the block.

OUTPUT

```
In Function var is -  Morning
Outside function, var is -  Good
```

- If we have a global variable and then create another global variable using the global statement, then changes made in the variable will be reflected everywhere in the program. This concept is illustrated in the code given below.

Example 5.13 Program to demonstrate modifying a global variable.

```
var = "Good"
def show():
        global var
        var = "Morning"
        print("In Function var is - ", var)
show()
print("Outside function, var is - ", var)
var = "Fantastic"
print("Outside function, after modification, var is - ", var)
```

OUTPUT

```
In Function var is -  Morning
Outside function, var is -  Morning
Outside function, after modification, var is -  Fantastic
```

- In case of nested functions (function inside another function), the inner function can access variables defined in both outer as well as inner function, but the outer function can access variables defined only in the outer function. The program code given below illustrates this concept.

Example 5.14 — Program to demonstrate access of variables in inner and outer functions.

```
def outer_func():
      outer_var = 10
      def inner_func():
            inner_var = 20
            print "Outer Variable = ", outer_var
            print "Inner Variable = ", inner_var
      inner_func()
      print "Outer Variable = ", outer_var
      print "Inner Variable = ", inner_var    #not accessible
outer_func()         #function call
```

> Arguments are specified within parentheses. If there is more than one argument, then they are separated using comma.

OUTPUT

```
Outer Variable = 10
Inner Variable = 20
Outer Variable = 10
Inner Variable =
NameError: global name 'inner_var' is not defined
```

- If a variable in the inner function is defined with the same name as that of a variable defined in the outer function, then a new variable is created in the inner function. Look at the code given below to understand this concept.

Example 5.15 — Program to demonstrate name clash variables in case of nested functions.

```
def outer_func():
      var = 10
      def inner_func():
            var = 20
            print("Inner Variable = ", var)
      inner_func()
      print("Outer Variable = ", var)
outer_func()
```

> You cannot assign value to a variable defined outside a function without using the global statement.

OUTPUT

```
Inner Variable =  20
Outer Variable =  10
```

In the above program, even if we use global statement, we would get the same result since global statement is applicable for the entire program and not for the outer function alone.

5.7.3 Resolution of Names

As discussed in the previous section, *scope* defines the visibility of a name within a block. If a local variable is defined in a block, its scope is that particular block. If it is defined in a function, then its scope is all blocks within that function.

When a variable name is used in a code block, it is resolved using the nearest enclosing scope. If no variable of that name is found, then a NameError is raised. In the code given below, str is a global string because it has been defined before calling the function.

Example 5.16 — Program that demonstrates using a variable defined in global namespace.

```
def func():
      print(str)
str = "Hello World !!!"
func()
```

> Try to avoid the use of global variables and global statement.

OUTPUT

```
Hello World !!!
```

You cannot define a local variable with the same name as that of a global variable. If you want to do that, you must use the global statement. The code given below illustrates this concept.

Example 5.17 Program that demonstrates using a local variable with same name as that of a global variable.

```
def f():
      print(str) #global
      str = "Hello World!"   #local
      print(str)
str = "Welcome to Python Programming!"
f()
```

OUTPUT
```
UnboundLocalError: local variable 'str'
    referenced before assignment
```

```
def f():
      global str
      print(str)
      str = "Hello World!"
      print(str)
str = "Welcome to Python Programming!"
f()
```

OUTPUT
```
Welcome to Python Programming!
Hello World!
```

5.8 THE return STATEMENT

In all our functions written above, nowhere have we used the `return` statement. But you will be surprised to know that every function has an implicit `return` statement as the last instruction in the function body. This implicit `return` statement returns nothing to its caller, so it is said to return NONE where NONE means nothing. But you can change this default behavior by explicitly using the `return` statement to return some value to the caller. The syntax of return statement is,

> A function may or may not return a value. A return statement with no arguments is the same as return None.

return [expression]

The expression is written in brackets because it is optional. If the expression is present, it is evaluated and the resultant value is returned to the calling function. However, if no expression is specified then the function will return **None**.

Example 5.18 Program to write a function without a `return` statement and try to print its return value. As mentioned earlier, such a function should return None.

```
def display(str):
    print(str)
#assigning return value to another variable
x = display("Hello World")
print(x)
#print return value without assigning it to another variable
print(display("Hello Again "))
```

OUTPUT
```
Hello World
None
Hello Again
None
```

The `return` statement is used for two things.
- Return a value to the caller
- To end and exit a function and go back to its caller

It should be noted that in the output None is returned from the function. The return value may or may not be assigned to another variable in the caller.

Example 5.19 To write another function which returns an integer to the caller.

```
def cube(x):
    return (x*x*x)
num = 10
result = cube(num)
print('Cube of ', num, ' = ', result)
```

OUTPUT
```
Cube of 10 = 1000
```

Example 5.20 Program to demonstrate flow of control after the return statement.

```
def display():
    print("In Function")
    print("About to execute return statement")
    return
    print("This line will never be displayed")
display()
print("Back to the caller")
```

OUTPUT
```
In Function
About to execute return statement
Back to the caller
```

Key points to remember

- The `return` statement must appear within the function.
- Once you return a value from a function, it immediately exits that function. Therefore, any code written after the return statement is never executed.

5.9 TYPES OF FUNCTION PARAMETERS

We have already discussed in the previous function, the technique to define and call a function. In this section, we will go a step forward and learn some more ways of defining a function. All these features make Python a wonderful language. Some of these features include: Required arguments, Keyword arguments, Default arguments and Variable-length arguments.

5.9.1 Required Arguments

We have already been using this type of formal arguments. In Required arguments, the arguments are passed to a function in correct positional order. Also, the number of arguments in the function call should exactly match with the number of arguments specified in the function definition.

Look at the three different versions of `display()` given below and observe the output. The function displays the string only when number and type of arguments in the function call matches with that specified in the function definition; otherwise a TypeError is returned.

Example 5.21

```
def display():
    print "Hello"
display("Hi")
```

OUTPUT

```
TypeError: display() takes no arguments (1 given)
```

```
def display(str):
    print str
display()
```

OUTPUT

```
TypeError: display() takes exactly 1 argument (0 given)
```

```
def display(str):
    print str
str ="Hello"
display(str)
```

OUTPUT

```
Hello
```

5.9.2 Keyword Arguments

When we call a function with some values, the values are assigned to the arguments based on their position. Python also allows functions to be called using keyword arguments in which the order (or position) of the arguments can be changed. The values are not assigned to arguments according to their position but based on their name (or keyword).

Keyword arguments, when used in function calls, help the function to identify the arguments by the parameter name. This is especially beneficial in two cases.

- First, if you skip arguments
- Second, if in the function call you change the order of parameters. That is, in any order different from that specified in the function definition.

> Having a required argument after keyword arguments will cause error.

In both the cases mentioned above, Python interpreter uses keywords provided in the function call to match the values with parameters.

Example 5.22 Program to demonstrate keyword arguments.

```
def display(str, int_x, float_y):
    print("The string is : ",str)
    print("The integer value is : ", int_x)
    print("The floating point value is : ", float_y)
display(float_y = 56789.045, str = "Hello", int_x = 1234)
```

OUTPUT

```
The string is:  Hello
The integer value is:  1234
The floating point value is:  56789.045
```

Example 5.23	Consider another program for keyword arguments in which during function call we use assignment operator to assign values to function parameters using other variables (instead of values).

```
def display(name, age, salary):
    print("Name : ", name)
    print("Age : ", age)
    print("Salary : ", salary)
n = "Aadi"
a = 35
s = 123456
display(salary = s, name = n, age = a)
```

OUTPUT

```
Name :  Aadi
Age :  35
Salary :  123456
```

Key points to remember

- All the keyword arguments passed should match one of the arguments accepted by the function.
- The order of keyword arguments is not important.
- In no case an argument should receive a value more than once.

> Keyword arguments make the program code easier to read and understand.

5.9.3 Default Arguments

Python allows users to specify function arguments that can have default values. This means that a function can be called with fewer arguments than it is defined to have. That is, if the function accepts three parameters, but the function call provides only two arguments, then the third parameter will be assigned the default (already specified) value.

The default value to an argument is provided by using the assignment operator (=). Users can specify a default value for one or more arguments.

Example 5.24	Program that uses default arguments.

```
def display(name, course = "BTech"):
    print("Name : " + name)
    print("Course : ", course)
display(course = "BCA", name = "Arav")   # Keyword Arguments
display(name = "Reyansh")         # Default Argument for course
```

> A default argument assumes a default value if a value is not provided in the function call for that argument.

OUTPUT

```
Name : Arav
Course :  BCA
Name : Reyansh
Course :  BTech
```

In the above code, the parameter name does not have a default value and is therefore mandatory. That is, you must specify a value for this parameter during the function call. But parameter course has already been given a default value, so it is optional. If a value is provided, it will overwrite the default value and in case a value is not specified during function call, the one provided in the function definition as the default value will be used.

Key points to remember

- You can specify any number of default arguments in your function.

- If you have default arguments, then they must be written after the non-default arguments. This means that non-default arguments cannot follow default arguments. Therefore, the line of code given below will produce an error.

Example 5.25 Program to demonstrate default arguments.

```
def display(name, course = "BTech", marks):  #error
    print("Name : " + name)
    print("Course : ", course)
    print("Marks : ", marks)
display(name = "Reyansh", 90)
SyntaxError: non-default argument follows default argument
```

> All the arguments to the right of the default argument must also have default values.

5.9.4 Variable-length Arguments

In some situations, it is not known in advance how many arguments will be passed to a function. In such cases, Python allows programmers to make function calls with arbitrary (or any) number of arguments.

When we use arbitrary arguments or variable length arguments, then the function definition uses an asterisk (*) before the parameter name. The syntax for a function using variable arguments can be given as,

```
def functionname([arg1, arg2,.... ] *var_args_tuple ):
    function statements
    return [expression]
```

Example 5.26 Program to demonstrate the use of variable-length arguments.

```
def func(name, *fav_subjects):
    print("\n", name, " likes to read ")
    for subject in fav_subjects:
        print(subject)
func("Goransh", "Mathematics", "Android Programming")
func("Richa", "C", "Data Structures", "Design and Analysis
    of Algorithms")
func("Krish")
```

> A positional argument is assigned based on its position in the argument list but a keyword argument is assigned based on parameter name.

OUTPUT
```
Goransh  likes to read  Mathematics Android Programming
Richa likes to read  C Data Structures Design and Analysis of Algorithms
Krish  likes to read
```

In the above program, in the function definition, we have two parameters – name and the variable length parameter fav_subjects. The function is called three times with 3, 4 and 1 parameter(s) respectively. The first value is assigned to name and the other values are assigned to parameter fav_subjects. Everyone can have any number of favorite subjects and some can even have none. So when the third call is made, fav_subjects has no value and hence the `for` loop will not execute as there is no subject available in fav_subjects.

Key points to remember

- The arbitrary number of arguments passed to the function basically forms a tuple before being passed into the function.
- Inside the called function, `for` loop is used to access the arguments.
- The variable-sized arguments, if present in the function definition, should be last in the list of formal parameters.
- Any formal parameters written after the variable-sized arguments must be keyword-only arguments.

5.10 PASSING STRINGS, LISTS, TUPLES, DICTIONARIES TO FUNCTIONS

We have already seen functions accepting strings as arguments. In this section, we will see how other objects like lists, tuples and dictionaries can be passed as arguments and manipulated within the function.

> A function cannot be used on the right side of an assignment statement. Therefore writing, *total(a, b) =s*; is invalid.

Example 5.27 Program to access a tuple in a function that is passed to it as an argument.

```
def Func(Tup):
    for i in Tup:
        print(i, end = ' ')
Tup = (1,2,3,4,5)
Func(Tup)
```

OUTPUT

```
1 2 3 4 5
```

We have studied that when we pass an argument by prefixing it with a *, it means that the argument is variable in size. Such arguments are passed using a tuple.

Example 5.28 Program to demonstrate variable-length arguments using tuple. The function adds the values it receives as arguments.

```
def sum(*args):
    '''Return the sum of each argument'''
    total = 0
    for i in args:
        total += i
    return total
tot = sum(1,2,3,4,5,6,7,8,9,10)
print("Sum of 1,2,3,4,5,6,7,8,9,10 = ", tot)
tot = sum(1,2,3,4,5)
print("Sum of 1,2,3,4,5 = ", tot)
```

OUTPUT

```
Sum of 1,2,3,4,5,6,7,8,9,10 =  55
Sum of 1,2,3,4,5 =  15
```

Passing Dictionary as an Argument

Python allows users to pass a dictionary as an argument to a function just as a normal variable is passed.

```
# A function that takes dictionary as an argument
def func(Dict):
    for key in Dict:
        print("Dict[",key,"] = ", Dict[key])
Dict = {'NAME':'Priya', 'MARKS': 92, 'GRADE':'A+'}
func(Dict)
```

OUTPUT

```
Dict[ NAME ] =  Priya
Dict[ MARKS ] =  92
Dict[ GRADE ] =  A+
```

We can even pass a dictionary as kwargs where "kwargs" means keyword arguments. Such arguments are useful when the user does not have a clue about the number of arguments. Therefore, the dictionary argument is passed by prefixing "**" it to the argument.

Example 5.29 Program to demonstrate passing dictionary as keyword arguments.

```
def Func(**name):
    print (name["fname"]+" "+name["mname"]+" "+name["lname"])
# passing dictionary key-value pair as arguments
Func(fname = "Lal", mname ="Bahadur", lname ="Shastri")
```

OUTPUT

```
Lal Bahadur Shastri
```

Apart from dictionary we can also pass other values to the function as illustrated in the program given below.

Example 5.30 Program to demonstrate passing dictionary as keyword arguments.

```
def Func(marks, avg, **name):
    print (name["fname"]+" "+name["mname"]+" "+name["lname"] + " Got Marks = "+
    str(marks) + " and Average = " + str(avg))
# passing dictionary key-value pair as arguments
Func(87,85.2, fname = "Parth", mname ="M", lname ="Patel")
```

OUTPUT

```
Parth M Patel Got Marks = 87 and Average = 85.2
```

5.11 DOCUMENTATION STRINGS

Docstrings (documentation strings) serve the same purpose as that of comments, as they are designed to explain code. However, they are more specific and have a proper syntax. As you can see below, they are created by putting a multiline string to explain the function. To understand the concept of documentation strings, let us first revisit the syntax of defining a function.

```
def functionname(parameters):
    "function_docstring"
    function statements
    return [expression]
```

As per the syntax, the first statement of the function body can optionally be a string literal which is also known as documentation string, or *docstring*. Docstrings are important as they help tools to automatically generate online or printed documentation. It also helps users and readers of the code to interactively browse through the code. Including docstrings in your code is a good programming habit.

Key points to remember

- As the first line, it should always be short and concise highlighting the summary of the object's purpose.
- It should not specify information like the object's name or type
- It should begin with a capital letter and end with a period.
- Triple quotes are used to extend the docstring to multiple lines. This docstring specified can be accessed through the __doc__ attribute of the function.
- In case of multiple lines in the documentation string, the second line should be blank to separate the summary from the rest of the description. The other lines should be one or more paragraphs describing the object's calling conventions, its side effects, etc.

- The first non-blank line *after* the first line of the documentation string determines the amount of indentation for the entire documentation string.
- Unlike comments, docstrings are retained throughout the runtime of the program. So, users can inspect them during program execution.

Example 5.31 Program to show a multi-line docstring.

```
def func():
    """The program just prints a message.
    It will display Hello World !!! """
    print("Hello World !!!")
print(func.__doc__)
```

> Function should be defined before it is called.

OUTPUT

```
The program just prints a message.
    It will display Hello World !!!
```

5.12 GOOD PROGRAMMING PRACTICES

While writing large and complex programs, you must take care of some points that will help you to develop readable, effective and efficient codes. For Python, **PEP 8** has emerged as the coding style guide that most projects adhere to, in order to promote a very readable and eye pleasing coding style. Some basic points that you should follow are:

- Instead of tabs, use 4-spaces for indentation.
- Insert blank lines to separate functions and classes, and statement blocks inside functions.
- Wherever required, use comments to explain the code.
- Use document strings that explain the purpose of the function.
- Use spaces around operators and after commas.
- Name of the classes should be written as ClassName (observe the capital letters, another example can be StudentInfo). We will read about classes in subsequent chapters.
- Name of the functions should be in lower case with underscores to separate words. For example, display_info(), get_data()
- Do not use non-ASCII characters in function names or any other identifier.

5.13 FUNCTION REDEFINITION

We know that in Python, we can redefine a variable. That is, you can change the value and even the type of value that the variable is holding. For example, in one line you can write *x* = 5.6 and in the other line you can redefine *x* by writing *x* = "Hello". Likewise, you can also redefine functions in Python.

Example 5.32 Program to demonstrate function redefinition.

```
import datetime
def showMessage(msg):
    print(msg)


showMessage("Hello")
def showMessage(msg):
    now = datetime.datetime.now()
    print(msg)
    print(str(now))
showMessage("Current Date and Time is : ")
```

> Trying to import a module that is not available causes an ImportError.

OUTPUT
```
Hello
Current Date and Time is :
2020-07-25 11:57:39.979856
```

In the above code, we have a function showMessage, which is first defined to simply display a message that is passed to it. After the function call we have again redefined the function to print the message as well as the current date and time.

5.14 MODULES

In the previous section, we have seen that functions help us to reuse a particular piece of code. Modules go a step ahead. They allow you to reuse one or more functions in your programs, even in the programs where those functions have not been defined.

Simply put, module is a file with a .py extension that has definitions of all functions and variables that you would like to use even in other programs. The program in which you want to use functions or variables to be defined in a module will simply import that particular module (or .py file).

> Modules are pre-written pieces of code that are used to perform common tasks like generating random numbers, performing mathematical operations, etc.

The basic way to use a module is to add import module_name as the first line of your program and then write module_name.var to access functions and values with the name var in the module. Let us first use the standard library modules.

Example 5.33 Program to print the PATH variable.

```
import sys
print("\n PYTHONPATH = \n", sys.path)
```

OUTPUT
```
PYTHONPATH =
 ['C:\\Users\\Reema\\AppData\\Local\\Programs\\Python\\Python38-32\\Lib\\idlelib',
  'C:\\Users\\Reema\\AppData\\Local\\Programs\\Python\\Python38-32\\python38.
  zip', 'C:\\Users\\Reema\\AppData\\Local\\Programs\\Python\\Python38-32\\DLLs',
  'C:\\Users\\Reema\\AppData\\Local\\Programs\\Python\\Python38-32\\lib', 'C:\\
  Users\\Reema\\AppData\\Local\\Programs\\Python\\Python38-32', 'C:\\Users\\Reema\\
  AppData\\Local\\Programs\\Python\\Python38-32\\lib\\site-packages']
```

In the above code, we *import* the sys module (short form of system) using the `import` statement to use its functionality related to the Python interpreter and its environment.

When the `import sys` statement is executed, Python looks for the sys.py module in one of the directories listed in its sys.path variable. If the file is found, then the statements in the module are executed.

The sys module provides functions and variables used to manipulate different parts of the Python runtime environment.

5.14.1 Module Loading and Execution

A module imported in a program must be located and loaded into memory before it can be used. Python first searches for the modules in the current working directory. If the module is not found there, it then looks for the module in the directories specified in the PYTHONPATH environment variable. If the module is still not found or if the PYTHONPATH variable is not defined, then a Python installation-specific path (like C:\Python27\Lib) is searched. If the module is not located even there, then an error ImportError exception is generated.

Until now, we have saved our modules in the same directory as that of the program importing it. But, if you want the module to be available to other programs as well, then the module should be either saved in directory specified in the PYTHONPATH, or stored in the Python installation Lib directory.

Once a module is located, it is loaded in memory. A compiled version of the module with file extension .pyc is generated. Next time when the module is imported, this .pyc file is loaded rather than the .py file, to save the time of recompiling. A new compiled version of a module is again produced whenever the compiled version is out of date (based on the dates when the .pyc file was created/modified). Even the programmer can force the Python shell to reload and recompile the .py file to generate a new .pyc file by using the `reload()` function.

5.14.2 The From...Import Statement

A module may contain definitions for many variables and functions. When you import a module, you can use any variable or function defined in that module. But if you want to use only selected variables or functions, then you can use the from...import statement. For example, in the given program you are using only the path variable in the sys module, so you could have better written from sys import path.

Example 5.34 Program that uses the from...import statement.

```
from math import pi
print("PI = ", + pi)
```

OUTPUT
3.141592653589793

To import more than one item from a module, use a comma-separated list. For example, to import the value of PI and sqrt() from the math module you can write

from math import pi, sqrt

However, to import all the identifiers defined in the sys module, you can use the from sys import * statement. However, you should avoid using the import * statement as it confuses variables in your code with variables in the external module.

You can also import a module with a different name using the as keyword. This is particularly more important when a module has either a long or confusing name.

For example,

> import * statement imports all names except those beginning with an underscore (_).

```
from math import sqrt as square_root
......
print(square_root(81))
```

Python also allows you to pass command line arguments to your program. This can be done using the sys module. The argv variable in this module keeps a track of command line arguments passed to the .py script as shown below.

```
import sys
print(sys.argv)
```

To execute this program code, go to Command Prompt (in Windows), write

```
C:\Python34> python main.py Hello World. You will get the output as,
['main.py', 'Hello', 'World']
```

Finally, you can use sys.exit([*arg*]) to exit from Python. arg is an optional argument which can either be an integer giving the exit status or another type of object. If it is an integer, zero signifies successful termination and any nonzero value indicates an error or abnormal termination of the program. Most systems require the value of arg to be in the range 0–127, and therefore produces undefined results otherwise. If another type of object is passed, None is same as passing zero, and any other object results in an exit code of 1. Generally, sys.exit("Error Message") is a quick way to exit a program when an error occurs.

Example 5.35 **Program to demonstrate sys.exit.**

```
import sys
print("HELLO WORLD")
sys.exit(0)
```

OUTPUT
```
HELLO WORLD
```

5.14.3 Name of Module

Every module has a name. You can find the name of a module by using the __name__ attribute of the module.

Example 5.36 **Program to print the name of the module in which your statement is written.**

```
print("Hello")
print("Name of this module is : ", __name__)
```

OUTPUT
```
Hello
Name of this module is :   __main__
```

Observe the output and always remember that for every standalone program written by the user, the name of the module is __main__.

5.14.4 Making Your Own Modules

You can easily create as many modules as you want. In fact, you have already been doing it since every Python program is a module. That is, every file that you save as .py extension is a module. The code given below illustrates this concept.

First write these lines in a file and save the file as MyModule.py

```
def display():            #function definition
   print("Hello")
   print("Name of called module is : ", __name__)
str = "Welcome to the world of Python !!!        #variable definition
```

Then, open another file and write the lines of code given below.

```
import MyModule
print("MyModule str = ", MyModule.str)   #using variable defined in MyModule
MyModule.display()                        #using function defined in MyModule
print("Name of calling module is : ", __name__)
```

When you run this code, you will get the following output.

```
MyModule str =  Welcome to the world of Python !!!
Hello
Name of called module is :  MyModule
Name of calling module is :  __main__
```

Note that we have been using the dot operator to access members (variables or functions) of the module. Assuming that MyModule had many other variables or functions definition, we could have specifically imported str and display() by writing the import statement as

from MyModule import str, display

> Modules should be placed in the same directory as that of the program in which it is imported. It can also be stored in one of the directories listed in sys.path.

5.14.5 Python Math Module

Python has a standard library that has many important and useful built-in functions (such as `print()`, `ord()` and `int()`). Besides these built-in functions, the library also has various modules that have functionalities for specified actions.

```
# Program to print the value of PI and e
import math
print("PI =", math.pi)
print("Epsilon = ",math.e)
```

OUTPUT
```
PI= 3.141592653589793
Epsilon =2.718281828459045
```

Some of the most popular mathematical functions are defined in the math module. These include trigonometric functions, representation functions, logarithmic functions, angle conversion functions, etc. In addition, two mathematical constants – PI and Epsilon are also defined in this module. Let us print the two values. Remember that before using the math module, we must first import it by writing **import math**. Then, the specific function can be used by writing, **math.function_name**.

Functions like sin, cos, tan, etc. that need an angle accepts the values in radians as an argument. In case you want to specify angle in degrees then the `math.degree()` function must be used. Table 5.2 list some commonly used built-in function in the math module.

Table 5.2 Built-in functions in math module

Function	Description	Example

`ceil(x)`	Returns the smallest integer greater than or equal to x.	`import math`
		`print(math.ceil(1.2345))`
		OUTPUT
		2

`fabs(x)`	Returns the absolute value of x	`import math`
		`print(math.fabs(-5.6))`
		OUTPUT
		5.6

Table 5.2 (*Continued*)

Table 5.2 Continued

Function	Description	Example

`factorial(x)`	Returns the factorial of x	`import math`
		`print(math.factorial(6))`
		OUTPUT
		`720`

`floor(x)`	Returns the largest integer less than or equal to x	`import math`
		`print(math.floor(-5.6))`
		OUTPUT
		`-6`

`fmod(x, y)`	Returns the remainder when x is divided by y	`import math`
		`print(math.fmod(-100,6))`
		OUTPUT
		`-4.0`

`modf(x)`	Returns the fractional and integer parts of x	`import math`
		`print(math.modf(-123.456))`
		OUTPUT
		`(-0.45600000000000307, -123.0)`

`trunc(x)`	Returns the truncated integer value of x	`import math`
		`print(math.trunc(-123.456))`
		OUTPUT
		`-123`

`exp(x)`	Returns e**x	`import math`
		`print(math.exp(10))`
		OUTPUT
		`22026.465794806718`

`log(x[, base])`	Returns the logarithm of x to the base (defaults to e)	`import math`
		`print(math.log(100,10))`
		OUTPUT
		`2.0`

`log2(x)`	Returns the base-2 logarithm of x	`import math`
		`print(math.log2(1024))`
		OUTPUT
		`10.0`

`log10(x)`	Returns the base-10 logarithm of x	`import math`
		`print(math.log10(1000))`
		OUTPUT
		`3.0`

`pow(x, y)`	Returns x raised to the power of y	`import math`
		`print(math.pow(10,4))`
		OUTPUT
		`10000.0`

`sqrt(x)`	Returns the square root of x	`import math`
		`print(math.sqrt(10000))`
		OUTPUT
		`100.0`

Table 5.2 (*Continued*)

Table 5.2 Continued

Function	Description	Example

`cos(x)`	Returns the cosine of x	`import math`
		`print(math.cos(90))`
		OUTPUT
		`-0.4480736161291701`

`hypot(x, y)`	Returns the Euclidean norm, sqrt(x*x + y*y)	`import math`
		`print(math.hypot(6,8))`
		OUTPUT
		`10.0`

`sin(x)`	Returns the sine of x	`import math`
		`print(math.sin(90))`
		OUTPUT
		`0.8939966636005579`

`tan(x)`	Returns the tangent of x	`import math`
		`print(math.tan(90))`
		OUTPUT
		`-1.995200412208242`

`degrees(x)`	Converts angle x from radians to degrees	`import math`
		`print(math.radians(90))`
		OUTPUT
		`1.5707963267948966`

`radians(x)`	Converts angle x from degrees to radians	`import math`
		`print(math.degrees(1.5707963267948966))`
		OUTPUT
		`90.0`

`uniform(a,b)`	It returns a floating-point number x, such that a <= x < b	`>>>random.uniform (5, 10)` `5.52615217015`
`randrange([start,] stop [,step])`	It returns a random item from the given range	`>>>random.randrange(100,1000,3)` `150`

PROGRAMMER'S ZONE

1. Write a program using functions to check whether two numbers are equal or not.

```
def check_relation(a,b):a
    if(a==b):
        return 0
    if(a>b):
        return 1
    if(a<b):
        return -1
a = 3
b = 5
res = check_relation(a,b)
```

```
if(res==0):
    print("a is equal to b")
if(res==1):
    print("a is greater than b")
if(res==-1):
    print("a is less than b")
```

OUTPUT

```
a is less than b
```

2. **Write a program to swap two numbers.**

```
def swap(a,b):
    a,b = b,a
    print("After swap : ")
    print("First number = ",a)
    print("Second number = ",b)
a = input("\n Enter the first number : ")
b = input("\n Enter the second number : ")
print("Before swap : ")
print("First number = ",a)
print("Second number = ",b)
swap(a,b)
```

OUTPUT

```
Enter the first number : 29
Enter the second number : 56
Before swap :
First number =  29
Second number =  56
After swap :
First number =  56
Second number =  29
```

3. **Write a program using functions and return statement to check whether a number is even or odd.**

```
def evenodd(a):
    if(a%2==0):
        return 1
    else:
        return -1
a = int(input("Enter the number : "))
flag = evenodd(a)
if(flag==1):
    print("Number is even")
if(flag==-1):
    print("Number is odd")
```

> Some of the modules in the Standard Library are written in Python, and some are written in C.

OUTPUT

```
Enter the number : 1091
Number is odd
```

4. **Write a program to convert time into minutes.**

```
def convert_time_in_min(hrs,minute):
    minute = hrs*60+minute
    return minute
h = int(input("Enter the hours : "))
m = int(input("Enter the minutes : "))
```

```
m = convert_time_in_min(h,m)
print("Minutes =",m)
```

OUTPUT

```
Enter the hours and minutes : 6
Enter the hours and minutes : 34
Minutes = 394
```

5. Write a program to calculate simple interest. Suppose the customer is a senior citizen. He is being offered 12 per cent rate of interest; for all other customers, the ROI is 10 per cent.

```
def interest(p,y,s):
    if(s=='y'):
        SI = float((p*y*12)/100)
    else:
        SI = float((p*y*10)/100)
    return SI
p = float(input("Enter the principle amount : "))
y = float(input("Enter the number of years : "))
senior = input("Is customer senior citizen(y/n) : ")
print("Interest :",interest(p,y,senior))
```

OUTPUT

```
Enter the principle amount : 200000
Enter the number of years : 3
Is customer senior citizen(y/n) : n
Interest : 60000.0
```

6. Write a program to calculate the volume of a cuboid using default arguments.

```
def volume(l,w=3,h=4):
    print("Length :",l,"\tWidth :",w,"\tHeight :",h)
    return l*w*h

print("Volume :",volume(4,6,2))
print("Volume :",volume(4,6))
print("Volume :",volume(4))
```

OUTPUT

```
Volume : Length : 4    Width : 6    Height : 2
48
Volume : Length : 4    Width : 6    Height : 4
96
Volume : Length : 4    Width : 3    Height : 4
48
```

7. Write a program that computes P(n,r).

```
def fact(n):
    f = 1
    if(n==0 or n==1):
        return 1
    else:
        for i in range(1,int(n+1)):
            f = f*i
        return f

n = int(input("Enter the value of n : "))
r = int(input("Enter the value of r : "))
```

```
result = float(fact(n))/float(fact(r))
print("P(",str(n),"/",str(r),") = ",str(result))
```

OUTPUT

```
Enter the value of n : 9
Enter the value of r : 4
P( 9 / 4 ) =  15120.0
```

8. **Write a program to computes C(n,r).**

```
def fact(n):
    f = 1
    if(n==0 or n==1):
        return 1
    else:
        for i in range(1,int(n+1)):
            f = f*i
        return f
n = int(input("Enter the value of n : "))
r = int(input("Enter the value of r : "))
result = float(fact(n))/(fact(r)*fact(n-r))
print("C("+str(n)+"/"+str(r)+") = "str(result))
```

OUTPUT

```
Enter the value of n : 10
Enter the value of r : 5
C(10/5) = 252.0
```

9. **Write a program to sum the series 1/1! + 4/2! + 27/3! + ...**

```
def fact(n):
    f = 1
    if(n==0 or n==1):
        return 1
    else:
        for i in range(1,int(n+1)):
            f = f*i
        return f

n = int(input("Enter the value of n : "))
s = 0.0
for i in range(1,n+1):
    s = s+(float(i**i)/fact(i))
print("Result :",s)
```

OUTPUT

```
Enter the value of n : 5
Result : 44.2083333333
```

10. **Write a program that uses docstrings and variable-length arguments to add the values passed to the function.**

```
def add(*args):
    '''Function returns the sum of values passed to it'''
    sum = 0
    for i in args:
        sum += i
    return sum
print(add.__doc__)
print("SUM = ",add(25, 30, 45, 50))
```

OUTPUT

```
Function returns the sum of values passed to it
SUM =  150
```

11. **Write a program that greets a person.**

    ```
    def greet(name, mesg):
        """This function
        welcomes the person passed whose name
        is passed as a
        parameter"""
        print("Welcome, " + name + ". " + mesg)
    mesg = "Happy Reading. Python is Fun !"
    name = input("\n Enter your name : ")
    greet(name, mesg)
    ```

    OUTPUT

    ```
    Enter your name : Goransh
    Welcome, Goransh. Happy Reading. Python is Fun !
    ```

12. **Write a program to print the following pattern using default arguments.**

    ```
    %%%%%%
    ^^^^^^
    ^^^^^^^^^^
    ^^^^^^^^^^^^^^
    ^^^^^^^^^^^^^^
    ```

    ```
    def pattern(c='%',n=6,r=1):
        for i in range(r):
            print()
            for j in range(n):
                print(c, end = ' ')
    c = input("Enter the character to be displayed : ")
    n = int(input("Enter the number of rows : "))
    m = int(input("Enter the number of columns : "))
    pattern()
    pattern(c)
    pattern(c,n)
    pattern(c,n,m)
    Example: Program that returns the full name of a person
    def name(firstName, lastName):
        separator = ' '
        n = firstName + separator + lastName
        return n
    print name('Janak', 'Raj')
    ```

    OUTPUT

    ```
    Janak Raj
    Example: Function that returns average of its arguments
    def avg(n1, n2):
        return (n1+n2)/2.0
    n1 = int(input("Enter the first number : "))
    n2 = int(input("Enter the second number : "))
    print "AVERAGE = ", avg(n1,n2)
    ```

    OUTPUT

    ```
    Enter the first number : 5
    Enter the second number : 7
    AVERAGE =   6.0
    ```

13. Write a program that defines a function large in a module, which will be used to find the larger of two values and called from a code in another module.

```
# Code in MyModule
def large(a,b):
    if a>b:
        return a
    else:
        return b

# Code in Find.py
import MyModule
print "Large(50, 100) = ", MyModule.large(50,100)
print "Large('B', 'c') = ", MyModule.large('B', 'c')
print "Large('HI', 'BI') = ", MyModule.large('HI','BI')
```

OUTPUT

```
Large(50, 100) =  100
Large('B', 'c') =  c
Large('HI', 'BI') =  HI
```

14. Write a program that accepts a dictionary and convert its keys to lowercase.

```
def func(Dict):
    for key in Dict:
        Dict[key.lower()] = Dict.pop(key)
Dict = {'NAME':'Priya', 'MARKS': 92, 'GRADE':'A+'}
func(Dict)
print(Dict)
```

OUTPUT

```
{'name': 'Priya', 'marks': 92, 'grade': 'A+'}
```

15. Write a program in which a function accepts a dictionary as an argument and squares its key to get its value.

```
def func(dict):
    for key in dict:
        dict[key] = key*key
Dict = {1:1, 2:2, 3:3, 4:4, 5:5}
func(Dict)
print(Dict)
```

OUTPUT

```
{1: 1, 2: 4, 3: 9, 4: 16, 5: 25}
```

Key Terms

Function: A piece of code that performs a well-defined task.

Arguments/parameters: The inputs that the function takes.

Function declaration: A declaration statement that identifies a function with its name, a list of arguments that it accepts and the type of data it returns.

Scope of the variable: Part of the program in which a variable is accessible is called its *scope*.

Lifetime of the variable: Duration for which the variable exists is called its *lifetime*.

Global variables: Variables which are defined in the main body of the program file. They are visible throughout the program file.

Module: A file with a .py extension that has definitions of all functions and variables that you would like to use even in other programs.

Package: A hierarchical file directory structure that has modules and other packages within it.

Chapter Highlights

- Understanding, coding and testing multiple separate functions are far easier than doing the same for one huge function.
- Large programs usually follow the DRY principle, that is, Don't Repeat Yourself principle. Once a function is written it can be called multiple times wherever its functionality is required.
- A bad repetitive code abides by the WET principle, i.e., Write Everything Twice, or We Enjoy Typing.
- A function f, that uses another function g, is known as the *calling function* and g is known as the *called function*.
- When a called function returns some result back to the calling function, it is said to *return* that result.
- Defining a function means specifying its name, parameters that are expected and the set of instructions. Once the structure of a function is finalized, the function can be executed by calling it.
- In nested functions, the inner function can access variables defined in both outer as well as inner function, but the outer function can access variables defined only in the outer function.
- Once you return a value from a function, it immediately exits that function. Therefore, any code written after the `return` statement is never executed.
- Keyword arguments, when used in function calls, help the function to identify the arguments by the parameter name.
- When the number of arguments passed to a function is not known in advance, then use arbitrary (or any) number of arguments in the function header.
- Docstrings (documentation strings) serve the same purpose as that of comments, as they are designed to explain code.

Review Questions

1. Define a function and give its advantages.
2. Can a function call another function? Justify your answer with the help of an example.
3. What do you understand by the term arguments? How do we pass them to a function?
4. What are user-defined functions? With the help of an example, illustrate how you can have such functions in your program.
5. The `return` statement is optional. Justify this statement with the help of an example.
6. Differentiate between local and global variables.
7. Define a function that calculates the sum of all numbers from 0 to its argument.
8. Arguments may be passed in the form of expressions to the called function. Justify this statement with the help of an example.
9. When you can have a variable with the same name as that of a global variable in the program, how is the name resolved in Python? Explain with the help of a program.
10. With the help of an example, explain the concept of accessibility of variables in nested functions.
11. Explain the use of `return` statement.
12. Explain the utility of keyword arguments.
13. What are docstrings?
14. What are modules? How do you use them in your programs?
15. What are variable-length arguments? Explain with the help of a code.

16. Write short notes on:
    a. Keyword arguments
    b. Default arguments
    c. Variable sized arguments.

Programming Exercises

1. Write a program that finds the greater of three given numbers using functions. Pass the numbers as arguments.
2. Write a program that prints the time taken to execute a program in Python.
3. Write a function that returns the absolute value of a number.
4. Write a function is_prime() that returns a 1 if the argument passed to it is a prime a number and a 0 otherwise.
5. Write a function that accepts an integer between 1 and 12 to represent the month number and displays the corresponding month of the year (For example, if month = 1, then display JANUARY).
6. Write a function is_leap_year, which takes the year as its argument and checks whether the year is a leap year or not and then displays an appropriate message on the screen.
7. Write a program to swap two variables that are defined as global variables.
8. Write a menu-driven program to add, subtract, multiply, and divide two integers using functions.
9. Write a program using function that calculates the hypotenuse of a right-angled triangle.
10. Write a function that accepts a number n as input and returns the average of numbers from 1 to n.
11. Write a program to calculate the area of a triangle using function.
12. Write a program using function to calculate x to the power of y, where y can be either negative or positive. Pass dictionary as an argument to the function.
13. Write a program using function to calculate compound interest, given the principal, rate of interest, and number of years.
14. Write a function that converts temperature given in Celsius into Fahrenheit.
15. Write a function to draw the following pattern on the screen
    ```
    ********
    !      !
    !      !
    !      !
    ********
    ```
16. Write a function called printStatus that is passed status code 'S', 'M', 'D', or 'U' and returns the string 'Separated', 'Married', 'Divorced', or 'Unmarried', respectively. In case an inappropriate letter is passed, print an appropriate message. Also include a docstring with your function.
17. Write a function that accepts three integers, and returns True if any of the integers is 0; otherwise it returns False
18. Write a function that accepts two positive numbers n and m where m<=n, and returns numbers between 1 and n that are divisible by m.
19. Write a function that displays "Hello name", for any given name passed to it.
20. Write a program to print the prime factors of a number.
21. Write a program that prompts the user to enter 10 numbers. Find the smallest and the second smallest number entered by the user.

Fill in the Blanks

1. In range(0, 100, 5) , the name of the function is _____ and it has _____ arguments.
2. _____ keyword allows you to have user-defined functions in your program.

3. _____ error is caused by importing an unknown module.
4. _____ consists of a function header followed by a function.
5. The _____ is used to uniquely identify the function.
6. _____ describes what the function does.
7. Fill in the blanks to define a function named display.
   _____ display()_____
   print("Hello World")
8. After the called function is executed, the control is returned to the_____.
9. A return statement with no arguments is the same as return_____.
10. Before calling a function, you must _____ it.
11. _____ variable can be accessed from the point of its definition until the end of the function in which it is defined.
12. To define a variable defined inside a function as global, _____ statement is used.
13. Every function has an implicit _____ statement as the last instruction in the function body.
14. The docstring specified can be accessed through the _____ attribute of the function.
15. You can find the name of a module by using the _____ attribute of the module.
16. Every package in Python is a directory which must have a special file called_____.
17. Fill in the blanks to define a function that takes two arguments and prints their sum.
    _____ mult(x,y)_____
    print(x*_____)
18. Fill in the blanks to define a function that prints "Positive", if its parameter is greater than 0 and "Negative" otherwise.
    _____ pos_neg(x):
       if x>0:
          _____ "Positive")
       _____
          print("Negative")
19. Fill in the blanks to define a function that compares the lengths of its arguments and returns the longest one.
    def max_len(x, y):
       if len(x)>=_____(y):
          _____x)
       else:
          _____y)
20. Fill in the blanks to pass the function cube as an argument to the function "test":
    _____ cube(x):
       return x*x*x
    def do(func,x)_____
       print(func(x))
    do(_____, 2)
21. To import the sqrt and cos function from the math module, write _____.
22. Trying to import a module that is not available results in _____.
23. Python's preinstalled modules form the _____.
24. The _____ command is used to force the reloading of a given module.
25. Packages have an attribute _____, which is initialized with a list having the name of the directory holding the _____init_____.py file.

State True or False

1. Docstring can contain multiple lines of text.
2. Every function can be written more or less independently of the others.
3. When a function call is encountered, the control jumps to the calling function.
4. A function can call only one function.
5. Code reuse is one of the most prominent reasons to use functions.
6. Large programs usually follow the WET principle.
7. We can have a function that does not take any inputs at all.
8. The calling function may or may not pass parameters to the called function.
9. The `return` statement is optional.
10. Python does not allow you to assign function name to a variable.
11. Names of variables in function call and header of function definition may vary.
12. Arguments may be passed in the form of expressions to the called function.
13. You can have a variable with the same name as that of a global variable in the program.
14. You should make extensive use of global variables and global statements.
15. The `return` statement can be used outside of a function definition.
16. Any code written after the `return` statement is never executed.
17. The order of keyword arguments is not important.
18. Default arguments should always be written after the non-default arguments.
19. You can specify only one default argument in your function.
20. The variable sized arguments, if present in the function definition, should be first in the list of formal parameters.
21. A function cannot be used on the left side of an assignment statement.
22. It is mandatory to place all import statements at the beginning of a module.
23. With the "import *moduleName*" statement, any item from the imported module must be prefixed with the module name.
24. All Python Standard Library modules must be imported before any programmer-defined modules.
25. If a particular module is imported more than once in a Python program, the interpreter will load the module only once.
26. A function can be called from anywhere within a program.
27. A statement can call more than one function.
28. Function calls may contain arguments that are function calls.
29. All functions that return a value must accept at least one parameter.

Multiple Choice Questions

1. DRY principle makes the code _____.
   a. Reusable   b. Loop forever   c. Bad and repetitive   d. Complex
2. How many times will the `print()` execute in the code given below?
   ```
   def display():
       print('a')
       print('b')
       return
       print('c')
       print('d')
   ```
   a. 1   b. 2   c. 3   d. 4

3. What is the output of this code?
   ```
   import random as r
   print(random.randomint(1, 10))
   ```
   a. An error occurs   b. 1   c. 10   d. Any random value

4. How would you refer to the `sqrt` function if it was imported like this?
   `from math import sqrt as square_root`
   a. math.square_root   b. math.sqrt   c. sqrt   d. square_root

5. The code will print how many numbers?
   ```
   def display(x):
       for i in range(x):
           print(i)
       return
   display(10)
   ```
   a. 0   b. 1   c. 9   d. 10

6. Which statement invokes the function?
   a. Function definition   b. function call   c. function header   d. __doc__

7. If number of arguments in function definition and function call do not match, then which type of error is returned?
   a. NameError   b. ImortError   c. TypeError   d. NumberError

8. _____ of a variable determines the part of the program in which it is accessible
   a. Scope   b. Lifetime   c. Data Type   d. Value

9. Arbitrary arguments have which symbol in the function definition before the parameter name?
   a. &   b. #   c. %   d. *

10. Modules are files saved with _____ extension
    a. .py   b. .mod   c. .mdl   d. .imp

11. The import * statement imports all names in the module except those beginning with _____
    a. %   b. $ c. ____   d. !

12. How would you refer to the `randint` function if it was imported by writing from random import randint as r_int
    a. random.rnd_int   b. r_int   c. randint.r_int   d. randint

13. Identify the correct way of calling a function named display() that prints Hello on screen
    a. print(display)   b. displayHello   c. result = display()   d. displayHello()

Give the Output

1. ```
   num = 10
   def show():
       var = 20
       print("In Function var is - ", num)

   show()
   print("Outside function, var is - ", num)
   ```

2. ```
   def f():
       s = "Hello World!"
       print(s)
   s = "Welcome to Python Programming"
   f()
   print(s)
   ```

3. ```
   def f():
           global var
           print(varr)
           var = 10
           print(var)
   var = 100
   f()
   ```
4. ```
   def display (str):
       print(str+"!")
   display ("Hello World")
   ```
5. ```
   def sqr(x):
       print(x*x)
   sqr(10)
   ```
6. ```
   def mul_twice(x,y):
           print(x*y)
           print(x*y)
   mul_twice(5, 10)
   ```
7. ```
   def func():
       global x
       print "x =", x
       x = 100
       print('x is now = ', x)
   x = 10
   func()
   print('x =', x)
   ```
8. ```
   def func1():
       var = 3
       func2(var)
   def func2(var):
       print(var)
   func1()
   ```
9. ```
   def func(x):
       print 'x = ', x
       x = 100
       print('In Function, x after modification = ', x)
   x = 50
   func(x)
   print('Outside Function, x = ', x)
   ```
10. ```
    def display( str ):
        print(str)
        return;
    display("Hello World !!")
    display("Welcome to Python Programming")
    ```
11. ```
    def sum( num1, num2 ):
        total = num1 + num2
        print("Inside function, Total = ", total)
        return total;
    ```
    ```

```
       total = sum( 10, 20 )
       print("Outside the function, Total = ", total)
12. def min(x,y):
       if x<y:
           return x
       else:
           return y
    print(min(4, 7))
13. def add(x, y):
       sum = x + y
       return sum
       print("This won't be printed")
    print(add(10,20))
14. def display(str):
       "This prints a passed string into this function"
       Print(str)
       return;
    display(str = "Welcome")
15. def say(message, repeat_it = 2):
       print(message * repeat_it)
    say('Hello')
    say('Hello', 5)
16. def func(x, y = 100, z = 1000):
       print('x = ', x, ' y = ', y, 'and z = ', z)
    func(5, 15, 25)
    func(35, z = 55)
    func(y = 70, x = 200)
17. def greet(*names):
       for name in names:
           print("Hello",name)
    greet("Aryan","Nikita","Cahitanya")
18. def func( arg1, *var):
       '"This prints arbitrary arguments"'
       print(arg1)
       for i in var:
           print(i)
       return;
    func("Score is : ", 10, 20, 30)
    func( "\n Average Score = ", 20)
19. def func():
       """Do nothing.
         Nothing doing.
       """
       pass
    print(func.__doc__)
```

20. ```
def C_to_F(c):
    return c * 9/5 + 32
print C_to_F(37)
```
21. ```
def pow(x, y=3):
    r = 1
    for i in range(y):
        r = r * x
        return r
print(pow(5))
print(pow(2, 5))
```
22. ```
def display(name, deptt, sal):
    print("Name: ", name)
    print("Department: ", deptt)
    print("Salary: ", sal)
display(sal = 100000, name="Tavisha", deptt = "IT")
display(deptt = "HR", name="Dev", sal = 50000)
```
23. ```
def display(mesg):
        return mesg + "!"
print_str = display
str = print_str("Hello")
print(str)
```
24. ```
from random import randint as r
for i in range(10):
        value = r(1,100)
        print(value)
```
25. ```
def is_even(x):
    if x==0:
        return True
    else:
        return is_odd(x-1)
def is_odd(x):
    return not is_even(x)
print(is_even(22))
```
26. ```
def display(x):
    for i in range(x):
        print(i)
        return
display(5)
```

## Find the Error

1. ```
import math as m
print(math.sqrt(25))
```
2. ```
def func():
            print("Hello World")
```
```

3. ```
   var1 = "Good"
   def show():
           var2 = "Morning"
           print(var1)
           print(var2)
   show()
   print(var1)
   print(var2)
   ```
4. ```
   def f():
           print var
           var = 10
           print(var)
   var = 100
   f()
   ```
5. ```
   def f():
       var = 100
       print(var)
   f()
   print(var)
   ```
6. ```
   def func(var):
       var+=1
       var *= 2
       print(var)
   func(9)
   print(var)
   ```
7. ```
   def func1():
       var = 3
       func2()
   def func2():
       print(var)
   func1()
   ```
8. ```
   def display(x,y):
       print (x+y)
   display(10)
   ```
9. ```
   def func(a, b):
       print(a)
       print(b)
   func(b=10, 20)
   ```
10. ```
    def func1():
        print("func1()")
    func1()
    func2()
    def func2():
        print("func2()")
    ```
11. ```
    def sum_to(x):
        return x+sum_to(x-1)
    print(sum_to(5))
    ```
    ```

Functions and Modules

Answers

Fill in the Blanks

1. range, 3
2. def
3. ImportError
4. Function definition
5. function name
6. docstring
7. def, :
8. calling program
9. None
10. define
11. local
12. global
13. return
14. docsting
15. __name__
16. __init__.py
17. def, :, y
18. def, print(, else:
19. len, return(, return(
20. def, :, cube
21. `from math import sqrt, cos`
22. ImportError
23. Python library
24. `reload()`
25. __path__

State True or False

1. True
2. True
3. True
4. False
5. True
6. False
7. True
8. True
9. True
10. False
11. True
12. True
13. true
14. False
15. False
16. true
17. True
18. True
19. False
20. False
21. True
22. False
23. True
24. False
25. True
26. True
27. True
28. True
29. False

Multiple Choice Questions

1. a
2. b
3. a
4. d
5. d
6. b
7. c
8. a
9. d
10.
11. c
12. d
13. a

Give the Output

1. ```
   In Function var is - 10
   Outside function, var is - 10
   ```
2. ```
   Hello World!
   Welcome to Python Programming
   ```
3. `100    10`
4. `Hello World!`
5. `100`
6. `50    50`
7. ```
   x =  10
   x is now = 100
   x = 100
   ```
8. `3`
9. ```
   x = 50
   In Function, x after modification = 100
   Outside Function, x = 50
   ```
10. `Hello World !!`
11. ```
    Welcome to Python Programming
    Inside function, Total = 30
    Outside the function, Total = 30
    ```
12. `4`
13. `This won't be printed`
14. `Welcome`
15. ```
    HelloHello
    HelloHelloHelloHelloHello
    ```
16. ```
    x =  5   y =  15 and z =  25
    x =  35  y =  100 and z =  55
    x =  200 y =  70 and z =  1000
    ```
17. ```
    Hello Aryan
    Hello Nikita
    Hello Cahitanya
    ```
18. `Score is :`

```
10
20
30
 Average Score = 20
```
19. Do nothing.
    Nothing doing.
20. 98.6
21. 5   2
22. 98.6
    Name: Tavisha

Department: IT
Salary: 100000
Name: Dev
Department: HR
Salary: 50000

23. Hello!
24. 78   88   85   65   94   15
    73   91   51   97
25. True
26. 0

Find the Error

1. `NameError: name 'math' is not defined`
2. `No output as function is not called`
3. `NameError: name 'var2' is not defined`
4. `brackets in print function missing`
5. NameError: name 'var' is not defined
6. NameError: name 'var' is not defined
7. NameError: name 'var' is not defined
8. `TypeError: display() missing 1 required positional argument: 'y'`
9. Keyword argument should be present as the last parameter in the function call statement
10. NameError: name 'func2' is not defined
11. Base condition is missing. RecursionError: maximum recursion depth exceeded

File Handling

6

Chapter Objectives

Today, there is hardly any real-time application that does not store data anywhere. This data is usually stored in files. In this chapter, we will therefore learn to do the following things:

- Perform basic operations operations on a text file like opening a file either by using relative or absolute file path in the desired mode, reading, appending, manipulating data stored in a text file and performing standard input/output and operations on them
- Perform basic operations on a binary file
- Use the Pickle Module for loading and dumping data in a binary file.
- Operations on CSV files

6.1 INTRODUCTION

A file is a collection of data stored on a secondary storage device like hard disk. Until now, we have been processing data that was entered through the computer's keyboard using the `input()`. But this task can become very tedious, especially when there is a huge amount of data to be processed. A better solution, therefore, is to combine all the input data into a file and then design a Python program to read this data from the file, whenever required.

When a program is being executed, its data is stored in *random access memory* (RAM). Though RAM can be accessed fast by the CPU, it is also **volatile**, which means that when the program ends, or the computer shuts down, all the data is lost. If you want to use the data in future, then you need to store this data on a permanent or non-volatile storage media like the hard disk, USB drive, DVD, etc.

Data on non-volatile storage media is stored in named locations on the media called **files**. You can think of working with files as working with a notebook. To use a notebook, you must first open it. Once the notebook is opened, you can read the contents that you had previously written in it or write some new content into it. After using the notebook, you close it. The same concept can be applied to files. We first open a file, read or write to it and then finally close it.

A file is basically used because real-life applications involve large amounts of data and in such situations the console-oriented I/O operations pose two major problems:

- First, it becomes cumbersome and time-consuming to handle huge amount of data through terminals.
- Second, when doing I/O using terminal, the entire data is lost when either the program is terminated or the computer is turned off. Therefore, it becomes necessary to store data on a permanent storage (the disks) and read whenever necessary, without destroying the data.

In order to use files, we have to learn file input and output operations, that is, how data is read or written to a file. Although file I/O operations are almost same as terminal I/O, the only difference is that when doing file I/O, the user must specify the name of the file from which data should be read/written.

6.2 FILE PATH

Files that we use are stored on a storage medium like the hard disk in such a way that they can be easily retrieved as and when required. Most file systems that are used today store files in a tree (or *hierarchical*) structure. At the top of the tree is one (or more) root node/s. Under the root node, there are other files and folders (or directories) and each folder

> The characters after the dot form the extension of the file. It is used to indicate the type of file. For example, .docx tells that the file is a Word document.

can, in turn, contain other files and folders. Even these folders can contain other files and folders and this can go on to an almost limitless depth. Consider the tree structure given in Fig. 6.1.

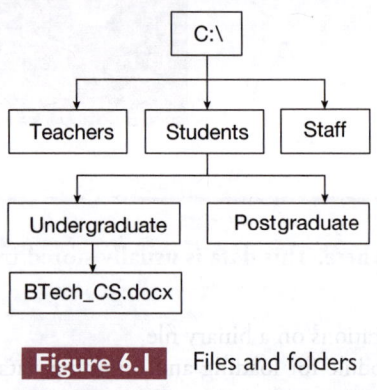

Figure 6.1 Files and folders

Every file is identified by its path that begins from the root node or the root folder. In Windows, C:\ (also known as C drive) is the root folder but you can also have a path that starts from other drives like D:\, E:\, etc. The file path is also known as pathname. For example, in the figure, the file BTech_CS.docx file is stored in the C:\. C: drive has a folder Students which, in turn, has a sub-folder (folder within a folder) named Undergraduate. The sub-folder Undergraduate has the desired file. So the path of this file can be written as,

C:\Students\Undergraduate\BTech_CS.docx

Note that the character used to separate the folder names (also called the *delimiter*) is specific to the file system. For example, while Solaris OS uses the forward slash (/), Microsoft Windows, on the other hand, uses the backslash slash (\).

> Folder names and file names are case sensitive in Windows but they are case insensitive in Linux.

6.2.1 Relative Path and Absolute Path

A file path can be either *relative* or *absolute*. While an absolute path always contains the root and the complete directory list to specify the exact location the file, relative path on the other hand, needs to be combined with another path in order to access a file. That is, relative pathnames start with respect to the current working directory and therefore lacks the leading slashes. For example, C:\Students\Undergraduate\BTech_CS.docx is the absolute path as all of the information needed to locate the file is contained in the path but Undergraduate\BTech_CS.docx is a relative path as only a part of the complete path is specified.

> A relative path is specified relative to the program's current working directory.

Note that when a relative file path is specified, the relative path is joined with the current directory to create an absolute file path. Therefore, in our example, if the current working directory is C:\Students, then the relative path Undergraduate\BTech_CS.docx is equivalent to using its absolute path.

6.3 TYPES OF FILES

Like C and C++, Python also supports two types of files – text files and binary files.

6.3.1 ASCII Text Files

A text file is a stream of characters that can be sequentially processed by a computer in the forward direction. For this reason, a text file is usually opened for only one kind of operation (reading, writing, or appending) at any given time. Because text files only process characters, they can only read or write data one character at a time. In Python, a text stream is treated as a special kind of file.

Depending on the requirements of the operating system and on the operation that has to be performed (read/write operation) on the file, newline characters may be converted to or from carriage-return/linefeed combinations. Besides this, other character conversions may also be done to satisfy the storage requirements of the operating system. However, these conversions occur transparently to process a text file.

> If you use a relative file path from the wrong directory, then either the wrong file will be accessed or no file will be accessed if no file of the specified name exists in the given path.

In a text file, each line contains zero or more characters and ends with one or more characters that specify the end of line. Each line in a text file can have a maximum of 255 characters. When data is written to a text file, each newline character is converted to a carriage return/line feed character. Similarly, when data is read from a text file, each carriage return/line feed character is converted to newline character.

Another important thing is that when a text file is used, there are actually two representations of data – internal and external. For example, an integer value will be represented as a number that occupies 2 or 4 bytes of memory internally but externally the integer value will be represented as a string of characters representing its decimal or hexadecimal value.

> In a text file, each line of data ends with a new line character. Each file ends with a special character called the end-of-file (EOF) marker.

6.3.2 Binary Files

A binary file is a file which may contain any type of data encoded in binary form for computer storage and processing purposes. It includes files like word processing documents, PDFs, images, spreadsheets, videos, zip files and other executable programs. Like a text file, a binary file is a collection of bytes. A binary file is also referred to as a character stream with the following two essential differences.

- A binary file does not require any special processing of the data and each byte of data is transferred to or from the disk, unprocessed.
- Python places no constructs on the file, and it may be read from, or written to in any manner the programmer wants.

While text files can be processed sequentially, binary files, on the other hand, can be either processed sequentially or randomly depending on the needs of the application. In Python, to process a file randomly, the programmer must move the current file position to an appropriate place in the file before reading or writing data. For example, if a file is used to store records (using structures) of students, then to update a particular record, the programmer must first locate the appropriate record, read the record into memory, update it and finally write the record back to disk at its appropriate location in the file.

> The contents of a binary file are not human-readable. If you want that data stored in the file must be human-readable, then store the data in a text file.

In a text file, an integer value 123 will be stored as a sequence of three characters – 1, 2 and 3. So each character will take 1 byte and therefore, to store the integer value 123 we need 3 bytes. However, in a binary file, the integer value 123 will be stored in 2 bytes in the binary form. This clearly indicates that binary files take less space to store the same piece of data and eliminates conversion between internal and external representations. Thus, binary files are more efficient than the text files.

Thus, we see that text files contain only basic characters and do not store any information about the color, font and size of the text. Examples of text files include files with .txt or .py extension. These files can be opened with Windows Notepad. They can be easily read and the contents of the file are treated as an ordinary string value. Binary files, on the other hand, cannot be read by text editors like Notepad. If you open a binary file in Notepad, you will see some scrambles, and absurd data.

> Binary files store data in the internal representation format. Therefore, an integer value will be stored in binary form as 2-byte value. The same format is used to store data in memory as well as in file. Like text file, binary file also ends with an EOF marker.

6.4 OPENING AND CLOSING FILES

Python has many in-built functions and methods to manipulate files. These functions and methods basically work on a file object.

> Binary files are mainly used to store data beyond text, like images, executables, etc.

6.4.1 The open() Function

Before reading from or writing to a file, you must first open it using Python's built-in open() function. **This function creates a file object,** which will be used to invoke methods associated with it. The syntax of open() is:

fileObj = open(file_name [, access_mode])

where,
file_name is a string value that specifies the name of the file that you want to access.
access_mode indicates the mode in which the file has to be opened, i.e., read, write, append, etc. Table 6.1 lists other possible values of access mode argument.

Note that the `open()` function returns a file object. This file object will be used to read, write or perform any other operation on the file. It works like a file handle.

You can also print the details of file object as shown in the code given below.

```
file = open("File1.txt", "rb")
print(file)
```

OUTPUT
`<open file 'File1.txt', mode 'rb' at 0x02A850D0>`

> Access mode is an optional parameter and the default file access mode is read (r).

Note that a file handle is different from a file. Try to understand it by using an analogy of TV and the TV remote control. You can use the remote control to switch channels, change the volume, etc. But whatever changes you try to do using remote control are actually applied on the TV. So, your file handle or the file object acts as a remote control of your file (TV). Whatever changes you want to perform on the file is actually carried out through the file object.

Table 6.1 Access modes

Mode	Purpose
r	This is the default mode of opening a file which opens the file for reading only. The file pointer is placed at the beginning of the file.
rb	This mode opens a file for reading only in binary format. The file pointer is placed at the beginning of the file.
r+	This mode opens a file for both reading and writing. The file pointer is placed at the beginning of the file.
rb+	This mode opens the file for both reading and writing in binary format. The file pointer is placed at the beginning of the file.
w	This mode opens the file for writing only. When a file is opened in w mode, two things can happen. If the file does not exist, a new file is created for writing. If the file already exists and has some data stored in it, the contents are overwritten.
wb	Opens a file in binary format for writing only. When a file is opened in this mode, two things can happen. If the file does not exist, a new file is created for writing. If the file already exists and has some data stored in it, the contents are overwritten
w+	Opens a file for both writing and reading. When a file is opened in this mode, two things can happen. If the file does not exist, a new file is created for reading as well as writing. If the file already exists and has some data stored in it, the contents are overwritten.
wb+	Opens a file in binary format for both reading and writing. When a file is opened in this mode, two things can happen. If the file does not exist, a new file is created for reading as well as writing. If the file already exists and has some data stored in it, the contents are overwritten.
a	Opens a file for appending. The file pointer is placed at the end of the file if the file exists. If the file does not exist, it creates a new file for writing.
ab	Opens a file in binary format for appending. The file pointer is at the end of the file if the file exists. If the file does not exist, it creates a new file for writing.
a+	Opens a file for both reading and appending. The file pointer is placed at the end of the file if the file exists. If the file does not exist, it creates a new file for reading and writing.
ab+	Opens a file in binary format for both reading and appending. The file pointer is placed at the end of the file if the file exists. If the file does not exist, a new file is created for reading and writing.

Table 6.2 File object attributes

Attribute	Information Obtained
fileObj.closed	Returns True if the file is closed and false otherwise
fileObj.mode	Returns access mode with which file has been opened
fileObj.name	Returns name of the file

6.4.2 The File Object Attributes

Once a file is successfully opened, a *file* object is returned. Using this file object, you can easily access different types of information related to that file. This information can be obtained by reading values of specific attributes of the file. Table 6.2 list the attributes related to a file object.

Example 6.1 Program to open a file and print its attribute values.

```
file = open("File1.txt", "wb")
print("Name of the file: ", file.name)
print("File is closed.", file.closed)
print("File has been opened in ", file.mode, "mode")
```

OUTPUT

```
Name of the file:  File1.txt
File is closed. False
File has been opened in wb mode
```

6.4.3 The `close()` Method

The `close()` method, as the name suggests, is used to close the file object. Once a file object is closed, you cannot further read from or write into the file associated with the file object. While closing the file object the `close()` flushes any unwritten information (means transfers the data that was supposed to be written in the file but was not yet transferred). Although Python automatically closes a file when the reference object of a file is reassigned to another file, it is always a good programming habit to explicitly use the `close()` method to close a file. The syntax of `close()` is **fileObj.close()**

The `close()` method frees up any system resources like file descriptors, file locks, etc. that are associated with the file. Moreover, there is an upper limit to the number of files a program can open. If that limit is exceeded then the program may even crash or work in an unexpected manner. Thus, you can waste lots of memory if you keep many files open unnecessarily. Also remember that open files always stand a chance of corruption and data loss.

Once the file is closed using the `close()` method, any attempt to use the file object will result in an error.

Example 6.2 Program that tries to access a file after it is closed.

```
file = open("File1.txt", "wb")
print("Name of the file: ", file.name)
print("File is closed.", file.closed)
print("FIle is now being closed.. You cannot use the File 
    Object")
file.close()
print("File is closed.", file.closed)
print(file.read())
```

> Python has a garbage collector to clean up unreferenced objects but still it is our responsibility to close the file and release the resources consumed by it.

OUTPUT

```
Name of the file:  File1.txt
File is closed. False
FIle is now being closed.. You cannot use the File Object
File is closed. True
Traceback (most recent call last):
  File "C:\Python27\Try.py", line 7, in <module>
    print(file.read())
ValueError: I/O operation on closed file
```

6.5 READING AND WRITING FILES

The `read()` and `write()` are used to read data from file and write data to files respectively. In this section, we will study both these functions to manipulate our data through files.

6.5.1 `write()` and `writelines()` Methods

The `write()` method is used to write a string to an already opened file. This string may include numbers, special characters or other symbols. While writing data to a file, you must remember that the `write()` method does not add a newline character ('\n') to the end of the string. The syntax of `write()` method is:

fileObj.write(string);

As per the syntax, the string that is passed as an argument to the `write()` is written into the opened file.

Example 6.3 To write a small program that writes a message in the file.

```
file = open("File1.txt", "w")
file.write("Hello All, hope you are enjoying learning Python")
file.close()
print("Data Written into the file.......")
```

> The `write()` method returns None.

OUTPUT

```
Data Written into the file......."
```

Now, if you open the File1.txt, you will see that it has the contents, "Hello All, hope you are enjoying learning Python" written in it. The file is created in the same directory where your program file (.py file) is stored, that is in the C:\Python27 folder.

The `writelines()` method is used to write a list of strings.

Example 6.4 Program to write to a file using the `writelines()` method.

```
file = open("File1.txt", "w")
lines = ["Hello World, ", "Welcome to the world of Python", "Enjoy Learning Python"]
file.writelines(lines)
file.close()
print("Data written to file........")
```

OUTPUT

```
Data written to file........
```

6.5.2 `append()` Method

Once you have stored some data in a file, you can always open that file again to write more data or append data to it. To append a file, you must open it using 'a' or 'ab' mode depending on whether it is a text file or a binary file. Note that if you open a file in 'w' or 'wb' mode and then start writing data into it, then its existing contents would be overwritten. So always open the file in 'a' or 'ab' mode to add more data to existing data stored in the file.

Appending data is especially essential when creating a log of events or combining a large set of data into one file. The code given below appends data to our File1.txt file.

Example 6.5 Program to append data to an already existing file.

```
file = open("File1.txt", "a")
file.write("\n Python is a very simple yet powerful language")
file.close()
print("Data appended to file........")
```

> If you open a file in append mode then the file is created if it did not exist.

OUTPUT

```
Data appended to file........"
```

6.5.3 The `read()` and `readline()` Methods

The `read()` method is used to read a string from an already opened file. As said before, the string can include alphabets, numbers, characters or other symbols. The syntax of `read()` method is

File Handling

fileObj.read([cout])

In the above syntax, count is an optional parameter which, if passed to the `read()` method, specifies the number of bytes to be read from the opened file. The `read()` method starts reading from the beginning of the file and if *count* is missing or has a negative value then, it reads the entire contents of the file (i.e., till the end of file).

Example 6.6 Program to print the first 10 characters of the file File1.txt.

```
file = open("File1.txt", "r")
print(file.read(10))
file.close()
```

OUTPUT

```
Hello All,
```

Note that if you try to open a file for reading that does not exist, then you will get an error, as shown below.

```
file1 = open("file2.txt","r")
print(file2.read())
```

OUTPUT

```
Traceback (most recent call last):
  File "C:\Python27\Try.py", line 1, in <module>
    file1 = open("file2.txt","r")
IOError: [Errno 2] No such file or directory: 'file2.txt'
```

> `read()` method returns newline as '\n'.

The `readline()` method is used to read a single line from the file. The method returns an empty string when the end of the file has been reached. Note that a blank line is represented by \n and the `readline()` method returns a string containing only a single newline when a blank line is encountered in the file.

Consider adding a few more lines in the file File1.txt and read its contents using the `readline()` method. The contents of the file are,

```
Hello All,
Hope you are enjoying learning Python
We have tried to cover every point in detail to avoid
    confusion
Happy Reading
file = open("File1.txt", "r")
print("First Line : ", file.readline())
print("Second Line : ", file.readline())
print("Third Line : ", file.readline())
file.close()
```

> Binary files are more efficient than text files, so we have opened the files using rb and wb access modes. You could have also opened using r or w access mode to work with text files.

OUTPUT

```
First Line :  Hello All,
Second Line :
Third Line :  Hope you are enjoying learning Python
```

You can also use the `readlines()` method to read all the lines in the file. The code for doing so is given below.

Example 6.7 Program to demonstrate `readlines()` function.

```
file = open("File1.txt", "r")
print(file.readlines())
file.close()
```

> After reading a line from the file using the `readline()` method, the control automatically passes to the next line. That is why, when you call the `readline()` again, the next line in the file is returned.

OUTPUT

```
['Hello All,\r\n', '\r\n', 'Hope you are enjoying learning Python\r\n', '\r\n', 'We have tried
    to cover every point in detail to avoid confusion\r\n', '\r\n', 'Happy Reading\r\n']
```
The `list()` method is also used to display entire contents of the file. You just need to pass the file object as an argument to the `list()` method.

Example 6.8 Program to display the contents of the file File1.txt using the `list()` method.

```
file = open("File1.txt", "r")
print(list(file))
file.close()
```

OUTPUT
```
['Hello All,\r\n', '\r\n', 'Hope you are enjoying learning Python\r\n', '\r\n', 'We have tried
      to cover every point in detail to avoid confusion\r\n', '\r\n', 'Happy Reading\r\n']
```

The last and probably a very fast, simple and efficient way to display a file is to loop over the file object to print every line in it. This is shown in the code given below.

Example 6.9 Program to display the contents of a file.

```
file = open("File1.txt", "r")
for line in file:
    print(line)
file.close()
```

OUTPUT
```
Hello All,
Hope you are enjoying learning Python
We have tried to cover every point in detail to avoid confusion
Happy Reading
```

> All reading methods return an empty string when end of file (EOF) is reached. That is, if you have read the entire file and then again call readline(), an empty string would be returned.

6.5.4 Opening Files Using `with` Keyword

It is a good programming habit to use the `with` keyword when working with file objects. Using this keyword ensures that the file is properly closed after it is used even if an error occurs during read or write operation or even when you forget to explicitly close the file. This difference is clearly evident from the codes given below.

```
with open("File1.txt", "rb") as file:
    for line in file:
        print(line)
print("Let's check if the file is closed : ", file.closed)
```

OUTPUT
```
Hello World
Let's check if the file is closed :  True
```

```
file = open("File1.txt", "rb")
for line in file:
    print(line)
print("Let's check if the file is closed : ", file.closed)
```

OUTPUT
```
Hello World
Let's check if the file is closed :  False
```

In the first code, the file is opened using the `with` keyword. After the file is used in the `for` loop, it is automatically closed as soon as the block of code comprising of the `for` loop is over. But when the file is opened without the `with` keyword, it is not closed automatically. You need to explicitly close the file after using it.

```
with open("file1.txt","r") as file:
    print(file.read()) # file is already closed after the last line is read
file.close()           # attempt to close a file that is already closed
```

OUTPUT
```
Hello
Welcome to the world of Programming
```

6.5.5 Splitting Words

Python allows you to read line(s) from a file and split the line (treated as a string) based on a character. By default, this character is space but you can also specify any other character to split words in a string.

Example 6.10 Program to split a line into a series of words and use space to perform the split operation.

```
with open('File1.txt', 'r') as file:
    line = file.readline()
    words = line.split()
    print(words)
```

> Calling close() on a file object that is already closed does not raise any error but fails silently.

OUTPUT

```
['Hello', 'World,', 'Welcome', 'to', 'the', 'world', 'of', 'Python', 'Programming']
```

Example 6.11 Program to perform split operation whenever a comma is encountered.

```
with open('File1.txt', 'r') as file:
    line = file.readline()
    words = line.split(',')
    print(words)
```

> When you open a file for reading or writing the file is searched in the current working directory. If the file exists somewhere else then you need to specify the path of the file.

OUTPUT

```
['Hello World', ' Welcome to the world of Python Programming\n']
```

6.5.6 Some Other Useful File Methods

Table 6.3 discusses some additional file methods.

Table 6.3 File methods

Method	Description	Example

`fileno()`	Returns the file number of the file (which is an integer descriptor)	`file = open("File1.txt", "w")`
		`print(file.fileno())`
		`OUPUT`
		`3`

`flush()`	Flushes the write buffer of the file stream	`file = open("File1.txt", "w")` `file.flush()`

`isatty()`	Returns True if the file stream is interactive and False otherwise	`file = open("File1.txt", "w")`
		`file.write("Hello")`
		`print(file.isatty())`
		`OUTPUT`
		`False`

`readline(n)`	Reads and returns one line from file. N is optional. If n is specified then atmost n bytes are read	`file = open("Try.py", "r")`
		`print(file.readline(10))`
		`OUTPUT`
		`file = ope`

`truncate(n)`	Resizes the file to n bytes	`file = open("File.txt", "w")`
		`file.write("Welcome to the world of programming....")`
		`file.truncate(5)`

`rstrip()`	Strips off whitespaces including new lines from the right side of the string read from the file.	`file = open("File.txt")`
		`line = file.readline()`
		`print(line.rstrip())`
		`OUTPUT`
		`Greetings to All !!!`

6.6 FILE POSITIONS

With every file, the file management system associates a pointer often known as *file pointer* that facilitates the movement across the file for reading and/or writing data. The file pointer specifies a location from where the current read or write operation is initiated. Once the read/write operation is completed, the pointer is automatically updated.

Python has various methods that tell or set the position of the file pointer. For example, the `tell()` method tells the current position within the file at which the next read or write operation will occur. It is specified as number of bytes from the beginning of the file. When you just open a file for reading, the file pointer is positioned at location 0, which is the beginning of the file.

The seek(offset[, from]) method is used to set the position of the file pointer. In simple terms, it moves the file pointer to a new location. The `offset` argument indicates the number of bytes to be moved and the `from` argument specifies the reference position from where the bytes are to be moved. Table 6.4 specifies the value of `from` argument and its corresponding interpretation. Note that the `from` value 2 is especially important when working with MP3 files that stores tags at the end of the file, so you directly issue a command to move the file pointer to a position 128 bytes from the end of the file.

Table 6.4 From and its position

From	Reference Position
0	From the beginning of the file
1	From the current position of
2	From the end of the file

Example 6.12 Program that tells and sets the position of the file pointer.

```
file = open("File1.txt", "rb")
print("Position of file pointer before reading is : ", file.tell())
print(file.read(10))
print("Position of file pointer after reading is : ", file.tell())
print("Setting 3 bytes from the current position of file pointer")
file.seek(3,1)
print(file.read())
file.close()
```

OUTPUT

```
Position of file pointer before reading is : 0
Hello All,
Position of file pointer after reading is : 10
Setting 3 bytes from the current position of file pointer
pe you are enjoying learning Python
```

PROGRAMMER'S ZONE

1. **Write a program that copies the first 10 bytes of a binary file into another.**

   ```
   with open("File1.txt", "rb") as file1:
       with open("file2.txt","wb") as file2:
           buf = file1.read(10)
           file2.write(buf)
   print("File Copied")
   ```

   OUTPUT

   ```
   File Copied
   ```

   > In Python, you don't need to import any library to read and write files. Just create a file object and call the open function to read/write to the file.

2. **Write a program that copies one Python script into another in such a way that all comment lines are skipped and not copied in the destination file.**

   ```
   with open("First.py", "rb") as file1:
       with open("Second.py","wb") as file2:
           while True:
               buf = file1.readline()
   ```

```
            if len(buf)!=0:
                if buf[0] == '#':
                    continue
                else:
                    file2.write(buf)
            else:
                break
print("File Copied")
```

OUTPUT

```
File Copied
```

3. Write a program that accepts filename as an input from the user. Open the file and count the number of times a character appears in the file.

```
filename = input("Enter the filename : ")
with open(filename) as file:
    text = file.read()
    letter = raw_input("Enter the character to be searched : ")
    count = 0
    for char in text:
        if char == letter:
            count += 1
print(letter, "appears ", count, " times in file")
```

OUTPUT

```
Enter the filename : File1.txt
Enter the character to be searched : a
a appears  7  times in file
```

4. Write a program that reads data from a file and calculates the percentage of vowels and consonants in the file.

```
filename = input("Enter the filename : ")
with open(filename) as file:
    text = file.read()
    count_vowels = 0
    count_consonants = 0
    for char in text:
        if char in "aeiou":
            count_vowels += 1
        else:
            count_consonants += 1
print("Number of vowels = ", count_vowels)
print("Number of consonants = ", count_consonants)
print("Total Length of File = ", len(text))
print("Percentatge of vowels in the file = ", ((count_vowels)*100)/len(text),"%")
print("Percentatge of consonants in the file = ", ((count_consonants)*100)/len(text), "%")
```

OUTPUT

```
Enter the filename : File1.txt
Number of vowels =   31
Number of consonants =   77
Total Length of File =   108
Percentatge of vowels in the file =   28 %
Percentatge of consonants in the file =   71 %
```

6.7 RENAMING AND DELETING FILES

The os module in Python has various methods that can be used to perform file-processing operations like renaming and deleting files. To use the methods defined in the os module, you should first import it in your program and then call any related functions.

The rename() method: The rename() method takes two arguments, the current filename and the new filename. Its syntax is:

    os.rename(old_file_name, new_file_name)

Example 6.13 — Program to rename file "FILE1.TXT" to "STUDENTS.TXT".

```
import os
os.rename("File1.txt", "Students.txt")
print("File Renamed")
```

> The *file* object provides functions to manipulate files

OUTPUT
```
File Renamed
```

You can check whether the above code renamed the right file by checking in the C:\Python27 directory. Now, there is no file named File1.txt but does have a file named Students.txt.

The remove() method: This method can be used to delete file(s). The method takes a filename (name of the file to be deleted) as an argument and deletes that file. Its syntax is:

os.remove(file_name)

Example 6.14 — Program to delete a file named File1.txt

```
import os
os.remove("File1.txt")
print("File Deleted")
```

OUTPUT
```
File Deleted
```
Check the contents of the directory. The file name File1.txt no longer exists.

PROGRAMMER'S ZONE

5. **Write a program that counts the number of tabs, spaces and new line characters in a file.**

```
filename = input("Enter the filename : ")
with open(filename) as file:
    text = file.read()
count_tab = 0
count_space = 0
count_nl = 0
for char in text:
    if char == '\t':
        count_tab += 1
    if char == ' ':
        count_space += 1
    if char == '\n':
        count_nl += 1
print("TABS = ", count_tab)
print("SPACES = ", count_space)
print("NEW LINES = ", count_nl)
```

OUTPUT
```
Enter the filename : File1.txt
TABS = 3
SPACES = 22
NEW LINES = 5
```

6. Write a program that generates a Quiz and uses Two Files- Questions.txt and Answers.Txt. The program opens Questions.txt and reads a question and displays the question with options on the screen. The program then opens the Answer.txt file and displays the correct answers.

    ```
    file1 = open("Questions.txt", "r")
    file2 = open("Answers.txt", "r")
    ques = file1.read()
    qlines= ques.split('\n')
    for lines in qlines:
        print(lines)
    ans = file2.read()
    alines= ans.split('\n')
    print("CORRCT ANSWERS")
    for lines in alines:
        print(lines)
    ```

7. Write a program that computes the total size of all the files in C:\Python27 folder.

    ```
    import os
    totalSize = 0
    for file in os.listdir("C:\Python27"):
        totalSize += os.path.getsize(os.path.join("C:\Python27",file))
    print("Total size of all the files in C:\\Python27 folder = ", totalSize)
    ```

    OUTPUT
    Total size of all the files in C:\Python27 folder = 799866

8. Write a program to check if a flash drive is connected to your computer.

    ```
    import os
    print("os.path.exists(\"G:\\") = ", os.path.exists("G:\\"))
    ```

    OUTPUT
    os.path.exists("G:\\") = True

9. Write a program that reads a file line by line. Each line read from the file is copied to another file with line numbers specified at the beginning of the line.

    ```
    file1 = open("file1.txt","r")
    file2 = open("File.txt","w")
    num = 1
    for line in file1:
        file2.write(str(num) + " : " + line)
        num = num + 1
    file1.close()
    file2.close()
    ```

10. Write a program that fetches data from a specified url and prints it on screen.

    ```
    import urllib.request
    x = urllib.request.urlopen('https://www.google.com/')
    print(x.read())
    ```
    Program 7.8 Write a program that fetches data from a specified url and writes it in a file.

    Hint: Use the urllib2 module that handles the url
    ```
    import urllib.request
    url = 'https://www.google.com/search?q=python'
    headers = {}
    headers['User-Agent'] = "Mozilla/5.0 (X11; Linux i686) AppleWebKit/537.17 (KHTML, like Gecko) Chrome/24.0.1312.27 Safari/537.17"
    Request = urllib.request.Request(url, headers = headers)
    Response = urllib.request.urlopen(Request)
    Data = Response.read()
    File = open('URL_File.txt','w')
    File.write(str(Data))
    File.close()
    ```

6.8 COMMA SEPARATED VALUES (CSV)

A CSV file is a plain-text file that contains data (including text and numbers) which can be easily exported to different applications. Though most often a comma is used to separate (or delimit) data, other characters like semicolons can also be used. As the name suggests, CSV files are saved with a .csv extension.

A CSV file has a very simple structure – data separated by commas. And this simplicity is its biggest strength. Data in a CSV file is human-readable and can be easily viewed with a text editor like Notepad or a spreadsheet program like Microsoft Excel, Google Sheets or LibreOffice.

Spreadsheet programs present the contents of a .CSV file as if it were formatted in rows and columns. While an xlsx file or any other spreadsheet file can have multiple sheets, CSV file can only have a single sheet. Moreover, unlike a spreadsheet file, CSV files do not store data in rows and columns. Despite these drawbacks, CSV files are popular because they can be easily created by website developers, easily imported to other applications and used to better organize large amounts of data.

Name	Class	State	Marks	Fees
Sahil	2018	Odisha	92	3.75
Bina Madan	2017	West Bengal	84	3.52
Jivham	2018	Karnataka	17	3.20
Krish	2019	Tamil Nadu	65	3.48

```
Sahil, 2018, Odisha, 92, 3.75

Bina Madan, 2017, West Bengal, 84, 3.52

Jivham, 2018, Karnataka, 17, 3.20

Krish, 2019, Tamil Nadu, 45, 3.48
```

Figure 6.2 Spreadsheet data represented in a CSV file

Figure 6.2 shows how a spreadsheet file is represented in a CSV file. Note that the fields of data in each row are delimited with a comma and individual rows are separated by a newline. Since the CSV file is a text file, it can be created and edited using any text editor.

6.8.1 Difference Between Excel vs. CSV

Excel	CSV
• It is a binary file.	• It is in plain-text format with a series of values separated by commas.
• An Excel file allows operations on the data.	• A CSV file is just a text file that only stores data. It does not allow formatting or other operations on data stored in it.
• Excel is a spreadsheet that saves files with extension .xlsx.	• CSV files are saved with extension .csv.
• Excel files cannot be opened or edited using text editors.	• CSV files can be opened or edited by text editors.
• It is very difficult to parse Excel data. The process of parsing is also very slow.	• CSV data can be parsed at a relatively faster speed.
• Excel files consume more memory while importing data.	• CSV files can be processed much faster and they consume less memory.
• Reading large files and manipulating Excel data is simpler in Excel for the end-user (for example, selecting individual cells for import, convert dates and time automatically, reading formulas and their results, filters, sorting, etc).	• Reading large files is slower. Moreover, CSV file does not permit automatically formatting data in the desired format.
• Besides, data, Excel files can store charts and graphs	• CSV cannot store charts or graphs
• Excel file can be opened with Microsoft Excel only.	• CSV can be opened with any text editor or even with a spreadsheet software like MS Excel.

6.9 WORKING WITH CSV FILES

Before reading data from or writing data to a csv file, we must import the csv module. This module has some important functions that help users to handle csv files in their programs.

6.9.1 Reading CSV Files with CSV

A CSV file is read using the reader object. The reader accepts the csv filename as input and returns a reader object.

The CSV file is opened as a text file with Python's built-in `open()` function, which returns a file object. The file object is then passed to the reader, for reading data from the file.

Example 6.15

```
import csv
with open('File1.txt') as csv_file:
    file = csv.reader(csv_file)
    line_count = 0
    for row in file:
        print(row)
        line_count += 1
print(f'Processed {line_count} lines.')
```

OUTPUT

```
['Welcome to the world of ....']
['Programming in Python !!!!']
['HAPPY PROGRAMMING']
Processed 4 lines.
```

6.9.2 Optional Python CSV Reader Parameters

Some additional parameters in the CSV reader object are:

- *delimiter* It specifies the character used to separate each field. By default, comma (',') is used.
- *quotechar* It specifies the character that will be used to surround fields containing the delimiter character. By default, a double quote (' " ') is used.
- *escapechar* It specifies the character used to escape the delimiter character if quotes are not used.

For example, if joining_year is written as Nov,2011 then there are three different ways to handle this situation.

- Use a different delimiter by using the delimiter option.
- Wrap the data in quotes because the chosen delimiter is ignored in quoted strings. The character to be used for quoting is specified with the `quotechar` parameter. You must use a `quotechar` that does not appear in the data.
- Escape the delimiter characters in the data using the `escapechar` parameter.

6.9.3 Reading CSV Files into a Dictionary with CSV

The CSV DictReader method is used to read a dictionary.

Example 6.16

```
import csv
with open('emp.txt', mode='r') as csv_file:
    file = csv.DictReader(csv_file)
    line_count = 0
    for row in file:
        print(f'{row["name"]} works in the {row["department"]} department, and was born in {row["joining_year"]}.')
        line_count += 1
    print(f'Processed {line_count} lines.')
```

OUTPUT

```
Kiyan works in the Accounting department, and was born in 2011.
Manan works in the HR department, and was born in 2012.
Karishma works in the IT department, and was born in 2013.
Processed 3 lines.
```

6.9.4 Writing CSV Files with CSV

Data can be written to a CSV file using a writer object and the `.writerow()` method. The writer accepts a csv filename as input and returns a writer object. The writer object converts the user's data into a delimited string. This string can later be used to write into CSV files using `writerow()` function.

Example 6.17

```python
import csv
with open('emp1.csv', mode='w') as employee_file:
    file = csv.writer(employee_file)
    file.writerow('The file contains details about employees')
    file.writerow(['Kiyan','Accounting',2011])
    file.writerow(['Manan','HR',2012])
    file.writerow(['Karishma','IT',2013])
print("DATA WRITTEN SUCCESSFULLY........")
```

OUTPUT

```
DATA WRITTEN SUCCESSFULLY........
```

Like the reader object, the writer object also has `quotechar` as an optional parameter that tells the writer which character is used to quote fields when writing to the file. However, whether to use quoting or not is determined by quoting the optional parameter. That is,

- If quoting is set to csv.QUOTE_MINIMAL, then `.writerow()` will quote fields only if they contain the delimiter or the quotechar. This is the default case.
- If quoting is set to csv.QUOTE_ALL, then `.writerow()` will quote all fields.
- If quoting is set to csv.QUOTE_NONNUMERIC, then `.writerow()` will quote all fields containing textual data. It will also convert all numeric fields to the float data type.
- If quoting is set to csv.QUOTE_NONE, then `.writerow()` will escape delimiters instead of quoting them. So another optional parameter escapechar must be specified in this case.

Example 6.18

```python
import csv
with open('emp1.csv', mode='w') as employee_file:
    file = csv.writer(employee_file)
    file.writerow('The file contains details about employees')
    file.writerow(['Kiyan','Accounting',2011])
    file.writerow(['Manan','HR',2012])
    file.writerow(['Karishma','IT',2013])
print("DATA WRITTEN SUCCESSFULLY........")
```

OUTPUT

```
DATA WRITTEN SUCCESSFULLY........
```

6.9.5 Writing CSV File from a Dictionary with CSV

We can even write a dictionary to a csv file using the DictWriter method as shown below. Note that here, the fieldnames parameter is required because this parameter uses the keys in fieldnames to write out the first row as column names. The DictWriter accepts a csv filename and fieldnames as parameters.

The `writeheader()` method can be used to write the first row of csv file using the pre-specified fieldnames. Subsequently, the `writerows()` method is used to write all the rows. In each row, only the values are written. Keys are not written in every row.

Example 6.19

```
import csv
with open('employee_file2.csv', mode='w') as csv_file:
    fieldnames = ['emp_name', 'dept', 'joining_year']
    writer = csv.DictWriter(csv_file, fieldnames=fieldnames)
    writer.writerow({'emp_name': 'Veronica', 'dept': 'Accounting', 'joining_year': 2009})
    writer.writerow({'emp_name': 'Natasha', 'dept': 'IT', 'joining_year': 2015})
print("DATA WRITTEN SUCCESSFULLY......")
```

OUTPUT
```
DATA WRITTEN SUCCESSFULLY......
```

6.10 PICKLE MODULE

Python pickle module is used for serializing and de-serializing Python objects. The process of converting any kind of Python object (for example, Booleans, Integers, Floats, Complex numbers, Strings, Tuples, Lists, Sets and dictionary) into byte streams (in the form of 0s and 1s) is called pickling or serialization or flattening or marshalling. Correspondingly, the process of converting byte stream (generated through pickling) back into Python objects is known as unpickling or de-serialization.

Pickling and unpickling are very important processes as they allow users to easily transfer data from one server/system to another and then store it in a file or database.

However, one must always make sure that data received from an untrusted source is not unpickled as such data may pose a serious threat to security. The pickle module has no way of knowing or raising alarm while pickling malicious data.

To pickle or unpickle a data object in Python, we must first import the pickle module.

```
import pickle
L = ['a', 'b', 'c', 'd']
with open('datafile.txt', 'wb') as file:
    pickle.dump(L, file)
print("Data Written Successfully .......")
```

In the above program, list L contains four elements ('a', 'b', 'c', 'd'). A binary file named "datafile.txt" is created in write mode in the current working directory. The list is pickled or serialized using the `dump()` method of pickle module and written to the file.

The `pickle.dump()` method takes three arguments. The first argument is the object that has to be serialized. The second argument is the file object that is obtained while opening the binary file in write mode. The third argument is the key-value argument which defines the protocol. There are two type of protocols – **pickle.HIGHEST_PROTOCOL** and **pickle.DEFAULT_PROTOCOL**.

The program given below unpickles the contents of datafile.txt and stores it in a list object that is then printed on the screen.

Example 6.20

```
import pickle
file = open ("datafile.txt", "rb")
L = pickle.load(file)
print(L)
```

OUTPUT
```
['a', 'b', 'c', 'd']
```

Example 6.21 Write a program to pickle a dictionary object.

```
import pickle
stud = {'RollNo': 1, 'Name':"Zack", 'Marks': 65, 'Course':"IT"}
file = open("Student.pickle","wb")
pickle.dump(stud, file)
file.close()
print("DATA WRITTEN SUCCESSFULLY .....")
file = open("Student.pickle", 'rb')
stud_details = pickle.load(file)
print(stud_details)
```

OUTPUT
```
DATA WRITTEN SUCCESSFULLY .....
{'RollNo': 1, 'Name': 'Zack', 'Marks': 65, 'Course': 'IT'}
```

6.10.1 Pickle Exceptions

While executing programs, we may get some exceptions (in simple terms, error though technically exception is different from error). Some of them are discussed below.

- Pickle.PicklingError is raised when the pickle object does not support pickling.
- Pickle.UnpicklingError if the file contains bad or corrupted data.
- EOFError if end of file is detected.

6.10.2 Advantages of Picking

- Can be used to save large amount of complicated data in the hard disk for future use
- Can be used to securely share large amount of data over a computer network
- Easy to use and can be done in just a few lines of code.
- The pickled file is not human-readable until it is unpickled. In this way, a pickled file provides some data security.

6.10.3 Disadvantages of Pickling

- Languages other than Python may not able to unpickle pickled files and will thus be unusable for them.
- There is always a security threat when unpickling data, from malicious or untrusted sources. Moreover, an attacker can access and modify the stored pickle files from caches, file systems, or databases.

> In Python, even functions and classes can be serialized.

Key Terms

Delimiter: One or more characters used to specify the boundary between different parts of text.

Directory: Collection of files, also called a folder. A directory can have other files and directories within it.

File: A stream of information that is usually stored on a permanent storage media such as hard drive, floppy disk, CD-ROM, etc.

File handle: An object that allows you to manipulate/read/write/close the file.

Non-volatile memory: Memory that can store data even when the power supply to the computer system is switched off. Hard drives, flash drives, and rewritable compact disks (CD-RW) are all examples of non-volatile memory.

File path: A sequence of directory names that specifies the exact location of a file.

Text file: A file having printable characters organized into lines separated by newline characters.

Volatile memory: Memory that loses data as soon as the computer system is switched off. RAM is an example of volatile memory.

Chapter Highlights

- If you want to use the data in future, then you need to store it on a permanent or non-volatile storage media like the hard disk, USB drive, DVD, etc.

- At the top of the tree structure of file storage is one (or more) root nodes. Under the root node, there are other files and folders (or directories) and each folder can, in turn, contain other files and folders.
- Every file is identified by its path that begins from the root node or the root folder.
- A file path can be either *relative* or *absolute*. While an absolute path always contains the root and the complete directory list to specify the exact location the file, relative path on the other hand, needs to be combined with another path in order to access a file.
- Each file ends with a special character called the end-of-file (EOF) marker.
- A binary file is a file which may contain any type of data encoded in binary form for computer storage and processing purposes.
- open() function creates a file object, which will be used to invoke methods associated with it.
- The close() method is used to close the file object. Once a file object is closed, you cannot further read from or write into the file associated with the file object.
- Python has a garbage collector to clean up unreferenced objects. However, it is still our responsibility to close the file and release the resources consumed by it.
- To append a file, you must open it using 'a' or 'ab' mode depending on whether it is a text file or a binary file.
- The read() method is used to read a string from an already opened file.
- The file pointer specifies a location from where the current read or write operation is initiated.
- The tell() method tells the current position within the file at which the next read or write operation will occur. It is specified as the number of bytes from the beginning of the file.
- The getcwd() method is used to display the current working directory.

Review Questions

1. What are files? Why do we need them?
2. Explain the significance of root node.
3. Differentiate between absolute and relative file path.
4. Differentiate between a file and folder.
5. Differentiate between text and binary files.
6. Explain the utility of open() function.
7. What are different access modes in which you can open a file?
8. With the help of an example, explain any three attributes of file object.
9. Is it mandatory to call the close() method after using the file?
10. Explain the syntax of read() method.
11. Give the significance of with keyword.
12. Write a short note on different methods to read data from a file.
13. With the help of suitable examples, explain the different ways in which you can write data in a file.
14. Discuss some directory methods present in the os module.
15. In the file, identify the delimiter and the line terminator characters.

Programming Exercises

1. Write a program that reads text from a file and writes it in another file but in the reverse order.
   Hint: Make the first line in the original file as the last line in the copied file.
2. Write a program that reads a file and prints only those lines that have the word 'print'.
3. Write a program that has several lines. Each line begins with a line number. Now read this file line by line and copy the line into another file but do not copy the numbers.
4. Write a program to compare two files.
5. Write a program to copy one file into another. Copy one character at a time.
6. Write a program to read and write the details of a student in a file.
7. Write a program to count the number of records stored in file 'employee'.
8. Write a program to edit a record stored in employee.txt file.
9. Write a program to read a file that contains lower case characters. Then write these characters into another file with all lower case characters converted into upper case.
10. Write a program to merge two files into a third file.
11. Write a program that reads a file and copies its contents to another file. While copying, replace all full stops with commas.

12. Write a program that exchanges the contents of two files.
13. Write a program that writes data to a file in such a way that each character after a full stop is capitalized and all numbers are written in brackets.
14. Write a program that takes a list of data values from the user and serializes it in a file. Also write the code to load this data and display it on the screen.
15. Write a program to create a dictionary that stores data of employee. Demonstrate the process of loading and dumping this data.

Fill in the Blanks

1. _____ function is used to access files.
2. Fill in the blanks to read a file using the "with" keyword.
   ```
   _____open("File.txt")_____file:
   data = file.read()
   ```
3. Fill in the blanks to open a file called `abc.bin` in binary read mode.
   ```
   File = open(_____,_____)
   ```
4. How many characters would be printed by this code (one character is one byte)?
   ```
   file=open("fILE.txt","r")
   for i in range(100):
   print(file.read(10))
   file.close()
   ```
5. Fill in the blanks to open a file, read its content and print its length.
   ```
   file=_____("File.txt","r")
   text = file._____()
   print (_____(text))
   file.close()
   ```
6. Fill in the blanks to open a file for reading using the `with` statement.
   ```
   _____open("File.txt")_____file:
   print(file._____())
   ```
7. Most file systems that are used today stores files in a _____ structure.
8. Every file is identified by its path that begins from the _____.
9. In Windows, _____ is the root folder.
10. A relative path is specified relative to the program's _____.
11. Each file ends with a special character called the _____.
12. `open()` function returns a _____.
13. The _____ method frees up any system resources like file descriptors, file locks, etc.
14. Any attempt to use the file object will result in a _____.
15. The write() method returns _____.
16. If you try to open a file for reading that does not exist, then you will get _____.
17. The `readline()` method returns _____ when the end of the file has been reached.
18. If you do not want the new file to be created in the current working directory, then you must specify the _____.
19. The _____ specifies a location from where the current read or write operation is initiated.
20. _____ method tells the current position within the file at which the next read or write operation will occur.
21. When you open a file for reading, the file pointer is positioned at _____.
22. If you try to change to a directory that does not exist _____ will be generated.
23. If you try to delete a non-empty directory, then you will get _____.
24. To remove a non-empty directory, use the _____ method defined inside the _____ module.
25. The method _____ is used to create more than one folder.
26. _____ method is used to create strings for filenames.
27. The _____ method uses the string value passed to it to form an absolute path.

State True or False

1. When a program is being executed, its data is stored in ROM.
2. RAM is an example of non-volatile memory.
3. You can have only one root in all the file systems.
4. Delimiters may vary from one operating system to another.
5. Folder names and file names are case insensitive in Windows
6. Absolute path always contains the root.
7. The contents of a binary file are human readable.
8. Text files include files like word processing documents, PDFs, images, spreadsheets, videos, zip files and other executable programs
9. Binary files are more efficient than text files.
10. *.py files are binary files
11. When you open a file for appending that does not exist, then a new file is created.
12. You can open any number of files without any sort of restriction.
13. The `read()` method starts reading from the beginning of the file.
14. If *count* is missing or has a negative value in the `read()` method then, no contents are read from the file.
15. The `readline()` method to read all the lines in the file
16. `tell()` moves the file pointer to a new location.
17. Before removing a directory, it should be absolutely empty.
18. `os.path.abs()` method accepts a file path as an argument and returns True if the path is an absolute path and False otherwise.
19. The `cwd()` method is used to display the current working directory.

Multiple Choice Questions

1. Identify the right way to close a file.
   a. `File.close()` b. `close(File)` c. `close("File")` d. `File.closed`
2. If the `File.txt` has `10` lines written in it, what will be the result?
   `len(open("File.txt").readlines())`
   a. 1 b. 0 c. 10 d. 2
3. If a file opened in `'w'` mode does not exist, then _____.
   a. Nothing will happen   b. a file will be created
   c. data will be written to a file that has name similar to the specified name d. an error will be generated
4. Identify the right way to write "`Welcome to Python`" in a file?
   a. `write(file,"Welcome to Python")`   b. `write("Welcome to Python",file)`
   c. `file.write("Welcome to Python")`   d. `"Welcome to Python".write(file)`
5. What will happen when a file is opened in write mode and then immediately closed?
   a. File contents are deleted.   b. Nothing happens.
   c. A blank line is written to the file. d. An error occurs.
6. A file is stored in _____ memory.
   a. Primary   b. Secondary   c. Cache   d. Volatile
7. _____ is an example of volatile memory.
   a. RAM   b. DVD   c. Hard Disk   d. Pen Drive
8. In the path `C:\Students\Undergraduate\BTech_CS.docx`, _____ is the sub-folder
   a. `C:`   b. `Students`   c. `BTech_CS`   d. `Undergraduate`
9. Identify the delimiter in the Solaris file system
   a. `/`   b. `\`   c. `:`   d. `|`
10. The default access mode is _____.
    a. `r`   b. `w`   c. `rb`   d. `wb`
11. By default, a new file is created in which directory?
    a. Root directory   b. Current working directory   c. Python directory   d. D drive
12. Which method is used to read a single line from the file?
    a. `read()`   b. `readline()`   c. `readlines()`   d. `reads()`
13. Which method is used to display entire contents of the file?
    a. `read()`   b. `readlines()`   c. `list()`   d. All of these.

14. In the `seek()` method, what will be the value of from if you want to specify number of bytes from the current location of the file pointer?
    a. 0   b. 1   c. 2   d. 3
15. Which method returns a string that includes everything specified in the path?
    a. `os.path.dirname(path)`   b. `os.path.basename(path)`
    c. `os.path.relpath()`   d. `os.path.abs()`

Fill in the Blanks and Identify the Usage of the Lines

1. `File = open("File.txt", "r")`
   The above statement _____ a text file.
2. `file.read()`
   The above statement _____ a text file.
3. `print(file.readline())`
   The above statement _____ a text file.
4. `print(file.readlines())`
   The above statement _____ a text file.
5. `file.write("Welcome")`
   The above statement _____ a text file.
6. `file = open("File.txt", "w")`
   The above statement _____ a text file.
7. `file.writelines(lines)`
   The above statement _____ a text file.
8. `file = open("File.txt", "a")`
   The above statement _____ a text file.
9. `file.close()`
   The above statement _____ a text file.
10. `file.read(10)`
    The above statement _____ a text file.
11. `file.seek(file.tell()-10)`
    The above statement _____ a text file.
12. `file = open("File.txt", "r+b")`
    The above statement _____
13. `file.seek(-10,2)`
    The above statement _____
14. `file.seek(20,1)`
    The above statement _____
15. `file.seek(30,0)`
    The above statement _____

Give the Output

1.  ```
    import os
    Files = ['BTech.txt', 'BCA.csv', 'BSc.docx']
    for file in Files:
        print(os.path.join('C:\\Users\\Students', file))
    ```
2.  ```
    with open("File.txt", "w") as file:
        file.write("Greetings to All !!! \n Welcome to the world of programming\n")
        with open("File.txt") as file:
    print(file.read())
    ```
3.  ```
    file=open("File.txt","r")
    text = file.read())
    print(len(text))
    file.close()
    ```
4.  ```
    str ="Welcome to Python Programming"
    file = open("File.txt","w")
    n = file.write(str)
    print(n)
    file.close()
    ```
5. What will be written in the file?
    ```
    file = open("File5.txt","w")
    file.write("Orient" + "Black" + "Swan")
    file.write(str(len("Orient Black Swan")))
    file.write("Clue".replace('C', 'B'))
    file.write("HELLO".lower())
    print("DATA WRITTEN.....")
    ```
6.  ```
    import csv
    fields = ['Name', 'Branch', 'Year', 'CGPA']
    rows = [ ['Nikhil', 'COE', '2', '9.0'],
             ['Sanchit', 'COE', '2', '9.1'],
             ['Aditya', 'IT', '2', '9.3'],
             ['Sagar', 'SE', '1', '9.5'],
             ['Prateek', 'MCE', '3', '7.8'],
             ['Sahil', 'EP', '2', '9.1']]
    ```
    ```

```python
    filename = "students.csv"
    # writing to csv file
    with open(filename, 'w') as csvfile:
        # creating a csv writer object
        csvwriter = csv.writer(csvfile)

        # writing the fields
        csvwriter.writerow(fields)

        # writing the data rows
        csvwriter.writerows(rows)
```

7.
```python
import csv
# my data rows as dictionary objects
mydict =[{'branch': 'COE', 'cgpa': '9.0', 'name': 'Nikhil', 'year': '2'},
         {'branch': 'COE', 'cgpa': '9.1', 'name': 'Sanchit', 'year': '2'},
         {'branch': 'IT', 'cgpa': '9.3', 'name': 'Aditya', 'year': '2'},
         {'branch': 'SE', 'cgpa': '9.5', 'name': 'Sagar', 'year': '1'},
         {'branch': 'MCE', 'cgpa': '7.8', 'name': 'Prateek', 'year': '3'},
         {'branch': 'EP', 'cgpa': '9.1', 'name': 'Sahil', 'year': '2'}]
# field names
fields = ['name', 'branch', 'year', 'cgpa']
# name of csv file
filename = "university_records.csv"
# writing to csv file
with open(filename, 'w') as csvfile:
    # creating a csv dict writer object
    writer = csv.DictWriter(csvfile, fieldnames = fields)
        # writing headers (field names)
    writer.writeheader()
        # writing data rows
    writer.writerows(mydict)
print("Data Written...")
```

8.
```python
import csv
with open("students.csv", 'r') as file:
    csv_file = csv.DictReader(file)
    for row in csv_file:
        print(dict(row))
```

9.
```python
import pickle
example_dict = {1:"6",2:"2",3:"f"}
pickle_out = open("dict.pickle","wb")
pickle.dump(example_dict, pickle_out)
pickle_out.close()
print("PICKLED....")
```

10.
```python
pickle_in = open("dict.pickle","rb")
example_dict = pickle.load(pickle_in)
print(example_dict)
print(example_dict[3])
```

11.
```python
import pickle
pickle_off = open ("datafile.txt", "rb")
emp = pickle.load(pickle_off)
print(emp)
```

Find the Error

1.
```python
with open("File.txt") as file
    file.write("Hello World")
with open(File.txt) as f:
data = f.read()
print data
```

2.
```python
filename = "File.txt"
file = open("filename", "r")
for line in file:
    print line,
```

3.
```python
filename = "File.txt"
file = open(filename, "r")
while True:
        print file.readline()
```

4.
```python
file = open("File.txt", "a")
write("Hello World again")
```

Answers

Fill in the Blanks

1. open()
2. with, as
3. "abc.bin", "rb"
4. 10
5. open, read, len
6. with, as, read
7. tree (or *hierarchical*)
8. root node or the root folder.
9. C:\ (also known as C drive)
10. Relative
11. end-of-file (EOF) marker
12. file object
13. close()
14. ValueError
15. None
16. IOError
17. an empty string
18. path
19. file pointer
20. tell()
21. remove()
22. WindowsError
23. OSError
24. rmtree(), shutil
25. mkdirs()
26. os.path.join()
27. os.path.abspath()

State True or False

1. False
2. False
3. False
4. True
5. False
6. True
7. False
8. False
9. True
10. False
11. True
12. False
13. True
14. False
15. False
16. False
17. True
18. False
19. False

Multiple Choice Questions

1. a
2. 10
3. b
4. (c)
5. (a)
6. b
7. a
8. d
9. a
10. a
11. b
12. b
13. d
14. b
15. a

Fill in the Blanks and Identify the Usage of the Lines

1. opens
2. reads
3. reads one line at a time from
4. reads a list of lines from
5. Writes to
6. opens for writing in
7. writes lines to
8. opens for appending
9. closes
10. reads first 10 bytes from
11. sets the file pointer 10 bytes to the left of the current position
12. opens a text file for reading as well as writing in binary mode
13. Moves the cursor to 10 bytes before the end of the file
14. moves the cursor to 20 bytes after the current position of the file pointer
15. moves the cursor to 30 bytes after the beginning of the file

Give the Output

1. C:\Users\Students\BTech.txt
   C:\Users\Students\BCA.csv
   C:\Users\Students\BSc.docx
2. Greetings to All !!!
   Welcome to the world of programming
3. 88
4. 29
5. DATA WRITTEN....
6. Data Written...
7. Data Written...
8. {'Name': 'Nikhil', 'Branch': 'COE', 'Year': '2', 'CGPA': '9.0'}
   {'Name': 'Sanchit', 'Branch': 'COE', 'Year': '2', 'CGPA': '9.1'}
   {'Name': 'Aditya', 'Branch': 'IT', 'Year': '2', 'CGPA': '9.3'}
   {'Name': 'Sagar', 'Branch': 'SE', 'Year': '1', 'CGPA': '9.5'}
   {'Name': 'Prateek', 'Branch': 'MCE', 'Year': '3', 'CGPA': '7.8'}
   {'Name': 'Sahil', 'Branch': 'EP', 'Year': '2', 'CGPA': '9.1'}
9. PICKLED....
10. {1: '6', 2: '2', 3: 'f'}
    f
11. ['a', 'b', 'c', 'd']

Find the Error

1. First line, File.txt should be opened in write mode and there should be a colon as the last character
   In the with block, there is no indentation
2. In second line filename should not be enclosed in double quotes
3. The while loop will never end, so put a break statement as
   if len(file.read())==0:
       break
4. It should be file.write(….)
   …

Rescursive Functions and Data Structures

7

Chapter Objectives

We have already studied in Chapter 5 about defining and calling user-defined functions. In addition to using Python built-in functions and importing some popular some important modules, we had also learnt how a user can create his own library (or module) in Python and use its functionality wherever required. In this chapter, we shall discuss some advanced topics that will help us to write programs that are more effective and use optimal computer resources. These topics include:

- Recursive functions
- Data structures like stacks and queues
- Understand the basic concept of calculating the efficiency of a program in terms of the number of operations it performs

7.1 RECURSIVE FUNCTIONS

A recursive function is defined as a function that calls itself to solve a smaller version of its task until a final call is made which does not require a call to itself. *Every recursive solution has two major cases, they are*

- **Base case**, in which the problem is simple enough to be solved directly without making any further calls to the same function
- **Recursive case,** in which first the problem at hand is divided into simpler sub-parts. Second, the function calls itself but with sub-parts of the problem obtained in the first step. Third, the result is obtained by combining the solutions of the simpler sub-parts.

Thus, we see that recursion utilizes the divide-and-conquer technique of problem solving. ***Divide-and-conquer technique means solving a problem by dividing it into two or more smaller parts. Each of these smaller parts is recursively solved, and the solutions are combined to produce a solution for the original problem.*** Therefore, recursion is defining a large and complex problem in terms of smaller and more easily solvable problems. In recursive function, a complicated problem is defined in terms of simpler problems and the simplest problem is given explicitly.

To understand recursive functions, let us take an example of calculating the factorial of a number. To calculate n!, what we have to do is multiply the number with the factorial of a number that is 1 less than the given number. In other words, n! = n × (n-1)!

Let us say we need to find the value of 5!...
5! = 5 × 4 × 3 × 2 × 1
   = 120

This can be written as
5! = 5 × 4!, where
4! = 4 × 3!
Therefore,
5! = 5 × 4 × 3!
Similarly, we can also write,
5! = 5 × 4 × 3 × 2!

> Every recursive function must have at least one base case. Otherwise, the recursive function will generate an infinite sequence of calls, thereby resulting in an error condition known as an infinite stack.

Expanding further,
5! = 5 × 4 × 3 × 2 × 1!
We know, 1! = 1

Therefore, the series of problems and solutions can be given as shown in Fig. 7.1.

PROBLEM		SOLUTION
5!		5 × 4 × 3 × 2 × 1!
= 5 × 4!	=	5 × 4 × 3 × 2 × 1
= 5 × 4 × 3!	=	5 × 4 × 3 × 2
= 5 × 4 × 3 × 2!	=	5 × 4 × 6
= 5 × 4 × 3 × 2 × 1!	=	5 × 24
	=	120

Figure 7.1 Recursive factorial function

Now if you look at the problem carefully, you can see that we can write a recursive function to calculate the factorial of a number. Note that we have said every recursive function must have a base case and a recursive case. For the factorial function,

- **Base case** is when n=1, because if n = 1, the result is known to be 1 as 1! = 1.
- **Recursive case** of the factorial function will call itself but with a smaller value of n, this case can be given as

$$factorial(n) = n \times factorial(n-1)$$

Example 7.1 Program to calculate the factorial of a number recursively.

```
def fact(n):
    if(n==1 or n==0):
        return 1
    else:
        return n*fact(n-1)
n = int(input("Enter the value of n : "))
print("The factorial of",n,"is",fact(n))
```

OUTPUT
```
Enter the value of n: 6
The factorial of 6 is 720
```

From the above example, let us analyze the basic steps of a recursive program.

Step 1: Specify the base case which will stop the function from making a call to itself.

Step 2: Check to see whether the current value being processed matches with the value of the base case. If yes, process and return the value.

Step 3: Divide the problem into a smaller or simpler sub-problems.

Step 4: Call the function on the sub-problem.

Step 5: Combine the results of the sub-problems.

Step 6: Return the result of the entire problem.

> The base case of a recursive function acts as the terminating condition. So, in the absence of an explicitly defined base case, a recursive function would call itself indefinitely.

7.1.1 Greatest Common Divisor

The greatest common divisor of two numbers (integers) is the largest integer that divides both the numbers. We can find the GCD of two numbers recursively by using the Euclid's algorithm that states:

$$\text{GCD}(a, b) = \begin{cases} b, \text{ if b divides a} \\ \text{GCD}(b, a \bmod b) \text{ otherwise} \end{cases}$$

GCD can be implemented as a recursive function because if b does not divide a, then we call the same function (GCD) with another set of parameters that are smaller and simpler than the original ones. (Here we assume that a > b. However, if a < b then interchange a and b in the formula given above).

Working

```
Assume a = 62 and b = 8
GCD( 62, 8)
    rem = 62 % 8 = 6
    GCD(8, 6)
        rem = 8 % 6 = 2
        GCD(6, 2)
            rem = 6 % 2 = 0
        Return 2
    Return 2
Return 2
```

Example 7.2 Write a program to calculate GCD using recursive functions.

```
def GCD(x,y):
    rem = x%y
    if(rem==0):
        return y
    else:
        return GCD(y,rem)

n = int(input("Enter the first number : "))
m = int(input("Enter the second number : "))
print("The GCD of numbers is", GCD(n,m))
```

OUTPUT
```
Enter the first number :  50
Enter the second number :  5
The GCD of numbers is 5
```

7.1.2 Finding Exponents

We can find the exponent of a number using recursion. To find x^y, the base case would be when y = 0, as we know that any number raised to the power 0 is 1. Therefore, the general formula to find x^y can be given as

$$\text{EXP}(x, y) = \begin{cases} 1, \text{if } y == 0 \\ x * \text{EXP}(x^{y-1}) \text{ otherwise} \end{cases}$$

> Recursive functions can become infinite if you don't specify the base case.

Working

```
exp_rec(2, 4) = 2 * exp_rec( 2, 3)
    exp_rec(2, 3) =  2 * exp_rec( 2, 2)
        exp_rec(2, 2) - 2 * exp_rec( 2, 1)
            exp_rec(2, 1)  = 2 * exp_rec( 2, 0)
                exp_rec( 2, 0) = 1
            exp_rec( 2, 1) = 2 * 1 = 2
        exp_rec( 2, 2) = 2 * 2 = 4
    exp_rec( 2, 3) = 2 * 4 = 8
exp_rec( 2, 4) = 2 * 8 = 16
```

Example 7.3 Write a program to calculate exp(x,y) using recursive functions.

```
def exp_rec(x,y):
    if(y==0):
        return 1
    else:
        return (x*exp_rec(x,y-1))

n = int(input("Enter the first number : "))
m = int(input("Enter the second number : "))
print("Result = ", exp_rec(n,m))
```

OUTPUT

```
Enter the first number : 5
Enter the second number : 3
Result = 125
```

7.1.3 The Fibonacci Series

The Fibonacci series can be given as:
0   1   1   2   3   5   8   13   21   34   55......

That is, the third term of the series is the sum of the first and second terms. On similar grounds, the fourth term is the sum of the second and third terms, and so on. Now we will design a recursive solution to find the nth term of the Fibonacci series. The general formula to do so can be given as

$$FIB(n) = \begin{cases} 1, \text{ if } n <= 2 \\ FIB(n-1) + FIB(n-2), \text{ otherwise} \end{cases}$$

As per the formula, FIB(1) = 1 and FIB(2) = 1. So we have two base cases. This is necessary because every problem is divided into two smaller problems (refer Fig. 7.2).

Working

If n = 7.

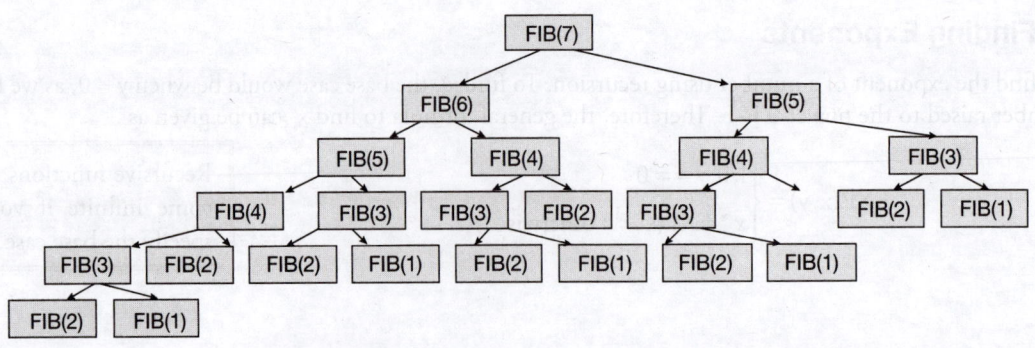

Figure 7.2 Recursion structure of FIB function

Example 7.4 Write a program to print the Fibonacci series using recursion.

```
def fibonacci(n):
    if(n<2):
        return 1
    return (fibonacci(n-1)+fibonacci(n-2))

n = int(input("Enter the number of terms : "))
for i in range(n):
    print("Fibonacci(",i,") = ",fibonacci(i))
```

OUTPUT
```
Enter the number of terms : 5
Fibonacci( 0 ) =  1
Fibonacci( 1 ) =  1
Fibonacci( 2 ) =  2
Fibonacci( 3 ) =  3
Fibonacci( 4 ) =  5
```

> Recursion can also be indirect. That is, one function can call a second function which in turn calls the first, which again calls the second, and so on. This can occur with any number of functions.

7.1.4 Recursion vs. Iteration

Recursion is more of a top-down approach to problem-solving in which the original problem is divided into smaller sub-problems. On the contrary, iteration follows a bottom-up approach that begins with what is known and then constructing the solution step-by-step.

Recursion is an excellent way of solving complex problems, especially when the problem can be defined in recursive terms. For such problems a recursive code can be written and modified in a much simpler and clearer manner.

However, recursive solutions are not always the best solutions. In some cases, recursive programs may require substantial amount of run-time overhead. Therefore, when implementing a recursive solution, there is a trade-off involved between the time spent in constructing and maintaining the program and the cost incurred in running-time and memory space required for the execution of the program.

Whenever a recursive function is called, some amount of overhead in the form of a run-time stack is involved. Before jumping to the function with a smaller parameter, the original parameters, the local variables and the return address of the calling function are all stored on the system stack. Therefore while using recursion, a lot of time is needed to first push all the information on the stack when function is called and then time is again involved in retrieving the information stored on the stack once the control passes back to the calling function.

To conclude, one must use recursion only to find solution to a problem for which no obvious iterative solution is known. To summarize the concept, let us briefly discuss the pros and cons of recursion.

Pros: The benefits of using a recursive program are:

- Recursive solutions often tend to be shorter and simpler than non-recursive ones.
- The code is clearer and easier to use.
- Recursion can be used to represent the original formula to solve a problem.
- It follows a divide-and-conquer technique to solve problems.
- In some (limited) instances, recursion may be more efficient.

> Recursive functions make the code look clean and elegant.

Limitations: The drawbacks of using a recursive program are:

- For some programmers and readers, recursion is a difficult concept.
- Recursion is implemented using system stack. If the stack space on the system is limited, recursion to a deeper level will be difficult to implement.
- Aborting a recursive process in midstream is slow and sometimes nasty.
- Using a recursive function takes more memory and time to execute as compared to its non-recursive counterpart.
- It is difficult to find bugs, particularly when using global variables.

Conclusion: The advantages of recursion pay off for the extra overhead involved in terms of time and space required.

7.2 ALGORITHM EFFICIENCY

If a function is linear (without any loops or recursions), the efficiency of that algorithm or the running time of that algorithm can be given as the number of instructions it contains. However, if an algorithm contains loops, then the efficiency of that algorithm may vary depending on the number of loops and the running time of each loop in the algorithm.

Let us consider different cases in which loops determine the efficiency of an algorithm.

Linear Loops: To calculate the efficiency of an algorithm that has a single loop, we need to first determine the number of times the statements in the loop will be executed. This is because the number of iterations is directly proportional to the loop factor. Greater the loop factor, more is the number of iterations. For example, consider the loop given below:

```
for i in range(100):
    statement block
```

Here, 100 is the loop factor. We have already said that efficiency is directly proportional to the number of iterations. Hence, the general formula in the case of linear loops may be given as

```
f(n) = n
```

However, calculating efficiency is not as simple as is shown in the above example. Consider the loop given below:

```
for i in range(0,100,2):
    statement block
```

Here, the number of iterations is half the number of the loop factor. So, here the efficiency can be given as

```
f(n) = n/2
```

Logarithmic Loops: We have seen that in linear loops, with every iteration the loop-controlling variable is either incremented or decremented. However, in logarithmic loops, the loop-controlling variable is either multiplied or divided during each iteration of the loop. For example, look at the loops given below:

```
i = 1
while(i<1000):
    print(i);
    i = i*2;
```

```
i = 1000
while(i>1):
    print(i);
    i = i//2;
```

Consider the first while loop in which the loop-controlling variable *i* is multiplied by 2. The loop will be executed only 10 times and not 1000 times because in each iteration the value of *i* doubles. Now, consider the second loop in which the loop-controlling variable *i* is divided by 2. In this case also, the loop will be executed 10 times. Thus, the number of iterations is a function of the number by which the loop-controlling variable is divided or multiplied. In the examples discussed, it is 2. That is, when $n = 100$, the number of iterations can be given by log 100, which is equal to 10.

Therefore, putting this analysis in general terms, we can conclude that the efficiency of loops in which iterations divide or multiply the loop-controlling variables can be given as

```
f(n) = log n
```

Nested Loops: Loops that contain loops are known as *nested loops*. In order to analyze nested loops, we need to determine the number of iterations each loop completes. The total is then obtained as the product of the number of iterations in the inner loop and the number of iterations in the outer loop.

In this case, we analyze the efficiency of the algorithm based on whether it is a linear, logarithmic, quadratic, or dependent quadratic nested loop.

Linear Logarithmic Loop: Consider the following code in which the loop-controlling variable of the inner loop is multiplied after each iteration. The number of iterations in the inner loop is log 10. This inner loop is controlled by an outer loop, which iterates 10 times. Therefore, according to the formula, the number of iterations for this code can be given as 10 log 10.

```
for i in range(10):
    j = 1
    while(j<10):
        print(j)
        j = j*2
```

In more general terms, the efficiency of such loops can be given as **f(n) = n log n**.

Quadratic Loop: In a quadratic loop, the number of iterations in the inner loop is equal to the number of iterations in the outer loop. Consider the following code in which the outer loop executes 10 times and for each iteration of the outer loop, the inner loop also executes 10 times. Therefore, the efficiency here is 100.

```
for(i in range(100)):
    for(j in range(100)):
        statement block
```

The generalized formula for quadratic loop can be given as **f(n) = n²**.

Dependent Quadratic Loop: In a dependent quadratic loop, the number of iterations in the inner loop is dependent on the outer loop. Consider the code given below.

```
for i in range(10):
    for j in range(i+1):
        print(j)
```

In this code, the inner loop will execute just once in the first iteration, twice in the second iteration, thrice in the third iteration, and so on. In this way, the number of iterations can be calculated as

1 + 2 + 3 + 4 + 5 + ... + 9 + 10 = 55

If we calculate the average of this loop (55/10 = 5.5), we will observe that it is equal to the number of iterations in the outer loop (10) plus 1 divided by 2. In general terms, the inner loop iterates (n + 1)/2 times. Therefore, the efficiency of such a code can be given as

```
f(n) = n (n + 1)/2
```

7.3 BIG-O NOTATION

In today's era of massive advancement in computer technology, we are hardly concerned about the efficiency of algorithms. Rather, we are more interested in knowing the generic order of the magnitude of the algorithm. If we have two different algorithms to solve the same problem where one algorithm executes in 10 iterations and the other in 20 iterations, the difference between the two algorithms is not much. However, if the first algorithm executes in 10 iterations and the other in 1000 iterations, then it is a matter of concern.

We have seen that the number of statements executed in a program for n elements of the data is a function of the number of elements, expressed as **f(n)**. Even if the expression derived for a function is complex, a dominant factor in the expression is sufficient to determine the order of the magnitude of the result, and hence, the efficiency of the algorithm. This factor is the Big-O, as in on the order of, and is expressed as **O(n)**.

The Big-O notation, where O stands for 'order of', is concerned with what happens for very large values of n. For example, if a sorting algorithm performs n^2 operations to sort just n elements, then that algorithm would be described as an **O(n²)** algorithm.

When expressing complexity using the Big-O notation, constant multipliers are ignored. So, an O(4n) algorithm is equivalent to O(n), which is how it should be written.

If f(n) and g(n) are the functions defined on a positive integer number n, then

f(n) = O(g(n))

That is, **f** of **n** is Big-O of **g** of **n** if and only if positive constants **c** and **n** exist, such that **f(n) ∈ cg(n)**. It means that for large amounts of data, **f(n)** will grow no more than a constant factor **g(n)**. Hence, g provides an upper bound. Note that here **c** is a constant which depends on the following factors:

- the programming language used
- the quality of the compiler or interpreter
- the CPU speed
- the size of the main memory and the access time to it
- the knowledge of the programmer, and
- the algorithm itself, which may require simple but sometimes time-consuming machine instructions.

We have seen that the Big-O notation provides a strict upper bound for **f(n)**. This means that function **f(n)** can do better but not worse than the specified value. Big-O notation is simply written as, **f(n) ∈ O(g(n))** or as **f(n) = O(g(n))**.
Examples of functions in O(n³) include: $n^{2.9}$, n^3, $n^3 + n$, $540n + 10$
Examples of functions not in O(n³) include: $n^{3.2}$, n^2, $n^2 + n$, $540n + 10$, $2n$

To summarize,

- Best-case O describes an upper bound for all combinations of input. It is possibly lower than the worst case. For example when sorting an array, the best case is when the array is already correctly sorted.
- Worst-case O describes a lower bound for worst case input combinations. It is possibly greater than the best case. For example, when sorting an array, the worst case is when the array is sorted in reverse order.
- If we simply write O, it means the same as worst-case O.

Table 7.1 Example of f(n) and g(n)

g(n)	f(n) = 0(g(n))
10	0(1)
$2n^3 + 1$	$0(n^3)$
$3n^2 + 5$	$0(n^2)$
$2n^3 + 3n^2 + 5n - 10$	$0(n^3)$

Now let us look at some examples of **g(n)** and **f(n)**. Table 7.1 shows the relationship between **g(n)** and **f(n)**. Note that the constant values will be ignored because the main purpose of the Big-O notation is to analyze the algorithm in a general fashion, so the anomalies that appear for small input sizes are simply ignored.

7.3.1 Categories of Algorithms

According to the Big-O notation, we have five different categories of algorithms:

1. Constant time algorithm: running time complexity given as O(1)
2. Linear time algorithm: running time complexity given as O(n)
3. Logarithmic time algorithm: running time complexity given as O(log n)
4. Polynomial time algorithm: running time complexity given as O(n^k) where k > 1
5. Exponential time algorithm: running time complexity given as O(2^n)

Table 7.2 shows the number of operations that would be performed for various values of n.

Table 7.2 Number of operations for different functions of n

n	o(1)	o(log n)	o(n)	o(n log n)	o(n^2)	o(n^3)
1	1	1	1	1	1	1
2	1	1	2	2	4	8
4	1	2	4	8	16	64
8	1	3	8	24	64	512
16	1	4	16	64	256	4096

7.4 DATA STRUCTURES

A *data structure* is a group of data elements that are put together under one name. It defines a particular way of storing and organizing data in a computer so that the data can be used efficiently.

Today, computer programmers do not write programs just to solve a problem. Their focus is to write an efficient program. For this, they first analyze the problem to determine the performance goals that must be achieved and then think of the most appropriate data structure for that job. However, program designers with a poor understanding of data structure concepts ignore this analysis step and apply a data structure with which they can work comfortably. The applied data structure may not be appropriate for the problem at hand and therefore may result in poor performance (like slow speed of operations).

Conversely, if a program meets its performance goals with a data structure that is simple to use, then it makes no sense to apply another complex data structure just to exhibit the programmer's skill. When selecting a data structure to solve a problem, the following steps must be performed.

Step 1: Analysis of the problem to determine the basic operations that must be supported. For example, basic operations may include inserting/deleting/searching a data item from the data structure.

Step 2: Quantify the resource constraints for each operation.

Step 3: Select the data structure that best meets these requirements.

This approach of selecting an appropriate data structure for the problem at hand supports a data-centred view of the design process because in this approach, the main focus is on data and the operations that are to be performed on them. The second concern is the representation of the data, and the final concern is the implementation of that representation.

There are different types of data structures that are supported by Python. While one type of data structure may permit adding of new data items only at the beginning, the other may allow it to be added at any position. While one data structure may allow updating data values, the other may not allow. So, selection of an appropriate data structure for the problem is a crucial decision and may have a major impact on the performance of the program.

Data structures are building blocks of a program. A program built using improper data structures may not work as expected. So as a programmer, it is mandatory to choose the most appropriate data structure for a program.

Data structures allow users to organize data in such a way that enables users to store collections of data, relate them and perform operations on them accordingly. It facilitates users to efficiently organize, store and maintain data.

7.4.1 Abstract Data Type and Data Structures

The main advantage of a data structure is that it helps the programmer to focus on the bigger picture rather than getting lost in the details. This is also referred to as data abstraction.

Data structures are an implementation of Abstract Data Types or ADT. This implementation requires a physical view of data using some collection of programming constructs and basic data types.

7.5 CLASSIFICATION OF DATA STRUCTURES

Data structures are generally categorized into two classes: *primitive* and *non-primitive* data structures as shown in Fig. 7.3.

7.5.1 Primitive and Non-primitive Data Structures

Primitive data structures are the fundamental data types which are supported by a programming language. Some primitive data structures include integer, float, string, and Boolean. The terms 'data type', 'basic data type', and 'primitive data type' are often used interchangeably.

Non-primitive data structures are those data structures which are created using primitive data structures. Examples of such data structures include arrays, lists, tuple, dictionary, sets and files.

Non-primitive data structures can further be classified into two categories: *linear* and *non-linear* data structures.

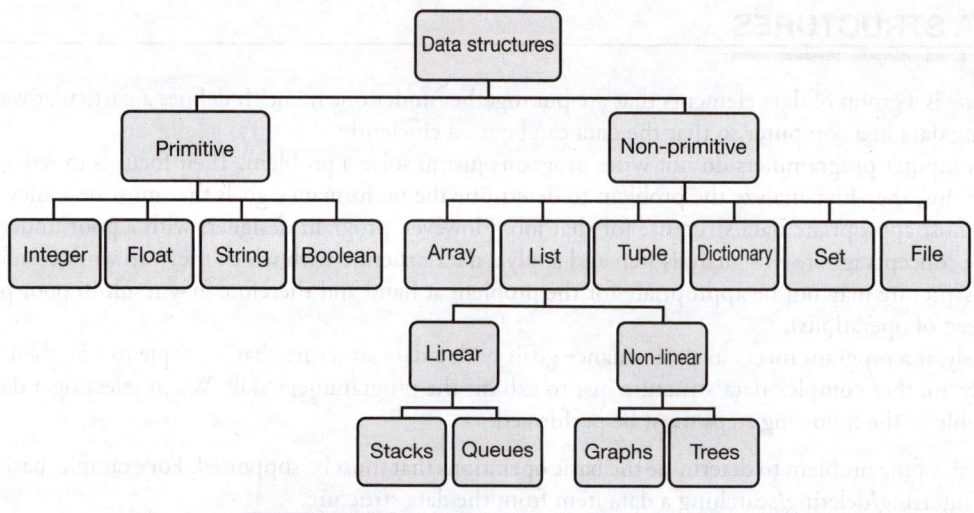

Figure 7.3 Classification of data structures

7.5.2 Linear and Non-linear Structures

If the elements of a data structure are stored in a linear or sequential order, then it is a linear data structure. Examples include stacks and queues. While stack is a LIFO data structure, queue on the other hand, is a FIFO data structure.

Non-linear data structures are the data structures in which there is no sequential linking of data elements. Any pair or group of data elements can be linked to each other and can be accessed without a strict sequence. Examples include graphs and trees. A binary tree starts with a root node and each of its data element can be connected to maximum two other data elements. However, a graph is an arrangement of vertices and nodes where some of the nodes are connected to each other through links.

7.6 USING LISTS AS STACK

Stack is an important data structure which stores its elements in an ordered manner. We will explain the concept of stacks using an analogy. You must have seen a pile of plates where one plate is placed on top of another as shown in Fig. 7.4. Now, when you want to remove a plate, you remove the topmost plate first. Hence, you can add and remove an element (i.e. a plate) only at/from one position which is the topmost position.

Stack is a linear data structure which uses the same principle, i.e., the elements in a stack are added and removed only from one end. Hence, a stack is called a LIFO (Last-In–First-Out) data structure, as the element that was inserted last is the first one to be taken out.

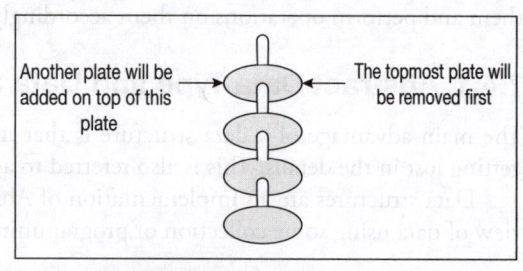

Figure 7.4 Stack of plates

Now the question is where do we need stacks in computer science? The answer is in function calls. Consider an example, where we are executing Function A. In the course of its execution, Function A calls another Function B. Function B, in turn, calls another Function C, which calls Function D. In order to keep track of the returning point of each active function, a special stack called system stack or call stack is used. Whenever a function calls another function, the calling function is pushed to the top of the stack. This is because after the called function gets executed, the control is passed back to the calling function. Look at Fig. 7.5 which shows this concept.

Now when Function E is executed, Function D will be removed from the top of the stack and executed. Once Function D gets completely executed, Function C will be removed from the stack for execution. The whole procedure will be repeated until all the functions get executed. Let us look at the stack after each function is executed. This is shown in Fig. 7.6. The system stack ensures a proper execution order of functions. Therefore, stacks are frequently used in situations where the order of processing is very important, especially when the processing needs to be postponed until other conditions are fulfilled.

Rescursive Functions and Data Structures

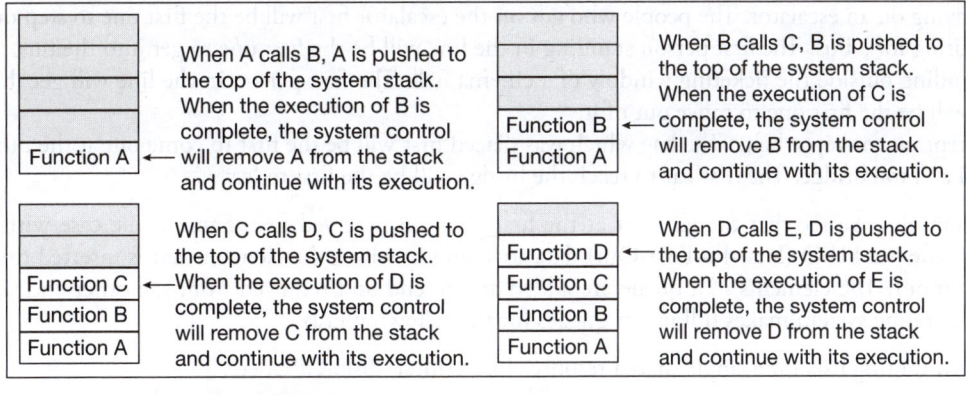

Figure 7.5 Calling a function from another function

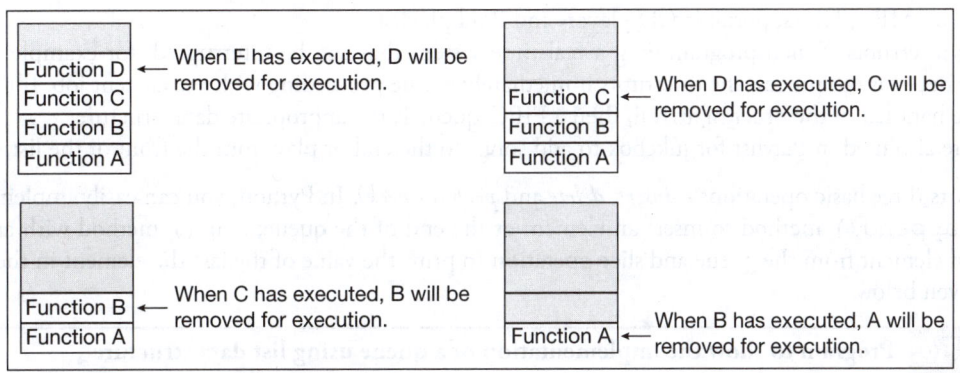

Figure 7.6 Function return using system stack

A stack supports three basic operations: *push, pop,* and *peep (or peek)*. The push operation adds an element at the end of the stack. The pop operation removes the last element from the stack. Lastly, the peep operation returns the value of the last element of the stack (without deleting it). In Python, the list methods make it very easy to use a list as a stack. For example, to push an element in the stack, you will use the `append()` method, to pop an element use the `pop()` method and for peep operation use the slicing operation as illustrated in the program given below.

Example 7.5 Program to illustrate operations on a stack.

```
stack = [1,2,3,4,5,6]
print("Original stack is : ", stack)
stack.append(7)
print("Stack after push operation is : ", stack)
stack.pop()
print("Stack after pop operation is : ", stack)
last_element_index = len(stack) - 1
print("Value obtained after peep operation is : ", stack[last_element_index])
```

Note: The del statement and the `pop()` method do the same thing. The only difference between them is that pop returns the removed item.

OUTPUT

```
Original stack is :  [1, 2, 3, 4, 5, 6]
Stack after push operation is :  [1, 2, 3, 4, 5, 6, 7]
Stack after pop operation is :  [1, 2, 3, 4, 5, 6]
Value obtained after peep operation is :  6
```

7.7 USING LISTS AS QUEUES

Queue is an important data structure which stores its elements in an ordered manner. Let us take a few analogies to understand it better.

- People moving on an escalator. The people who got on the escalator first will be the first one to step out of it.
- People waiting for a bus. The first person standing in the line will be the first one to get into the bus.
- People standing outside the ticketing window of a cinema hall. The first person in the line will get the ticket first and thus will be the first one to move out of it.
- Luggage kept on conveyor belts. The bag which was placed first will be the first to come out at the other end.
- Cars lined at a toll bridge. The first car to reach the bridge will be the first to leave.

In all these examples, we see that the element at the first position is served first. Same is the case with queue data structure. A queue is a FIFO (First-In–First-Out) data structure in which the element that is inserted first is the first one to be taken out. The elements in a queue are added at one end and removed from the other end. In computer systems, the operating system makes full use of queues for the following tasks.

- To maintain waiting lists for a single shared resource like printer, disk, CPU, etc.
- To transfer data asynchronously (data not necessarily received at the same rate as sent) between two processes (IO buffers), e.g., pipes, file IO and sockets
- As buffers on MP3 players, portable CD players and iPod playlist.
- Handling interrupts. When programming a real-time system that can be interrupted, for example, by a mouse click, it is necessary to process the interrupts immediately before proceeding with the current job. If the interrupts have to be handled in the order of arrival, then a FIFO queue is the appropriate data structure.
- Queues are also used in Playlist for jukebox to add songs to the end or play from the front of the list.

Queue supports three basic operations – *insert, delete* and *peep (or peek)*. In Python, you can easily implement a queue by using the `append()` method to insert an element at the end of the queue, `pop()` method with an index 0 to delete the first element from the queue and slice operation to print the value of the last the element in the queue. The program is given below.

Example 7.6 Program to show the implementation of a queue using list data structure.

```
queue = [1,2,3,4,5,6]
print("Original queue is : ", queue)
queue.append(7)
print("Queue after insertion is : ", queue)
queue.pop(0)
print("Queue after deletion is : ", queue)
print("Value obtained after peep operation is : ", queue[(len(queue) - 1)])
```

OUTPUT
```
Original queue is :  [1, 2, 3, 4, 5, 6]
Queue after insertion is :  [1, 2, 3, 4, 5, 6, 7]
Queue after deletion is :  [2, 3, 4, 5, 6, 7]
Value obtained after peep operation is :  7
```

Key Terms

Recursive function: A function that calls itself to solve a smaller version of its task until a final call is made which does not require a call to itself.

Divide-and-conquer technique: A problem-solving technique that works by *dividing* a problem into two or more smaller instances.

Nested loops: Loops that contain loops are known as *nested loops*.

Data structure: A group of data elements that are put together under one name. It defines a particular way of storing and organizing data in a computer so that the data can be used efficiently.

Primitive data structures: The fundamental data types which are supported by a programming language.

Non-primitive data structures: Data structures which are created using primitive data structures.

Linear data Structure: If the elements of a data structure are stored in a linear or sequential order, then it is a linear data structure. Examples include stacks and queues.

Queue: A FIFO (First-In–First-Out) data structure in which the element that is inserted first is the first one to be taken out. The elements in a queue are added at one end and removed from the other end.

Chapter Highlights

- Recursion utilizes divide-and-conquer technique of problem solving.
- Each of the sub-problems in recursion is *recursively* solved, and the solutions are combined to produce a solution for the original problem.
- Every recursive function must have at least one base case. Otherwise, the recursive function will generate an infinite sequence of calls thereby resulting in an error condition.
- Recursion is more of a top-down approach to problem solving.
- A linear program without any loops or recursions will have running time equal to the number of instructions it contains.
- To calculate the efficiency of an algorithm having loop(s), we need to first determine the number of times the statements in the loop will be executed
- The Big-O notation provides a strict upper bound for f(n).
- The main advantage of a data structure is that it helps the programmer to focus on the bigger picture rather than getting lost in the details.
- Data structures are generally categorized into two classes: *primitive* and *non-primitive* data structures.
- Non-primitive data structures can further be classified into two categories: *linear* and *non-linear* data structures.
- A stack is a linear and a LIFO (Last-In–First-Out) data structure, as the element that was inserted last is the first one to be taken out.
- A stack supports three basic operations: *push, pop,* and *peep (or peek)*. The push operation adds an element at the end of the stack. The pop operation removes the last element from the stack. The peep operation returns the value of the last element of the stack (without deleting it).

Review Questions

1. Define a recursive function and explain how it works.
2. With the help of an example, explain the technique of finding factorial of a number using recursion.
3. With the help of an example, explain the technique of finding GCD of a number using recursion.
4. With the help of an example, explain the technique of finding Fibonacci series.
5. Discuss the pros and cons of recursive functions.
6. How will you calculate the algorithmic efficiency of:
   a. Linear loop   b. Logarithmic loop   c. Nested loop.
7. Define recursive function. Give an example and state how you will calculate its algorithmic efficiency.
8. What is the significance of Big-O notation?
9. What is a data structure? How is it useful to the programmer?
10. How will you choose the most appropriate data structure for a particular problem?
11. Differentiate between primitive and non-primitive data structures.
12. How is linear data structure different from a non-linear data structure?
13. Write a short note on stack as a data structure.
14. Explain the mechanism of storing and accessing data in a queue.
15. Give some applications of queue in a computer system.

Programming Exercises

1. Write a program to concatenate two strings using recursion.
2. Write a program to calculate P(n,r).
3. Write a program to calculate C(n,r).
4. Write a program to read an integer number. Print the reverse of this number using recursion.
5. Write a program to compute F(x, y) where
   F(x, y) = F(x–y, y) + 1 if y ≤ x
6. Write a program to compute F(n, r) where F(n, r) can be recursively defined as
   F(n, r) = F(n–1, r) + F(n–1, r–1) .
7. Write a program to compute Lambda(n) for all positive values of n where, Lambda(n) can be recursively defined as
   Lambda(n) = Lambda(n/2) + 1 if n > 1
8. Write a program to compute F(M, N) where F(M,N) can be recursively defined as
   F(M,N) = 1 if M = 0 or M ≥ N ≥ 1
   and F(M,N) = F(M–1,N) + F(M–1, N–1) otherwise .
9. Write a program to reverse a string using recursion.
10. Write a program to calculate exp(x,y) using recursion.
11. Write a program to print the Fibonacci series using recursion.
12. Write a function to print a table of binomial coefficients which is given by the formula:
    B(m, x) = m!/ (x! (m-x)!) where m > x
    Hint: B (m,0) = 1, B(0,0) = 1 and B(m,x) = B(m, x-1) * [(m – x + 1)/x]
13. Write a program that creates a stack and adds the names of students in the stack. Demonstrate the pop and peep operations on this stack.
14. Write a program that creates a queue of all the students who wish to demonstrate their projects. Demonstrate how you will remove names of those students who have already exhibited their projects from this queue?

Fill in the Blanks

1. A _____ function is defined as a function that calls itself.
2. Recursion utilizes _____ technique of problem solving.
3. A recursive function without a _____ case will result in an infinite function calls.
4. A linear program without any loops or recursions will have running time equal to the number of _____ it contains.
5. Loops that contain loops are known as_____.
6. The efficiency of a linear logarithmic loop is _____.
7. The efficiency of a _____ loop can be given as f(n) = n².
8. The _____ notation provides a strict upper bound for f(n).
9. Best case O describes an _____ bound for all combinations of input.
10. _____ is a group of data elements that are put together under one name.
11. Stacks and Queues are examples of _____ and _____ data structure.
12. _____ is a LIFO data structure.
13. _____ and _____ are examples of non-primitive non-linear data structures.

State True or False

1. The recursive case solves the problem directly without making any further calls to the same function.
2. Divide-and-conquer technique means solving a problem by dividing a problem into two or more smaller instances.
3. Every recursive function can have only one base case.

4. The recursive case acts as the terminating case for the recursive function.
5. Recursive solutions provide the best solutions.
6. Recursive function takes more memory and time to execute.
7. A data structure helps the programmer to focus on details rather than looking at the bigger picture.
8. Arrays, lists, tuple, dictionary, sets and files are examples of primitive data structures.
9. A queue is a LIFO data structure.
10. The peep operation removes the last element from the stack.
11. In a queue, elements are added at one end and removed from the other end.

Multiple Choice Questions

1. Which of the following is not a function of the recursive case?
   a. Divide the problem into simpler sub-parts   b. Calls itself with sub- problem
   c. Calculates the final result   d. None of these.
2. In recursion, each sub-problem is solved _____.
   a. Iteratively   b. recursively   c. sequentially   d. None of these.
3. Recursion is a _____ approach to problem solving.
   a. top-down   b. bottom-up   c. Both a and b.   d. None of these.
4. Algorithmic efficiency of a linear loop is _____.
   a. f(n) = n/2   b. f(n) = n   c. f(n) = log n   d. f(n) = log n
5. The value of constant c while calculating complexity does not depend on _____.
   a. programming language   b. quality of compiler
   c. programmer   d. CPU speed
6. Examples of functions in $O(n^4)$ is _____.
   a. $n^{3.2}$ b. n^2 c. $n^3 + n$ d. $540n^4 + 10$
7. Which case describes a lower bound for worst-case input combinations?
   a. Best   b. Worst   c. Average   d. All of these.
8. A data structure helps users to _____ data efficiently.
   a. Store   b. Organize   c. Access   d. All of these.
9. Which of the following is not a primitive data structure in Python?
   a. String   b. Boolean   c. List   d. Float
10. Which operation returns the value of the last element of the stack?
    a. Push   b. Pop   c. Peep   d. All of these
11. Which data structure will you use to maintain waiting lists for the CPU?
    a. String   b. List   c. Stack   d. Queue

Give the Output

1. ```
   def is_even(x):
       if x==0:
           return True
       else:
           return is_even(x-1)
   print(is_even(10))
   ```
2. ```
   queue = ["Amar", "Akbar", "Anthony"]
   queue.append("Ram")
   queue.append("Iqbal")
   print(queue)
   print(queue.pop(0))
   print(queue)
   print(queue.pop(0))
   print(queue)
   ```
3. ```
   def mult3(n):
       if n == 1:
           return 3
       else:
           return mult3(n-1) + 3
   for i in range(1,10):
       print(mult3(i), end = ' ')
   ```
   ```

Find the Error

1. ```
   def factorial(x):
   return x*factorial(x-1)
   print(factorial(6))
   ```
2. ```
   def sum_to(x):
   return x+sum_to(x-1)
   print(sum_to(5))
   ```
3. ```
   def factorial(x):
       if x != 1:
           return 1
       else:
           return (x *
   factorial(x-1))
   num = 3
   print("The factorial of", num,
   "is", factorial(num))
   ```
4. ```
   s = []
   s.append('eat')
   s.append('sleep')
   s.append('code')
   s.pop()
   s.pop()
   s.pop()
   s.pop()
   ```
5. ```
   def is_odd(x):
       return not is_even(x)
   print(is_even(22))
   ```
6. ```
   def is_even(x):
       return not is_even(x)
   print(is_even(22))
   ```

Answers

Fill in the Blanks

1. recursive
2. Divide-and-conquer
3. base
4. instructions
5. nested loops
6. f(n) = n log n.
7. quadratic
8. Big-O
9. upper
10. Data Structure
11. Non-primitive,
12. stack
13. Graphs, trees.

State True or False

1. False
2. True
3. False
4. False
5. False
6. True
7. False
8. False
9. False
10. False
11. True

Multiple Choice Questions

1. d
2. b
3. a
4. b
5. c
6. c
7. b
8. d
9. c
10. d
12. d

Give the Output

1. True
2. ['Amar', 'Akbar', 'Anthony', 'Ram', 'Iqbal']
   Amar
   ['Akbar', 'Anthony', 'Ram', 'Iqbal']
   Akbar
   ['Anthony', 'Ram', 'Iqbal']
3. 3 6 9 12 15 18 21 24 27

Find the Error

1. RecursionError: maximum recursion depth exceeded
2. RecursionError: maximum recursion depth exceeded
3. The factorial of 3 is 1 (wrong result)
4. IndexError: pop from empty list
5. NameError: name 'is_even' is not defined
6. RecursionError: maximum recursion depth exceeded

Computer Networks

8

Chapter Objectives

These days, a single computer in isolation is not of much use. To make full use of a computer, you must connect it with other computer(s). When two or more computers are connected, they communicate with each other and share each other's resources. This is where a computer network comes into picture.

We cannot even imagine our day without the Internet today. This statement, in itself, is sufficient to reveal the importance of a computer's network in today's scenario. In this chapter, we will therefore learn about the following details:

- Use of computer network
- Wired and wireless networks
- Network topologies
- Types of computer networks
- VoIP
- Malware
- Network structure
- Network protocols
- Cookies
- Firewalls, Intellectual Property Rights
- Network devices
- IT ACT 2000
- Cyber crime
- World Wide Web
- HTML, DNS, URL
- Static and dynamic websites
- Web hosting and web scripting
- Web 2.0, E-commerce and E-payments

8.1 INTRODUCTION

A computer communication network or a computer network or a network, as it is simply known as, is a ***collection of computers and devices interconnected to facilitate sharing of resources (printer, CD-ROM), information and electronic documents among interconnected devices.*** The advantages of interconnecting computing devices include:

File Sharing: It facilitates users to share and access files that are stored on a remote computer. The users can sit at their workstation and easily view the files stored on other computers that are connected to the same network, provided they are authorized to do so. This saves the time required to copy a file from one system to another, by using a storage device like pen drive or a CD-ROM.

> File sharing allows multiple users to work together on the same project.

Moreover, users can access or update the information stored in a database, keeping it up-to-date and accurate. Hence, network file sharing is more flexible than using pen drives or optical drives (like CD, DVD or Blu Ray). It allows users to share photos, music files, and documents with other users.

Resource Sharing: It facilitates users to share the limited and otherwise expensive resources among a number of computing devices. For example, in your computer lab there may be 30 computers but only one or two printers. In order to allow every computer to use the printer, there are two options. First, to buy an individual printer for every computer; and second, to connect the already available printers to all the computers and printers in the lab via a network.

Increased Storage Capacity: A number of computers attached to the network enable sharing of files. Files stored on one computer can be easily accessed by another computer. A stand-alone computer may have limited storage capacity but when several computers are connected, the memory of all the computers can be used (Fig. 8.1).

Increased Cost Efficiency: The software available in the market are costly and take time for installation. Computer network is a feasible solution as it allows software to be stored or installed on one computer and then be shared among other computers connected on the same network.

Load Sharing: If one computer is designated to carry out all the jobs, then it is very likely that the computer will slow down thereby taking hours to complete all the jobs. So, a better option is to transfer extra jobs to another machine (connected on the same network) for execution. This drastically improves the performance of the system.

Facilitate Communications: Using a network, users can communicate efficiently and easily through email and instant messaging, thereby allowing users to pass important messages in a speedy manner without wasting paper.

Figure 8.1 Connecting devices

8.1.1 Limitations of Computer Network

However, on the downside, there are also a few problems associated with networking:

- If the server fails, applications cannot be accessed.
- If the server fails, it can lead to data loss.
- The server, if hacked, can lead to misuse of data.
- When the number of computers and computing devices exceed the permissible number, the performance and efficiency of the system can decrease considerably.
- Network management is a difficult and tedious job.

8.2 HISTORY OF INTERNET

The roots of the Internet can be traced back to 1969 when the Advanced Research Projects Agency (ARPA) of the US government formed the first network that was widely known as the Advanced Research Projects Agency Network (ARPANET).

This network was initially created to interconnect computers so that users in research organizations and universities could communicate with each other and share information. However, it was in 1989 that the US government had lifted restrictions on the use of Internet and allowed it to be used for commercial purposes as well. Since then, the Internet has grown rapidly to become the world's largest network that connects thousands of networks, billions of computers, and hundreds of countries across the world.

8.3 THE INTERNET

The Internet is a global network that connects billions of computers all over of the world. It is a network of networks. Thus, the Internet links different organizations, academic institutions, government offices and home users to share information among a large group of users.

Each computer on the internet is called a *host*. To connect to the Internet, the user must gain access through a commercial Internet Service Provider (ISP). The Internet, sometimes known as "the Net", allows the users to:

- Connect easily through ordinary personal computers and local phone numbers to share a huge pool of information
- Exchange electronic mail (email) with friends and colleagues. The email service has practically replaced the Postal Service for short written transactions. It has undoubtedly become the most widely used application on the Net.
- Converse with other users on the internet. The conversation can be text-based, voice-based, video-based or a combination of all.
- Share important piece of information in a timely manner
- Access multimedia information that includes sound, photographic images and even video
- Browse the information and websites using a Web browser. The most popular Web browsers are Microsoft Edge, Opera, Google Chrome and Mozilla Firefox.

An additional feature of the Internet is that it lacks a central authority that controls it. Although there are different governing boards that work to establish policies and standards, the Internet is bound by few rules and answers to no single organization.

8.4 DATA SWITCHING

We have seen that data can be transmitted between two devices only when they are directly connected with each other. However, this is impossible in large networks. In such big networks, there are numerous intermediate devices between the sending and the receiving machine. All these devices together make a path for the data to be transmitted between the sending and receiving devices. This process of creating a path for data transmission is called switching. For example, when you call your friend, there is no direct connection between the two phones but there are numerous junctions that move data from the caller to the called. There are two main switching techniques which are described as below.

8.4.1 Circuit Switching

When we call a friend, a circuit is established between our phone and the friend's phone. This circuit may pass through a number of telephone exchanges. Once the call has been set up, the dedicated path will continue to exist until the call is finished. Thus, in circuit switching, an end-to-end path is set up before any data can be sent. However, if no circuit can be established between the sender and receiver due to lack of resources, the connection is said to be *blocked*.

In some cases, especially when distance is very short or when there is frequent communication, users may opt for a permanent leased line which is a permanent dedicated link between the sender and the receiver (as shown in Fig. 8.2). For example, a leased line is helpful in a company with its headquarters at one location and a branch office at the other.

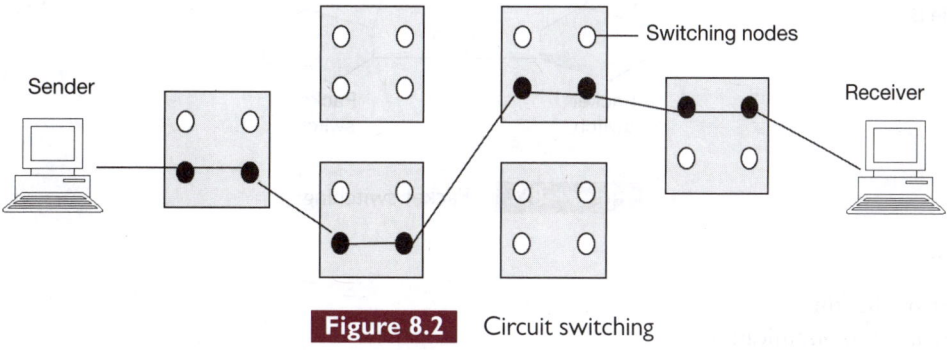

Figure 8.2 Circuit switching

Advantages

- Simple technique for transmitting data
- Useful for long distance communications
- Communication takes place in real time – no delays other than the time taken for transmission
- Once the call is setup, full capacity of the circuit is exclusively used by the sender and receiver.
- No restriction or constraint on the size of data to be transmitted.

Disadvantages

- Before data transmission, some time is taken to set up a circuit. This leads to delay in data transfer.
- Line utilization is poor.
- If the line is busy, no connection can be set up.
- Data is not checked for any error.

8.4.2 Packet Switching

The packet switching method is similar to message switching. While in message switching the message could have unlimited length, in packet switching, on the other hand, a message is split into packets of fixed size.

A packet consists of a header part that stores the address of the receiver, control information, packet number, etc.; a data part that stores information to be transferred; and a trailer at the end that contains error checking information. The packets (of a message) may take totally different routes to reach the receiver and may also reach the receiver at different times. In such a scenario, it is the responsibility of the receiver to reassemble the packets in correct order, to obtain the complete message. For example, if a message is split in three packets, then packets 1, 2 and 3 may be sent to the receiver via different paths. And it may happen that packet 2 may arrive at the destination before packets 1 and 3. So the receiver must arrange the packets in correct sequence (according to packet number specified in the header) to get the message.

Figure 8.3 shows the packet switching technique. In this technique, the switches called routers maintain a routing table that stores information about the next device to which the packet can be sent. This next device can be the receiver itself or any other device through which the receiver can be reached.

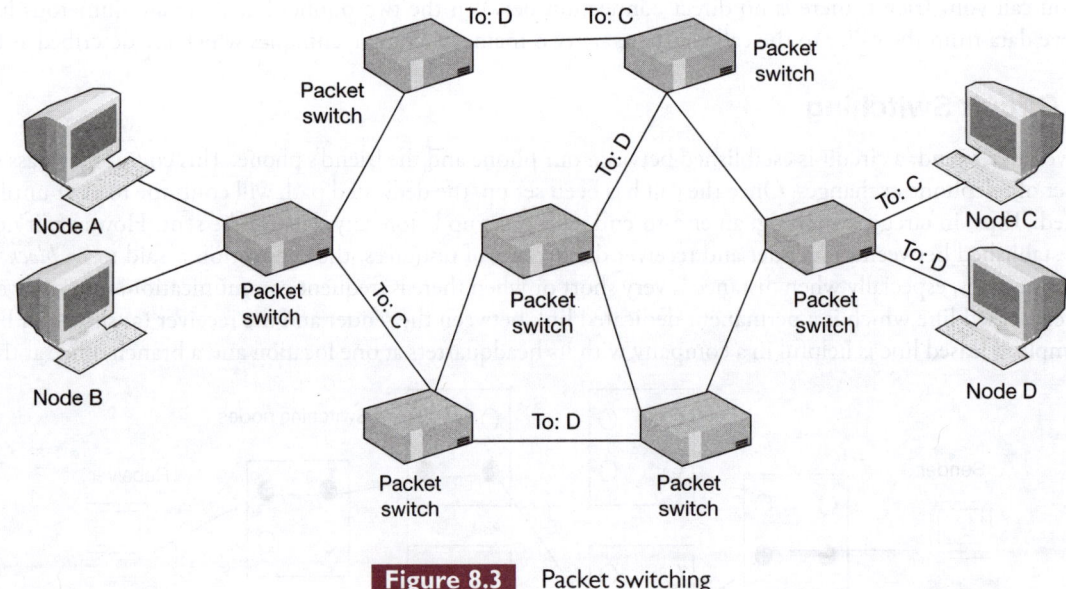

Figure 8.3   Packet switching

Advantages

- Provides error checking
- Provides reliable communication
- Does not allow the receiver to be blocked if some other device is also sending it data
- Efficient utilization of the communications channel
- More advantageous when messages are short and frequent since there is no scope for the line to be busy
- Better than circuit switching as it does not require circuit establishment and termination before and after data transmission
- Even when one router or switch or line is unavailable, the packet can still reach the receiver via another route.
- Since size of a packet is smaller than the message, the data storage requirement at the intermediate nodes is less than that required in message switching.

Disadvantages

- Transmission delays occur because data is temporarily stored at intermediate devices.
- The need to buffer the whole packet makes either the router design expensive and/or slower, or the size of packets is limited.
- Lot of overhead is involved in splitting a message at the sender' end and then reassembling the packets in correct sequence in the receiving device.
- There is no guarantee of how much time the packets of a message will take or in what sequence they will arrive at the destination.

8.5 CONCEPT OF CHANNEL

In a network, a node is a device that either sends or receives data to the other nodes on the network. A node can be a computer, printer or any other device capable of sending/receiving data. Links connecting the devices are known as **communication channels**.

Through these devices, data is shared between two or more nodes. A computer network can be thought of as a telecommunication channel that allows nodes to share data with other nodes connected to the same network. The best example of a computer network is the Internet.

Every network must meet certain criteria like performance, reliability and scalability.

Performance of a network can be measured using Transit Time and Response Time.

Transit Time: It is the time taken by a message to travel from one device to another.

Response Time: It is defined as the time elapsed between a request sent and a response received.

Reliability: It indicates how frequently network failure takes place. More the failures, lesser is the network's reliability.

Scalability: Scalability of a network means how easily a new node can be added to a network.

Security: It refers to the protection of data from any unauthorised user or access.

8.6 DATA TRANSMISSION MODE OF CHANNELS

Transmission of data on a communication channel between two machines can take place in several different mechanisms. This transmission can be characterized by the following features:

- Direction of data flow
- Number of bits sent simultaneously
- Synchronization between the sending and receiving devices

8.6.1 Simplex, Half-duplex, and Full-duplex Connections

The data transmission mode refers to the direction of flow of data. Based on this characteristic, a connection can be further classified into three categories—simplex, half-duplex, and full-duplex.

In the *simplex mode*, data flows in only one direction, from the sending device to the receiving device. A simplex connection (Fig. 8.4) is often desirable where the data need not flow in both directions. For example, the computer can send a message to the printer, but the printer need not send any data or message to the computer.

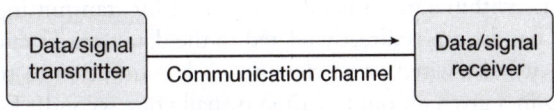

Figure 8.4 Simplex connection

In the real world, simplex mode of data transmission is not very popular because most of the communications require bi-directional exchange of data. However, this mode of communication is used in business, at certain point-of-sale terminals where sales data is entered without the need for a corresponding reply. It is also used in radio and TV transmissions.

In a simplex transmission, only one device transmits data and all other connected devices can only receive data. Hence, this type of transmission is similar to a one-way traffic, as data flows only in one direction. Note that in simplex mode, direction of data flow cannot be reversed. That is, the device which has assumed the role of sending data can only send and not receive. Similarly, the receiver can only receive data but can never send it.

In the **half-duplex mode**, also known as an alternating connection or semi-duplex, there is only one communication channel (a wire or a cable) to carry data. However, both the devices can be either a transmitter or a receiver. That is, devices can share the channel but only one of them can transmit at a time. While one device is transmitting the data/signals, the other will be in receiving mode, and vice-versa. This is shown in Fig. 8.5.

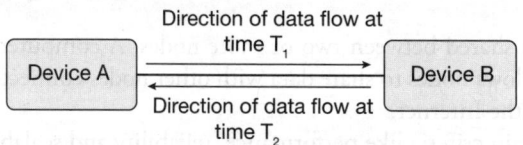

Figure 8.5 Half-duplex connection

In the half-duplex mode, the data is sent and received alternately. Hence, it can be thought of as a one-lane bridge, where vehicles can come from both the directions, but not at the same time. Vehicles on one side must wait until traffic coming from the opposite direction has crossed the bridge. In the real world, the half-duplex mode is utilized in web browsing. For example, if the user sends a request to download a particular web page, then that page is downloaded and displayed to the user.

In a **full-duplex connection**, data flows in both the directions simultaneously as shown in Fig. 8.6. That is, each end of the line can transmit and receive the data/signals at the same time. The number of communication channels in a full-duplex connection can either be one or two. Two separate communication channels can carry data in both directions and can be thought of as the combination of two simplex lines, one in each direction. However, if there is only one single communication channel, then the bandwidth of the channel is divided into two – one for each direction of data transmission.

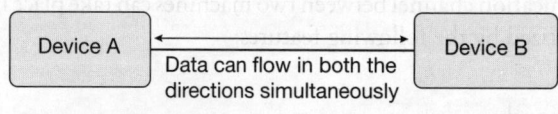

Figure 8.6 Full-duplex connection

A full-duplex connection can be thought of as a two-lane bridge where vehicles can simultaneously travel in both the directions but only in their respective lanes. In the real world, the full-duplex data transmission mode is widely applied in telephone systems, where both the caller and the receiver can talk at the same time.

8.7 BANDWIDTH

Bandwidth is a range of frequencies within a given band that is used for transmitting an analog signal. It is usually expressed in Hz, KHz, and MHz. Bandwidth is directly related to the data transfer rate.

Data transfer rate is the capacity of a wired or wireless network connection to transmit the maximum amount of data from one point to another in a given amount of time (usually one second). Data rates are often measured in megabits (million bits) or megabytes (million bytes) per second. The data transfer rate can be specified as given below.

bps	bits per second	Bps	bytes per second
Kbps	Kilobits per second	KBps	kilo bytes per second
Mbps	megabits per second	MBps	megabytes per second
Gbps	giga bits per second	GBps	giga bytes per second
Tbps	tera bits per second	TBps	tera bytes per second

You can compare bandwidth with the amount of water that can flow through a water pipe, as shown in Fig. 8.7. The bigger the pipe, the more water can flow through it at a time. Similarly, the more the bandwidth a data connection has, the more data it can send and receive at a time.

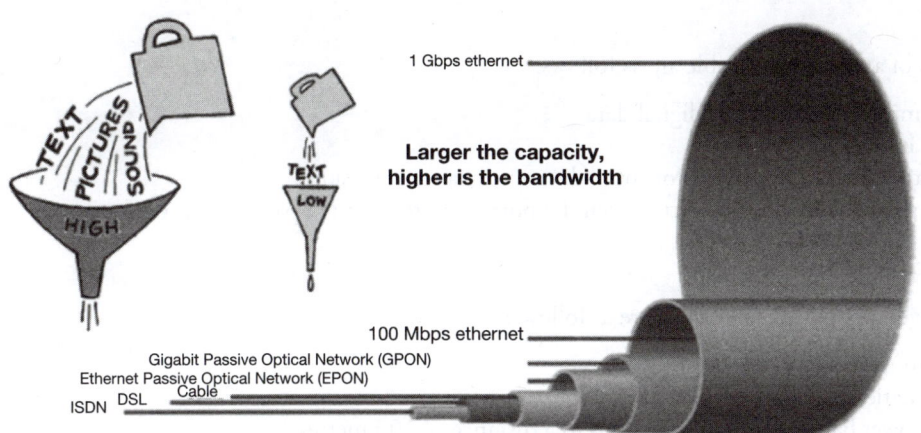

Figure 8.7 Amount of bandwidth

Bandwidth connections can be symmetrical or asymmetrical.

Symmetrical bandwidth means that the data capacity is the same in both directions to upload (transferring data from your computer to the Internet) or download data (transferring data from the Internet to your computer).

Asymmetrical bandwidth means download and upload capacity are not equal. In this case upload capacity is smaller than download capacity.

End users pay for the capacity of their network connections; so the greater the bandwidth of the connection, the more expensive it is.

How Much Bandwidth is Required?

In companies, a calculation is done to find out how much bandwidth is required to run all the applications on their networks. For this, the maximum number of users who would be using the network at a time is multiplied by the number of times the bandwidth capacity is required by each application.

8.8 WIRED COMMUNICATION MEDIA

The computers on a network can be separated by a few metres as in a lab or nearly unlimited distances as in the case of the Internet. Computers and other computing devices are connected through a variety of media, which include twisted-pair cable, coaxial cable, optical fibre, and various wireless technologies.

8.8.1 Twisted Pair Cable

It consists of copper wires that are twisted into pairs and is the most widely used medium for telecommunication. Figure 8.8 shows each bunch of twister pair cables being enclosed in a plastic insulation. While ordinary telephone wires consist of two insulated copper wires twisted into pairs, computer network cables, on the other hand, consist of four pairs of copper cables that can be utilized for both voice and data transmission.

Twisted wires help to reduce crosstalk and electromagnetic induction. The transmission speed of twisted pair cable varies from two million bits per second to 100 million bits per second.

Figure 8.8 Twisted pair cable

Twisted pair cables are cheap and easy to install and use. However, these cables easily pick up noise signals and thus, become prone to error when their length extends beyond 100 metres.

Advantages

The advantages of a twisted pair cable are as follows:

- It can transmit analog as well as digital data.
- It is easy to install.
- It is cheap and the least expensive for short-distance data transmission.
- The entire network remains unaffected even if a portion of the twisted pair cable is damaged.

Disadvantages

The disadvantages of a twisted pair cable are as follows:

- It is prone to noise.
- Signal attenuation and distortion are very high.
- It supports lower bandwidth—10 mbps up to a distance of 100 metres
- It is not secure as it is easy to tap.
- It may break easily because of its thin size.

Applications: The applications of twisted pair cables are as follows:

- Telephone lines use twisted pair cables to carry voice and data.
- Some LANs use twisted pair cables to connect computing devices

8.8.2 Coaxial Cable

It is a highly preferred connecting media for cable television systems and for connecting computers within an office building or within short distances to form a network. A coaxial cable consists of a single copper conductor at its centre encapsulated inside a plastic layer that provides insulation between the centre conductor and a braided metal shield (refer to Fig. 8.9). The metal shield blocks any interference from the outside environment and is protected by an outer shield of plastic material.

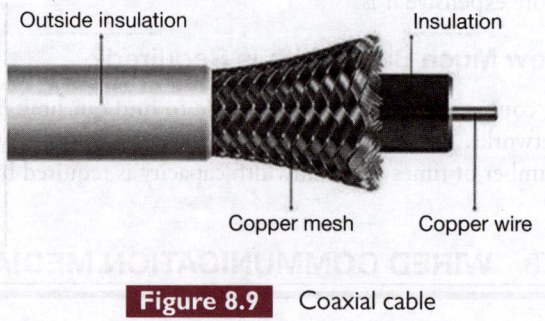

Figure 8.9 Coaxial cable

Coaxial cable is highly resistant to signal interference and can support greater cable lengths between network devices than a twisted pair cable. Its transmission speed varies from 200 million to more than 500 million bits per second. However, the downside of this cable is that it is difficult to install.

Advantages: The advantages of a coaxial cable are as follows:

- It can span longer distance at higher bandwidth or data rate.
- It is less susceptible to interference.
- It has better shield against electromagnetic interference than a twisted pair cable.
- It can carry analog as well as digital data.
- It is reasonably priced but more expensive than a twisted pair cable.
- It is easy to handle.
- There is less attenuation and distortion of data.
- It is less prone to noise and crosstalk.

Disadvantages: The disadvantages of a coaxial cable are as follows:

- It is not secure as it can be easily breached.
- It is prone to error and noise.
- It is more expensive than a twisted pair cable.

- It is thicker and heavier than a twisted pair cable and thus difficult to install.
- It may be damaged by lightning strikes.

Applications: The applications of a coaxial cable are as follows:

- It is used to bring cable TV connection to customers' homes.
- It is used to attach a personal antenna to a television set or digital converter box.

8.8.3 Fibre-optic Cable

A fibre-optic cable (Fig. 8.10) is constructed in several layers. The core is the actual glass or fibre, a conductor which is covered with a refractive coating called cladding that causes light to travel in a controlled path along the entire length of the glass core. The next layer is a protective covering or an insulating jacket made of Teflon or PVC to protect the core and coating from any kind of damage. It also prevents light from escaping the assembly.

Optical fibre cables carry data by means of pulses of light. They transmit light which can travel over extended distances. Fibre-optic cables are not affected by electromagnetic radiation and are, thus, best suited for environments that contain a large amount of electrical interference. The transmission speed of an optical fibre cable is hundreds of times faster than for coaxial cables and thousands of times faster than for a twisted-pair wire. This capacity has helped broaden the communication possibilities by including services such as video conferencing and other interactive services.

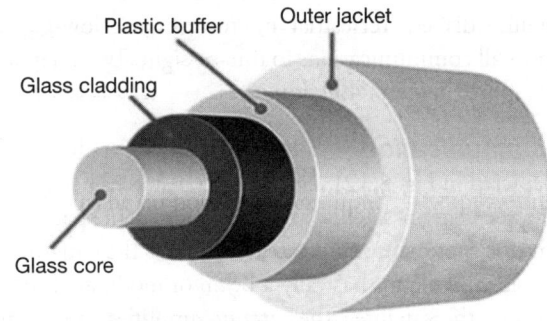

Figure 8.10 Fiber optic cable

Moreover, nowadays, the trend is moving towards using coloured light rather than white light. Initially, only one message could be carried in a stream of white light impulses, but with this technology, multiple signals can be carried in a single go.

Advantages: The advantages of optical cables are as follows:

- They support higher bandwidth.
- There is less signal attenuation.
- They are not affected by power surges, electromagnetic interference, or power failures.
- They are lighter than copper.
- They are secure as they are difficult to tap.

Disadvantages: The disadvantages of optical cables are as follows:

- Being a new technology, people must be trained to use these cables.
- They are expensive.
- They are delicate as they are made of glass.
- They are comparatively difficult to install.

Applications: The applications of optical cables lie in the following:

- They are used by doctors as light guides, imaging tools, and lasers for surgeries.
- They are used for transmitting voice, data, or video over long distances.
- They are employed in applications such as HDTV and video on demand.
- Cable television companies use them for delivery of digital video and data services.
- They are used in intelligent transportation systems such as smart highways with intelligent traffic lights, automated tollbooths, and changeable message signs.
- They are used in biomedical industry for transmission of digital diagnostic images.
- They are increasingly being used to form the backbone of local area networks.

8.9 WIRELESS AND SATELLITE COMMUNICATION

The wireless technologies that connect computers and other devices to form a network include terrestrial microwave, communication satellites, cellular systems and infrared systems.

Terrestrial Microwave: Terrestrial microwaves (refer Fig. 8.11) use Earth-based transmitter and receiver. Microwave antennas are usually placed on top of buildings, towers, hills, and mountain peaks and resemble satellite dishes. Terrestrial microwaves use low-gigahertz range, which limits all communications to line-of-sight. Two relay stations are separated by (approximately) 40 kilometers.

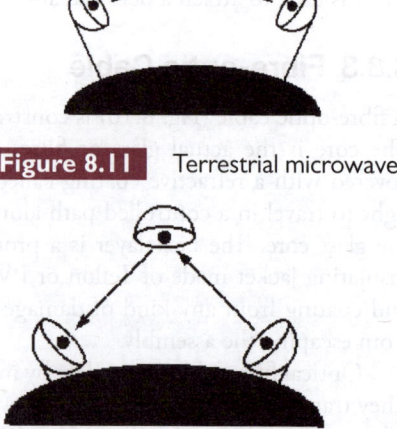

Figure 8.11 Terrestrial microwave

Communication Satellites: In satellite communication (depicted in Fig. 8.12), signals are transferred between the sender and receiver using a satellite that is stationed in space, typically 35,400 km (for geosynchronous satellites) above the equator. In this process, the signal which is basically a beam of modulated microwaves is sent towards the satellite. The satellite amplifies the received signal and transmits it back to the receiver's antenna present on the earth's surface. This means that all the signals are transferred in space. Satellites can be used to relay voice, data, and TV signals.

Figure 8.12 Communications satellite

Infrared Communication: Infrared light is widely used by TV remote controls. In computers, the infrared technology enables computing devices to communicate via short-range wireless signals. These signals are used to transfer digital data. Infrared communication has become an alternative to cables and floppy disks and provides a point-to-point, low-cost way to connect computers with each other or with other devices and appliances. Moreover, cellular phones are also equipped with infrared ports to enable them to be connected to a computer for dial-up networking connections.

> Infrared signals can be transmitted within small distances not more than 10 meters (face-to-face) without any object in the line of transmission.

8.10 WIRELESS OR WI-FI NETWORK

Nowadays, the number of networks operating without cables (wireless) is constantly increasing. Wireless LANs use high-frequency radio signals, infrared light beams, or lasers to communicate with remote computers. Information is exchanged among devices as if they are physically connected with each other. For longer distances, wireless communication is also done through cellular telephone technology, microwave transmission, or by satellite.

Wireless network enables laptop computers or other portable devices to connect to the LAN. They are also preferred in older buildings where it may be difficult or impossible to install additional cables.

A wireless network (Fig. 8.13) is a cost-effective means to access the Internet. When we take our laptop to hotels, airports, or other public places and access Internet, we are actually working through a wireless network.

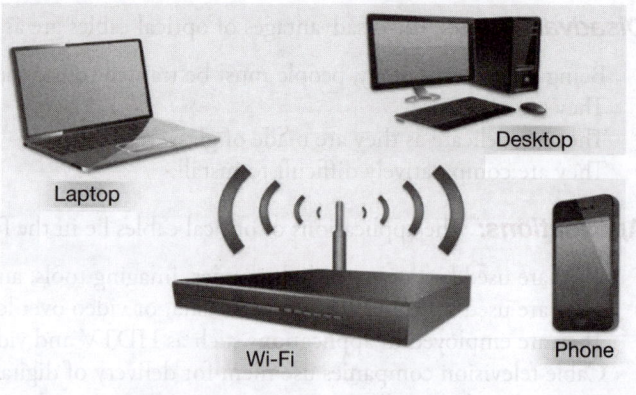

Figure 8.13 Wireless network

8.10.1 Advantages

The advantages of wireless networks are as follows:

- With a laptop computer or other hand-held mobile devices, users can access the Internet throughout the university campus, in a mall, or in an airplane.
- If your computer has a wireless adapter, locating a wireless network is extremely simple. Moreover, in some cases, users automatically get connected to networks within a range.
- Setting up a wireless network is cheaper as it eliminates the need to buy and install network cables.
- New devices can be easily added to a wireless network, provided the maximum number of devices is not exceeded.
- Wireless networks enable users to conveniently access the network resources from any location within its coverage area.
- With wireless networks, users are no longer tied to the desk as in case of a wired connection. Users can change locations or be mobile while accessing the network.
- Wireless access helps users to be more productive as they can work as per their convenience.
- Since wireless networks eliminate or reduce wiring costs, they are a cheaper option than their wired counterparts.
- In a wireless network, radio signals can be transmitted at any of the three frequency bands it supports. Moreover, radio signals may even do frequency hopping—rapidly hop between the different bands to reduce interference and allow multiple devices use the same wireless connection simultaneously.

> Wi-Fi networks use Ethernet protocol.

8.10.2 Disadvantages

The disadvantages of wireless networks are as follows:

- As wireless networks are more susceptible to unauthorized use, users must enable specially designed security schemes to prevent virtual intruders and freeloaders.
- Wireless networks are susceptible to interference from lights and electronic devices as they use radio signals and similar techniques for transmission.
- Due to the interference caused by electrical devices and/or items blocking the path of transmission, wireless connections are not as stable as their wired counterparts.
- The wireless transmitter in a laptop requires a significant amount of power, so it affects the battery life of laptops.
- The transmission speed of wired networks is much higher than that offered by wireless networks.

> A wireless network is often referred to as Wi-Fi and an area with an accessible wireless network is called a Wi-Fi hotspot. Wi-Fi hotspots that we often use at a public space (like cafes and airports) may be either free or they may demand a small fee for use.

8.11 NETWORK DEVICES

There are three main devices that may be used to connect one computer to another computer. These are the hub, switch, and router. To understand which device to use when, we shall read about them in detail in this section.

> There are seven layers in the OSI model.

8.11.1 MODEM (MOdulator DEModulator)

A modem is a hardware device that allows a computer to send and receive data over a telephone line or a cable or satellite connection. Earlier, when dial-up connection was used by most Internet users, the modem was used to convert digital data coming from the computer into analog data (in the form of waves) which could be sent on the telephone lines. At the receiving end, the modem converted the analog signals coming from telephone lines into digital data that the computer could understand.

Therefore, MODEM is the short form of Modulator Demodulator. Modulation is the process of converting digital data (coming from the sending computer) into an analog signal. At the receiving end we have demodulation, which takes the analog signal and turns it back into digital data that can be read by the receiving computer as shown in Fig. 8.14.

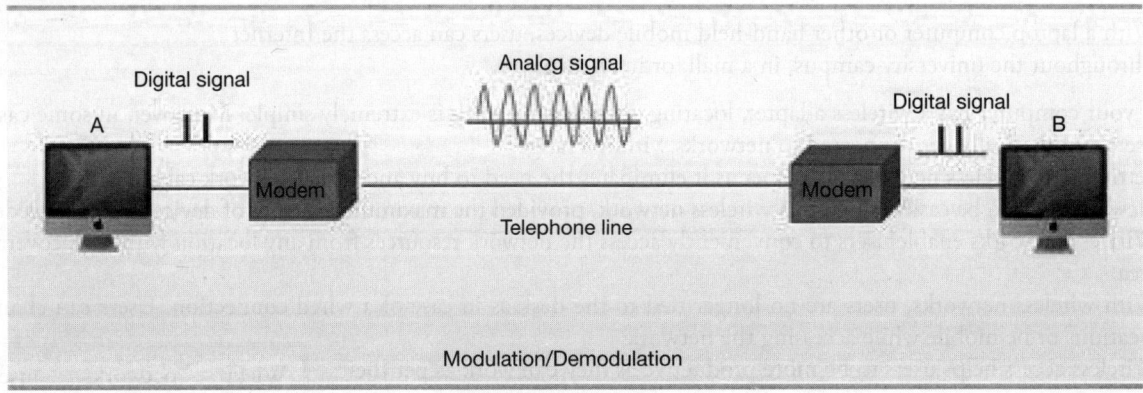

Figure 8.14 Modem

However, these days most people use high-speed broadband connection to access the Internet. In such a scenario, the work of a modem (also known as a broadband modem) has become much simpler as it is no longer required to perform analog-to-digital conversion.

Broadband modems transfer data at a faster speed and do not interfere with phone calls.

Other Types of Modem

Cellular Modems: establish Internet connectivity between a mobile device and a cell phone network.

Cable Modems: send and receive data over standard cable television lines. Modern cable modems provide an efficient way of transmitting TV, cable Internet, and digital phone signals over the same cable line.

Onboard Modems: are the modems which are built onto the computer motherboard. Though onboard modems cannot be removed, they can be disabled easily.

Speed: The speed of a modem is measured in Bits per Second (bps) or Kilo Bits per Second (kbps). Speed signifies the number of bits that a modem can send or receive in one second. While the speed of the fastest dial-up modem is 56 kbps, the speed of broadband modems is higher.

8.11.2 RJ45 Connector

RJ45 is a type of commonly used connector for computer (Ethernet) networking. Though it resembles a telephone jack, it is slightly wider. Since Ethernet cables which are used to connect two computing devices have RJ45 connectors at both the ends, these cables are often known as RJ45 cables (Fig. 8.15).

In RJ45, "RJ" stands for "registered jack". Registered jack indicates that it is a standardized networking interface and "45" is the number of the interface standard. Each RJ45 connector has eight pins spaced about 1mm apart. This means that an RJ45 cable connects eight separate wires. All these eight wires have different colours. Four of them are solid colours and other four are striped.

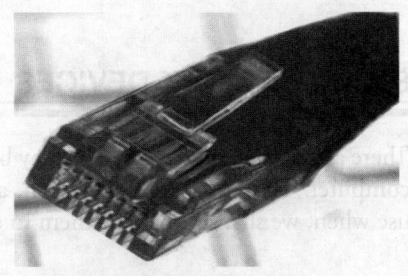

Figure 8.15 RJ45 cable

RJ45 cables are available in two versions – T-568A and T-568B. Though T-568B wiring scheme is more commonly used, some networking applications require a T-568A connector on one end and a T-568B connector on the other. Such an arrangement is often used for direct computer-to-computer connections when there is no router, hub, or switch available.

8.11.3 Network Interface Card or the Ethernet Card

One can use the network services through a network interface card (NIC), also known as a network adapter or a LAN card (Fig. 8.16). That is, no computer can communicate with other devices without a properly installed and configured LAN card. The communication cables that connect different devices to form a network are connected via this card. An NIC acts as a liaison for a computer to send and receive data on a LAN. Every LAN follows a set of protocols. The most common protocol being used is the Ethernet and a lesser used protocol is token ring.

Figure 8.16 NIC

Hence, when forming a LAN, an NIC must be installed in each computer on the network, and all NICs in the network must support the same protocol. NICs are available in two varieties—wired and wireless. While most modern desktop computers use a wired NIC, laptops, on the other hand, come with both wired and wireless LAN cards. However, if a computer does not have an NIC, then we may use a USB-based adaptor that can be plugged into the USB port of the computer. This is a portable adaptor and is again available in two varieties—wired and wireless.

8.11.4 Switch

A switch (as shown in Fig. 8.17) is a high-speed network device that is used to connect multiple computers. Switches are usually small, flat boxes with 4 to 8 ports. Through these ports, one can connect computers, modems, and even other switches. A high-end switch may have more than 50 ports.

A switch receives incoming data packets and sends them to their destination on a local area network (LAN). A switch operates at the data link layer (Layer 2) or the network layer of the OSI Model.

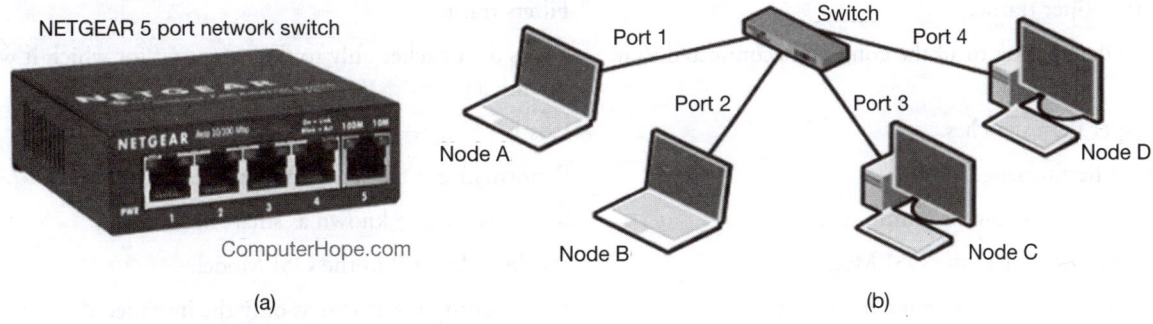

Figure 8.17 (a) Switch; (b) Computers connected through ports of switch

Basically, every data packet sent over a network has a destination address written in it. This destination address is used by the switch to determine the output port to which the data should be sent so that it reaches its intended destination.

Therefore, we can say that a switch filters the data packets and sends it only to the port which is connected to the destination of that packet. To do this filtering work, a switch maintains a table of addresses (of computers) and their port. When it receives a packet, it reads the port number from the table and forwards the packet

> The first network device that was added to the Internet was a switch called the IMP, which helped send the first message on October 29, 1969.

only to that particular port. For example, if the switch receives a packet to be sent to Node C, it will send that packet only on Port 3.

8.11.5 Hub

A hub, also known as a network hub, is a device that is used to connect computers, printers, servers, or other devices so that they can communicate with each other. Like a switch, a hub has many ports through with multiple devices can be connected. A typical hub has 4–24 ports (Fig. 8.18).

Every computer on the network is directly connected with the hub. Hubs are usually used for a private or small and simple network (typically LAN) which is not connected to the Internet. When a hub receives a packet of data from a connected device, it broadcasts (sends it to every device) that data packet to all other devices connected to it. This means that unlike switches, hubs do not have the intelligence to filter data. Hence, every device picks the message but only the destined device processes the packet and all the other computers just discard it.

In the past, network switches and routers were expensive. So, most users preferred to buy hubs but with a decline in cost of switches and routers, these days, switches and routers are used to connect computers. Note that a switch is a device that can be used in all places where a hub is used. Some important differences between a switch and a hub are highlighted in Table 8.1.

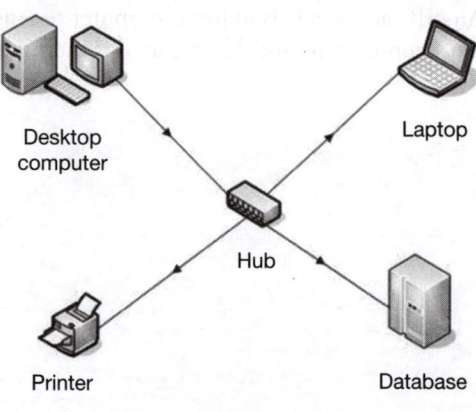

Figure 8.18 Hub

Applications of Hub

- Hubs are used to create small Home Networks.
- Hubs are used to monitor networks.
- Hubs are used in Organizations and Computer Labs to connect computers.
- It enables a computer or any other hardware device to be available to all other devices on the network.

Table 8.1 Comparison between a switch and a hub

Hub	Switch
Cannot filter traffic.	Filters traffic.
Sends data packet to all the computers connected to it.	Sends data packet only to the computer for which it was intended.
Cheaper than switches.	Costly
Slower performance.	Performance is higher than hub.
Hubs are also known as dumb switches	Switches are also known as smart hubs.
Works at Layer 1 of the OSI Model.	Works at Layer 2 of the OSI Model.
No data security as everyone receives it.	Data security is ensured as only the intended destination receives the data.

> A USB hub is a device that allows multiple devices to connect through a single USB port. It is designed to increase the number of USB devices that can be connected to a computer. For example, if your computer has two USB ports, and you want to connect five USB devices, then you can connect a 4-port USB hub to one of the ports. The hub will create four ports out of one, giving you five total ports. With this hub, you can connect up to 127 devices to a single computer.

8.11.6 Router

A router is a network device that connects multiple computer networks together using either wired or wireless connections. It works at Layer 3 of the OSI model and moves data from one network to the other.

A router (shown in Fig. 8.19) is an intelligent device that routes data to destination computers. It is used to connect two logically and physically different networks, two LANs, two WANs, and a LAN with a WAN. Routers use special software known as routing table that stores the addresses of devices connected to the network.

Figure 8.19 Router

Wireless Routers, also known as Wi-Fi routers or Travel routers are used by people and families who want to use the functions of a router at other locations besides home. Wireless routers connect to the modem and create a wireless signal in home or office. So, any computer within range can connect to the wireless router and use broadband Internet.

> Routing devices called mobile hotspots share a mobile (cellular) Internet connection with Wi-Fi clients.

How a Router Works

To reach your school from your home, there may be more than one route. But which route you take depends on factors like shortest distance, traffic on that route, whether that route is safe, etc., as shown in Fig. 8.20. Similarly, when we send data packets for a computer on the Internet, there may be several paths available to reach that computer. But it is the router which will evaluate all the routes and then forward the packet on the best possible route.

Routers have a small memory that stores an embedded operating system. It maintains a table in its memory (also known as **Routing Table**) that contains information about the available routes and their conditions (like traffic on that route, cost involved, etc.) This information is then used to determine the best route for a given packet.

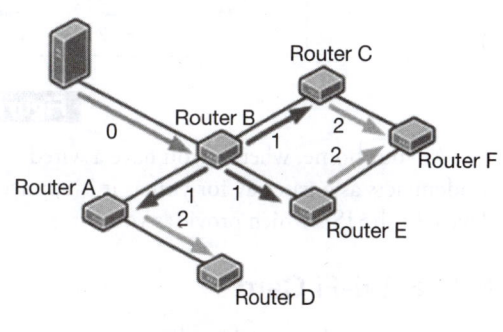

Figure 8.20 Router

Thus, a router has a lot more capabilities than other network devices (like hub and switch). Note that if you just want to form a LAN, then you may either use a switch or a hub. But if you want to connect two or more LANs or any other network among themselves or to the Internet, then you must have a router.

There are several companies that make routers, including Cisco, Linksys, Juniper, Netgear, Nortel (Bay Networks), Redback, Lucent, 3Com, HP, Dlink and Belkin, to name a few.

8.11.7 Gateway

Gateway (as shown in Fig. 8.21) is a device that joins two networks using different protocols (set of rules followed for data transmission). It works on the 7th layer and in fact any layer of the OSI model since a device working at a higher layer supports functionalities for all the lower layers as well. For example, a device at Layer 3 can perform functions for Layers 1, 2 as well as of Layer 3. Similarly, a device at Layer 7 can be used to provide functions for all seven layers in the OSI model.

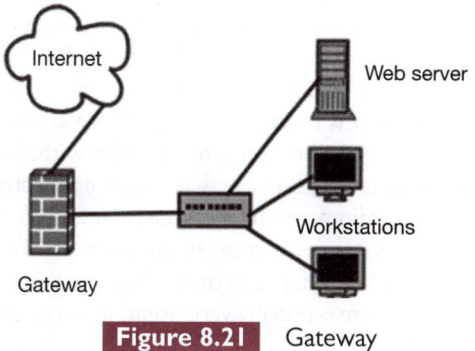

Figure 8.21 Gateway

The most common gateway is a router that connects a home or enterprise network to the Internet. When two networks are connected, devices on one network can communicate with the devices on another network.

A gateway can be implemented completely in software, hardware, or in a combination of both.

When to Use a Router and When to Use a Gateway

Routers connect two networks using the same protocol. Gateways connect two networks using different protocols. If two networks that follow the same protocol are to be connected, then a router is enough.

As you see in Fig. 8.22, gateways serve as the entry and exit point of a network. All data that come inside a network or go out of the network have to first pass through the gateway.

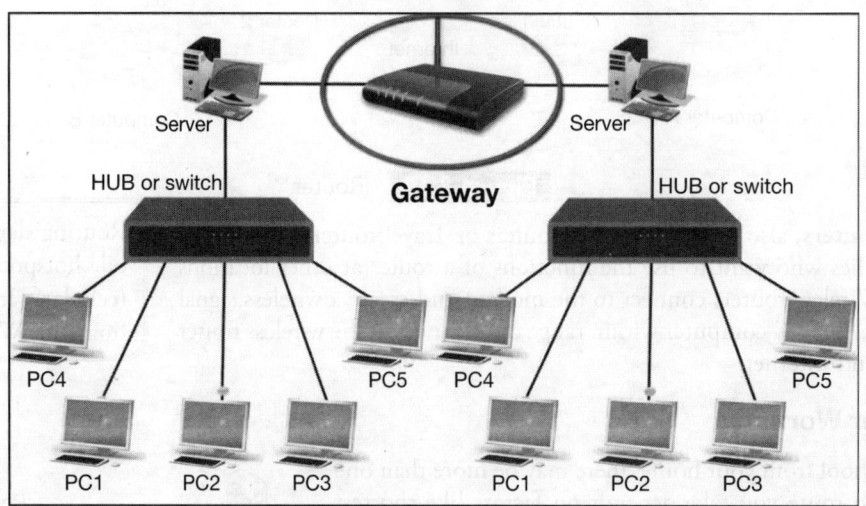

Figure 8.22 Router and gateway

At your home, whether you have a wired Internet connection or wireless, your modem acts as a gateway for you as it is connected with the router or the gateway device of the ISP which provides you Internet access.

> Like the router, the gateway also decides the best possible path to send data packets.

8.11.8 Wi-Fi Card

You must have observed that whenever you walk around in a public place, your school campus or in a hotel, you are connected to the internet using a wireless connection. To provide wireless connectivity, Wi-Fi hot spots are scattered throughout the city. These hotspots are usually connected to computers using radio frequencies from a cell phone tower. The computers pick up the radio signal using a wireless Internet card, which is also known as the Wi-Fi card. The Wi-Fi card is a small device about the size of a credit card that provides internet capability to laptops, desktops, PDAs and other hand-held devices. These days, computers come with one pre-installed wireless card. Those that did not come with such a card can also be used simply by inserting a portable Wi-Fi card (Fig. 8.23) into a suitable slot (PCI slot, PCI Express slot or USB port) on the side of the computer.

Figure 8.23 Wi-Fi card

The Wi-Fi card must be in the range of a wireless Internet signal dedicated to the network it is trying to connect. Once connected, the Wi-Fi card acts as both a receiver and transmitter of wireless signal to allow users access to the Web with their portable devices. For a wireless network to work, there must be a router which has antennae that enable connectivity. However, the strength of the connectivity totally depends on the quality of radio waves being received at any particular time.

With massive increase in number of Wi-Fi hot spots, the demand for wireless Internet cards has gone up tremendously. Today, everyone wants to share Internet connection and go wireless when moving around the city. Wi-Fi cards are especially very useful in areas where network cables are not available to provide connectivity of various devices.

8.12 NETWORK TOPOLOGY

A network topology is an arrangement of computers or other computing devices. Topology describes the pattern in which different devices on the network are connected and the way data flows between them. There are different network topologies in use.

8.12.1 Bus Topology

Bus topology (Fig. 8.24) is a type of network in which every computer or computing device is connected to single cable. Bus topology is mainly used in cable broadband distribution networks.

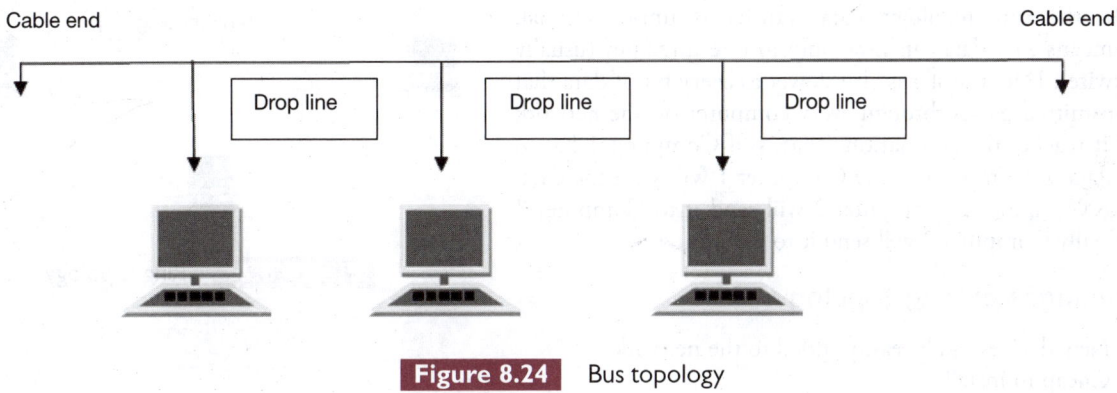

Figure 8.24 Bus topology

Advantages of Bus Topology

1. Requires less cost
2. Less cable length required as compared to other network topologies
3. Used in small networks
4. Easy to implement
5. Additional devices can be easily added to the network.

Disadvantages of Bus Topology

1. If there is a fault in the main cable, the entire network fails.
2. Performance of the network decreases with more number of devices.
3. Limited number of devices can be connected to a bus network.
4. Data transmission is usually slower and prone to errors.
5. Data is transmitted only in one direction.

8.12.2 Star Topology

In the star network topology (Fig. 8.25), a central computer, also known as the hub or the server, is directly connected to all other computers or computing devices. In this topology, all data transmission is possible only through the hub. For example, if one device has to send data to the other, there is no way for direct data transfer. The sending device sends data to the hub and the hub sends it to the other device.

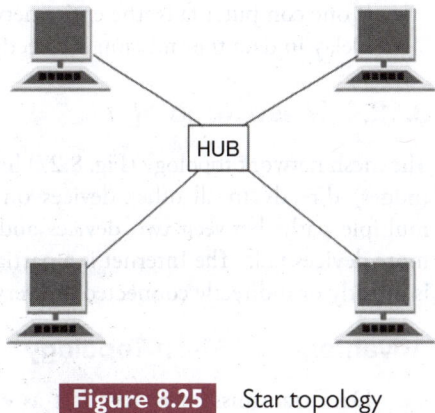

Figure 8.25 Star topology

Advantages of Star Topology

1. Fast performance in a network that has a few devices and less data transmission requirements
2. Easy to find and correct errors or failures
3. Easy to setup
4. If a device fails, the network will not be affected; it will continue to work smoothly.

Disadvantages of Star Topology

1. Cost of installation is high.
2. If the hub fails, then the entire network fails.
3. Performance of the network depends on the hub's capacity.

8.12.3 Ring Topology

In the ring topology (Fig. 8.26), every computer is connected to two of its neighbours – one on the left and the other on its right, thereby forming a closed loop. The last computer is connected to the first.

In the ring topology, data transfer is uni-directional. This means that data can flow only in one direction (usually clockwise). Data transfer is also slower as every bit of data that is transmitted passes through every computer on the network until it reaches the destination. That is, if Computer 1 has to send data to Computer 4, the Computer 1 will send the data, first to Computer 2, Computer 2 will send it to Computer 3 and finally Computer 3 will send it to Computer 4.

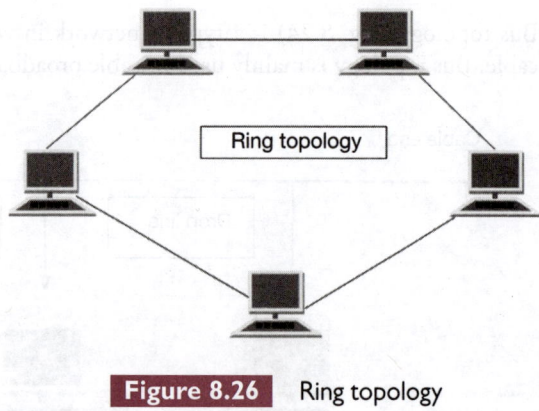

Figure 8.26 Ring topology

Advantages of Ring Topology

1. New devices can be easily added to the network
2. Cheap to install
3. Best suited for networks that do not have a hub
4. More reliable than star topology as the communication does not depend on a single hub
5. Easy to install
6. Can span over larger distances
7. Every node has equal chance to transmit data

Disadvantages of Ring Topology

1. Finding and correcting errors in the network is difficult.
2. Adding or removing a computer disturbs the entire network.
3. If one computer fails, the entire network is affected.
4. Delay in data transmission is directly related to number of devices connected on the network.

8.12.4 Mesh Topology

The mesh network topology (Fig. 8.27) links all computers or computing devices (nodes) directly to all other devices on the network. Mesh topology creates multiple paths between two devices and provides connectivity even if one or more devices fail. The Internet is a partial mesh network in which every device is directly or indirectly connected to every other device.

Advantages of Mesh Topology

1. Data transmission is very fast as every connection between two devices carries its own data.
2. If one computer fails, the entire network is not affected.
3. Easy to find and correct errors.
4. Provides data security as data is transferred only through the dedicated connection between two devices leaving no scope for any other device to intercept the data.

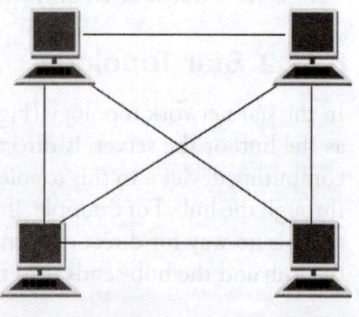

Figure 8.27 Mesh topology

Disadvantages of Mesh Topology

1. Difficult to install
2. Lot of cables are required, so cabling cost is more.
3. It is the most expensive network as, for n nodes, $n \times (n-1) / 2$ physical links (cables) are required

8.12.5 Tree Topology

A tree topology (Fig. 8.28) is also known as a hierarchical topology because all the computers are connected by forming a hierarchy. This topology has at least three levels to the hierarchy.

The easiest way to understand a tree topology is to visualize it as a *star of star network* where star topologies are themselves connected in a star configuration. The tree topology is usually used to connect computers in a WAN.

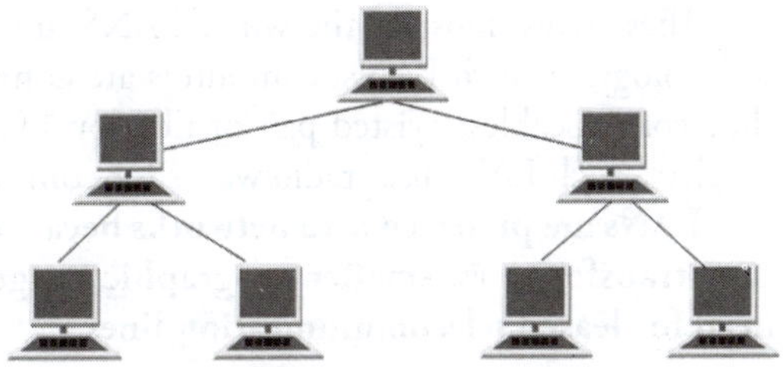

Figure 8.28 Tree topology

Advantages of Tree Topology

1. New devices can be easily added to the network
2. Easy to manage and maintain the network
3. Finding and correcting faults in the network is easy.

Disadvantages of Tree Topology

1. Lot of cables are required; this also increases the cost of the network
2. Difficult to manage when the number of devices increases beyond a limit
3. If the central hub fails, the entire network fails.

8.12.6 Hybrid Topology

Hybrid topology (Fig. 8.29) is a combination of two or more topologies. For example, in your school if the computers in one lab are connected using bus topology and in the other lab, they are connected using star topology, then when we connect the two topologies, a hybrid topology will be formed.

Since hybrid topology is a mixture of two or more topologies, it reaps the advantages of the individual topologies.

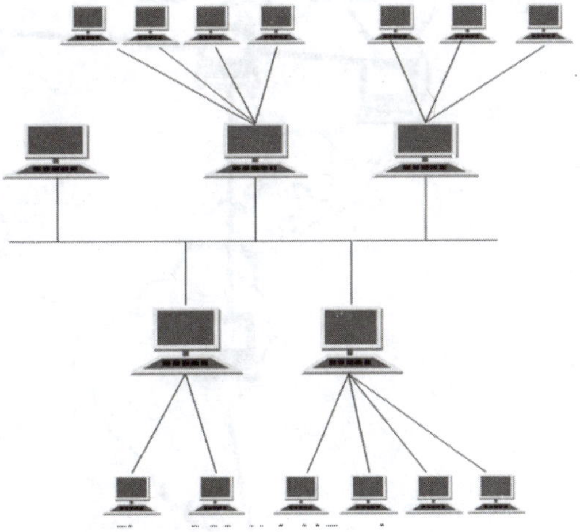

Advantages of Hybrid Topology

1. Detecting and correcting errors is easy
2. More effective than other topologies
3. New devices can be easily added
4. More flexible than other topologies.

Disadvantages of Hybrid Topology

1. Complex in design
2. Expensive.

Figure 8.29 Hybrid topology

8.13 TYPES OF NETWORK

There are different types of computer networks that are widely used, both in homes and in business. These networks vary in terms of their scale, scope, design and implementation. In this section we will read about these types of networks which include: LAN, WAN, MAN, CAN and PAN. Of these, LAN and WAN are the original categories of area networks and the others have gradually emerged over many years with advancement in technology.

8.13.1 LAN – Local Area Network

LAN (Fig. 8.30) supports communication between two or more computers/computing devices in a limited geographical area such as home, school, computer laboratory, office building, or closely positioned group of buildings. Owing to limited scope and cost of operation, LANS are typically owned, controlled, and managed by a single person or organization.

These days, most of the wired LANS are based on Ethernet technology. In such LANs, computers are connected using cables (like coaxial cables, twisted pair or fiber optic). LANs can also be wireless. Such LANs uses radio waves for communication.

LANs are preferred area networks because they have higher data transfer rates, smaller geographic range, and there is no need for leased telecommunication lines.

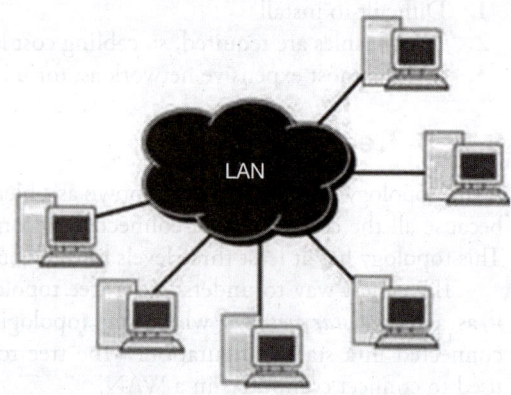

Figure 8.30 Local Area Network (LAN)

8.13.2 WAN – Wide Area Network

WANs span a large geographic area such as a city, country, or even intercontinental distances (Fig. 8.31), using a communication channel that combines many types of media such as telephone lines, cables, and air waves. A WAN often uses transmission facilities provided by common carriers, such as telephone companies. WAN can be created by linking LANs together.

When individual networks connect together to form a larger network (or a bigger WAN), the resulting network is called an **internetwork**, generically abbreviated to 'an internet'. Moreover, when WANs from all over the world connect to form a global internet, it is called **The Internet**. The Internet is therefore, the largest WAN, spanning the Earth.

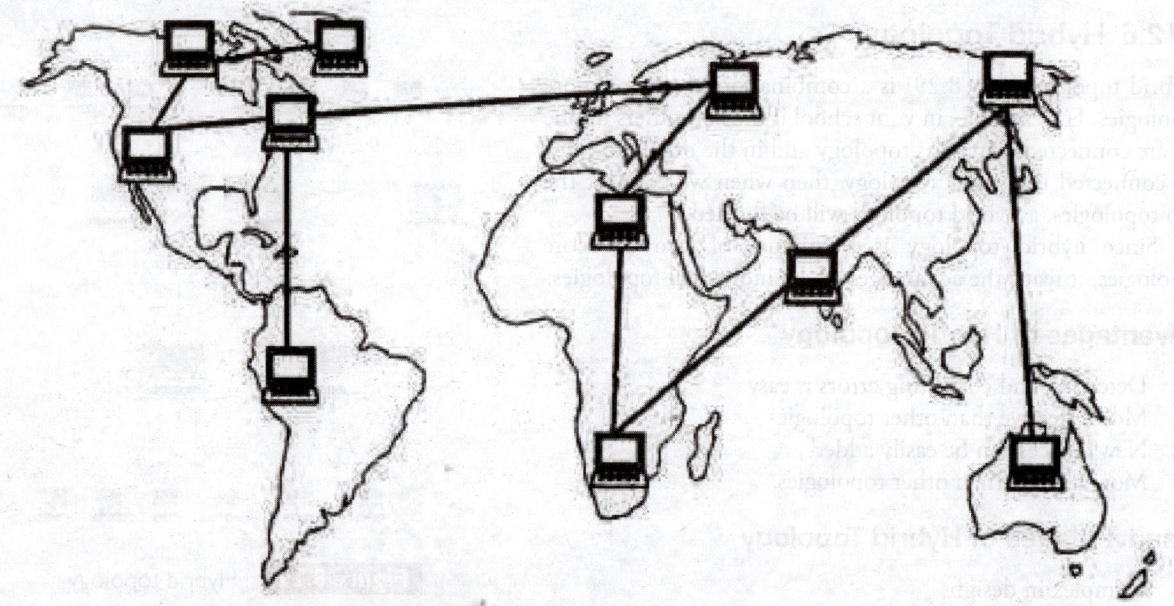

Figure 8.31 Wide Area Network (WAN)

A WAN is a geographically dispersed collection of LANs. A LAN can be easily connected to a WAN by using a special network device called *router*. WAN and LAN can be easily distinguished from each other in several important ways. Most WANs (like the Internet) are not owned by any one individual or organization. Rather, they exist under collective or distributed ownership and management.

The Internet is a public WAN, but organizations can also form private WAN, which is basically two or more LANs connected to each other. For example, a company with offices in Delhi, Kolkata, Chennai and Mumbai having a LAN setup at each office can connect their LANs through leased telephone lines, thereby forming as WAN. Table 8.2 highlights the underlying difference between a LAN and a WAN.

Table 8.2 Difference between LAN and WAN

LAN	WAN
• Covers a restricted geographical area • Usually confined to a single or very few buildings • Owned and controlled by a single person or organization • Higher data transmission rate ranging from 10 Mbps to 1 Gbps • Lower error rate • Comparatively less cost is involved in its deployment • Devices are physically connected by coaxial or fiber optic cable	• Covers a wider geographical area • Installed nationwide and/or world wide • Owned and controlled collectively • Data transmission rate is comparatively slower • Error rate is higher • High costs involved in its setup • Devices are connected through telephone lines, microwave links or satellite links

8.13.3 MAN – Metropolitan Area Network

MAN is a network that interconnects computers and other devices in a geographic area or region larger than that covered by LAN but smaller than that covered by a WAN. A MAN (Fig. 8.32) may interconnect networks in a city or a campus or a community to form a single larger network (which may then be connected to a WAN). MAN may be formed by interconnecting several LANs by bridging them with backbone lines with the help of fiber optical cables. In areas where cabling is not possible, wireless alternatives like microwave, radio, or infra-red laser links are used to connect two or more LANs.

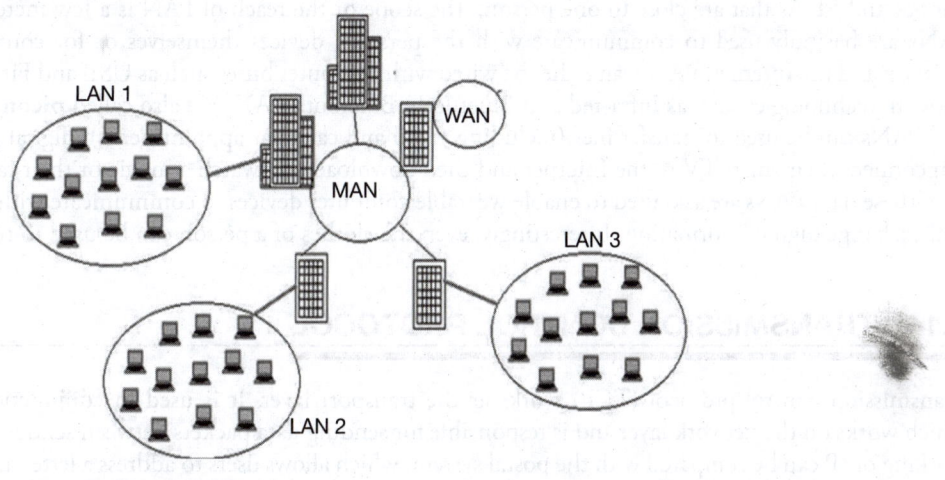

Figure 8.32 Metropolitan Area Network (MAN)

A MAN can be distinguished from a LAN or WAN in the following ways:

1. The size of the network varies in between that of a LAN and WAN. MAN typically covers an area of between 5 and 50 km range. MANs can cover area as small as a group of buildings to an area the size of a city.
2. MAN (like WAN) is usually not owned by a single individual or an organization. It is generally owned by either a consortium of users or by a network service provider who sells the service to the users.
3. MAN is a high-speed network that allows sharing of regional resources.

Though MAN is not a very widely used area network, it does have its own importance for some government bodies and organizations on larger scale.

8.13.4 CAN – Campus Area Network or Corporate Area Network

CAN is a computer network created by interconnecting LANs within a limited geographical area (Fig. 8.33). The network is almost entirely owned by the campus of an enterprise, university, government, military bases, etc. The size of the area that CAN covers is larger than that of LAN and smaller than that of MAN or WAN.

For example, in case of a university having multiple labs or multiple buildings, it is called the Campus Area Network and in case of an organization with multiple offices or multiple departments in the buildings, it is termed as the corporate area network.

These days, CANs are mostly formed using wireless communication mediums rather than cabling and wirings because wireless communication has become more economical than the use of long wires and cables. CANs are economical, beneficial and easy to implement in specific areas of a locality. Therefore, they are widely used by universities and other corporate organizations to work from any block and receive the same speed of data transfer.

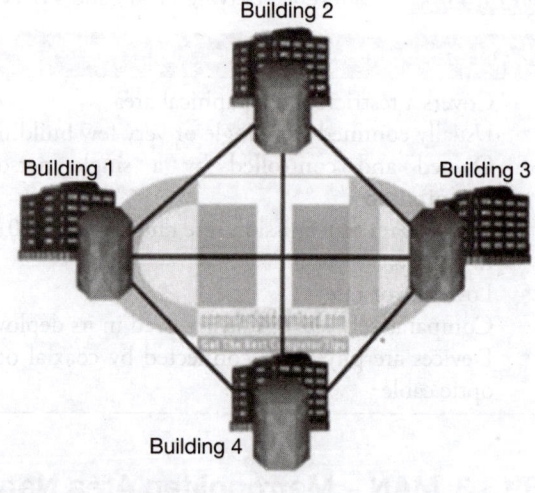

Figure 8.33 Campus Area Network (CAN)

8.13.5 PAN – Personal Area Network

PAN is a computer network designed for communication between computer devices like mobile computers, cell phones and PDAs that are close to one person. The scope or the reach of PAN is a few meters (less than 10 meters). PANs are basically used to communicate with the personal devices themselves or for connecting to a higher-level network and the Internet. PANs can either be wired with computer buses such as USB and FireWire or be wireless with network technologies such as Infra-red and Bluetooth. Bluetooth PANs are also called **piconets**.

PANs can be used to transfer files (including email and calendar appointments), digital photos and music. Users can connect their smart TV to the Internet and then download and watch a movie or their favorite serial using PAN.

These days PANs are also used to enable wearable computer devices to communicate with other nearby computers and exchange digital information. Interestingly, even the clothes of a person can be used to transfer the data.

8.14 TRANSMISSION CONTROL PROTOCOL

Transmission control protocol (TCP) works at the transport layer. It is used in conjunction with the IP protocol which works on the network layer and is responsible for sending data packets between sender and receiver devices. The working of IP can be compared with the postal system, which allows users to address a letter and submit it to the postal system that has no direct link between the sender and the receiver. The main responsibility of the TCP is, therefore, to establish a connection between the sender and the receiver so that reliable and error-free data transmission can take place. The connection established by TCP exists until both the devices have finished their data transmission.

Another important responsibility of TCP is segmentation and reassembly as shown in Fig. 8.34. At the sender's site, TCP breaks the message into several smaller segments and at the receiver's site, TCP reassembles the fragmented data to form the complete message. Since each data packet of the same message may reach the receiver through different routes, it may happen that packet 3 arrives before packet 1. Therefore, the TCP at the receiver's site rearranges the packets in the correct sequence and then assembles them to form the complete message.

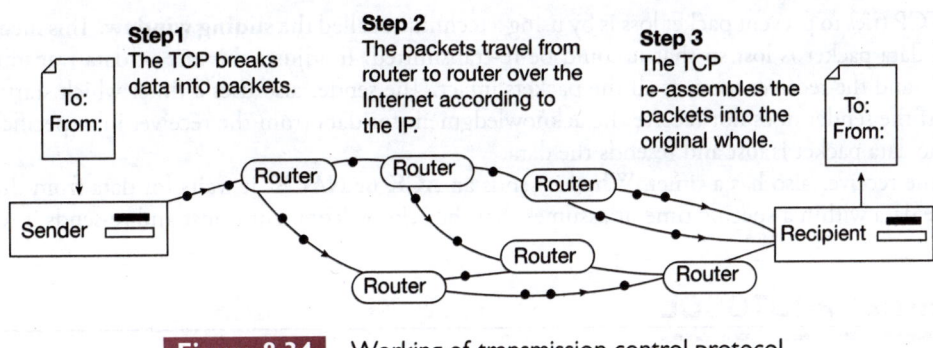

Figure 8.34 Working of transmission control protocol

8.15 RE-TRANSMISSION AND RATE MODULATION

TCP is a reliable protocol that does its best to transfer data without any error, and without any part being lost or duplicated. TCP ensures this level of reliability using error control techniques. For error control, following steps are performed by TCP.

- Error detection mechanism is used to identify corrupted data packets.
- If any erroneous data packet is present, TCP first tries to correct the error by itself.
- If it is not able to correct the error(s), then it sends a Negative Acknowledgment (NACK) to the sender thereby asking the sender to resend that particular data packet.

Note that error control also includes mechanisms for detecting lost segments, out-of-order segments, and duplicated segments. Error detection and correction in TCP is done by using concepts of checksum, acknowledgment, and timeout.

TCP uses **acknowledgments** to confirm the receipt of data packets. Every packet exchanged, be it a data packet or a packet carrying control information has to be acknowledged. However, ACK segments are never acknowledged.

Re-transmission lies at the heart of error control mechanism. TCP asks the sender to re-transmit one or more data packets when they are erroneous, lost, or delayed, as shown in Fig. 8.35.

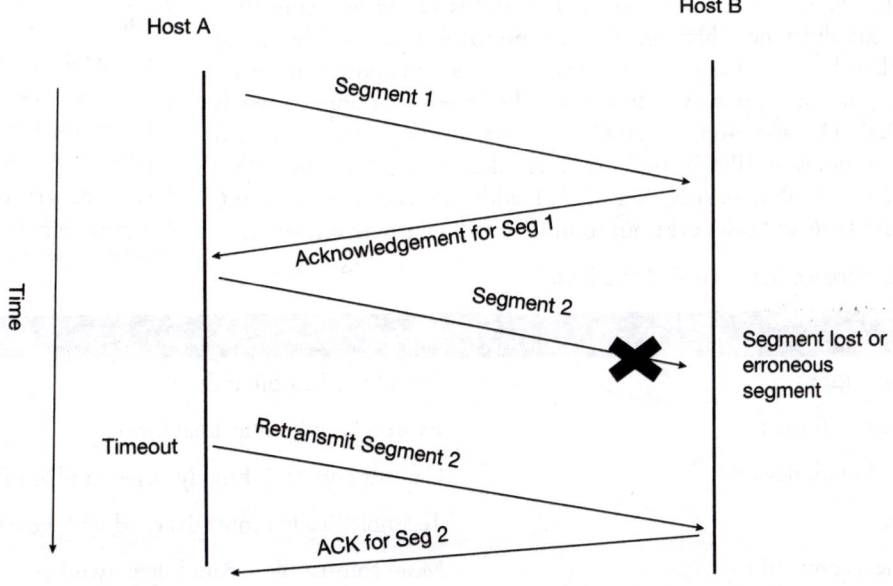

Figure 8.35 Sending and receiving acknowledgments for error and flow control

Basically, TCP tries to prevent packet loss is by using a technique called the **sliding window**. This mechanism easily detects when a data packet is lost so that it could be re-transmitted. It adjusts the rate of data transmission so that no packet is lost and the receiver receives all the packets intact. The sender also uses a timer which starts when a data packet is sent. If the sender does not receive the acknowledgment for data from the receiver in a specific time, then it assumes that the data packet is lost and resends the data.

Similarly, the receiver also has a timer. When it sends an **ACK or NACK**, it waits for data from the sender. If it does not receive data within a specific time, it assumes that the acknowledgment is lost and re-sends it to the receiver.

8.16 INTERNET PROTOCOL

The Internet Protocol (IP) is the address system of the Internet. Its main responsibility is to deliver data packets from the sender device to the destination device. However, since IP does not handle packet ordering or error checking, it is usually coupled with TCP. TCP/IP together forms the backbone of reliable data delivery over any network.

To better understand the difference between TCP and IP, think of an analogy. IP address is the phone number assigned to your computing device, and TCP is the technology that makes the phone ring and allows users to talk to each other.

Currently, two versions of IP are being used—IPv4 and IPv6 where v stands for version.

IP Version 4: Currently, IPv4 (Fig. 8.36) is being widely used by most network devices. It is a 32-bit number (in binary) and can support a maximum of 2^{32} or 4.3 billion devices on the Internet. Addresses in IPv4 consist of 32 binary bits. The 32 bits are divided into four groups of eight bits where each group is separated by a dot. For example, 216.27.61.137 is an IP address written in decimal notation for better readability and understandability. The same address, when written in binary, can be given as 11011000.000110111.00111101.10001001.

An IPv4 address (dotted-decimal notation)

172. 16. 254. 1

10101100.00010000.11111110.00000001

One byte = Eight bits

Thirty-two bits (4*8), or 4 bytes

Figure 8.36 IPv4 address

Although simple, the problem with version 4 is that as more and more devices are being added to the Internet every year, IPv4 addresses are getting exhausted.

IP version 6: The newer version of IP is IPv6 and is slowly replacing IPv4. Table 8.3 lists some differences between the two protocol versions. IPv6 is not more advanced than IPv4 but has many new features. Since an address in version 6 is 128-bits long, it can support 2^{128} devices on the Internet or approximately, 340, 282, 366, 920, 938, 463, 463, 374, 607, 431, 768, 211, 456 devices. Due to their large size, the address in IPv6 is specified in hexadecimal separated by colons. For example, 1124:1:0:C:0:42:0:512C is a valid IP address specified in version 6. Presently, IPv4 and IPv6 addresses exist but soon IPv6 will take over version 4.

> IPv5 is an experimental protocol for Unix-based systems and was never released to be used by the general public. All odd-numbered versions are developed for experimental purposes.

Table 8.3 Difference between IPv4 and IPv6

IPv4	IPv6
Provides a 32-bit address	Provides a 128-bit address
Expressed in decimal format	Expressed in hexadecimal format
Can support 4.3 billion devices	Can support an infinitely large number of devices
Getting obsolete	Technologically more advanced with new features
Comparatively less compatible	More compatible for mobile networks
Comparatively small -sized data can be sent	Bigger-sized data can be sent
Comparatively less secure	More secure than IPv4

8.17 FILE TRANSFER PROTOCOL

FTP is the preferred method of exchanging files because it is faster and reliable. It is usually used to perform the following functions:

- Enable users to share files, computer programs, and/or data.
- Enhance the use of remote computers.
- Provide authentication and security to stored files and programs.
- Transfer data reliably and efficiently.

Generally, FTP is used to transfer web page files from computers to the server so that the pages can be available for everyone on the Internet. Using FTP, users can easily update (delete, rename, move and copy) files on a server. However, it is also used to download programs and other files to the user's computer from other servers. The FTP program can be invoked either by typing the FTP commands on a simple command line interface (like the MS-DOS Prompt window) or with a commercial program that offers a graphical user interface (GUI). Even the Web browser can make FTP requests to download the selected programs.

In FTP terminology, the following rules are adopted:

- The machine on which the file exists is called the server and the machine that requests that file is called the client.
- Copying files from a client to a server is called uploading, whereas transferring files from a server to a client is called downloading.
- The term 'get' refers to receiving files from the server and 'put' refers to sending files (synonymous with download and upload respectively).

8.17.1 How to Use FTP

Nowadays, using the FTP is as simple as using Windows Explorer. FTP is widely being used to upload web pages on the Internet. Users create web page files on their computers and transfer them to the ISP's web server by using FTP.

To enable this, an FTP client software is already installed in the user's computer. This software allows users to log in to a remote computer. The software has two window panes; the one on the left displays all files and directories in the user's computer and the pane on the right displays all files and folders present in the remote computer. Files can be easily transferred by simply dragging and dropping them from one pane to another.

Steps for Using FTP

The following are the steps for using FTP:

- Open the FTP client software installed in computer. You can also use the FTP through your web browser by just typing the URL of the FTP server. However, web browsers are slower and less reliable than dedicated FTP clients.
- Enter the name of the FTP host (e.g., ftp.microsoft.com).
- Enter your username and password. If it is an anonymous FTP server like Cyberduck for Mac or WinSCP for Windows, then type anonymous as username and your email_id as your password.

Usually, all publicly available files are accessed using anonymous FTP server.

Using FTP Through Command Line Instructions

While GUI-enabled FTP clients need to be downloaded from the Internet, users can also use FTP through command line instructions in Windows, Mac OS X, and Linux by typing ftp.microsoft.com.

Basic FTP support is provided by all computers.

Provide your username and password. In case of an anonymous FTP site, enter anonymous as username and email address as password.

FTP also allows users to delete, rename, move, and copy files on the server.

Modes of File Transfer

FTP can transfer files in the following three modes.

Stream Mode: It is that mode in which it transfers files as a continuous stream with no intervention or processing of information into different formats.

Block Mode: In this mode, the data to be transferred is di

Compressed Mode: In this mode, FTP compresses the

In Fig. 8.37, FTP uses two connections for data exchange—one for sending commands and the other for sending or receiving data.

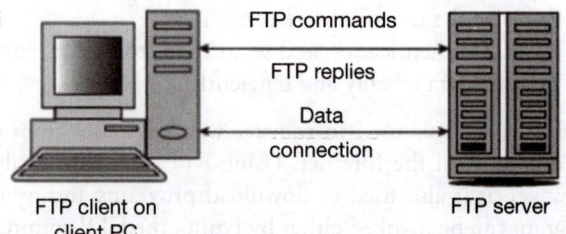

Figure 8.37 FTP connections

Active and Passive Connection Mode: FTP supports two modes of connection—active and passive.

In active mode, the client initiates the connection. Once the server gets connected with the client, the data can be exchanged.

In passive mode, the server is always waiting for any request from the client. Most FTP clients use passive connection mode by default.

8.18 POINT-TO-POINT PROTOCOL (PPP)

PPP is a communication protocol that works at the second layer of the OSI model. It is used to transmit multi-protocol data between two computers that are directly connected point-to-point with each other. PPP is a byte-oriented protocol that is widely used in broadband communications having heavy loads and high speeds. Being a layer 2 protocol, PPP transmits data in frames.

PPP is a full-duplex protocol that can be used on any physical media including twisted pair, coaxial cable, fiber optic or satellite links.

Key services provided by Point-to-Point Protocol include defining procedure for:

- the frame format of the data to be transmitted
- establishing link between two points and exchange of data
- exchanging data between two points
- encapsulating network layer data in a frame
- authenticating rules for the communicating devices.

Apart from the above functionalities, PPP also provides address for network communication and connections over multiple links.

8.18.1 Components of PPP

Point-to-Point Protocol is a layered protocol having a family of supporting protocols including:

- **High-level Data-link Control (HDLC) protocol** that encapsulates the datagram so that it can be transmitted over the specified physical layer
- **Link Control Protocol (LCP)** that is responsible for establishing, configuring, testing, maintaining and terminating links for transmission
- **Authentication Protocols (AP)** that are used to authenticate endpoints for use of services. The three authentication protocols supported by PPP are
  - Password Authentication Protocol (PAP)
  - Challenge Handshake Authentication Protocol (CHAP)
  - Extensible Authentication Protocol (EAP)
- **Network Control Protocols (NCPs)** that are used for negotiating the parameters and features for the network layer. For every higher-layer protocol supported by PPP, a different NCP exists.

- o Top of Form
- o Bottom of Form.

PPP is widely used by Internet service providers (ISPs) to enable dial-up connections to the Internet. The LCP establishes a session between a user's computer and an ISP.

8.19 HTTP (HYPERTEXT TRANSFER PROTOCOL)

HTTP is the most commonly used protocol on the Internet. It specifies a set of rules for transferring web pages that include text, graphic images, sound, video, etc. and other multimedia files) on the World Wide Web. Whenever a user types the URL in the address bar of the web browser, he is indirectly using HTTP.

> HTTP, hypertext and hyperlink lay the foundation of data communication for the World Wide Web.

Since most web browsers use HTTP as the default protocol, even if you type a domain name like google.com, the web browser will automatically insert "http://" and the complete URL will then be read as, www.google.com.

HTTP uses a request-response model in which the client makes a request and the server sends the response containing the requested information.

From Fig. 8.38, we can see that HTTP defines rules for communication between client computers and web servers. This protocol specifies how messages are formatted and transmitted, what actions web servers and browsers should take in response to various commands, and how files, including text, graphics, audio, and video, are to be transferred on the World Wide Web. The clients and servers communicate with each other by sending HTTP requests and HTTP response packets. The process can be understood as given below:

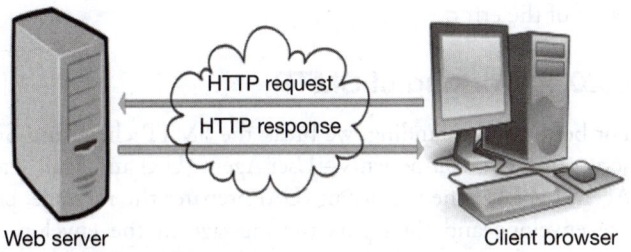

Figure 8.38 HTTP request/response model

Step 1: The user enters a URL in the address bar of the web browser or clicks a hyperlink to open a particular web page.

Step 2: The web browser of the user's computer acts as a client and sends an HTTP request to the web server (for example, www.google.com).

Step 3: The web server receives the request.

Step 4: The server runs an application stored on it to process the request (for example, to fetch the requested web page).

Step 5: The server returns an HTTP response (output) to the browser.

Step 6: The client receives the response and displays the output on the user's screen.

HTTP is known for its simplicity. But in present times, this simplicity has rather become its limitation. Therefore, HyperText Transfer Protocol-Next Generation (HTTP-NG) project has emerged to replace HTTP. HTTP-NG not only provides better performance but also supports efficient commercial applications. It also simplifies HTTP's security and authentication features.

8.20 SIMPLE MAIL TRANSFER PROTOCOL (SMTP)

SMTP is a very popular and powerful protocol used for sending and receiving email over the Internet. However, SMTP is always used along with another protocol like POP3 or the IMAP. In this scenario, SMTP is used for sending email and either POP3 or IMAP is used for receiving email. The use of IMAP or POP3 is important as SMTP cannot save messages on the server and download them when required for access.

Figure 8.39 shows that SMTP is used to send a message to the server (or the mail server) and the server uses SMTP to relay that message to the receiving server. However, the receiving server uses IMAP or POP3 to store your messages on the server and then allows the user to access these messages whenever required.

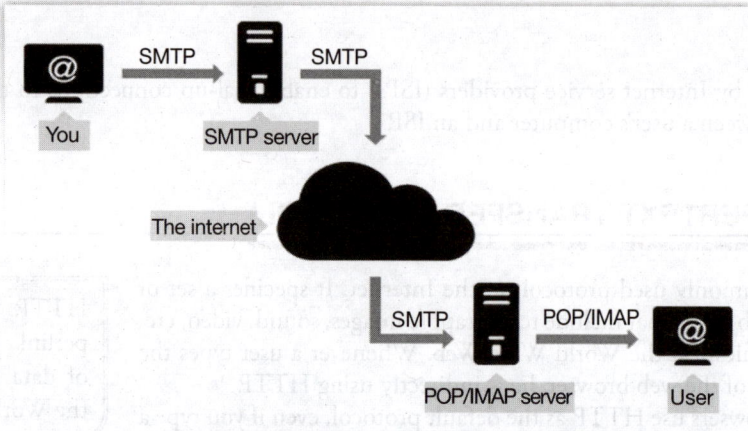

Figure 8.39 SMTP architecture

The servers can also handle errors like incorrect email address. For example, if the recipient address is wrong, then the receiving server replies with an error message indicating the cause of the error.

8.20.1 Working of SMTP

For better understanding, we break the SMTP client and SMTP server into two components – User Agent (UA) and Mail Transfer Agent (MTA). The user agent (UA) prepares the message, creates the envelope and then puts the message in the envelope. The mail transfer agent (MTA) transfers this mail across the internet. Several MTAs may come into picture to relay the message from the sender to the receiver (Fig. 8.40).

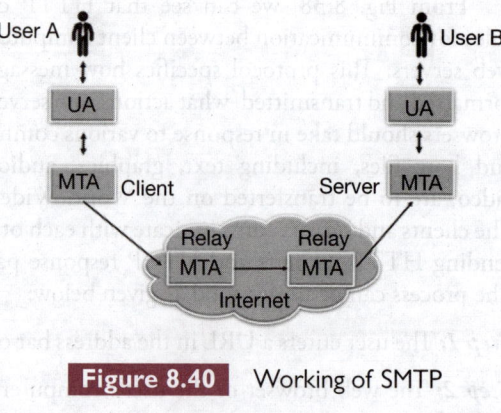

Figure 8.40 Working of SMTP

8.21 POST OFFICE PROTOCOL 3 (POP3)

The SMTP protocol expects the destination machine and mail server receiving the mail to be on-line all the time as otherwise TCP connection cannot be established. But the destination machine cannot be online all the time. Therefore, the server receives the mail on behalf of its clients.

A POP3 server stores messages for each user until the user connects to download and read them using a POP3 client (like Microsoft Outlook, Microsoft Mail, etc.) as shown in Fig. 8.41.

To retrieve a message from a POP3 server, the destination machine (also known as the POP3 client) establishes a TCP session with the server and then issues a series of POP3 commands to retrieve email messages from it.

Some commonly used POP3 commands include the following:

LIST: command that lists the contents of the user's mailbox

RETR: command, used to retrieve messages from the server

DELE: command, used to delete a particular email message

QUIT: command, used to end the transaction state and enter the update state.

In the name POP3, 3 indicates the version number of the widely used protocol POP. The main work of POP3 is to receive and hold email(s) for a user until he/she picks it up. When the user downloads his/her email(s) from the server, POP3 automatically deletes the copy of those emails stored on the server. In this way, POP3 makes it easy for anyone to check his/her email from any computer in the world. However, this is possible if and only if the email application on the computer is configured to use POP3.

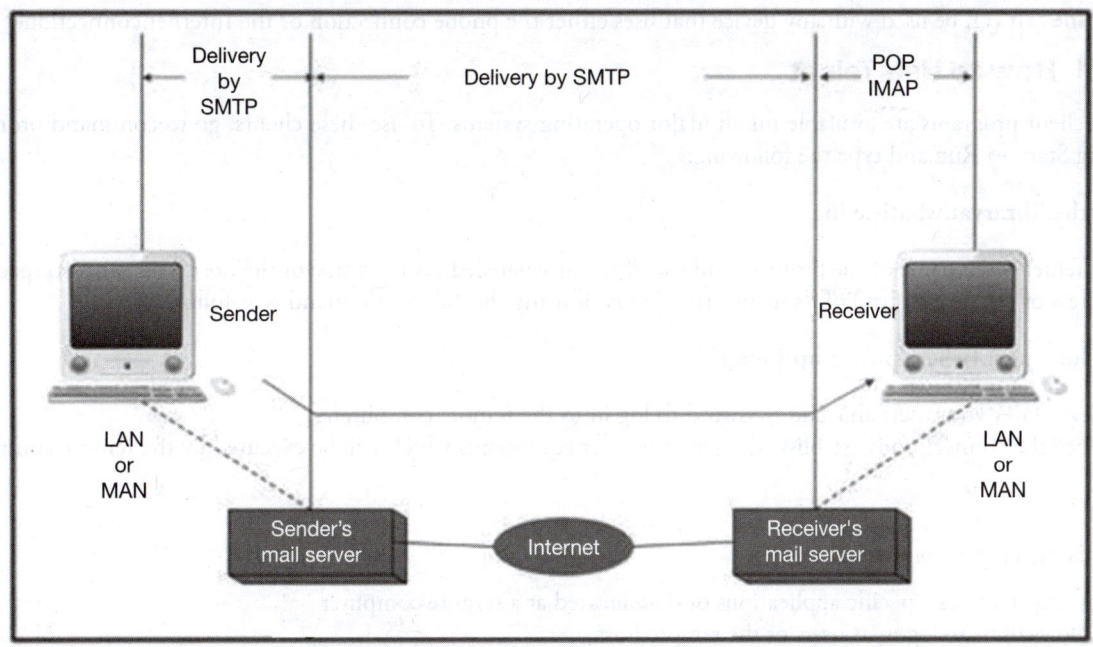

Figure 8.41   Delivery by POP3 and IMAP

Users can configure POP3 to "store" email on the server for a certain period of time thereby allowing users to download it multiple times within that given time frame.

Though IMAP is an alternative protocol to POP3, POP3 is more commonly used because of its simplicity, high rate of success and minimum errors. POP3 can work with virtually any email program, as long as the email program is configured to use the protocol. Many popular email programs like Eudora and Microsoft Outlook are automatically designed to work with POP3.

8.22   TERMINAL EMULATION

Terminal emulation or Telnet is a text-based protocol that uses the underlying TCP/IP technology for accessing a remote computer's (called host) data and application programs. Users can use the Telnet client software to connect with the Telnet server (or the remote host) as shown in Figure 8.42. Once the Telnet client establishes a connection to the remote host, the client becomes a virtual terminal and can communicate with the remote host from his/her computer.

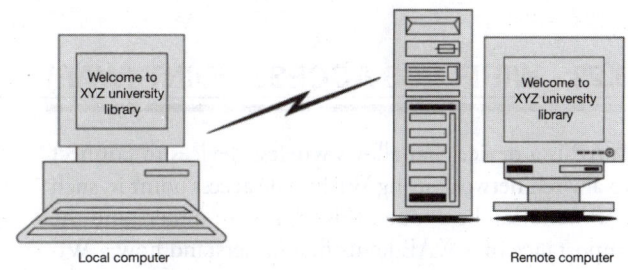

Figure 8.42   Telnet protocol

Features

The following are the features of Telnet.

Bidirectional: It is used to send and receive information. This means that data travels in both directions.

Interactive: It accepts a command from the user, executes it on the remote computer, and displays the result on the user's screen.

Text-oriented: It is a text-based protocol that lacks usage of GUI.

Versatile: It can be used with any device that uses either the phone connection or the Internet connection.

8.22.1 How to Use Telnet

Telnet client programs are available for all major operating systems. To use these clients, go to command prompt by clicking Start → Run and type the following:

telnet the.libraryat.whatis.edu

where Telnet is the name of the protocol and the.libraryat.whatis.edu is the name of the host. You can also specify the IP address of the host instead of its name. The syntax of using the Telnet command is as follows:

telnet host port (where port is optional)

Next, enter your username and password to log in to the remote computer.
Once the connection is established, users can enter commands which will be executed by the remote computer.

Uses

Telnet is used in the following areas:

- It is used to access specific applications or data located at a remote computer.
- It allows users to log in as users of the remote host.
- Even a dumb terminal can use the applications hosted on the world's most powerful computer.
- It enables users to control the server and communicate with it over the network.
- It enables research scholars and professors to log in to the university's computer from any terminal.
- It allows users to access databases, library catalogues, and other information resources around the world.

Telnet has now evolved as secure shell (SSH) and is used by network administrators to manage Unix and Linux computers from a remote computer.

Shortcomings

The drawbacks of Telnet are as follows:

- It is a text-based computer protocol and lacks a fancy screen with images, animation, and hyperlinks.
- It is insecure because it transfers all data in clear text.
- Users cannot transfer files using Telnet.

8.23 WIRELESS ACCESS POINT (WAP)

WAP is a device that allows wireless devices to connect to a wired network using Wi-Fi. The access point in such a scenario can be a router (Fig. 8.43). To understand the importance of a WAP, let us first understand how a Wi-Fi network operates.

Like walkie-talkies, cell phones, radios and televisions, a wireless network uses radio waves for a two-way communication in the following manner.

Step 1: A computer's wireless adapter receives the user's data and translates it into a radio signal.

Step 2: A wireless router receives the radio signal and decodes it.

Step 3: The router sends the decoded data to the Internet via a physical, wired connection.

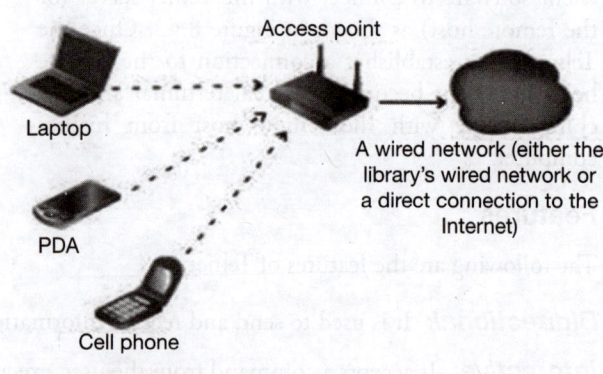

Figure 8.43 Wireless Access Point (WAP)

At the receiver's site, the same set of process takes place but in reverse. The router receives the data from the Internet via a wired connection. It translates data into radio signals and transmits it to the sender's wireless adapter.

If many computers are present, each with its own wireless adapter, then all these computers can use a single router to connect to the Internet (Fig. 8.43). However, if the router fails or if too many users access high-bandwidth applications at the same time then users may either suffer from electromagnetic interference or may get disconnected.

> Interference which degrades the signal is a common problem in wireless networks. Electromagnetic interference can either occur due to other networks or because of devices that generate radio waves that are within, or close to the radio bands used for communication.

8.24 WORLDWIDE INTEROPERABILITY FOR MICROWAVE ACCESS (WiMAX)

WiMAX is a wireless communications standard that has been specifically designed for creating metropolitan area networks (MANs). It is similar to the Wi-Fi standard, but unlike Wi-Fi that can provide connectivity in limited range of distance (within few hundred feet), Wimax supports a greater coverage in terms of area (up to 30 miles). Moreover, mobile WiMAX stations can broadcast up to 10 miles.

While Wi-Fi can be used to provide internet connectivity for home networks and coffee shops, multiple Wi-Fi repeaters should be set up to cover larger areas. This is not just an inefficient way to provide wireless access but also something that requires a lot of maintenance. WiMAX, on the other hand, can cover several miles using a single station thereby providing greater coverage with less maintenance efforts.

The technical name of WiMAX is "IEEE 802.16", and that of Wi-Fi is 802.11. WiMAX is considered to be the second generation of broadband wireless access standard and will be used along with Wi-Fi. WiMAX aims to provide wireless internet connectivity across cities and even other large areas. In fact, some proponents of WiMAX predict that it will eventually provide Internet access across the globe. Therefore, we can say that WiMAX operates at higher speeds over greater distances and for a greater number of users. WiMAX can provide service even in areas where wired infrastructure is difficult to install.

WiMAX provides quality-of-service capabilities for applications ranging from downloading text files to real-time streaming video.

WiMAX provide two forms of wireless service:

Non-line-of-sight service uses a small antenna on your computer to connect to the WiMAX tower.

Line-of-sight service in which a fixed dish antenna points straight at the WiMAX tower from a rooftop or pole. This service provides a stronger and more stable connection to send more data with fewer errors.

> The WiMAX wireless coverage is measured in square kilometers (miles) while that of Wi-Fi is measured in square meters (yards).

WiMAX supports very high peak data rates – about 25 Mbps and 6.7 Mbps for downloading and uploading data, respectively. It has the potential to allow millions of devices to access the Internet wirelessly, cheaply and easily.

8.25 VOICE OVER INTERNET PROTOCOL (VoIP)

VoIP is a technology that allows users to make voice calls using a broadband Internet connection instead of a regular (or analog) phone line. Users can talk to anyone having internet connection or at least a telephone number be it local, long distance, or an international number.

> VoIP (voice over IP) is the transmission of voice and multimedia content over Internet Protocol (IP) networks.

8.25.1 How VoIP / Internet Voice Works

VoIP services convert our (analog) voice into a digital signal that can be sent over the Internet. However, if a user is calling another person's regular phone number, the signal is converted to a regular telephone signal before it reaches the destination.

VoIP allows users to make a call directly from their computer, a special VoIP phone, or a traditional phone connected to a special adapter. Moreover, wireless hot-spots in airports, parks, cafes, etc. allow users to connect to the Internet and use VoIP service wirelessly.

What Kind of Equipment Do I Need?

To use VoIP services, we need to have the following:

A broadband high-speed **Internet connection** is required.

A **computer** (or even a smartphone), **adaptor**, or **specialized phone** for making calls. When using a computer, some software and an inexpensive microphone are also required. Special VoIP phones plug directly into the broadband connection and operate like a traditional telephone. When using a traditional telephone with a VoIP adapter, you just need to dial the number. The service provider may also provide a dial tone.

Once we have the required set-up (Fig. 8.44), we can make a local or a long-distance call using our equipment. The increasing usage of VoIP can be easily understood from the graph given in Fig. 8.45, which shows the market size of VoIP applications from the year 2014 to 2024.

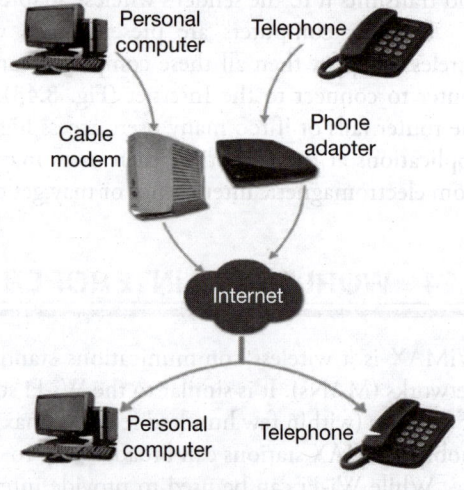

Figure 8.44 VoIP setup

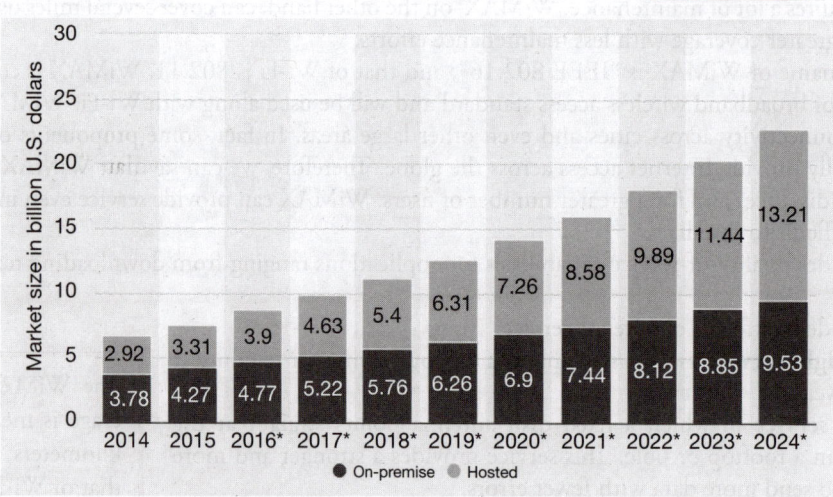

Figure 8.45 Market size of VoIP applications

Sources: Statista estimates; grand view research; © Statista 2019

Advantages of VoIP

Users can access features and services that are not available with a traditional phone, or are available but only for an additional fee.

Users do not need to pay for both a broadband connection and a traditional telephone line (Fig. 8.46).

VoIP applications integrate voice, video and text chat. Apple's FaceTime, Zoom, Google Meet and WhatsApp are all examples of VoIP applications.

- VoIP applications allow users to place a conference call involving more than one user simultaneously. This makes VoIP systems much more scalable.

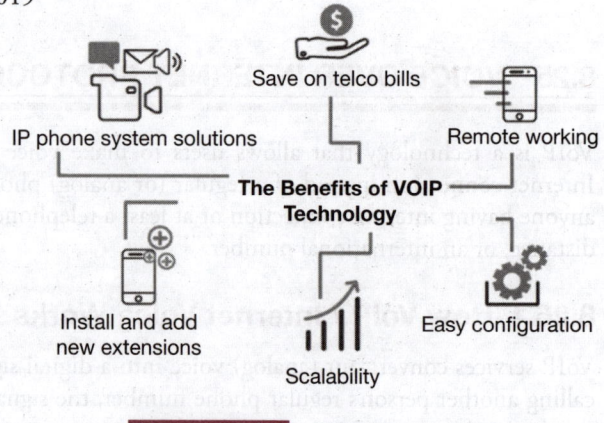

Figure 8.46 Benefits of VoIP

- Services that are usually charged by telecommunication companies like call forwarding, caller ID or automatic redialling, are offered for free using VoIP technology.
- A VoIP system provides significant cost savings over a traditional phone system. Users can make free national and international calls and also avail other services.
- Organizations can enhance their relationship with customers by providing them free 24 × 7 customer support services.
- Working with manpower at remote locations has become much easier with VoIP systems.
- Fax machines are now out-dated, but still VoIP offers fax-to-email services for those who still prefer to use it.
- The infrastructure is less expensive and the system can be setup very easily.
- With a high-speed broadband internet connection, a good VoIP service can provide excellent call quality with very little downtime.

Disadvantages of VoIP

- Some VoIP services do not work during power outages. The service provider also does not offer backup power.
- If users do not have high-speed internet connection, then VoIP is of limited use.
- Poor internet connection can affect the quality of calls.
- VoIP services are vulnerable to cyber-attacks. Though reliable service providers and software systems implement tools and measures to protect against such vulnerabilities, the risk is always there.

8.26 MALWARE

Malware or malicious software means software designed with wrong intentions. A malware is specifically written to gain access to a computer, either to harm it by disturbing its operations or to gather sensitive information from it. Moreover, a malware is usually embedded or hidden within legitimate software that is either useful or attractive.

No doubt, malware is a big threat to computer security. When we say malware, it includes all the terms like computer virus, spyware, worms, Trojan horse, etc. (Fig. 8.47)

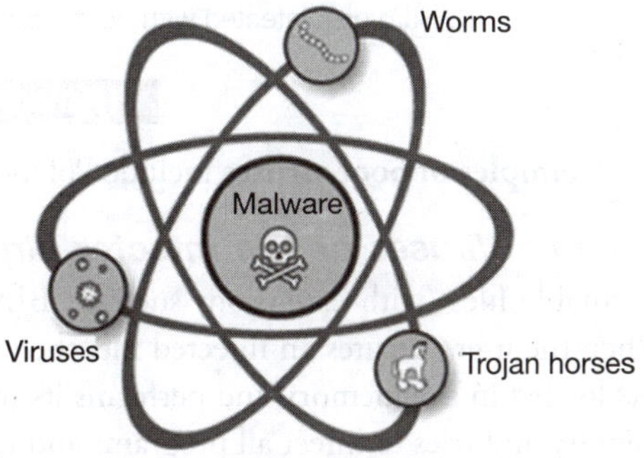

8.26.1 VIRUS (Vital Information Resources Under Seige)

Figure 8.47 Malware

A computer virus is a small program that gets loaded in the computer without the user's knowledge and replicates (repeats) itself. Virus is harmful for the computer as by copying itself repeatedly in the computer's memory, it quickly uses all available memory and finally halts the system. A virus can even corrupt or delete files from the computer and may spread itself to other computers by using the user's email.

Therefore, computer viruses are always undesirable as they slow down the computer's performance, cause erratic behavior, loss of data, and frequent crashes.

Features of Virus: A virus replicates itself. It is always embedded in a legitimate file. Moreover, a virus gets activated by an external action. For example, when a user downloads and opens a file that contains virus.

Sources of Virus: Sources of computer virus (Fig. 8.48) include the following:

- Files that are either attached in email messages or sent while chatting

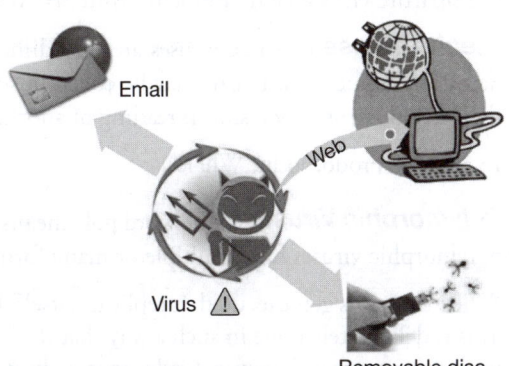

Figure 8.48 Sources of virus

- Embedded in funny images, greeting cards and in audio/video files
- Some files downloaded from the Internet may contain virus

Examples of virus are: W32.Sfc!mod, ABAP.Rivpas.A, Accept.3773, ILOVEYOU, Code Red, Melissa, Stuxnet.

8.26.1.1 Types of Virus

We can broadly classify computer viruses under different categories like,

Boot Viruses: Back when floppy disks were used to transfer data, these viruses were used to infect them. However, as floppy disks are no longer used, the boot virus infects only the master boot records of the hard disk.

The boot record stores the code that loads the operating system in the memory when the computer is turned on. Boot record viruses either overwrite the boot record or move it to a different location in the hard disk. When the operating system is somehow loaded in memory, the virus also gets loaded along with the operating system as shown in Fig. 8.49. Once loaded, the virus performs all malicious activities without getting noticed.

> The master boot record on the hard disk is the first sector on the hard disk.

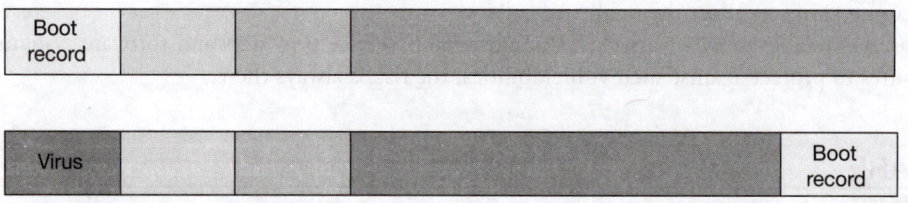

A. Hard disk before virus attack
B. Hard disk infected with boot record or the boot sector virus. The virus has relocated the boot record.

Figure 8.49   Working of boot sector virus

Examples of boot viruses include Polyboot.B, AntiEXE, Disk Killer, and Stoned.

Program Viruses or File Infector Viruses: These are the most common type of viruses. They infect only executable files (with extensions such as .BIN, .COM, .EXE, .SYS) of applications, music files, videos, games, etc. When the user executes an infected file, the virus also gets executed along with the file. On being executed, the virus gets loaded in the memory and performs its intended task (like overwriting or deleting files, etc.). A file virus stays in memory and tries to infect all programs and files that are loaded in memory at that particular point of time.

Examples of file virus are Snow.A, Jerusalem, and Cascade.

Multipartite Viruses: Multipartite viruses are a combination of boot viruses and program viruses. Like program viruses, they infect an executable file. When the user unknowingly executes the infected file, the multipartite virus infects the master boot records in the hard disk just like the boot record virus. Examples of multipartite virus include Emperor, Anthrax, Tequilla, and One_Half.

> It is easier to identify and remove program virus than the boot virus.

Stealth Viruses: These viruses are very difficult to detect as they make use of different techniques to avoid their detection. Some stealth virus may be coded in such a way that if the user has instructed the computer to read one file then stealth virus may result in reading of another file.

Examples: Frodo, Joshi, Whale.

Polymorphic Viruses: The word poly means many and polymorphic means 'many forms'. So, as the name implies, polymorphic viruses have multiple or many forms.

When this virus gets executed, it replicates itself. However, while replicating, the virus makes small changes in the code. This is deliberately done in such a way that the code is slightly different but the malicious intentions and harm caused to the computer is the same. Codes that replicate in this way are difficult to be detected by anti-virus.

Examples include Elkern, Marburg, Satan Bug, and Tuareg.

Macro Viruses: A macro virus infects documents that contain macros (a special type of program). Programs like Microsoft Word, PowerPoint and Excel are easily prone to this type of virus as they support macros.

For example, whenever users open any Word document, the uninfected document also gets infected. Once infected, the repairing of that file is very difficult. Moreover, when a macro virus-infected file is opened on another computer, the virus spreads on that computer also.

Examples of macro viruses are Relax, Melissa.A, Bablas, O97M/Y2K, and WM.NiceDay.

Resident Viruses: A resident virus, as the name suggests, resides in the computer's memory (RAM) and perform all its intended tasks (like corrupting other opened files and programs). A resident virus can run independently even without the originally infected file.

Examples include Randex, CMJ, Meve, and Mr Klunky.

Direct Action Viruses: These viruses replicate and perform their intended action only when the infected file is being executed. At other times, the virus becomes dormant (in sleep mode). Direct action viruses get activated (or come in action) when a specific condition is met. It then infects all the files in its directory and some other files (in the directories specified in the AUTOEXEC.BAT file PATH). Example is the Vienna virus.

Overwrite Viruses: The overwrite virus deletes the data stored in the infected file so that it is no longer usable. There is no way to recover the deleted contents; so the only option that the user has is to delete the entire file.

Examples are Way, Trj.Reboot, and Trivial.88.D.

Directory Virus: As the name suggests, directory virus affects the directories. The virus changes the file path (or file location). When the user opens a file whose location has been changed, the virus gets executed.

> Autoexec.bat is a batch file stored in the root directory of hard disk. It is used to perform some vital operations when the computer is booted.

Network Virus: As the name implies, network viruses rapidly spread through a network. They replicate through files shared on the network.

Examples are Nimda and SQL Slammer.

FAT Virus: File allocation table (FAT) is a table maintained by the operating system that stores information about location, size, and other details of files stored on the hard disk. The FAT virus attacks on the file allocation table.

Once the FAT is infected, it becomes impossible for the computer to locate files. Moreover, the virus spreads to other files when the FAT tries to access them. A file infected by the FAT virus becomes inaccessible to the users.

8.26.1.2 Virus Symptoms and Harm Caused by Virus

As discussed earlier, viruses operate in different ways. While some viruses are active only when the application to which it is attached is running, others will be running as long as the computer is on. Although virus executes without getting noticed by the user, the user can still get some symptoms that will indicate that his/her computer has been infected. Some of these symptoms are:

- Your computer is running slower than normal.
- Computer applications are not working correctly.
- Some important files cannot be accessed.
- You are unable to take a print-out.
- Unusual error messages are being flashed on the screen.

Many viruses arrive by email

- Dialog boxes and menus are not being displayed properly.
- Files have double (two) extensions on attachments.
- The antivirus program is suddenly disabled or not working.
- You are not able to install any antivirus program in your computer.
- You get some new and unusual icons the computer's desktop as shown in Fig. 8.50.
- Strange music or sounds can be heard from the speakers.
- A program that you were using has disappeared from the computer without you deleting it.
- Unwanted programs start running automatically.
- The home page of your web browser gets changed.
- Advertisements are being displayed even when you are not browsing the Internet.
- Hardware devices are not responding.

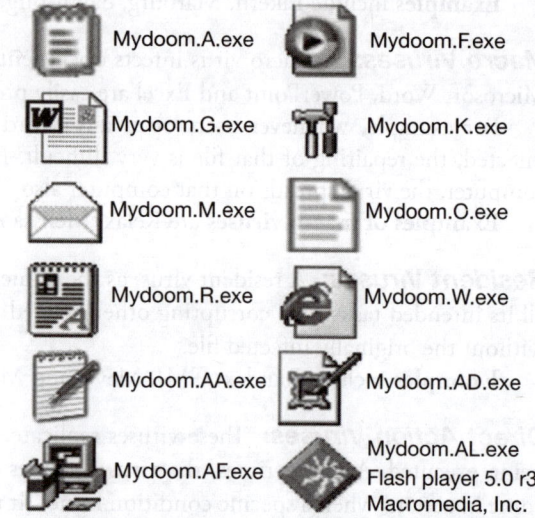

Figure 8.50 Virus files with their icons

8.26.2 Worms

Worms are malicious programs that take control over the computers on which they get installed and steal confidential data from it.

Like viruses, worms also replicate themselves and spread to other computers through a network (Fig. 8.51). Once a worm gets installed, it uses the email program of the user to send a copy of itself to everyone whose email address is present in the user's address book.

However, unlike viruses, most worms do not interfere with the normal use of a computer. They do not harm any file stored on the computer. Moreover, they exist as separate entities and do not attach themselves to other files or programs.

Due to replication, worms take a lot of space in the hard disk, take more time of the CPU (to replicate and spread its infection to other computers), and also take more time on the Internet connection. This, in turn, slows down the computer. The user will not be able to access the Internet properly at a good speed and ultimately the computer may even stop responding (hang).

Examples of worm are: W32.SillyFDC.BBY, Packed.Generic.236, W32.Troresba.

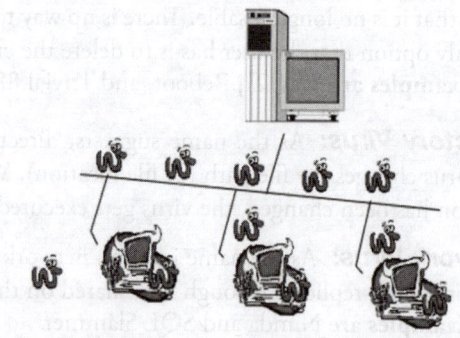

Figure 8.51 Worms spreading through internet

> A computer virus is more dangerous than a worm as it makes changes or deletes your files while worm only replicates itself with out making changes to your files/data.

8.26.3 Trojan Horse

A Trojan horse is a **non-replicating** malicious program that pretends to be harmless so that users can easily download it on their computer. It is usually **embedded within a harmless program.**

When the program containing a Trojan horse is executed, the Trojan also gets executed along with it (as shown in Fig. 8.52). This may result in slow response from the computer, display of annoying messages on the computer screen, theft of data (stealing email addresses, passwords and other confidential information like credit card number) and loss of data (by deleting files). Some Trojans may even give unauthorized access of the victim's computer to its controller, ruin the FAT, and install a virus.

> The name Trojan Horse came from the wooden horse used by the Greek army to conquer the city of Troy and save the beautiful Helen.

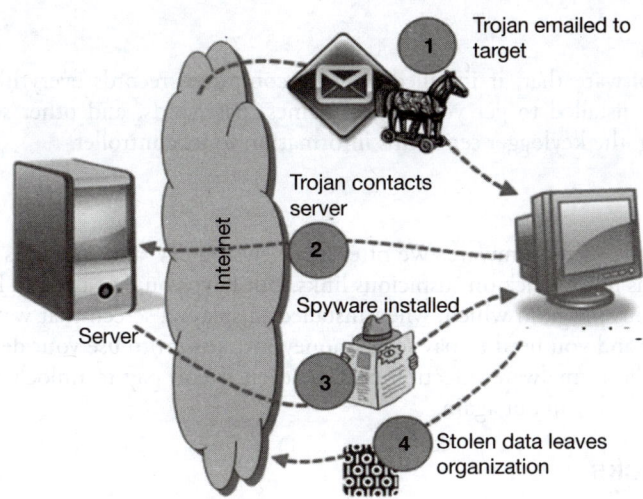

Figure 8.52 Working of a Trojan horse

The only solution to get rid of the Trojan is to delete the infected file or program from the computer.

Example: JS.Debeski.Trojan

> Most antivirus software can detect and remove Trojan horses.

8.26.4 Adware

Adware is an **advertising-supported software**. It is usually embedded within a software, especially software that can be freely downloaded from the Internet. When users download a software that has adware inside it, the adware gets installed in the user's computer. Adware can also be spread through email attachments and shared files on the network. Moreover, some adware can automatically get downloaded while browsing any website.

> Adwares are used by companies for marketing purpose.

Once an adware is installed, advertising banners and pop-ups are displayed while the user is working on the Internet. Adware comes under the category of malware because most of the times, the ads that they display are unwanted and are displayed without the user's permission. Adware displays so many unwanted advertisements that it starts annoying the user and distracts them from doing their work.

8.26.5 Spyware

Spyware is a malicious program that monitors users' activity on their computer and reports it to another person with malicious intentions. Spyware sends all this information without the user's permission. Usually, spyware is used for the following:

> Spyware is a big threat to a user's privacy and security while working on the Internet.

- Monitoring the user's Internet browsing patterns to collect information about his/her login-ids, passwords, bank, or credit card information
- Installing adware, virus, Trojan horse or any other malicious program
- Redirecting web browsers to untrusted sites.

Spyware, like other malicious programs, is embedded in a software that can be freely downloaded from the Internet. Once installed, it is very difficult to remove them from the computer.

> Unlike spyware, adware does not transfer the user's personal information to another location. Both, however, slow down the computer and display unwanted advertisements to annoy the user.

8.26.6 Keyloggers

Keylogger is a malicious software that, if installed in your computer, records everything that you type on your computer. This is especially installed to get your log-in names, passwords, and other sensitive information. After recording what we are typing, the keylogger sends this information to its controller.

8.26.7 Ransomware

You must have heard the name of ransomware. We often get news on TV and messages on WhatsApp about some new ransomware that alerts us not to click on suspicious links. But have you ever tried to know what is ransomware?

Ransomware is a malicious program which, when installed, displays a screen that warns you that you have been locked out of your computer and you need to pay some money (or ransom) to use your device. Such messages are not real notices. They clearly indicate malware infection because even if you pay to unlock the system, the system will either not unlock you or will lock you out again.

8.26.8 Sweeper Attacks

Sweeper attack is another type of malicious program used by unscrupulous people to delete all the data from the computer system.

Some Interesting Facts

Look at the pie-charts given in Fig. 8.53. What do you interpret?

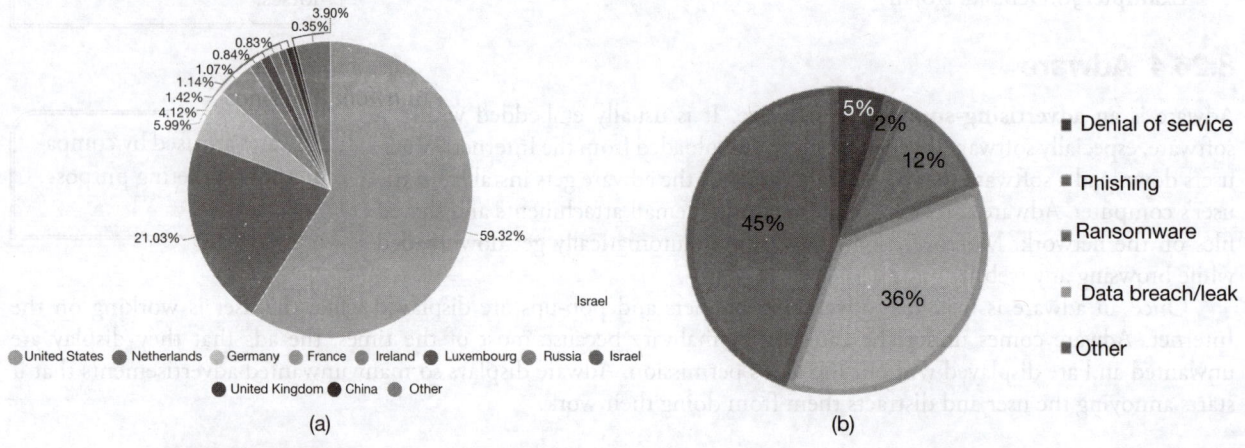

Figure 8.53 (a) USA is the most affected country; (b) Cyber incident types – 2020

Sources: (a) https://securelist.com/it-threat-evolution-q1-2020-statistics/96959/; (b) https://www.govtech.com/policy/2020-marks-a-record-breaking-year-for-cyber-attacks-against-schools.html

8.26.9 Spamming

Spamming means sending unwanted emails in bulk (to a large number of recipients). Spam is considered to be an electronic junk mail, which is usually sent for advertising products. Most spam emails often advertise dubious (not trustworthy) products, get-rich-quick schemes, enticing business opportunities, winning of a lottery or get-easy-loan schemes.

Though spam email is a very cost-effective medium to commercially advertise a product, for the receiver it is a waste of time (Fig. 8.54). Spammers get email addresses which are publicly available on the Internet and use those addresses to send mails to the masses.

In many countries, spamming is considered to be an illegal activity and a person found guilty of spamming has to appear before the court. Therefore, very often spammers either hide or forge the origin of their messages to circumvent laws and anti-spammer lists used by anti-spam software.

Figure 8.54 Spamming

These days, spam is increasingly sent from computers that are infected by **computer viruses.** Virus-makers and spammers have together come up with an idea to use the infected computers as spam-sending "drones" or "zombies". We know that virus spreads rapidly and generate massive amounts of spam, that too when sent from legitimate addresses. Now, even if someone is to be punished, it will be the owner of the infected computer system who is himself a victim.

> There was a time when 95% of email messages sent worldwide were recognized as spam.

Therefore, it becomes even more important to install effective **anti-virus software** to prevent your computer from being infected and possibly become a source of spam even without your knowledge.

Preventive Measure

- **Never ever open and reply** to a spam message.
- Identify the spam email by reading its subject and just delete it right away. Messages with subjects like a more youthful appearance, prescription drugs without a doctor's approval, love, thicker hair, or a better mortgage rate are all spam.
- Even if you open the spam, **don't click** *any* **links** in that email. Not even the unsubscribe link.
- **Do not forward** an email from someone you don't know to a list of people. There are many messages on WhatsApp, Facebook and email that ask the recipient to forward the email or message to 20 people, for example, and expect a miracle etc. These messages are spam and when they are forwarded, each time 20 more people get affected. Messages like sign-and-forward emails that often appear in the form of a petition are also spam.
- **Do not buy any product** advertised in spam mails or messages. If you do so, you not only encourage the spammer but also open the doors for infecting your computer with malware.
- Never share your email address everywhere. Instead keep an email address exclusively for professional purpose and another one for personal purpose (like shopping websites, social networking, etc.).
- Block the spam messages.
- Many email programs as well as ISPs use a spam filter to automatically block all spam messages as shown in Figure 8.55.
- The user also has an option to mark an email as Spam, so that next time it comes from the same sender, it is automatically sent to the 'Spam' or 'Junk' folder.

Figure 8.55 Spam folder in email

> If your email account receives lot of spam messages then it is better to delete that account and create a new one with a different id.

8.27 HTTP COOKIE

Also known as a web cookie, an Internet cookie or a browser cookie indicates information that is stored on a computer by a web server. The browser stores each message in a small file, called **cookie.txt**. The computer sends this information back to the server each time the user visits that website. The computer does not change the information it receives from the web server.

Cookies are files that contain information like a username and password that are exchanged between a user's computer and a web server to identify a particular user and improve his/her overall browsing experience.

For example, cookies allow websites to retain the user's login credentials and preferences, such as colours, themes, sports, news, etc. The computer remembers cookies using the **name=value pair.** When the user re-visits the website in future, the web browser automatically returns the user's information previously stored on the web server in the form of a cookie.

There are two types of cookies:

Session Cookies are used only while navigating a website. They are stored in the RAM and are never written to the hard drive. Therefore, as soon as the session ends, these cookies are automatically deleted. In this way, session cookies maintain user privacy.

Persistent Cookies are stored on the computer's hard disk and are thus retained even after the session ends. Usually these cookies have an expiration date and are automatically removed when that date is reached.

Persistent cookies are used for two main reasons:

Authentication: Cookies track the username and password with which a particular user has logged in to the website. They are a big help to users as they have to no longer remember passwords for that site. (Note that when you click on the Save Password option, the username and password are actually stored as cookies on the computer).

Tracking: Cookies can also be used to track multiple visits to the same site over time. Some online websites use cookies to track pages visited by a particular user and products ordered or added to their wish lists. This information is then used to suggest other products in which the user may be interested.

8.27.1 Security Concerns

- Usually, cookies cannot transfer viruses or malware to the user's computer.
- Cookies cannot pass any confidential information to the web server as cookies are the information sent by the server and this information cannot be changed in any way. Because the data in a cookie does not change when it travels back and forth, it has no way to affect how your computer runs.
- Computer cookies not only keep track of data for websites, but they also hold a host of personal information.
- Some cyber-attacks can hijack cookies and get all information regarding user's browsing sessions.

8.27.2 Removing Cookies

Deleting or prohibiting all sorts of cookies will make navigation to some websites difficult. Without cookies, users may have to re-enter their data for each visit. Before removing cookies, users must evaluate the ease of use expected from a website that uses cookies because cookies always improve the web experience. Users can just handle them carefully to make a balance between ease and security concerns.

However, we can practise some control over third-party and tracking cookies to protect our privacy.

Third-party cookies pose serious security threat as they are generated by websites other than those that the user is currently surfing. These websites may be linked to ads on web page(s) being visited by users. Therefore, visiting a site with 10 ads may generate 10 cookies, even if users do not click on them.

> Zombie cookies are used by web analytics companies to track unique individuals' browsing histories or even to ban specific users.

Some third-party cookies may be zombies. **Zombie cookies,** also known as flash cookies, are permanently installed on users' computers, even when they opt not to install cookies. They also reappear after they have been deleted, so it is very difficult to remove them.

8.28 FIREWALL

Firewall is either a hardware or a software that is installed between the network of an organization and the rest of Internet. We have already seen that a computer connected to the Internet is open to several types of attacks. In organizations, a lot of confidential data is stored on the computers. No company would want their sensitive data to be disclosed to an unauthorized person or deleted or overwritten by a malicious program. Therefore, a sound protection of computers in an organization is of prime importance.

In Fig. 8.56, we see that the main purpose of a firewall is to separate a secure area from a less secure area and to control communications between the two.

> In our home computers, we usually use software firewall (or personal firewalls).

We can use a software firewall in our home computer to prevent unwanted access to the computer over a network connection. For example, you can set the firewall to limit Internet access to email only, so that no other types of information can pass between your computer and the Internet.

> A firewall is a software program or piece of hardware that helps screen out hackers, viruses, and worms that try to reach your computer over the Internet.

In many schools, you cannot open Facebook, YouTube or download a song or movie. This is because the firewall is configured to reject any data going to or coming from these websites. Firewalls have become so important today that every operating system including Windows, Mac, Linux, etc. offer built-in support for maintaining and testing firewalls on the computer and the firewall is turned on by default.

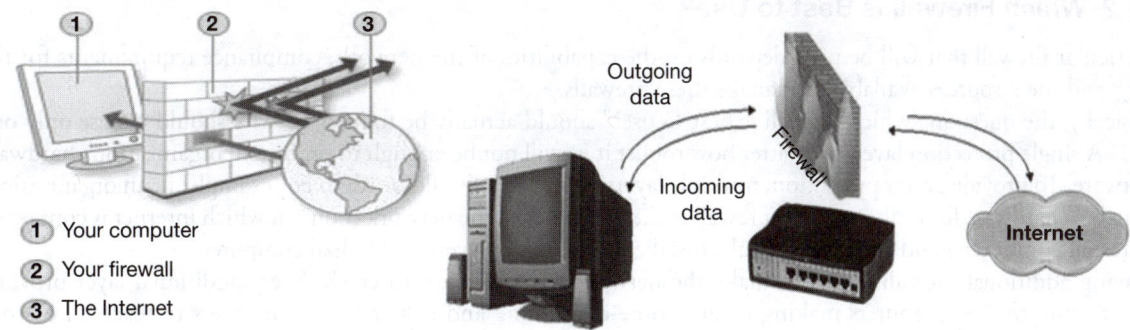

Figure 8.56 All incoming and outgoing data packets have to pass through the firewall

8.28.1 Types of Firewalls

The different types of firewalls are explained in this section.

Packet Filtering: This technique examines each data packet that either enters or leaves the network. Based on the result of examination, it accepts or rejects the packet depending on user-defined rules.

Although packet filtering is a fast, efficient, and effective technique, it is difficult to configure and is susceptible to spoofing. Moreover, packet-filter firewalls cannot tell whether a packet is part of an existing data exchange or a new one. This is because each packet is treated in isolation. Thus, packet filtering can allow or reject data packets based on the IP address of the sender and receiver machines.

Stateful Firewalls: Stateful firewall overcomes the drawback of packet filters by recording all connections passing through it. This gives enough information to determine whether a packet is the start of a new connection, an existing connection, or not a part of any connection. When the state of the packet is known, the firewall can speed up packet processing by allowing a packet of an existing connection without further analysis and evaluating only those packets (based on rules) that are coming through a new connection. Stateful firewall analyses data packets irrespective of IP address; they check the state of the data packets.

Application-layer Firewalls or Proxy Firewalls: With increasing attacks against web servers, a firewall is required to protect servers and the applications running on them. For this, application firewalls that inspect and filter packets are implemented to block specific content (such as malware or certain websites) and report when applications are misused.

However, practically speaking, most firewalls use more than one technique to implement security mechanisms. Proxy firewalls block or allow traffic based on its rule set. These rules can be based on the following features.

IP addresses Block data coming from or going to a certain IP address or a range of IP addresses.

Domain names Allow or disallow data from certain specific domain names or domain name extensions such as .edu, .com, gov, .net, .mil.

Protocols Allow or disallow data that uses protocols such as IP, SMTP, FTP, UDP, ICMP, and Telnet. Every protocol supports a different type of service.

Keywords Allow or disallow data flow that contains certain keywords or phrases. This is done to block offensive or unwanted data from flowing in.

8.28.1.1 Cloud Firewalls

When cloud computing technology is used to deliver a firewall service, it is called a cloud firewall, or firewall-as-a-service (FaaS). Cloud firewalls usually have proxy firewalls installed but it is not mandatory that only a proxy firewall should be used to provide firewall service through cloud.

The main advantage of using cloud-based firewalls is that they are very easy to scale when demand for such a firewall grows in an organization. In such a case, additional capacity has to be added to the cloud server to filter larger traffic loads.

8.28.1.2 Which Firewall is Best to Use?

The particular firewall that will be used depends on the capabilities of the network, compliance requirements for the industry, and the resources available to manage these firewalls.

Basically, the question "which firewall is best to use?" should actually be framed as "why should we use only one firewall?" A single protection layer, no matter how robust it is, will not be enough to protect an organization's hardware and software. To provide better protection, multiple layers of firewalls should be used. For example, in an organization, there can be a hardware firewall or a cloud firewall at the perimeter of the network (point at which internet is connected with internal computers) and software firewalls installed and used on every individual computer.

Having additional firewalls helps to make the network more difficult to crack. Every additional layer provides extra protection to the computers making it more time-consuming and riskier for the attackers to reach all of your most sensitive information

8.29 HTTPs

HTTPs is a secure version of HyperText Transfer Protocol (HTTP). The 's' stands for secure. HTTPs ensures secure communication between a user's browser and a web server. A website supporting HTTPs protocol has its URL beginning with https://. Moreover, whenever you are accessing a secured website, you can always see a green address bar or padlock in the browser window.

HTTPs is very much important for e-commerce websites and those websites that accept online payments or confidential data. It sends this data securely to the server to prevent it from being stolen by malicious users. Besides these reasons, HTTPs has also become important because Google has recently announced that HTTPs will be a factor in their ranking of the websites. HTTPs either uses SSL or TLS (Transport Layer Security) for encrypting data.

To summarize, the benefits of using HTTPs over HTTP include the following:

- It enhances trust of customers by reassuring them that they are using a secure and responsible business.
- Customers are sure about the identity of the business.
- HTTPs increases the ranking by search engines. Besides providing confidentiality, HTTPs also provides authentication. To use HTTPs, a website needs to authenticate itself to prove that it is the site it says it is. For this, the website's administrator asks a CA (certification authority such as Comodo or Symantec) to issue the site a certificate that includes a cryptographic key that, in theory, cannot be forged.
- HTTPs prevents tampering of data by ISPs or hackers. They can no longer insert ads or inject codes designed to compromise a user's computer.

Without HTTPs, a government censor can choose to block certain pages of a site or even just parts of a page. Figure 8.57 shows a comparison of HTTP and HTTPs.

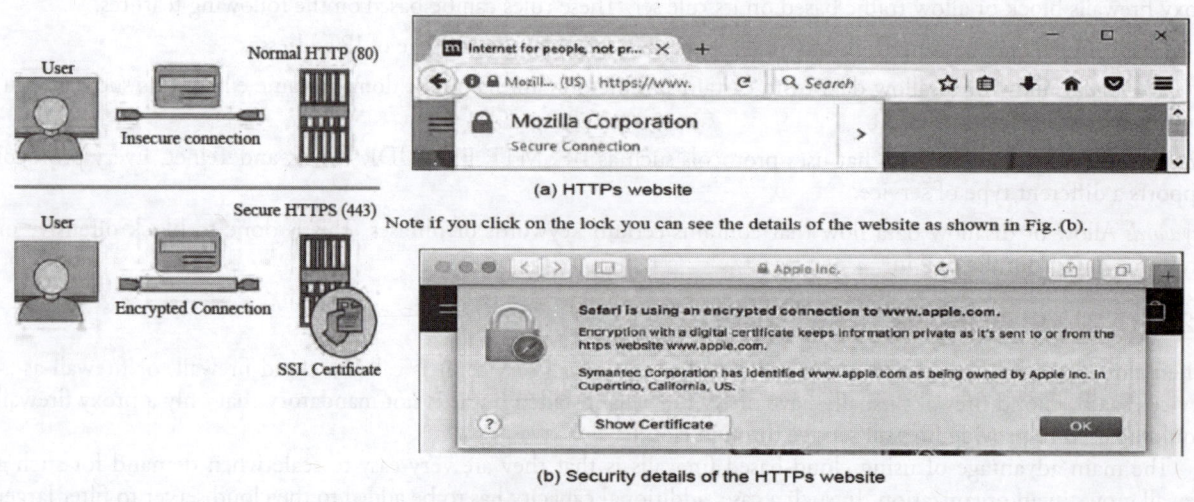

Figure 8.57 HTTP vs. HTTPs

8.29.1 HTTP vs. HTTPs

On a website supporting HTTP, confidential data can be intercepted, spied on and even altered by anyone between the user's website and the web server.

When HTTP website is accessed, the web server responds to user's requests (from the browser). All the data is exchanged in an unencrypted form. On the other hand, with HTTPs website, the user's web browser and the server first exchange cryptographic keys. These keys are then used by the web browser and the web server to send messages that only the other side can decrypt, thereby locking out all hackers.

HTTPs also provides additional privacy for normal web browsing, making your normal web browsing confidential. Hence, any other person will not be able to know the pages you have visited

8.30 INFORMATION TECHNOLOGY ACT 2000

High-speed Internet connectivity has no doubt brought about a communication revolution. However, on the flipside, it has led to an increase in online crimes. A rise in these offences necessitated effective laws for protection online. Keeping this in mind, the Indian Parliament passed the Information Technology Act 2000 (No. 21 of 2000). This was conceptualized on the United Nations Commissions on International Trade Law (UNCITRAL) model.

The Government of India enacted the Information Technology (IT) Act with the objective to deliver and facilitate lawful electronic, digital, and online transactions, and mitigate cybercrimes. It defines the offences, along with the penalties for each category of offence, in detail.

The IT Act of India provides legal recognition for transactions involving exchange of electronic data and other means of electronic communication, commonly referred to as electronic commerce (or e-commerce). E-commerce involves alternatives to paper-based methods of communication and storage of information.

8.30.1 Salient Features of IT Act

Some of the key features of the IT Act are listed here:

1. Digital signatures have been replaced with electronic signatures.
2. A detailed note on offences, penalties, and breaches is given.
3. It talks about the justice dispensation systems for cybercrimes.
4. It provides details for the constitution of the Cyber Regulations Advisory Committee.
5. The Act is based on The Indian Penal Code, 1860; The Indian Evidence Act, 1872; The Bankers' Books Evidence Act, 1891; The Reserve Bank of India Act, 1934; etc.
6. It adds a provision to Section 81, which states that *nothing contained in the Act shall restrict any person from exercising any right conferred under the Copyright Act 1957.*

Some important sections of the Act are given in Table 8.4.

Table 8.4 IT Act sections and punishments

Sections	Particulars	Punishment for the Offence
Section 43	Damage to computer system etc.	Compensation to the person affected.
Section 66	Computer-related offence	Imprisonment for term of 3 years or fine for 5 lakh rupees or both
Section 67	Publication or transmission of obscene material in e-form	Fine of 5 lakh rupees, and imprisonment of 3 years and double conviction on second offence
Section 68	Not complying with directions of controller	Fine up to 1 lakh or imprisonment of 2 years or both.
Section 70	Protected system	Imprisonment up to 10 years and shall also be liable for a fine.
Section 72	Breaking confidentiality of the information of computer	Imprisonment for term of 2 years or fine of 1 lakh rupees or both
Section 73	Publication of false digital signatures	Imprisonment for term of 2 years or fine for 1 lakh rupees or both
Section 74	Publication of digital signatures for fraudulent purpose	Imprisonment for term of 2 years or fine for 1 lakh rupees or both

8.31 CYBERCRIME

Cybercrime is a criminal activity that either targets or uses a computer, a computer network or a networked device. Cybercrimes are purposely committed for financial, political or personal gains.

The professionalization and proliferation of cybercrime results in massive loss to the country every year, thereby impacting individuals, businesses, and even governments. Experts estimate that cybercrime damages will reach $6 trillion annually by the end of 2021. With widespread use of IoT (Internet of Things) devices, cybercriminals have found increased opportunities to penetrate security measures, gain unauthorized access, and commit crimes.

8.31.1 Common Examples of Cybercrime

Malware: Malware infections are used to infect computer systems, destroy files and adversely impact their overall functionality. They are programmed to self-replicate to jump to other devices and systems. As discussed, malware includes virus, worms, Trojan horse, adware, spyware and ransomware.

Hacking: Hacking is a cybercrime that involves unauthorized use of a system.

Phishing: Phishing is the act of sending an email or messages to a user falsely claiming to be a legitimate authority. Phishing is done to scam the user to get his personal information (this is an example of identity theft).

A phishing email usually asks the user visit a website (that is actually bogus) to update his/her personal information like password, credit card number, social security number, or bank account numbers. All this information is already available with the legitimate website. The bogus website captures the details entered by the user and steals it to commit a crime.

The bogus website is created in such a way that it looks exactly like the original website. This is done so that the user does not suspect the website before entering the information. The graph given in Fig. 8.58 shows that the number of phishing cases are constantly increasing worldwide.

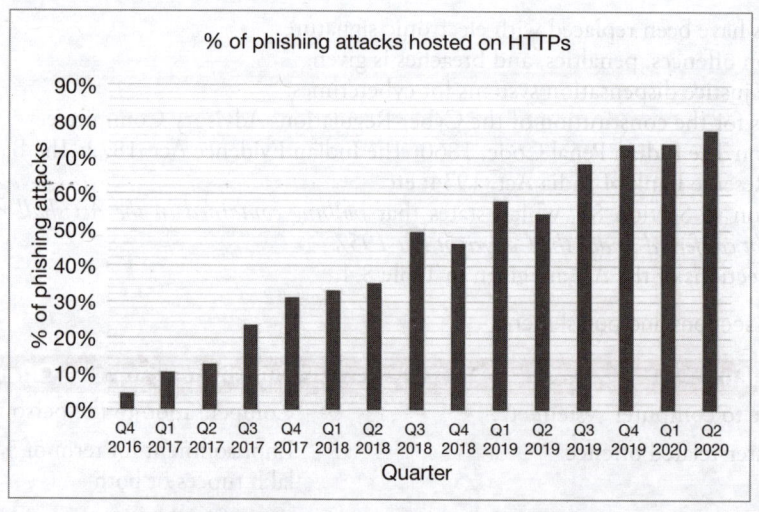

Figure 8.58 Phishing attacks worldwide

Source: APWG

Spoofing: The word *spoof* means to hoax, trick, or deceive. Correspondingly, spoofing means tricking or deceiving computer systems or other computer users. This is either done by hiding one's identity or faking the identity of another user on the Internet.

Spoofing can be done in several ways. In the first variant, ***email spoofing***, messages are either sent using a bogus email address or faking the email address of another user. However, since most of the email servers today have security features, it is extremely difficult for unauthorized users to send spoofed emails.

In the second variant of spoofing, which is also known as *IP spoofing*, the IP address of a certain computer is masked so that it becomes difficult for other systems to determine the sender (real sender) of the data. For example, if I send you a letter and in the **From** address, I write your friend's address instead of mine then you will think that you got the letter from your friend. It will be very difficult for you to know that it was me and not your friend who had sent that letter.

In its third variant, the cyber criminals *fake an identity* (like an online username). For example, when posting on a web discussion forum, a user may pretend to be a representative of a company, when actually he/she has no association with it. Moreover, in online chat rooms, users may fake their age, gender and location.

Eavesdropping: Eavesdrop, in general terms, means the practice of actually standing under the eaves of a house and listening to the conversations inside. In computers, eavesdropping means unauthorized real-time interception of a private communication, such as a phone call, email, instant message, video conference or fax transmission.

Voice over IP (VoIP) Internet calling systems that do not use encryption make it relatively easy for an intruder to intercept calls. These calls can be recorded without being observed by the callers.

Even systems that use encryption are vulnerable to such attacks. In August 2009, a Trojan known as Peskyspy was found, which was specifically designed to access Skype call audio before it was encrypted.

The activities of eavesdropping do not disrupt the normal operation of the systems being eavesdropped on. Obviously, when we are overhearing someone else's private conversation, we will never want to disturb the conversation so that we can get maximum information. While eavesdropping, both parties of the communication – the sender and receiver are completely unaware that their communication is being intercepted and data is being stolen.

Devices with microphones including laptops and cell phones can also be hacked to remotely activate their microphones and send data to the attacker.

An eavesdropping attack, which is also known as a **sniffing or snooping attack**, is difficult to detect because it does not cause any operational abnormalities in network transmissions.

> Encryption means changing the actual information in such a way that it appears to be some random data. For example, **HELLO** can be sent as KHOOR. Did you notice that here, 3 is added to every character making it difficult to understand what information was originally sent?

> Eavesdropping on a conventional telephone line is known as wiretapping.

Child Pornography: Child pornography is defined as "any visual depiction of sexually explicit conduct involving a child, which includes photograph, video, digital or computer-generated image indistinguishable from an actual child and an image created, adapted or modified to appear to depict a child".

In simple terms, Child Sexual Abuse Material or CSAM, legally known as child pornography refers to any content that depicts sexually explicit activities involving a child. CSAM is often circulated for personal consumption. More recently, live-streaming sexual abuse has been reported in large numbers. In such instances, some people pay to watch the live abuse of a child through video conferencing software. This type of abuse is far more difficult to detect because of its real-time nature and the lack of digital evidence left behind following the crime.

CSAM is a global issue and the United States remains one of the largest producers and consumers of child abuse content in the world. Researchers have listed the risk factors that may increase the potential for children of any age group and background to be exposed to sexual abuse.

Child sexual abuse images and videos found online have both boys and girls who are in the age group 0–18 years. The severity of this abuse can be understood from the fact that the Canadian Centre for Child Protection found that in 78.30% of the images and videos, children under 12 years were depicted and 63.40% of those children were under 8 years of age. Also, they found that 80.42% of the children were girls, while 19.58% were boys.

CSAM causes trauma that carries into adulthood. Most of the times, CSAM victims are abused by their known people whom they trust. These offenders have close access to the children they are abusing. This closeness helps them to normalize sexual contact and maintain secrecy.

Spreading Rumour and Cyber Bullying: Cyber bullying or Internet bullying is a form of teen violence that has already caused lasting harm to young people. Some teens use Internet to bully or harass another person (classmates or neighbourhood friends). As a result, the victim goes in depression or inculcates anxiety problems. In many cases victims have even committed suicide (Fig. 8.59).

Figure 8.59   Cyber bullying and its effects

In cyber bullying, teens have been found involved in the following activities. We have laid special emphasis on this point so that students can understand the sensitivity of the matter and avoid such practices.

- Sending threatening messages through smart phones or emails
- Spreading rumors through social networking websites or through group messages
- Stealing someone's email_id and password and using it to send threatening or damaging messages to a third person
- Taking pictures of someone and spreading it through the Internet
- Sexting, or circulating sexually suggestive pictures or messages about a person.

> **SERIOUS NOTE:** Teens often think that cyber bullying is only for fun. But remember that such activities can get you out of your school, affect your admission in college and in getting a job in a reputed organization. Parents of such children can face legal charges for cyber bullying.
> If cyber bullying involved sexting then the offender can be registered as a sex offender.
> Even if teens use fake email ids, there are many ways to find out who had sent these messages.

Internet Frauds and Scams

The downside of using Internet services includes activities such as stealing personal information, conducting fraudulent transactions, or transmitting the proceeds of fraud to financial institutions. Such frauds can occur in chat rooms, email, message boards, or on websites. Some common Internet frauds are discussed below.

Purchase Fraud: occurs when a criminal purchases a product or service online and pays for it through fraud, for example, using a stolen or a fake credit card. As a result, merchants do not get paid for the transaction and lose money.

Online Auction Fraud: occurs when a fraudster starts an online auction of high-priced items on a website. He then accepts payment from the auction winner, but either does not deliver the product or delivers a product that is less valuable than the one offered. This is the most common fraud on the Internet.

Online Retail Fraud: is similar to the auction fraud in which, after receiving the payment, either the product is not delivered or an inferior product is delivered.

Work from Home: scam occurs when business opportunities are advertised on the Internet and users are asked to pay nominal to substantial sums of money to get themselves registered. The fraudster collects thousands of dollars but never delivers the promised material or adequate information to the subscribers. Instead, he or she sends advice to the subscriber on how to place ads similar to the one through which the subscriber got recruited. In another scenario, the scammer accepts services from the victims (like writing directories, data entry, reading books, etc.) but then refuse to reimburse them by rejecting their work considering it sub-standard.

Pharming: occurs when a hacker exploits vulnerability in the Domain Name System (DNS) to redirect website traffic from a legitimate website to his/her fraudulent website. This process of making the victim's computer to communicate with the wrong server is called domain hijacking.

The fraudster constructs a fake web site that looks similar to the legitimate site and asks for user's personal information like his bank password, PIN number, bank account number, credit card number, etc. to steal his information and misuse it. This combination of domain hijacking with a phishing website constitutes pharming.

Stock Market Fraud: includes attempts to manipulate securities prices on the market for the personal profit of the scammer. The scammer usually follows any of the two methods to do this fraud. First is the pump-and-dump scheme in which false information is spread to cause a dramatic increase in price of thinly traded stocks chat rooms, forums, internet boards, or email (as spam). This is called the "pump". The moment prices reach the desired level, scammers sell their stocks (called "dump") to innocent victims thereby making a substantial profit. Later when the prices again fall to their usual prices, the victims realize that it was all a fraud.

In the second technique, called short-selling or scalping, the scammer spreads false information that causes dramatic decrease in prices. Once the stock price falls to the desired level, the scammer buys them in bulk and then reverses the false information or waits for the company to disapprove the information in the media. Once the stock regains its original price, the fraudster sells it making high profits.

Distributed Denial-of-Service Attacks (DDoS)

In DDoS, cybercriminals attack an important computer (like server) to bring down a system or the entire network. For this, large networks of infected devices known as Botnets are created by depositing malware on users' computers. The hacker then hacks into the system once the network is down.

> Botnets comprise of compromised computers that are controlled by remote hackers. The remote hackers send spam or attack other computers through these botnets.

A DoS attack can also be caused by sending a flood of fake data packets to a website to overload the server thereby causing the web server to temporarily malfunction or in some cases, crash completely.

Cyberstalking

Cyberstalking is done by harassing the victim online by sending a plethora of online messages and emails. Cyber-stalkers usually use social media, websites and search engines to intimidate a user and instil fear. Most often, these cyber-stalkers know their victim and want the victim to live in constant fear or be concerned for their safety.

Prohibited/Illegal Content

Sharing and distributing inappropriate content that can be considered highly distressing and offensive also comes under cyberattack. Any content depicting sexual activity between adults, videos with intense violence, videos of criminal activities, advocating terrorism-related acts and child exploitation material are all examples of offensive content.

Cyberextortion

A crime involving an attack or threat of an attack to demand money to stop the attack. Ransomware attack is an example of cyberextortion.

Cryptojacking

An attack that uses scripts to mine cryptocurrencies within browsers without the user's consent. The criminal loads cryptocurrency mining software in the victim's system.

Cyberespionage

A cybercrime in which the cybercriminal hacks into systems or networks to gain access to confidential information held by a government or other organization. It is purposely done to gather, modify or destroy data, as well as use network-connected devices like webcams or closed-circuit TV (CCTV) cameras, to spy on a targeted individual or groups and monitor communications, including emails, text messages and instant messages.

8.32 INTELLECTUAL PROPERTY RIGHTS (IPR)

Intellectual Property Rights (or IPR) are rights that are applicable to creative work which can be treated as an asset or physical property. They can be categorized into four main areas – copyright, trademarks, design rights and patents. Each of these are applicable in various situations and with their own set of technical rules. To protect your idea(s) effectively when launching a new product or doing any other important business activity, you may have to utilize one or more of the IPR types.

© Copyright

Copyright applies to creative work such as literature, art, music and drama as well as in films, sound recordings, drawings, paintings, photography, typographical arrangements or any work that is recorded in some way. These rights protect the author's work by prohibiting unauthorised actions. The author is empowered to take legal action against instances of infringement or plagiarism.

Therefore, while obtaining permission to use creative works, we are talking about copyright law. To use someone else's work, we must take the author's permission.

Trademarks

A trademark can be a name, word, slogan, design, symbol or any other item that is used to identify a product or organisation. Trademarks which are unique for a product or company are to be registered with an appointed government body. The process of registering trademarks may take up to two years in India. However, once registered, a trade mark is valid for ten years and can be renewed thereafter indefinitely for further ten-year periods

Once registered, trademarks are identified by the abbreviation 'TM', or the '®' symbol. In most countries, the national patent office also administers trademarks. You must have observed that all big brands have a trademark (Fig. 8.60).

Figure 8.60 Popular companies' trademarks

Design Rights

Designs (Fig. 8.61) must also be protected by both copyright and design rights. They may also be registered like patents. Once registered, designs are valid for a maximum of ten years and renewable for a further five years.

Crocs D'517,789 Infringing   Apple D'604,305 Infringing

Figure 8.61 Violating design rights

> Unlike copyrighted works, trademarks have different degrees of protection depending on factors including the consumer awareness of the trademark, the type of service and product it identifies, and the geographic area in which the trademark is used.

Patents

Patents are applied to industrial processes and inventions. They also provide protection against unauthorized implementation of the invention. In general terms, patents are grants made by national governments that give the creator of an invention an exclusive right to use, sell or manufacture the invention. All patents must be registered. The process of registering, however, may take 2 to 3 years to complete.

In India, the regulatory authority for patents is the Patent Registrar under the office of the Controller General of Patents, Designs and Trade Marks, which is part of India's Ministry of Commerce and Industry. Once registered, patents are valid for 20 years from the date of filing an application (subject to an annual renewal fee).

India's patent law operates under the 'first to file' principle which states that if two people apply for a patent on a similar invention, then the first one to file the application is awarded the patent.

Right of Publicity

A patchwork of state laws known as the right of publicity protects the image and name of a person against unauthorized use for commercial purposes. For example, no company can use a celebrity's or even a common man's name and picture to advertise their product.

> Internet piracy of films, music, games and software is an issue in India, as is unauthorized copying of physical books.

Trade Secrets

The Trade Secret laws provide protection against sensitive business information. For example, a marketing plan, launch of a new product must be kept confidential as it gives the business an advantage over its competitors (Fig. 8.62).

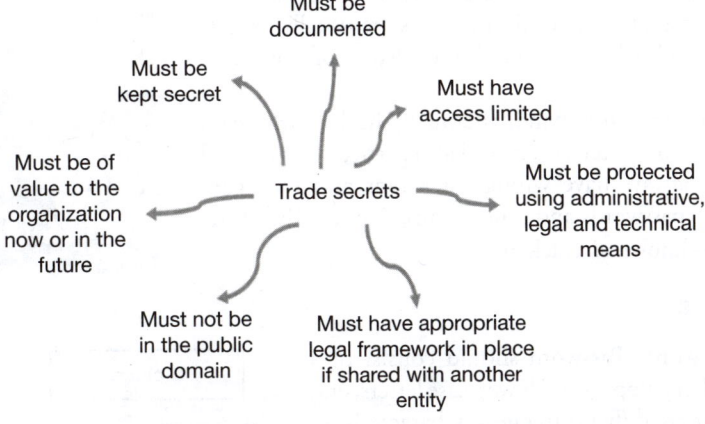

Figure 8.62 The 7 'Musts' of trade secrets

Table 8.5 given below summarizes these techniques.

Table 8.5 Comparison between patents, trademarks, copyrights and trade secrets

		Protects	Infringement	Registration Process	Term	Comparative Costs
Patent	Utility patent	Functional aspects	Make, use, offer, sale, import	Yes	20 years upon filing	Expensive
	Design patent	Ornamental features	Make, use, offer, sale, import	Yes	15 years upon filing	Moderate
Trademarks		Brands	Used in commerce	Optional	Potentially indefinite, limited by use	Inexpensive
Copyrights		Works of authorship	Copying, etc.	Optional	Life plus 70 years	Inexpensive
Trade secrets		Information	Misappropriation	No	Potentially indefinite, limited by secrecy	Depends

8.33 HACKING

Hacking means the act of identifying weakness in a computer system or even a network. Once the weakness is identified, it is exploited to gain access to that computer. For example, if someone has set a very weak password then a hacker (people who hack) can break the password to access the system.

Hacking is a very serious problem today as computers have become a must-have device for all of us and a stand-alone computer without being connected to any network or the Internet is just not enough in today's era. We need to be connected for more information, for better ways to do routine tasks, to socialize and to run a successful business. But this exposes our computers to hackers. **Hackers hack computer systems to commit fraudulent acts such as privacy invasion, stealing corporate/personal data, etc.**

Hacking can either be ethical or unethical. Ethical hacking is done when someone deliberately accesses the computer, but not to break its security and steal data. It is done only to identify any weakness in the system so that they can be overcome. Ethical hackers are usually experts in computer technology who have a sound knowledge of computer hardware and software.

Unethical hacking, on the other hand, is done by hackers who gain unauthorized access to the computer system and also get access to secured accounts. These hackers always have wrong intentions and they gain access usually by cracking passwords and other security codes. Therefore, unethical hackers are also known as crackers.

Preventive Measures

- Create complex passwords. Password should consist of a combination of numbers, upper- and lower-case letters, and special characters that are difficult to guess. Characteristics of an ideal password are given in Fig. 8.63.
- Create a different password for every account. This ensures that even if the hacker has broken your password of one account at least the others are safe.
- Never reveal your passwords to anyone. Not even to your close friend. Do not even write it down on the last page of your notebook or at places that can be easily accessed by others.
- Change your passwords often. You must at least change it once in every 4–5 months.
- Do not repeat your password. Always set a new one. Websites like Gmail never allows you to choose a previous password.
- After checking your emails and using your other accounts, do not forget to log out.
- Install anti-virus software and firewalls
- Download software only from trusted websites
- Do not open emails with attachments coming from unknown people.

Figure 8.63 Features of an ideal passwoard

Include	Do not include
More characters	Dictionary words
More numbers/symbols	Repeated words
Memorable combinations	Personal information
Uppercase and lowercase	The word "Password"

Hackers

A hacker is a person who finds and exploits weakness in a computer system and/or networks to gain unauthorized access to it. Hackers are usually classified into different categories based on their intent (Fig. 8.64).

Ethical Hacker (White Hat Hacker): A hacker who gains unauthorized access to computer or network systems to fix the identified weaknesses.

Cracker (Black Hat Hacker): Also known as unethical hackers, they gain unauthorized access to a computer or network system for personal gains. They do this with intent to steal confidential data, violate privacy rights, transfer funds from bank accounts, etc.

WHITE HAT
Considered the good guys because they follow the rules when it comes to hacking into systems without permission and obeying responsible disclosure laws

GRAY HAT
May have good intentions, but might not disclose flaws for immediate fixes
......
Prioritize their own perception of right versus wrong over what the law might say

BLACK HAT
Considered cybercriminals; they don't lose sleep over whether or not something is illegal or wrong
......
Exploit security flaws for personal or political gain– or for fun

Figure 8.64 White, gray and black hat comparison

Grey Hat Hackers: These hackers lie between ethical and unethical hackers. They deliberately gain unauthorized access into computer or network to identify weaknesses in the system and then reveal them to the system owner. They have no malicious intentions to harm anyone. Some grey hat hackers also hack the system to test their knowledge and skills to see how easily they can break into a system.

Script Kiddies: A non-skilled person who uses available tools to gain unauthorized access to a computer system or network.

Hacktivist: A hacker who hacks a website to post social, religious, and political, etc. messages on it comes under this category.

Phreaker: A hacker who identifies and exploits weaknesses in telephones rather than in computers and computer networks.

8.34 WORLD WIDE WEB

The technical definition of the World Wide Web (WWW) can be given as 'all the resources and users on the Internet that are using the hypertext transfer protocol (HTTP)'. On the web, all documents are formatted in a special markup language called HyperText Markup Language (HTML) that supports links to other documents, graphics, audio, and/or video files. This feature enables users to jump from one document to another simply by clicking on hot spots.

You must have noted that when you position your cursor on a hotspot, also known as hyperlink, the cursor changes to a hand-shaped figure. When you click on the hyperlink, you are taken to another part of the information. Sometimes, there are buttons, images, or portions of images that can be clicked.

In simple terminology, the WWW is a part of the Internet that allows easy navigation through the use of GUIs and hypertext links between different addresses. The WWW that is simply referred to as Web was created in 1989 by Tim Berners-Lee.

The Web can be perceived as the user part of the Internet. Novice or professional users make use of the Web to communicate and access information for business and recreational purposes. Application programs called web browsers make it easy to access the web. Some popular web browsers are Mozilla Firefox, Opera, Google Chrome, and Microsoft Edge (Fig. 8.65).

Figure 8.65 Popular Web browsers

Many a time, we think that the Internet and the WWW are the same, but this notion is not correct. *The Internet and the Web work together. While the Internet provides the underlying structure, the Web on the other hand, utilizes that structure to offer content, documents, multimedia, etc.* For example, the Internet is like the highway, and the WWW is like a truck that uses the highway to get from one place to another.

8.35 HYPERTEXT MARKUP LANGUAGE

HyperText Markup Language (HTML) is rightly said to be the mother tongue of web browsers. It is a standard language understood by all web browsers. HTML consists of a set of markup symbols or codes (commonly known as tags) inserted in a file to be displayed by the web browser such as Google Chrome, Mozilla Firefox, etc. In order to understand HTML, let us first break up these words and try to understand their individual meaning.

Hypertext: The term 'hypertext' is opposite to linear. It is a method by which we browse the Web. By clicking on a hypertext (where the mouse pointer turns into a finger), another text on the same Web page or a different Web page is displayed.

Markup: Markups are the building blocks of HTML. A markup is a code embedded in a file that instructs the web browser how to display the page. Tags are displayed within angular brackets (e.g., <bold>)

Language: HTML is a means of communicating instructions for formatting a hypertext document. It consists of codes and syntax like any other language.

HTML consists of numerous predefined tags to describe page content. Each opening tag (<…>) has a corresponding closing tag (</…>). The content to be displayed is written in between the tags. The tags instruct the web browser to display the content as specified by the tag. For example, the statement in HTML code,

```
<bold> Hello, World!!! </bold>
```

will be displayed as

Hello, World!!!

on the screen. From the example, we can observe that the tags themselves do not appear on the web page when you view it through a web browser. The Web browser reads the tag, interprets it, and applies its effect while displaying the page. Some tags are also used to insert images, text, videos, tables, and forms in a web page.

> You can view the HTML code of a web page by right clicking on a web page and selecting the 'View Source' option from the pop-up menu.

Uses

The following are the uses of HTML:

- It is used for designing Web pages. With HTML, Web page designers can embed text, images, audio, video and interactive forms in a Web page.
- It allows designers to embed scripts (such as JavaScript or VBScript) within a Web page to design interactive pages.

Although HTML is easy to learn and is improved every year, presently, Web pages are rarely designed using only HTML.

8.36 EXTENSIBLE MARKUP LANGUAGE

Like HTML, Extensible Markup Language (XML) is a markup language that defines a set of rules for encoding documents in a format that is readable by humans as well as computers. XML is used to share information in a consistent way. It has been specifically designed for web documents. Like HTML, the basic building block of an XML document is a tag.

Features

Some of the features of XML are as follows:

- It is a flexible markup language as it allows web page designers to create their own customized tags.
- It is a text-based data format.
- It is easy to use and specifies a general format for describing data, which enhances its usability over the Internet.
- It is widely used for representing arbitrary data structures.
- It is designed to be self-descriptive.
- It supports the use of nested tags to represent hierarchical data.

Table 8.6 summarizes the differences between HTML and XML.

Table 8.6 Differences between HTML and XML<message>

HTML	XML
It is designed to display data.	It is designed to describe data.
HTML tags are predefined.	XML tags are not predefined.
It focuses on how data looks.	It focuses on what data is.
It is about displaying information.	It is about carrying information.
It does not need any extra piece of software to display data.	It just describes data. It needs another piece of software to display that data.

Let us take an example to see how data is described in XML with customized tags. In the example, Aditya sends a message to Sarthak:

```
<to>Sarthak</to>
<from>Aditya</from>
<heading>Reunion</heading>
<body>This Friday we have an alumni meet in our school. Let's meet there.
</body>
</message>
```

As we can see from the example, the message is self-descriptive. It has customized tags that represent information about sender, receiver, heading, and body message. These tags are not defined in any XML standard and are invented by the author of the XML document.

The example justifies that XML is self-describing or self-defining. Since the structure of the data is embedded with the data, it can be easily understood. It is, therefore, used to share information in a consistent way.

Final Note

XML is not a replacement for HTML; rather, it complements HTML. In web applications, XML and HTML are used together. While XML is used to describe data, HTML is used to format and display that data.

XML provides a flexible way to create information formats. It allows structured data to be shared electronically through the Internet, Intranet, or Extranet. From this discussion, let us try to conclude the meaning of the individual words in XML.

Extensible: XML is extensible since it allows designers to define their own tags.

Markup: The basic building blocks of XML are markups or tags.

Language: XML is not just a language like HTML. Rather, it is a metalanguage—a language that allows users to create or define other languages. For example, with XML, languages such as RSS, MathML (a mathematical markup language), and even tools like extensible stylesheet language transformation (XSLT) can be created.

8.37 DOMAIN NAME SYSTEM

When you want to talk to a friend, you do not type his number. You may be having several friends and memorizing everyone's number is just not possible. Therefore, you save all important phone numbers along with their names in your phonebook. To connect with your friend, instead of dialling his 10-digit cell number, you just search for his name in the phonebook and click the *Call* button. Although you use the name, your call is not connected based on the name. The name is converted into a number which is then used to establish the connection.

Coming back to the Internet, we have seen that every device has a unique IP address. To connect with a particular device, you need to specify its address. However, we do not really type the IP address. For example, if we want to connect to google.com, we just type www.google.com. Then where is the IP address and how are we able to access the Website? The answer to this question is the domain name system (DNS). Similar to the phonebook service, the Internet has a corresponding DNS service that translates domain names into IP addresses (for example, www.google.com translates to 74.125.224.72). This means that every time we use the Internet, we always use the DNS.

> DNS is a service that automatically converts domain names into IP addresses.

The DNS system works as a network of DNS servers. As maintaining a central database of all the computers on the Internet along with their names and IP address is quite unpractical, the DNS distributes the responsibility of storing domain names and their corresponding IP addresses to authoritative name servers. These name servers are responsible for the domain they support. The authoritative name servers may even delegate authority to other sub-domain servers. Besides providing speedy mapping, this authority delegation process ensures distributed and fault-tolerant service to Internet users.

In such a networked DNS environment, if one DNS server does not know the IP address of a particular domain name, it asks another server for the same. The process is repeated until a proper match between IP address and domain name is found. This concept is shown in Fig. 8.66.

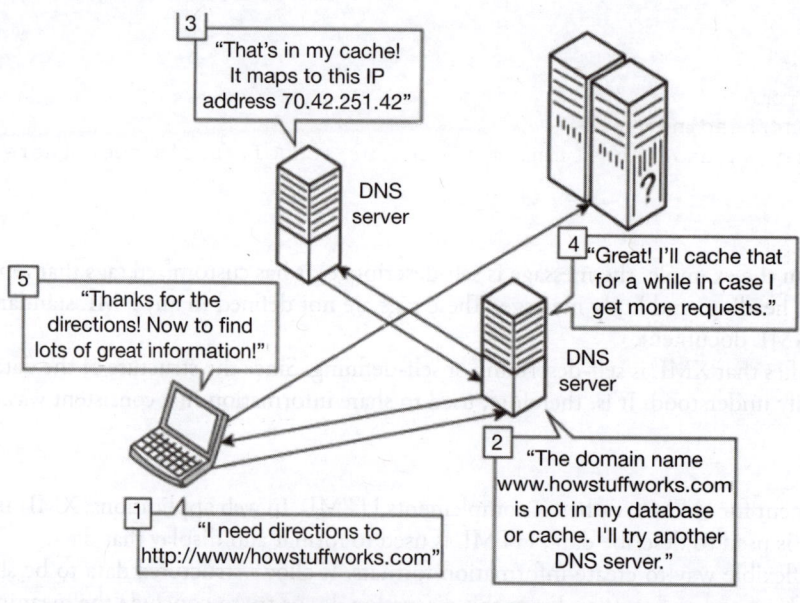

Figure 8.66 Working of DNS

Key points to remember

Here are some key points about DNS:

- It assumes that IP addresses are assigned statically and will not change.
- It supports caching of requests.
- ISPs maintain their own DNS servers to resolve name to IP address mapping.

- Since DNS translation causes additional overhead when accessing any website on the Internet, ISPs cache DNS mapping in their DNS server so that it can automatically direct subsequent requests to the appropriate IP address.
- Some commonly used domains are as follows:
  - **gov** Government agencies
  - **org** Non-profit organizations
  - **com** Commercial business
  - **int** International organizations
  - **edu** Educational institutions
  - **mil** Military
  - **net** Network organizations

- Some country domains are as follows:
  - **ca** Canada
  - **us** Unites States of America
  - **th** Thailand
  - **fr** France
  - **uk** United Kingdom
  - **jp** Japan
  - **in** India

- Other domain names include .museum (for museums), .info (informational websites), .name (personal websites), .pro (for professionals), .aero (for aeronautical companies), .coops (for co-operative organizations), .jobs (for job posting), .mobl (for mobile communication networks), etc.

Like our full names in which the general name or surname comes on the right and our specific name comes on the left, domain names are also organized from right to left, with general domains to the right, and specific domains to the left.

For example, in the domain name **www.google.com**, there are three domain names, each separated by a dot. Here, **.com** is a general domain and **google** is a sub-domain, and **www** is a sub-domain prefix for the World Wide Web.

8.38 UNIFORM RESOURCE LOCATOR OR UNIVERSAL RESOURCE LOCATOR

A uniform resource locator (URL) specifies the unique address for a file that is accessible on the Internet. It is provided by the user in the address bar. For example, when you type www.google.com, after pressing the Enter key, there is a long sequence of characters in the address bar. This is the URL. This means that to access any page on the Internet, we need to provide its URL.

The file on the Internet that we want to access can be a web page, an audio file, video file, or image with extensions such as .htm, .php, .mp4, .avi, .jpg, .bmp, .gif, .asp, .cgi, .xml, etc. The syntax for a URL is as follows:

Protocol://domain-name/path

where **protocol** specifies the name of the protocol to be used to access the file resource. Commonly used protocols are http, https, ftp, telnet, news, gopher, mailto, etc. These fields specify how to connect.

Domain Name: identifies the name of the website. This means that the domain field identifies where to connect.

Path is a hierarchical description that indicates the location of the file. It indicates to the web server what to connect.

For example, when we just write **http://www.google.com**, http is the protocol, www.google.com is the domain name, and by default, the home page which is saved as index.htm is displayed to the user. Refer to Fig. 8.67 which shows another sample URL.

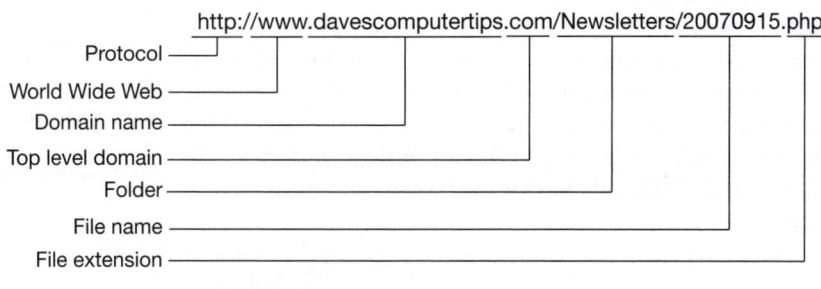

Figure 8.67 Components of a URL

If we provide the URL as **http://www.example.com/Student/ABC.TXT**, then http is used to fetch the file ABC.TXT from Student directory stored in the computer on which the website www.example.com is hosted.

There are basically two types of URLs as shown in Fig. 8.68. While an absolute URL specifies the complete URL containing all three fields (protocol, domain, and path), relative URLs, on the other hand, contain only the one field, which is the domain name.

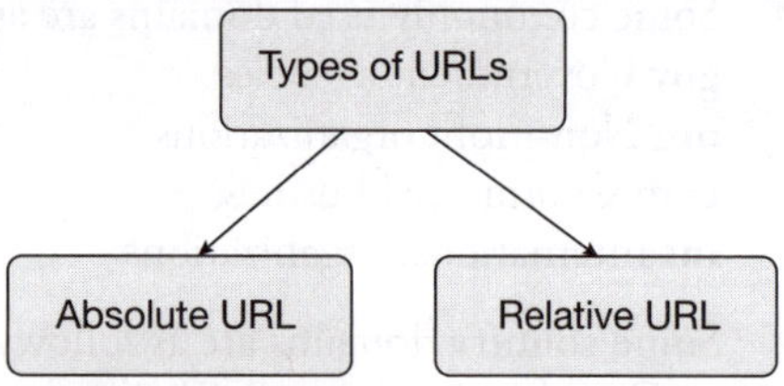

Many a time, you must have observed a complex URL as the one given here, especially when you log in to your email account or search for a string on google.

http://www.google.com/cgi-bin/search.cgi?q=computer%20fundamentals

Figure 8.68 Types of URL

Although it seems complex, it is actually very simple to interpret. In the query, http is in the protocol, www.google.com is the domain, and search.cgi is a file in the cgi-bin directory.

Anything following the question mark (?) in a URL is a pair of variable(s) and its value(s). In the URL, q=computer%20fundamentals means that q is a variable name, and computer%20fundamentals is the value of q. Since blank spaces are not allowed in a URL, blank space has been written as %20. Spaces can also be written as a **+** (plus) sign. In the query, the user is trying to search computer fundamentals on Google.

These values are sent by the user's computer to Google's server. Google will find relevant pages and will display the result on the user's screen. Similarly, when we log in to our email account, we supply two values to the server—username and password. In such a situation, multiple variables are separated with an ampersand (&) sign as shown here:

> A domain name is not the same as URL because it is just a small part of the entire URL.

http://www.gmail.com/config/passwd.cgi?u=erree&p=s2ejmd3

In the URL, there are two different variables—u with value erree and p with value s2ejmd3.

8.39 WEB PAGE

A Web page is a document that is accessed through the Internet or other network using a Web browser. It is commonly written in HyperText Markup Language (HTML). A Web page may contain text, graphics, video and hyperlinks to other Web pages and files.

> You can view the source code of the Web page.

Usually, a Web page has a .htm or .html file extension. However, it may also have extensions like .cgi, .php, .pl,, etc.

To access a Web page, you must enter its URL address in the address bar of the Web browser. If you are not sure of the URL of the Web page then you can use a search engine to find the Web page or use the search on the website containing the Web page.

Web pages can be either static or dynamic.

Static Web pages show the same content each time they are viewed.

Dynamic Web pages have content that can change each time they are accessed. For example, the Web pages that display date, time, current temperature, availability of seats in a train or flight, etc. fall under this category. Dynamic Web pages are written using scripting languages like PHP, Perl, ASP, or JSP. However, the information is returned as HTML code so that the browser can easily display them on the user's screen.

> The first Web page was created at CERN by Tim Berners-Lee on August 6, 1991. You can visit and browse the first website and first Web page at the http://info.cern.ch/ address.

> A Web page is an individual document on a website.

8.40 WEBSITE

A website is a collection of related Web pages. It may contain one or more Web pages. In fact, a website may even have thousands of Web pages.

To access a website, we must enter its URL in the address bar of the Web browser. When no particular web page is mentioned in the URL, the home page or the index page which is stored as index.htm is displayed on the screen by default. If you remember, home page is the first page or the starting page of a website.

However, to refer to a particular Web page on a website, the user must enter the complete path of the web page. We have learnt in the previous sections that name and path of the file is mentioned as the last part of the URL (sub directory and filename).

For example, if we write, www.abc.com then the index.htm page on the abc website is displayed. But if we write www.abc.com/contacts/customer.htm, then the customer.htm Web page stored in the contacts folder is displayed.

A website is stored on a Web server (Fig. 8.69). A very large website may be spread over a number of servers in different geographic locations. For example, the website of IBM consists of thousands of files and web pages that are spread out over many servers across the globe. However, one web server can also store the files and Web pages of several small websites.

> Any business, government, or person can create a website on the Internet. Today, there are billions of websites on the Internet that have been created by billions of different people.

> Multiple pages of a large website can be stored on several servers. In contrast, a single server can host pages of several small websites.

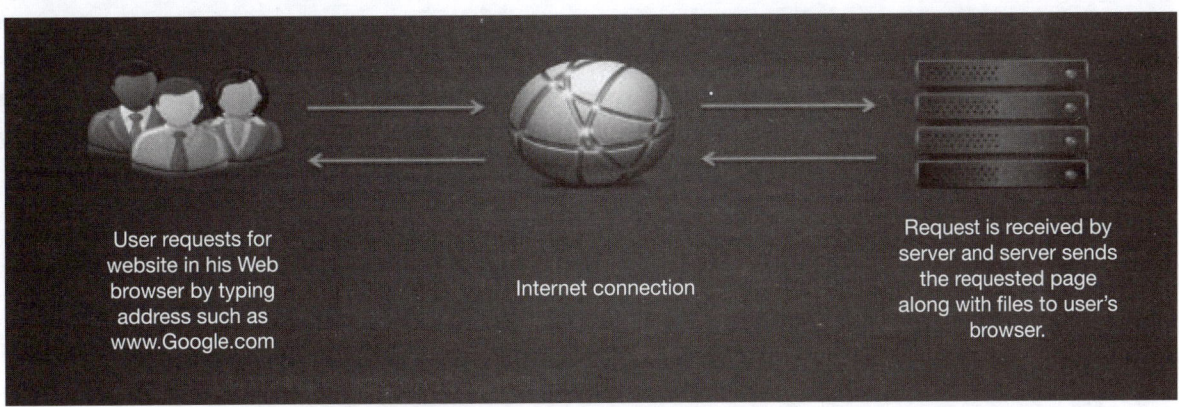

Figure 8.69 Accessing a website across Internet

All websites hosted through the Internet constitute the World Wide Web (WWW). To be useful, a website must have well-structured information and be presented in a user-friendly look and feel.

8.40.1 Static and Dynamic Websites

Like static Web pages, we have **static websites**. A static website has all static Web pages. That is, it has Web pages that always display the same content/information. For example, a company's website that provides details about the company's portfolio, contacts, future projects etc. A static website can be developed by anyone who has a basic knowledge of HTML.

Dynamic websites, however, use database (a collection of tables) to store and create information as and when required or requested by the user (Fig. 8.70). Refer Table 8.7 to better understand the difference between a static and dynamic website. The information on a dynamic website changes automatically. Some examples of dynamic website that we frequently use are online shopping, airline/railway reservation and social networking websites to name a few. To create a dynamic website, one must know PHP, JSP, Perl, ASP or other technologies.

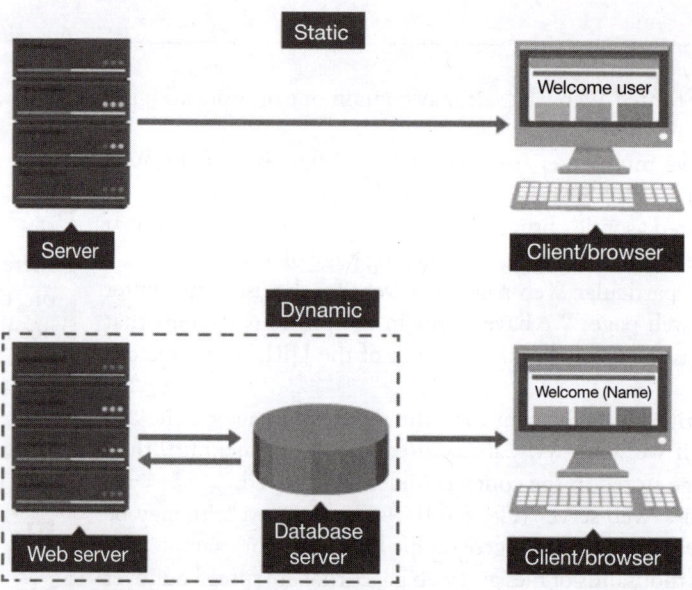

Figure 8.70 Static website vs. dynamic website

Table 8.7 Difference between static and dynamic websites

Static Websites	Dynamic Websites
The same information is displayed always.	Information may change every time the user requests it.
A basic knowledge of HTML is sufficient to develop a static website.	A user must know ASP, JSP, PHP, Perl or any other technology in addition to HTML to create a dynamic website.
Information must be manually changed to update it.	Information changes automatically based on underlying logic.
Example, a website listing the profile, products, prices, contacts of key persons, etc.	Example, online shopping and online reservation websites.

8.41 WEB SERVERS

A Web server is a computer that uses protocols like HTTP, SMTP, etc. to respond to client requests made over the World Wide Web (WWW). Web server software controls how clients access files hosted on it. Usually, clients type URLs of the websites; it is the role of the Web server to deliver the site's content to the client requesting it (Fig. 8.71). The Web server stores all files related to the website, including HTML documents, images and JavaScript files. Web servers are connected to the Internet 24 × 7 to facilitate data to be exchanged with other connected devices.

Thus, the Web server works on the client-server model. All computers that host websites must have Web server software. Some popular Web servers include Apache, Microsoft's Internet

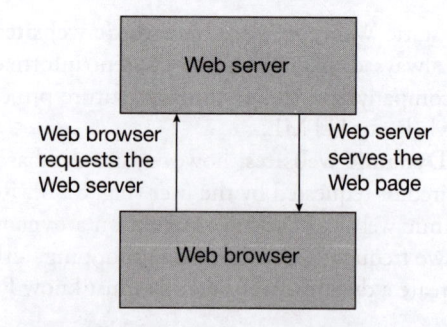

Figure 8.71 Interaction between Web browser and Web server

Information Server (IIS) and Nginx – pronounced *engine X*. Other Web servers include Novell's NetWare server, Google Web Server (GWS) and IBM's family of Domino servers.

These Web servers are often used for:

- Sending and receiving emails
- Handling requests for File Transfer Protocol (FTP) files
- Building and publishing Web pages
- Caching Web pages for fast delivery of frequently requested pages. This process is also known as Web acceleration.
- Limiting the speed of response to different clients to prevent a single client from dominating resources to satisfy requests from a large number of clients.

For choosing an appropriate Web server, the user must consider how well a Web server works with the operating system installed in his computer, how efficient it is in searching for relevant information, managing server-side programming and security characteristics.

A single Web server can host one or multiple websites using the same software and hardware resources. This is known as virtual hosting.

> A Web server can even be embedded in a device such as a digital camera to allow users to communicate with the device through any Web browser.

8.42 WEB HOSTING

Web hosting is an online service that enables users to publish their website or Web applications on the Internet. When opting up for a Web hosting service, the user takes some space on rent on a Web server to store all the files and data necessary for his or her website to work properly as shown in Fig. 8.72. Once the pages of a website are stored on the Web server, they can be accessed by other computers connected to the internet.

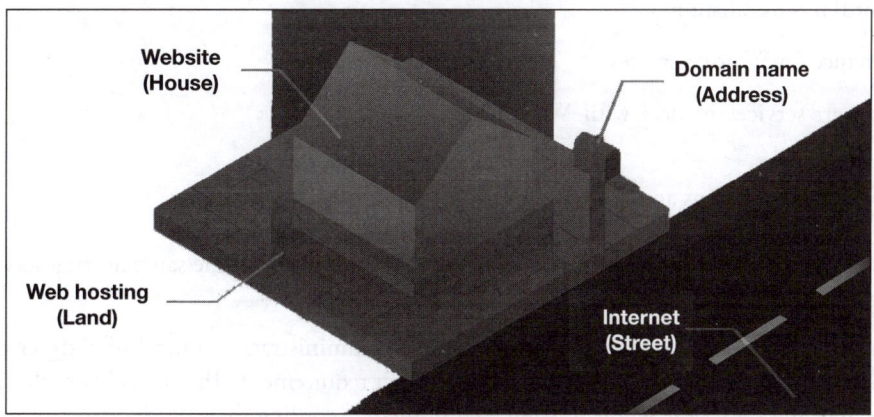

Figure 8.72 Web hosting

The server runs 24 × 7 and has full protection against malicious attacks. Whenever someone types the URL in the address bar of the Web browser, the Web server transfers all the files necessary to serve that request.

Users must choose a hosting plan that best fits their needs. In fact, you can think of a Web hosting service as housing rentals. Users have to pay the rental amount regularly to keep the server running continuously.

8.42.1 Types of Web Hosting Services

The different types of Web hosting services available are:

Shared Hosting: For a blogging website or for a website of a small business, Shared Hosting is the right choice. This service is quite affordable as it allows the Web server's space to be shared by other websites. However, since resources of the Web server are shared with other websites, the speed and performance of a website suffers. Moreover, users have minimal control over the server.

Pros	Cons
• Less expensive	• Little or no control over server configuration
• Excellent option for small online business websites	• Increased traffic on one or more websites can slow down another website
• Domain specific technical knowledge not required	
• Website maintenance and server administration is done by the hosting company.	

WordPress Hosting: This is also a particular form of shared hosting created for WordPress site owners. The server is configured specifically for WordPress and the website also has pre-installed plugins for crucial tasks, such as caching and security. This allows a website to open much faster and run with fewer problems. WordPress hosting plans also include features like pre-designed WordPress themes, drag-and-drop page builders, and specific developer tools.

Pros	Cons
• Less expensive	• The hosting plan is optimized only for WordPress sites.
• User-friendly interface	• Hosting any other website on the server may pose several challenges.
• One-click WordPress installation	
• Good performance for WordPress sites	
• Customer support services to deal with WordPress issues	
• Pre-installed WordPress plugins and themes	

Reseller Hosting: The reseller hosting plan allows users to rent out or re-sell the same hosting services provided by the parent hosting company.

Dedicated Hosting: Dedicated hosting gives users complete administrative control of a server that is dedicated solely to their website. Users can manage their websites as per their requirement. They can choose the operating system and software to be used and set up the whole hosting environment according their needs.

Dedicated hosting is as powerful as owning your own server. Therefore, it is best suited for large online businesses that deal with heavy traffic.

Pros	Cons
• Full control over server configuration	• High cost, more oriented towards larger businesses
• High reliability and security options	• Technical and server management knowledge is a must
• Root access to your server	

VPS Hosting: VPS hosting is an advanced form of shared hosting. It assigns users, resources that are not shared with the other websites. These services are expensive as the Web server allocates dedicated partition for websites on that server. This means that users get exclusive server space and a reserved amount of resources and memory. It is a great medium for businesses with a rapidly increasing traffic.

Pros	Cons
• Dedicated server space	• More expensive than other types of hosting
• Increase in traffic on other websites does not affect performance	• Technical and server management knowledge is a must
• Complete control and access to the server	
• Easy scalability and high customizability	

Cloud Hosting: Cloud hosting is the most reliable solution on the market. It provides users with a cluster of servers. All files and resources are replicated on each server.

When one of the cloud servers is busy or encounters a problem, Web traffic coming to it is automatically routed to another server in the cluster. This results in little or no downtime of services. Hence, it is a preferred choice for busy websites.

Pros	Cons
• Little or no downtime	• Hard to estimate the actual costs
• Server failures have no effect on your website	• Root access is not always provided
• Allocates resources on demand	
• Pay-as-you-go pricing strategy - you only pay for what you use	
• More scalable than other Web hosting types	

Selecting the Right Web Hosting Package

There are several Web hosting options available. The answer to which service a user must opt for varies from business to business. For example, the right option to be chosen depends on:

- The type of website – blogging website, ecommerce portal, news website, etc. – that has to be hosted
- The amount of web traffic and robustness of the infrastructure required depends on the type of website chosen
- Speed at which the online business will expand
- Storage space and bandwidth requirement
- Cost that the user can afford to pay.

8.43 WEB SCRIPTING

We have read that there are two types of Web pages – static and dynamic. While we can design a static Web page using simple HTML, we must use a Web scripting language to add some dynamic features to it.

Dynamic Web pages can be designed using a variety of **scripting languages** like JavaScript, VBScript, Perl, PHP, ASP that can be run either on the client (Web browser) or on the web server. Scripts that run on the Web browser are called **client-side scripts** and those that run on the web server are called **server-side scripts**.

Client scripting and server scripting both serve different purposes and a Web page can be composed using both. While client scripting is used for rendering some special effects or for form validation and basic computation, server scripting is used for accessing online databases, providing forums, feedback forms etc.

8.43.1 Client Scripting

Client scripting is used to make interactive web pages. The users enter some information and the client displays the content based on what the user has entered. For example, a Web page may use client scripting to validate data entry fields on an HTML form so that the user gets immediate feedback when they make a mistake. You must have seen that when you enter a password with 4 or 5 small-case characters, you are immediately prompted to enter a password of at least 8 characters having upper case, lowercase, digits and special symbols.

The two popularly used scripting languages are JavaScript and VBscript. VBscript is usually supported on Microsoft products and is therefore not a good choice for writing client scripts. Since **JavaScript** is supported on almost all modern Web browsers, it is the standard choice of web programmers.

> JavaScript and the programming language Java are not related. Java is a product of Sun Microsystems and JavaScript came from Netscape. However, the syntax for both languages is very similar.

To understand how client-side scripting works, observe the steps listed below.

Step 1: The user clicks on a link. The Web browser sends the request for the Web page say, http://local host/my Page.html

Step 2: The web server gets the request for myPage.html. If this is a static Web page, then the server simply sends it to the Web browser and the Web browser displays it on user's screen and there is no need to proceed with other steps in the sequence (Step 3 onwards).

Step 3: However, if the Web page has some client-side scripting code in it, the client (or the Web browser) passes the script to the interpreter. The choice of interpreter will depend on the scripting language that has been used to write the script.

Step 4: The interpreter executes the instructions written in the script, and places the result on the same HTML page.

Step 5: The Web browser displays the HTML page on the user's screen. The entire process is given in Fig. 8.73.

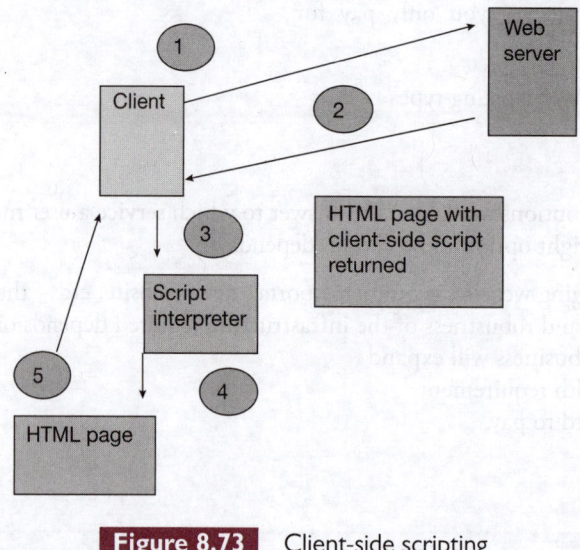

Figure 8.73 Client-side scripting

8.43.2 Server Scripting

Server scripting languages like ASP, PHP, Perl and CGI are used to create dynamic Web pages on the Web server. These pages are then sent to the browser. For example, when we send a query to be executed on a database server (for example, to see your marks on CBSE website), your request page is designed using HTML and a server-side scripting code. The server executes the script and sends back to the client a HTML page with its response. The HTML page is simply displayed by the server. This means that all server scripting process takes place before the page is sent to the browser.

The browser sees pure HTML and not the script. The entire process of request and response is given below and illustrated in Fig. 8.74

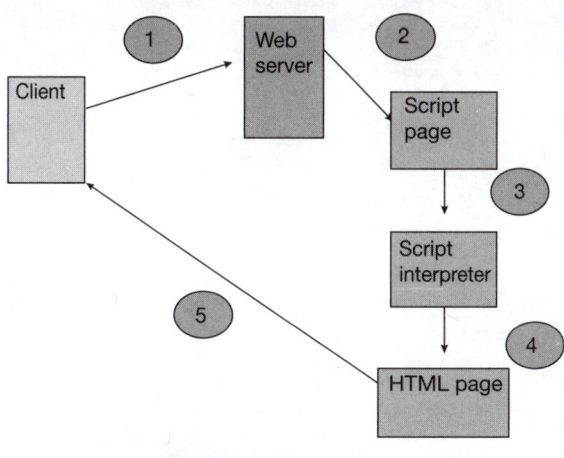

Figure 8.74 Server-side scripting

Step 1: The user clicks on a link or types a URL in the address bar of the Web browser. The Web browser sends the request for the Web page say, http://localhost/my Page.php.

Step 2: The Web server gets the request and sees that it is a .php file, which needs to be handled by the PHP Interpreter. So, it passes the request to the PHP interpreter to process the PHP code. (The choice of interpreter depends on the type of script).

Step 3: The interpreter places the result into an HTML page.

Step 4: The HTML page is returned to the client and the Web browser displays the HTML page on the screen.

Popular server-side scripting languages include PHP, Perl, ASP, JSP, Python and Ruby. However, PHP and Python are the ones that are most widely.

> Popular websites like Facebook and WordPress are written using PHP. HTML and CSS are not categorized as scripting languages.

8.44 WEB 2.0

The term Web 2.0 refers to Internet applications that allow users to share information and collaborate with other people. It is an improved version of the first worldwide web that brought more demand for dynamic Web pages than static ones. Web 2.0 led to the growth of social media. It changed the way in which Web pages are designed and used by the end-users, without changing the technical specifications of Web 1.0.

Web 2.0 Applications

While Web 1.0 was meant to search for information and connect devices and people, Web 2.0 goes a step ahead and does everything to allow users to collaborate with people. Some very popular examples of Web 2.0 include services like Google Maps, Google Docs, Flickr, Video sharing sites (like YouTube), wikis (like MediaWiki), blogs (like WordPress), social networking (like Facebook), folksonomies (like Delicious), Microblogging (like Twitter), podcasting (like Podcast Alley), online shopping portals (like Amazon), online gaming websites, content hosting services and many more.

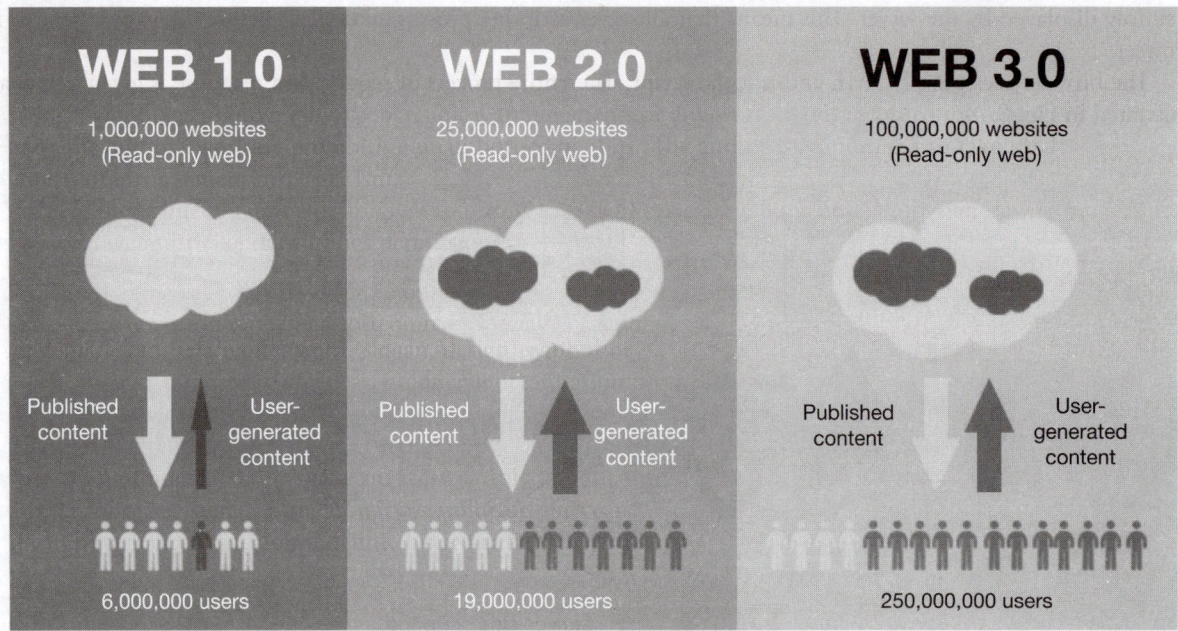

Figure 8.75 Evolution of the Web

Source: https://www.f5buddy.com/basic-definitions-of-web-1-0-web-2-0-and-web-3-0/

From Fig. 8.75, it is clearly evident that Web 2.0 websites enable users to create, share, collaborate and communicate their work with others. Any user without prior knowledge of Web design or publishing can also use these websites to upload their content. These capabilities were absent in the Web 1.0 environment.

Advantages of Web 2.0

Web 2.0 moved netizens from a read-only Internet to a "read/write" Internet. Users can now not only access information, but also send information back to the server to get more customized results.

Web 2.0 got a major boost from cloud technology that allowed companies to use more powerful Web-delivered services (Fig. 8.76). Some other main advantages of Web 2.0 include:

- It is available anywhere, anytime (with smart and portable devices).
- It uses a variety of media including text, audio, video, animation, etc.
- It is user-friendly.
- Learners can actively be involved in knowledge building.
- It allows users to create dynamic learning communities.
- Any user can author and/or edit the content available on the Internet. For example, Wikipedia allows any user to post reliable content on its website.
- Users can give their feedback on any content published online by writing comments and reviews.
- Users can even add to or enhance the content already published on the Internet.
- It facilitates real-time discussion.
- It offers optimized search engine results as well as an enhanced user experience.

> With Web 3.0, Internet experts are trying to develop a semantic Web with data mapping features that will transform the Web into a "read, write and execute" Web that will help automation programs take over from purely user-driven Internet activity.
>
> Internet bots will do the actual work of generating the HTTP requests and responses and surf the web instead of human users.

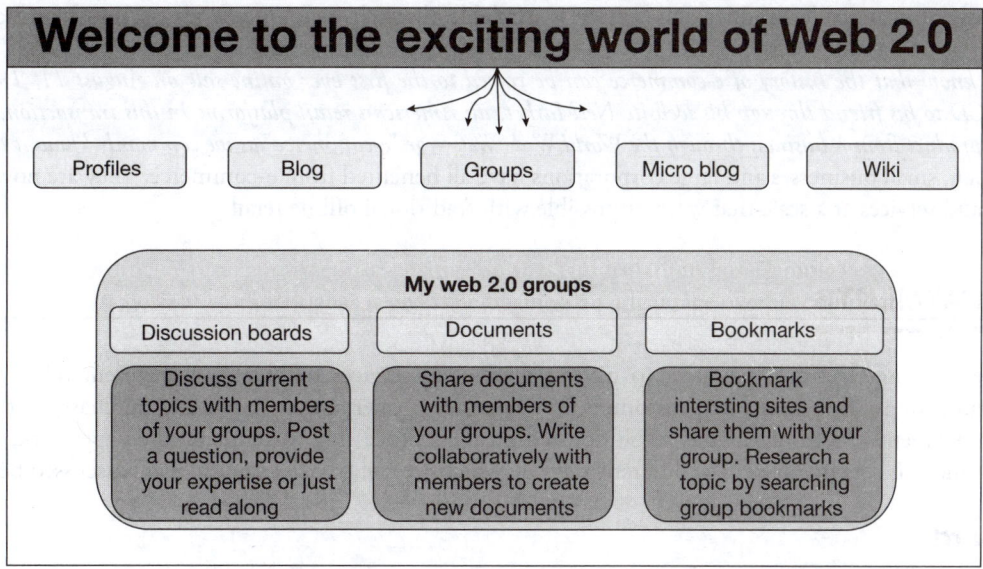

Figure 8.76 What can be done in Web 2.0

8.45 ELECTRONIC COMMERCE

E-commerce, also known as electronic commerce or internet commerce, refers to the buying and selling of goods or services using the internet. It also involves the transfer of money and data to execute these transactions. Online marketing, online advertising, online sales, product service, online billing and online payments are also a part of e-commerce activities.

While doing e-business covers all aspects of operating an online business, e-commerce on the other hand, refers specifically to the transaction of goods and services. Therefore, e-business concept is wider than e-commerce.

Nearly every imaginable product and service is available through e-commerce transactions, including books, music, plane tickets, and financial services such as stock investing and online banking.

Do you know that the history of e-commerce can be traced to the first ever online sale on August 11, 1994, when a man sold a CD to his friend through his website NetMarket, an American retail platform? In this transaction, a consumer purchased a product from a business through the World Wide Web—or "e-commerce" as we commonly know it today.

Since then, small businesses and large corporations have all benefited from e-commerce. They are now able to sell their goods and services at a scale that was not possible with traditional offline retail.

8.46　E-PAYMENTS

E-commerce sites use electronic payment to pay for goods and services purchased. E-payment refers to paperless monetary transactions. This means that customers no longer need paper money in hand to purchase anything.

Making payments electronically has revolutionized business processing by reducing the paperwork, labour cost, transaction time and cost involved. The different ways by which we can pay electronically are discussed below.

8.46.1　Cards

Cards are the most common form of electronic payments. There are three types of cards: credit, debit and prepaid cards. These cards are made of plastic and have a magnetic chip at the back of the card.

Credit Card

A credit card is basically a small plastic card with a unique number attached with an account (Fig. 8.77). When a customer purchases a product using credit card, the amount is paid by the bank on behalf of the customer. The customer gets a certain time period after which he/she can pay the credit card bill, which is usually calculated and sent to the credit card holder every month.

While using the credit card, the customer gives the merchant (from whom he buys) the card while shopping. The merchant swipes the card through a Point-of-Sales (PoS) machine, which delivers the bill to the credit card company. The company sends a confirmation message back to the merchant that the purchase was completed. This process typically takes only a few seconds to complete. When doing online shopping using credit card, the customer just has to enter his credit card number and its expiry date along with a CVC code (printed at the backside of the card). The processing of credit card is shown in Fig. 8.78.

Figure 8.77　Card of payments

Debit Card

Debit card has a unique number engraved on it, which is mapped with the bank account number. This means that to have a debit card, you must have a bank account. The main difference between a debit card and a credit card is that with a debit card, the amount gets deducted from the card holder's bank account immediately. So, to buy a product or service using debit card, there must be sufficient balance in the card holder's bank account. There is no such requirement in the case of a credit card. Thus, a debit card helps the customer to keep a check on his/her spending and allows him/her to spend only what he/she has.

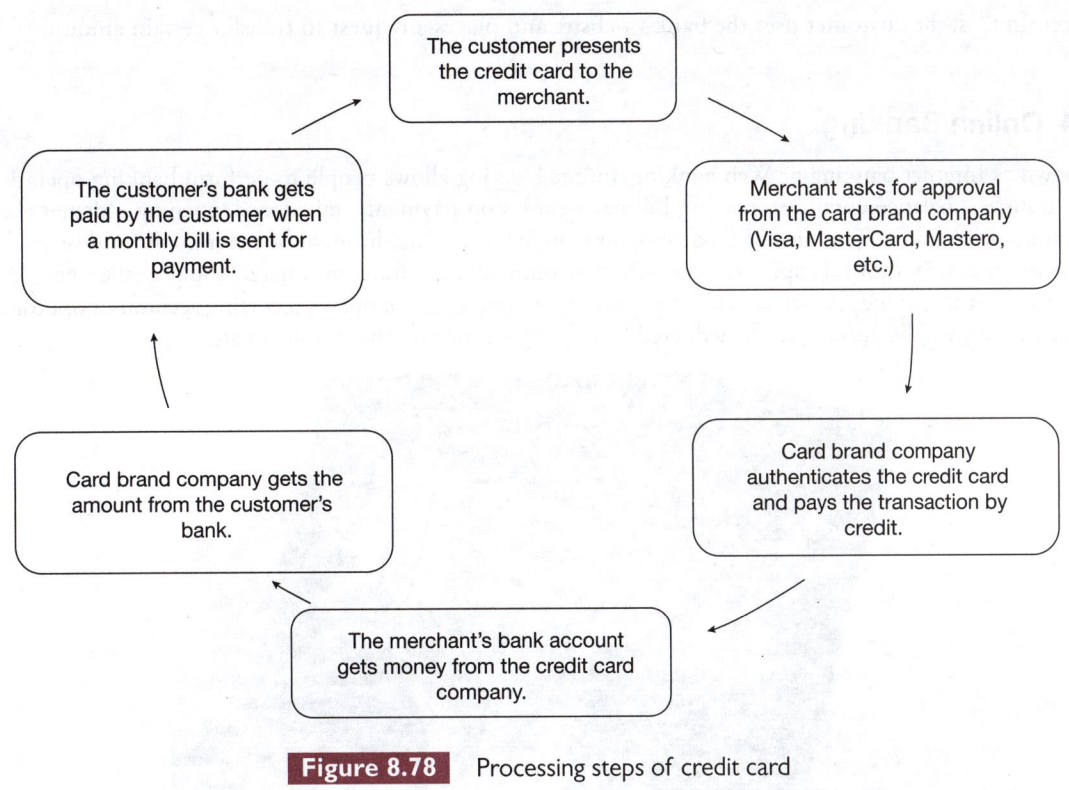

Figure 8.78 Processing steps of credit card

Smart Card

Smart card looks like a credit card or a debit card (Fig. 8.79). It has a small microprocessor chip embedded in it. This chip is used to store the amount of money. Whenever the card holder uses the card, the amount gets deducted from that stored on the card. Correspondingly, when the card holder recharges the card, the amount gets added to the money stored in it. You must have used smart cards in a games parlour, metro trains, food courts, etc.

Smart cards are used like debit cards and credit cards. The card holder has to enter a PIN that is assigned to him/ her to use it. Mondex and Visa Cash cards are examples of smart cards.

Figure 8.79 Smart card for payments

8.46.2 E-money

E-money transactions involve payment done over the network. With e-money, the amount gets transferred from one financial body to another financial body in a faster and convenient manner, thereby saving a lot of time.

Online payments done using credit/ debit/ smart cards are examples of e-money transactions. Another popular example is e-cash. To use e-cash, both customer and merchant have to sign up with the bank or company issuing e-cash (like bitcoin).

> Some online retailers also have their own gift cards which are sold to customers.

8.46.3 Electronic Fund Transfer

Electronic Fund Transfer (EFT) is a very popular way of transferring money from one bank account to another bank account. These accounts may be in the same bank or different. EFT can be done using ATM or using a computer. In this, the customer uses the bank's website and places a request to transfer certain amount to another account.

8.46.4 Online Banking

Also known as Internet banking or Web banking, online banking allows people to perform banking operations (like account transfers, balance enquiries, making bill payments, stop payments, take loans, opening a demat account to trade in the stock market, opening an FD, or shopping online by paying through the debit/credit card issued by bank) using the Internet (Fig. 8.80). People can access their account anytime from anywhere. Going further, people can also schedule their future payments to occur automatically. For example, if you open a recurring account or opt for an EMI, then that amount will be automatically deducted from your account on the specified date.

Figure 8.80 Online banking

Today more and more people are moving towards Internet banking not only because it is faster and convenient but also because it is secure. To use Internet banking, a bank customer must have a computer with Web browser software installed in it to access the bank's website. Users just need to enter their login name and password to access the services provided by that bank. The bank does not charge any extra amount for making online transactions.

Other very popular applications of Internet banking include the tie-up between Indian Railways and ICICI to allow passengers to make their railway pass for local trains online. The pass is delivered to the passenger's home. But the facility is limited to Mumbai, Thane, Nashik, Surat and Pune.

Although Internet banking is very beneficial, you must take some security precautions that are given below.

- You should never share personal information such as PIN numbers, passwords, etc. with anyone. Not even the bank's employees.
- Never share your PIN and passwords over emails or phone. If you have done it, change the PIN/password immediately.
- PIN and/or passwords should be changed frequently.
- Sign out properly after making an online transaction.

> Online fund transfer may take place in a day or so but with traditional banking it takes about three working days.

8.46.5 Bank on Your Mobile

These days, almost everybody has a mobile phone. So, it is a good idea to manage your bank account through your mobile device. A mobile device may be a smart phone, tablet, PDA or any device other than your desktop. In this section we will read about two important techniques in which a customer can do banking transactions on his/her mobile phone.

Mobile Banking: Mobile banking is the act of doing financial transactions on a mobile device like cell phone, tablet, etc. It can be as simple as a bank sending an alert message whenever money is deposited or withdrawn from the account or as complex as a customer transferring a huge amount to another account.

These days, mobile banking is used by customers to pay their bills, check their account balances, deposit check, transfer money, notify the bank of a lost or stolen credit card, stop payment on a check, receive a new PIN, or view a monthly statement, among other transactions. This type of banking offers more convenience to the consumers who have to no longer physically go to a bank, log on from their home computer, or make a phone call. Mobile banking is also referred to as M-banking or SMS banking.

To assist their customers, banks have made mobile apps that can be conveniently used for funds management. This amazing technology has helped people to carry out bank transactions anytime and from anywhere. However, on the down side of mobile banking, we can say that security is a big concern. Thus, establishing a secure connection before logging into a mobile banking app is very important, as otherwise the client's personal information may be compromised. Some steps that one must take to avoid security threats include:

- The customers must closely monitor their bank accounts by analyzing the balance and transactions performed from time to time
- Take immediate action when the mobile device is lost or stolen.
- While connecting to your bank's mobile app, make sure that your wireless network is secure.
- Never send sensitive information over an unsecured wireless network (for example, in a hotel or café).
- Use additional layers of authentication in which the account holder authorizes various transactions via text message or phone calls with the bank to give an additional code.
- Configure your device to auto-lock after a short period of non-use.
- Do not store sensitive data (passwords, etc.) on your mobile device.
- Use mobile security protection features that include anti-theft, antivirus, antispyware, anti-phishing and app protection.
- Use an alphanumeric password.
- Change your password often, and do not set your pets' names, your child's name, or any birthdays as the password.

To provide additional security, banks are now sending one-time use password to a cell phone or other devices when the customer wishes to log into his/her account. The customer is then asked to enter both passwords within a certain period of time. The first password is one that he had already set and the second is the one-time use password. The one-time use password expires, naturally, after it is used once or after a time limit has passed.

8.46.6 Mobile Wallet

Also known as e-wallets wallets, mobile wallets are prepaid accounts that allow users to store different bank accounts, credit card or debit card information in a secure environment. Mobile wallets enable customers to make all payments faster and in a safer manner. For example, we can use Paytm, Google Pay, Mobikwik or Phone Pe accounts to pay our bills, book tickets and make payments. Table 8.8 lists some details about popular e-wallet companies in India.

Also called m-wallet, digital wallet or e-wallet, is a mobile technology that is used similar to a real wallet. Mobile wallets use the technology that everyone has – the smart phone; for example – to allow the user to make in-store payments quickly and securely without having to locate his credit or debit card. Mobile wallet is a convenient way of holding anything like rewards cards, medical records, credit and debit cards, an ID or social security card, driving license, and other personal items that a real physical wallet can hold.

> E-wallet allows customers to store multiple credit cards, debit card and bank account numbers in a secure environment.

While mobile wallets make it extremely simple for customers to conduct transactions with a specific company via their reward cards, for example, they are also very useful to store important documents like medical records, which need to be available on hand at all times. Credit and debit cards make transactions simple to conduct via a mobile device. The mobile wallet is secure enough to store sensitive information. It can also be used by customers to purchase their products online with greater ease.

Finally, the mobile wallet can also be used to store personal items such as photos and files and give us a feel of using a real wallet.

Table 8.8 Different e-wallet/mobile wallet companies in India

E-Wallet	Industry	Company	Bank Transfer Allowed?	Mobile Platform
Paytm	Private	One97 Communications	Yes	Android, iOS, Windows Phone, Ovi, Blackberry
MobiKwik	Private	One MobiKwik Systems Private Limited	Yes	Android, iOS, Windows Phone
Oxigen Wallet	Private	Oxigen Services India Pvt. Ltd.	Yes	Android, iOS, Windows Phone
Citrus Wallet	Private	Citrus Pay	Yes	Android, iOS
ItzCash	Private	Itz Cash Card Ltd.	Yes	Android, iOS
Freecharge	Private	Snapdeal	No	Android, iOS, Windows Phone
Axis Bank Lime	Banking	Axis Bank	No	Android, iOS, Windows Phone
Airtel Money	Telecom	Airtel	Yes	Android, iOS
ICICI Pockets	Banking	ICICI Bank	Yes	Android, iOS
Jio Money	Telecom	Reliance	No	Android, iOS, Windows Phone
mRupee	Telecom	Tata Teleservices Limited	Yes	Android, iOS, Windows Phone
SBI Buddy	Banking	State Bank of India	Yes	Android, iOS
Vodafone M-Pesa	Telecom	Vodafone	Yes	Android, iOS, Windows Phone
HDFC PayZapp	Banking	HDFC Bank	Yes	Android, iOS

Advantages of Mobile Wallet

- Easily accessible through mobile devices
- Easy to add or load money using net banking, credit card or debit card.
- Cannot be stolen or lost
- Money is stored according to the user's requirement.
- The money is safe and users do not have to share their debit or credit card details frequently.
- Even small payments that may include a figure after decimals (pay even in paise, say Rs. 54.50).
- No need to carry cash every time as mobile wallet allows users to shop anytime, anywhere.
- Ensures timely payment using the auto facility to make future bill payments automatically from wallet balance on a pre-determined date.
- E-wallets offer money-saving features through the discount, cashback, offers, promo codes and free gifts.

Disadvantage of Mobile Wallet

- Mobile wallets can be used only by those having mobile devices with a net connection.
- Mobile wallets can be used by those who are comfortable working with technological advances.
- Not every merchant and shopkeeper uses mobile wallets.

8.46.7 Mobile Payments

For making mobile payments, the user needs to download the software and link it with credit card or mobile billing information. Once this link is made, users can pay by sending text messages.

8.46.8 Mobile Money

In a country like ours, many people either do not have a bank account or do not have balance in their account. But most of them have a mobile phone. And even for small transactions that costs anywhere between Rs 50 – Rs 500 (like to buy things like games, music, e-books, etc), people use mobile money in which payments are deducted from the mobile's prepaid balance or billed to their postpaid account (Fig. 8.81).

Benefits

- Cheaper transactions for both customer as well as merchants
- Micro-payments and reduced charges increase sales
- Offers special promotions for their products
- Reduced fraud as mobile wallets are harder to steal or duplicate than cards or cash
- Decreased payment time, especially in high-volume businesses
- Lower processing fees as compared to traditional cards
- Better customer loyalty.

Figure 8.81 E-payment

8.46.9 E-cheque

This payment system serves the same functions as the paper ones. It is an obligation of a bank to transfer money from the payer's account to a payee. In an e-cheque, the payer uses digital signatures to sign. The payee gives that cheque to the bank or any other payment system. After checking the authenticity of the digital signature, the funds are transferred to the payee.

Advantages of E-payment

- Helps to conduct electronic commerce.
- Saves time and is more efficient.
- Convenient to use as customers can make payments anytime and anywhere. They just need an internet-connected device.
- Even a non-technical person can easily make online payments.

Disadvantages of E-payment

- E-commerce fraud is growing at 30% per year.
- Users' sensitive data is at risk of theft.
- Internet connection is a must to complete online transactions.

> Electronic payments use a Payment Gateway provider which is an e-commerce application service provider that processes credit card payments. It gets its revenues from the merchants to whom they provide these services. In turn, the Payment Gateway has to share some of its merchant fee with the banks and payment systems companies.
>
> Payment gateways provide a safer platform for money exchange. They have their own fraud protection system to provide protection from fraudsters. In India, some well-known payment gateways are CCAvenue and Tech Process. Pay by Amazon has also recently launched its service.

8.46.10 When to Use Which Technique

- For shopping or paying bills use cards or e-wallets.
- For small transactions, mobile payments, e-wallets or mobile money is preferred.
- For transfer of large amount, EFT must be used.
- To transfer money to your friends or family, EFT or Internet banking can be used.

Key Terms

Computer network: A collection of computers and devices interconnected to facilitate sharing of resources (printer, CD-ROM), information and electronic documents among interconnected devices.

Communication channel: Link connecting the devices on a network are known as communication channels.

Transit time: It is the time taken by a message to travel from one device to another.

Response time: It is defined as the time elapsed between a request sent and a response received.

Reliability: A measure that indicates how frequently network failure takes place. More the failures, less is the network's reliability.

Bandwidth: Range of frequencies within a given band that is used for transmitting analog signals. It is usually expressed in Hz, KHz, and MHz.

Data transfer rate: Capacity of a wired or wireless network connection to transmit the maximum amount of data from one point to another in a given amount of time (usually one second).

Modulation: The process of converting digital data (coming from the sending computer) into an analog signal.

Demodulation: The process of converting an analog signal into a digital data that can be read by the receiving computer.

Gateway: A device that joins two networks using different protocols.

Network topology: An arrangement of computers, or other computing devices. It describes the pattern in which different devices on the network are connected and the way data flows between them.

Server: The machine on which the file(s) that have to be shared with different users are stored.

Client: The machine that requests access to a particular file stored on the server machine.

Uploading: The process of copying files from a client to a server

Downloading: The process of transferring files from server to a client

VoIP: A technology that allows users to make voice calls using a broadband Internet connection instead of a regular (or analog) phone line.

Malware: Also known as malicious software is software designed with wrong intentions. A malware is specifically written to gain access to a computer either to harm it by disturbing its operations or gather sensitive information from it.

Computer virus: A small program that gets loaded in the computer without the user's knowledge, where it replicates itself. It harms the computer by copying itself repeatedly in the computer's memory, corrupting or deleting files from the computer.

Trojan horse: A non-replicating malicious program that pretends to be harmless so that users can easily download it on their computer. It is usually embedded within a harmless program.

Spyware: A malicious program that monitors the user's activity on his/her computer and reports it to another person with malicious intentions.

Keylogger: Malicious software that, once installed in your computer, records everything that you type on your computer.

Ransomware: A malicious program which when installed, displays a screen that warns you that you have been locked out of your computer and you need to pay some money (or ransom) to use your device.

Spamming: Sending unwanted emails in bulk (to a large number of recipients).

Firewall: Hardware or software that is installed between the network of an organization and the rest of Internet.

Cybercrime: A criminal activity that either targets or uses a computer, a computer network or a networked device. Cybercrimes are purposely committed for financial, political or personal reasons.

Hacking: The act of identifying weakness in a computer system or even a network. Once the weakness is identified, it is exploited to gain access to that computer.

Phishing: The act of sending an email or messages to a user falsely claiming to be a legitimate authority. Phishing is done to scam the user to get his personal information. (This is an example of identity theft.)

Email spoofing: Sending messages either using a bogus email address or faking the email address of another user.

IP spoofing: Masking the IP address of a certain computer so that it becomes difficult for other systems to determine the sender (real sender) of the data.

Spoofing: Tricking or deceiving computer systems or other computer users. This is either done by hiding one's identity or faking the identity of another user on the Internet.

Eavesdropping: Unauthorized real-time interception of a private communication, such as a phone call, email, instant message, video conference or fax transmission.

Child pornography: Any visual depiction of sexually explicit conduct involving a child, which includes photograph, video, digital or computer-generated image indistinguishable from an actual child and an image created, adapted or modified to appear to depict a child.

Pharming: The act of exploiting vulnerability in the Domain Name System (DNS) to redirect website traffic from a legitimate website to a fraudulent website. This process of making the victim's computer to communicate with the wrong server is called domain hijacking.

Cyber extortion: A crime involving an attack or threat of an attack to demand money to stop the attack. Ransomware attack is an example of cyber extortion.

Cryptojacking: An attack that uses scripts to mine cryptocurrencies within browsers without the user's consent. The criminal loads cryptocurrency mining software in the victim's system.

Cyber espionage: A cybercrime in which the cybercriminal hacks into systems or networks to gain access to confidential information held by a government or other organization. It is purposely done to gather, modify or destroy data, as well as use network-connected devices, like webcams or closed-circuit TV (CCTV) cameras, to spy on a targeted individual or groups and monitor communications, including emails, text messages and instant messages.

Intellectual Property Rights (or IPR): Rights that are applicable to creative work which can be treated as an asset or physical property.

Trademarks: A name, word, slogan, design, symbol or any other item that is used to identify a product or organization. It is unique for a product or company and needs to be registered with an appointed government body.

Ethical hacker (white hat hacker): A hacker who gains unauthorized access to a computer or network systems to fix the identified weaknesses.

Cracker (black hat hacker): Also known as unethical hackers, they gain unauthorized access to a computer or network system for personal gains.

Grey hat hackers: Hackers who deliberately gain unauthorized access into computer or network to identify weaknesses in the system and then reveal them to the system owner.

Script kiddies: A non-skilled person who uses available tools to gain unauthorized access to a computer system or network.

Hacktivist: A hacker who hacks a website to post social, religious, and political, etc. messages on it comes under this category.

Phreaker: A hacker who identifies and exploits weaknesses in telephones rather than in computers and computer networks.

Markup: A code embedded in a file that instructs the web browser on how to display the page.

Uniform Resource Locator (URL): The unique address for a file that is accessible on the Internet.

Web page: A document that is accessed through the Internet or other networks using a web browser. It is commonly written in HyperText Markup Language (HTML).

Web site: A collection of one or more related web pages.

Web server: A computer that uses protocols like HTTP, SMTP, etc. to respond to client requests made over the World Wide Web (WWW).

Web acceleration: Caching web pages for fast delivery of frequently requested pages.

Virtual hosting: A single web server that can host one or multiple websites using the same software and hardware resources.

Web hosting: An online service that enables users to publish their web sites or web applications on the Internet.

Client-side scripts: Scripts that run on the web browser.

Server-side scripts: Scripts that run on the web server.

Ecommerce: Also known as electronic commerce or internet commerce, it refers to the buying and selling of goods or services using the internet.

Mobile banking: The act of doing financial transactions on a mobile device like cell phone, tablet, etc. It can be as simple as a bank sending an alert message whenever money is deposited or withdrawn from the account or as complex as a customer transferring a huge amount to another account.

E-wallets: Also known as mobile wallets, they are prepaid accounts that allow users to store different bank accounts, credit card or debit card information in a secure environment and allow them to make all payments in a faster and safer manner.

Chapter Highlights

- The internet is a global network that connects billions of computers all over of the world. It is a network of networks.
- In a network, a node is a device that either sends or receives data to/from the other nodes on the network.
- The data transmission mode refers to the direction of flow of data. Based on this characteristic, a connection can be classified into three categories—simplex, half-duplex, and full-duplex.
- A modem is a hardware device that allows a computer to send and receive data over a telephone line or a cable or satellite connection.
- In RJ45, "RJ" stands for "registered jack". Registered jack indicates that it is a standardized networking interface and "45" is the number of the interface standard. Each RJ45 connector has eight pins spaced about 1 mm apart.
- A switch is used to filter data packets and send them only to the port which is connected to the destination of the packets.
- Router is a network device that connects multiple computer networks together using either wired or wireless connections.
- When a hub receives a packet of data from a connected device, it broadcasts (sends it to every device) that data packet to all other devices connected to it.
- Routers maintain in their memory, a table (also known as **Routing Table**) that contains information about the available routes and their conditions (like traffic on that route, cost involved, etc). This information is then used to determine the best route for a given packet.
- Hotspots are usually connected to computers using radio frequencies from a cell phone tower. These computers pick up the radio signal using a wireless Internet card which is also known as the Wi-Fi card.
- The mesh network topology links all computers or computing devices nodes directly to all other devices on the network.
- TCP is a reliable protocol that does its best to transfer data without any error, and without any part being lost or duplicated.
- The Internet Protocol (IP) is the address system of the Internet. Its main responsibility is to deliver data packets from the sender device to the destination device.
- File Transfer Protocol (FTP) is used to transfer web page files from individual computers to the server.
- The term 'get' refers to receiving files from the server and 'put' refers to sending files (synonymous with download and upload respectively).
- PPP is used to transmit multi-protocol data between two computers that are directly connected point-to-point with each other.

- HTTP specifies a set of rules for transferring web pages (that include text, graphic images, sound, video, etc. and other multimedia files) to the World Wide Web.
- SMTP is used for sending email and either POP3 or IMAP is used for receiving email. The use of IMAP or POP3 is important as SMTP cannot save messages on the server and download them when required.
- SMTP server has two components – User Agent (UA) and Mail Transfer Agent (MTA).
- Terminal emulation or Telnet is a text-based protocol that uses the underlying TCP/IP technology for accessing a remote computer's (called host) data and application programs.
- WiMAX is a wireless communications standard that has been specifically designed for creating metropolitan area networks (MANs).
- Unlike virus, worms exist as separate entities and do not attach themselves to other files or programs.
- Cookies are small pieces of information that are stored on a computer by a web server. The browser stores each message in a small file, called **cookie.txt**.
- When cloud computing technology is used to deliver a firewall service, it is called a cloud firewall, or firewall-as-a-service (FaaS).
- HTTPs is a secure version of HyperText Transfer Protocol (HTTP). The 's' stands for secure.
- E-commerce involves alternatives to paper-based methods of communication and storage of information.
- Trade-secret laws provide protection against sensitive business information. For example, a marketing plan for launch of a new product must be kept confidential as it gives the business an advantage over its competitors.
- The term Web 2.0 refers to internet applications that allow users to share information and collaborate with other people. It is an improved version of the first worldwide web that brought more demand for dynamic web pages than static ones

Review Questions

1. Define the term 'computer networks' and list some reasons why such networks have been created.
2. How is the internet different from a computer network? Give some applications of the internet.
3. Explain the different data transmission modes.
4. Which type of communication cable will you prefer to create a computer network? Justify your answer.
5. Discuss wireless communication techniques of creating a computer network.
6. Write a short note on networking devices.
7. Differentiate between a hub and a switch.
8. How does a router work?
9. Explain the role of Wi-Fi in networking.
10. What is network topology? Explain any three of them.
11. Differentiate between LAN, MAN, WAN and PAN.
12. Explain the role of TCP and IP protocols in data transmission.
13. Differentiate between IPv4 and IPv6.
14. Explain the advantages and working of FTP.
15. Give the use of PPP.
16. Explain the working of HTTP.
17. Write a short note on Telnet protocol.
18. How does a wireless network send or receive messages over the internet?
19. Differentiate between Wi-Fi and Wi-max.
20. What is VoIP technology? List some advantages.
21. Define malware and discuss some its popular types.
22. Discuss any three types of computer viruses.
23. List a few symptoms of virus attack.
24. How is a virus different from a worm and a Trojan horse?
25. How is a spyware, keylogger and ransomware a threat to computer security?
26. What are cookies? How are they useful?
27. What is a firewall? Explain the features of different types of firewalls.
28. How is phishing used for identity theft?
29. Define spoofing and explain its types.
30. Why is cyber bullying treated as a serious cybercrime?
31. List some common ways of frauds on the internet.
32. Explain the term IPR.
33. Differentiate between ethical and unethical hacking.
34. Write a short note on the different types of hackers.
35. How is XML better than HTML?
36. How does DNS work?
37. With the help of an example, explain the meaning of a URL.

38. Differentiate between absolute and relative URL.
39. What is a Web page? How is a Web page related to a website?
40. Differentiate between a static and a dynamic website.
41. What is Web hosting? Explain the different ways in which it can be done.
42. How will you choose a Web hosting service for your website?
43. Differentiate between client-side and server-side scripting languages
44. Differentiate between Web 1.0 and Web 2.0
45. What is e-commerce? How is payment done for e-commerce transactions?

Fill in the Blanks

1. _____ is a global network that connects billions of computers all over of the world.
2. In _____ switching, an end-to-end path is set up before any data can be sent.
3. The internet is designed using _____ switching technology.
4. _____ of a network means how easily a new node can be added to a network.
5. _____ is the range of frequencies within a given band that is used for transmitting analog signals.
6. _____ use Earth-based transmitter and receiver.
7. _____ is the process of converting an analog signal into a digital data that can be read by the receiving computer.
8. _____ Modems are the modems which are built onto the computer motherboard.
9. _____ are used for direct computer-to-computer connections when there is no router, hub, or switch available.
10. No computer can communicate with other devices without a properly installed and configured _____ card.
11. The strength of wireless connectivity totally depends on the quality of _____ being received at any particular time.
12. _____ is an arrangement of computers or other computing devices.
13. In _____ topology, every computer or computing device is connected to single cable.
14. In _____ topology, all data transmission is possible only through the hub.
15. _____ topology is also known as star of stars topology.
16. _____ topology is a combination of two or more topologies.
17. A LAN can be connected to a WAN by using a _____.
18. Error control and flow control are managed by _____ protocol.
19. TCP uses _____ to confirm the receipt of data packets.
20. _____ is the address system of the Internet. It delivers data packets from the sender device to the destination device.
21. All publicly available files are accessed using _____ FTP server.
22. _____ protocol is used in PPP to encapsulate the datagram so that it can be transmitted over the specified physical layer.
23. _____ protocol will soon replace HTTP.
24. _____ is used for sending email and either _____ or _____ is used for receiving email.
25. The _____ transfers this mail across the internet.
26. _____ is a technology that allows users to make a local or a long-distance call using broadband connection.
27. Computer virus, spyware, worms, Trojan horse, etc. are all examples of _____.
28. _____ viruses either overwrite the boot record or move it to a different location in the hard disk.
29. _____ is a table maintained by the operating system that stores information about location, size, and other details of files stored on the hard disk.

30. _____ is an advertising-supported software.
31. _____ attacks delete all the data from the computer system.
32. Email programs as well as ISPs use a _____ to automatically block all the spam messages.
33. Web browser stores cookies in a file called _____.
34. _____ cookies are created by ads on Web page(s) being visited by users.
35. Packet filtering can allow or reject data packets based on the _____ of the machines.
36. _____ prevents tampering of data by ISPs or hackers. They can no longer insert ads or inject code designed to compromise a user's computer.
37. _____ involves alternatives to paper-based methods of communication and storage of information.
38. _____ is a criminal activity that either targets or uses a computer, a computer network or a networked device.
39. In _____, messages are either sent using a bogus email address or faking the email address of another user.
40. In _____, cybercriminals send a flood of fake data packets to a website to overload the server thereby causing the web server to temporarily malfunction or in some cases, crash completely.
41. In DoS attack, _____ are created by depositing malware on users' computers.
42. _____ is an attack that uses scripts to mine cryptocurrencies within browsers without the user's consent.
43. _____ are applied to industrial processes and inventions to protect them from unauthorised implementation.
44. _____ protects the image and name of a person against unauthorized use for commercial purposes.
45. Unethical hackers are also known as _____.
46. _____ hat hackers hack the system to test their knowledge and skills to see how easily they can break into a system.
47. _____ Language supports links to other documents, graphics, audio, and/or video files.
48. By clicking on a _____, another text on the same web page or a different web page is displayed.
49. _____ is a self-describing or self-defining markup language.
50. Domain Name Service convert domain names into corresponding _____.
51. Anything written after ? in the URL specifies_____.
52. _____ web pages show the same content each time they are viewed.
53. By default, when no particular web page is mentioned in the URL, _____ is displayed on the screen.
54. Caching web pages for fast delivery of frequently requested pages is known as _____.
55. _____ hosting gives users complete administrative control of server that is dedicated solely to their website.
56. Validating a HTML form is done through _____-side scripting.
57. _____ interprets and displays a webpage on the screen.
58. _____ is the best option for making payments for those who have a mobile phone but either do not have a bank account or do not have balance in their account.
59. _____ is an example of e-cash.
60. While shopping _____ should be used for paying bills.

State True or False

1. The advantage of Internet is that it lacks a central authority that controls it.
2. A permanent leased line is an example of packet switching.
3. Full-duplex data transmission mode can be implemented using a single cable between the sender and the receiver.
4. Symmetrical bandwidth means download and upload capacity are not equal.
5. Twisted Pair cables can connect telephones, TVs as well as computers.

6. Infrared signals can be used only within small distances (> 10 m).
7. Wireless networks are susceptible to interference from lights and electronic devices.
8. The transmission speed of wireless network is much higher than that offered by wired networks.
9. Hub is an intelligent network device.
10. Routers can perform the function of a hub as well as a switch.
11. The bus topology links all computers or computing devices nodes directly to all other devices on the network.
12. Data transfer rate and data error rate is less in LANs than WANs.
13. IP does not handle packet ordering or error checking.
14. FTP servers usually work in active mode.
15. NCP is used in PPP for establishing, configuring, testing, maintaining and terminating links for transmission.
16. Telnet is a text-based protocol that lacks usage of GUI.
17. Users cannot transfer files using Telnet.
18. Antivirus software can detect Trojan horse and protect users from spam emails.
19. As soon as the web browsing session ends, permanent cookies are automatically deleted from the computer.
20. Cookies can transfer viruses or malware to the user's computer.
21. Deleting or prohibiting cookies will make some websites difficult to navigate.
22. We must use HTTP for financial transactions.
23. HTTPs exchanges all data in an unencrypted form.
24. In phishing attack, the IP address of a certain computer is masked so that it becomes difficult for other systems to determine the sender (real sender) of the data.
25. Cyber espionage is a cybercrime in which the cybercriminal hacks into systems or networks to gain access to confidential information.
26. Copyrights are not applicable on films, sound recordings, drawings, paintings, and photography.
27. Trademarks provide protection against sensitive business information.
28. HTML supports customized tags.
29. Domain name is a part of the URL.
30. A single web server can host one or multiple websites.
31. Web 2.0 moved netizens from a read-only Internet to a "read/write" Internet.
32. Client scripting is used for accessing online databases, providing forums, feedback forms etc.
33. Using mobile banking, users can check their balance amount and make payments but cannot stop payment on a cheque.
34. Users can store multiple card information and bank account details in a wallet.
35. For small transactions, EFT should be used.

Multiple Choice Questions

1. Which of the following is not a feature of circuit switching technique?
   a. Expensive
   b. Fast delivery
   c. Efficient utilization of the communications channel
   d. Reliable data delivery
2. _____ indicates how frequently network failure takes place.
   a. Reliability   b. Scalability   c. Security   d. Availability
3. A computer and printer work in _____ mode of data transmission.
   a. simplex   b. half-duplex   c. full-duplex   d. All of these.
4. Which of the following cable is more prone to noise and has signal attenuation issues?
   a. Fibre Optic   b. Twisted Pair   c. Coaxial   d. Wi-Fi

5. TV programmes are broadcasted using _____.
   a. terrestrial microwaves
   b. communication satellites
   c. infrared waves
   d. laser beam
6. _____ is used to filter data packets and send them to only the port which is connected to the destination of that packet.
   a. Hub
   b. Router
   c. Switch
   d. Modem
7. _____ is a network device that is used at the third layer of OSI model to connect multiple computer networks.
   a. Hub
   b. Router
   c. Switch
   d. Modem
8. _____ is a device that joins two networks using different protocols.
   a. Hub
   b. Router
   c. Switch
   d. Gateway
9. In which topology, the entire network fails if there is a fault in the main cable.
   a. Ring
   b. Bus
   c. Mesh
   d. Star
10. Which of the following protocol works on the second layer of OSI model?
    a. TCP
    b. IP
    c. PPP
    d. FTP
11. Which of the following is not true about PPP?
    a. Byte oriented protocol
    b. Layer 3 protocol
    c. Works in full-duplex mode
    d. Can be used with satellite links
12. Which protocol specifies a set of rules for transferring web pages that include text, graphic images, sound, video, etc. and other multimedia files on the World Wide Web?
    a. TCP
    b. IP
    c. PPP
    d. HTTP
13. Which protocol is used for relaying emails?
    a. SMTP
    b. IMAP
    c. POP3
    d. FTP
14. Which of the following is used to prepare the message, create the envelope and then put the message in the envelope?
    a. POP3
    b. IMAP
    c. MTA
    d. UA
15. Programs like Microsoft Word, PowerPoint and Excel are easily prone to _____ virus.
    a. Stealth
    b. Macro
    c. Polymorphic
    d. Resident
16. _____ cookies reappear after they've been deleted.
    a. Persistent
    b. Session
    c. Zombie
    d. Third-party
17. _____ firewall can prevent or provide access based on protocols used.
    a. Packet filtering
    b. Proxy
    c. Cloud
    d. Stateful
18. On a website supporting HTTP, which of the following cannot happen to confidential data?
    a. Intercepted
    b. spied
    c. altered
    d. All of these.
19. _____ means unauthorized real-time interception of a private communication.
    a. Phishing
    b. Hacking
    c. Eavesdropping
    d. Spoofing
20. Domain hijacking is also known as _____.
    a. Phishing
    b. Pharming
    c. Eavesdropping
    d. Sniffing
21. Ransomware is an example of _____.
    a. Cyber extortion
    b. Cryptojacking
    c. Cyber espionage
    d. Cyber stalking
22. _____ is a name, word, slogan, design, symbol or any other item that is used to identify a product or organisation.
    a. Trademark
    b. Copyright
    c. Patent
    d. Trade Secret
23. _____ is a non-skilled person who uses available tools to gain unauthorized access to a computer system or network.
    a. Phreaker
    b. Hacktivist
    c. Script kiddies
    d. Cracker
24. Nignix, Microsoft IIS and Apache are examples of _____.
    a. Web pages
    b. websites
    c. Web servers
    d. search engines

25. A shared hosting technique in which users get a dedicated server space and a reserved amount of resources and memory.
   a. Dedicated   b. VPS   c. Shared   d. Reseller

26. Which of the following is not a server-side scripting language?
   a. ASP   b. PHP   c. JavaScript   d. Perl

27. Which card has a small microprocessor chip embedded in it to store the amount of money?
   a. Smart card   b. Debit card   c. Credit card   d. All of these.

28. CC Avenue, Pay Pal, pay by Amazon are examples of _____.
   a. Mobile wallets   b. Prepaid cards   c. Payment gateways   d. Mobile apps

Answers

Fill in the Blanks

1. Internet
2. circuit
3. packet
4. Scalability
5. Bandwidth
6. Terrestrial microwaves
7. Demodulation
8. Onboard
9. RJ45 cables and RJ connector
10. NIC or LAN
11. radio waves
12. Network Topology
13. bus
14. star
15. Tree
16. Hybrid
17. router
18. TCP
19. acknowledgments
20. The Internet Protocol (IP)
21. anonymous
22. High-Level Data-Link Control (HDLC)
23. HyperText Transfer Protocol - Next Generation (HTTP-NG)
24. SMTP, IMAP, POP3
25. mail transfer agent (MTA)
26. VoIP
27. malware
28. Boot record
29. File allocation table (FAT)
30. Adware
31. Sweeper
32. spam filter
33. cookie.txt
34. Third-party
35. IP address
36. HTTPs
37. E-commerce
38. Cybercrime
39. email spoofing
40. Denial-of-Service attack
41. Botnets
42. Cryptojacking
43. Patents
44. Right of publicity
45. crackers
46. Grey
47. HyperText Markup
48. hypertext
49. XML
50. IP address
51. a variable and its value
52. Static
53. the home page or the index page
54. web acceleration
55. Dedicated
56. client
57. Web browser
58. Mobile money
59. Bitcoin
60. cards or e-wallets.

State True or False

1. True
2. False
3. True
4. False
5. False
6. True
7. True
8. False
9. False
10. True
11. False
12. True
13. True
14. False
15. False
16. True
17. True
18. True
19. False
20. False
21. True
22. False
23. False
24. False
25. True
26. False
27. False
28. False
29. True
30. True
31. True
32. False
33. False
34. True
35. False

Multiple Choice Questions

1. c
2. a
3. a
4. b
5. b
6. c
7. b
8. d
9. c
10. c
11. b
12. d
13. a
14. d
15. b
16. c
17. b
18. d
19. c
20. b
21. a
22. a
23. c
24. c
25. b
26. c
27. a
28. c

Data Management

Chapter Objectives

In this chapter, we will read about storing data in databases for fast and efficient access and manipulation, with focus on the following:

- Problems with file management system
- Database approach – Applications, pros and cons
- ACID property
- Relational databases
- Components of DBMS
- Database keys
- Data integrity rules

9.1 FILE MANAGEMENT SYSTEM

When computers were first used for business applications, a related group of records were stored in a file. Each department had its own files that were specifically designed for applications or services provided by that particular department. For example, you may have noticed that in that in your school, there are three departments – academics, accounts and library. Each of these departments maintain a student's file that has details of a student that are specific for their purpose.

Although maintaining a separate student's file (computerized file) in each department to be a good and easy way of storing details, this approach suffers from various drawbacks.

Data Redundancy: Redundancy means repetition. From Fig. 9.1, it is clear that if a particular data is required by two different applications, then it may be stored in two or more files. Here, name, class, roll number, address and phone number of a student is recorded in three different files.

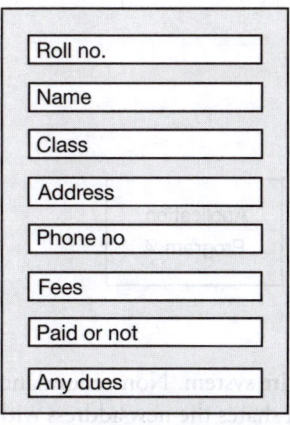

Figure 9.1 File management system

Lack of Flexibility: When we store data in separate files, the user can generate only limited reports and execute a limited number of queries. Such systems cannot respond to un-anticipatory queries or be amenable to any kind of investigative or trend analysis that has now become mandatory for any business to survive in the competitive world.

Difficulty in Accessing Data: Storing data in separate files does not allow data to be retrieved in a convenient and efficient manner. For example, if there is a need to make a list of all the students who have not paid their fees and also have some library dues, then two files have to be accessed for the purpose. Making such a list will also be a time-consuming and cumbersome task.

Data Isolation: Since data is scattered in different files in distinct departments and stored in different formats, retrieving data from different files is very difficult.

Data Integrity Issues: Data stored in files must satisfy certain types of consistency constraints. For example, the student cannot be issued more than three books. It is very difficult for computer programmers to write applications or programs that can retrieve as well as store only the data that satisfies the specified constraints. For example, the moment a student is issued the fourth book, the program must disallow this task.

Data Atomicity Issues: In case of a failure, data must be restored to the correct state that existed prior to the failure. It is difficult to accomplish this when separate files are used. For example, if a user is running a banking software to transfer Rs 10K from his account to another account and if the computer automatically shuts down because of some failure, then either the money should be deducted from his account and added to another or nothing should happen. Just imagine how difficult it would be if the amount was deducted from the account but not added in the other account. So, either the work should be done in entirety or not at all.

9.2 DATABASE

A database is a collection of related data organized in a way that allows users to easily access, update and maintain the data. It stores non-redundant data that can be shared by different application systems (as shown in Fig. 9.2).

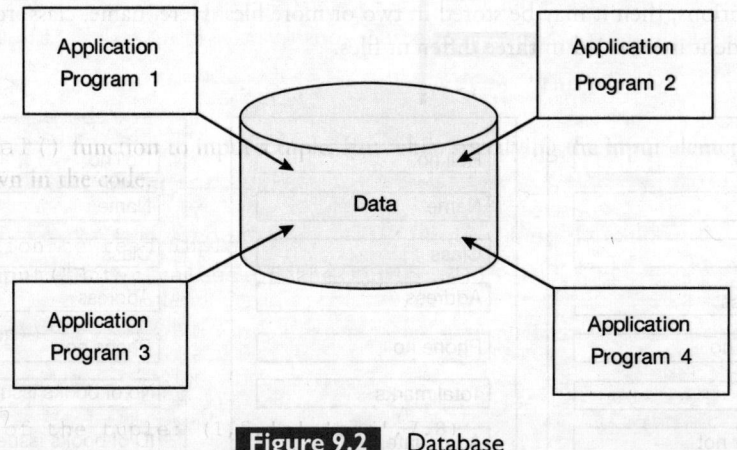

Figure 9.2 Database

'Non-redundant' means that only a single copy of data exists in the entire system. Non-redundancy ensures **data consistency**. For example, if a student changes his/her residence address and shares the new address with the academic department then that department will have the updated value but others will have the incorrect old value. This is called inconsistent data which occurred due to redundancy of data (existence of same data at multiple locations). In databases, only a single copy of data exists that is shared by all the applications running in every department.

9.2.1 Advantages of Database

The following are the advantages of using database to store data:

- It reduces data redundancy because databases are shared instead of being stored as independent files.
- It minimizes data inconsistencies.
- It maintains data integrity and quality.
- Information about the stored data including its meaning and interpretation can be saved in the data dictionary.
- Data stored is secured as a database with appropriate security tools to control access.
- Data can be easily searched by using keywords.
- Data can be shared among multiple branches of the same organization.
- Data can be used to analyze trends such as which product is most popular among customers.

9.2.2 Application of Database System

Database systems are widely used in almost every area we can think of. They have been successfully implemented for the following applications:

- Databases are used for reserving air as well as train tickets.
- Airlines and railways use databases for displaying the route and schedule of trains and flights.
- In hospitals, databases are used to store details of patients, their medical history and other details.
- Financial institutions (like banks) use database for storing details of customers, their accounts, loans, and other transactions. They also use databases to record purchases on credit cards for generating monthly bills.
- Databases are used in schools and colleges to store the information about students.
- Database are used in every organization to maintain records of all their employees, their salaries, perks, taxes, etc.
- In telecommunication departments, databases are used to store information about the telephone numbers. They also store record of calls, for generating monthly bills, etc.
- Online shopping websites and other business activities use database to store details of products, customers, transactions and other payment details.
- The world wide web maintains enormous amount of textual and multimedia data in databases.
- Databases are used in online trading for storing information about sales and purchases of stocks and bonds.

9.3 ACID PROPERTY

Every operation that takes place in a database system must maintain ACID properties where ACID means **A**tomicity, **C**onsistency, **I**solation and **D**urability. ACID ensures accuracy, completeness, and data integrity.

Atomicity: It states that an operation must either complete fully or must not be performed at all. There should not be any middle state, especially when updating the data. So, this rule says "All or Nothing".

Consistency: When any operation takes place, it should not have any adverse effect on the data stored in the database. If the database was in a consistent state before the execution of an operation, it must remain consistent even after the execution of the operation. For this, a database ensures that only valid data that satisfies all rules and constraints are written in the database.

Isolation: In a database system, when more than one transaction is executed at the same time, the property of isolation states that all the transactions will be carried out and executed as if it is the only transaction in the system. No transaction will affect any other transaction.

For example, if user A withdraws Rs 10000 and user B withdraws Rs 15000 from user C's account, which has a balance of Rs. 50,0000, then only one person will be allowed to draw from C's account and the other person will have to wait until the first operation is completed. After both operations, the balance in C's account will be Rs 50,000 – Rs 10,000 – Rs 15,000.

However, if they both are allowed to withdraw at the same time then both operations will read balance as 50,000, draw their amount and will update accordingly. Rs. 50,000 - Rs. 10,000 or Rs.50,000 – Rs. 15,000.

Durability: External factors like system crash or power failure, should not affect the data once the database operation is completed on the server.

In the above example, user B may withdraw Rs. 15,000 only after user A's transaction is completed and is updated in the database. If the system fails before A's transaction is logged in the database, then A cannot withdraw any money, and amount in C's account is not affected.

Thus, we see that every database must guarantee all the above properties to ensure reliability, robustness and consistency. All of the major relational DBMSs support ACID principles. They all include features that ensure that data remains consistent throughout software and hardware crashes, as well as any failed transactions.

9.4 COMPONENTS OF A DATABASE SYSTEM

An effective database system comprises of four main components (as shown in Fig. 9.3). They can be described as:

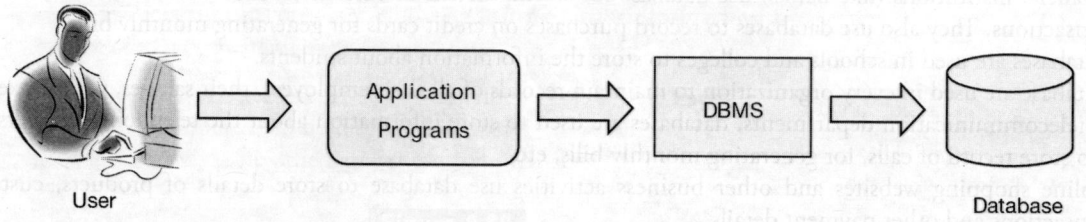

Figure 9.3 Components of a database-oriented approach

Data: The most crucial component of a database is the data stored in it. This data can be accessed by users through application programs. A database stores two types of data – user data and metadata. While user data contains data to supports user applications, the metadata on the other hand, stores data about data. It describes the structure of the database and includes information regarding number of tables and table names, number of fields and field names, primary key fields, types of pre-defined queries, etc.

Hardware: The hardware consists of the secondary storage devices on which data is stored. These include input and output devices for receiving/ giving data to users and processor and main memory for processing the data in a fast and efficient manner.

Software: The software consists of the Database Management System (DBMS) which acts as a bridge between the user and the database. The DBMS software interacts with the user's application programs and database to insert, update, delete and retrieve data. DBMS is responsible for maintaining the integrity and security of stored data and for recovering information in case of system failure. Some common examples of DBMS are MS ACCESS, SQL Server, Oracle, dBase and FoxPro.

Users: Users are the people who access the data from the database. They may vary from clerical staff to managers and executives. Based on the job profile, these users are either given full or partial access to the database data. Database users (refer Fig. 9.4) can be broadly classified into the following categories:

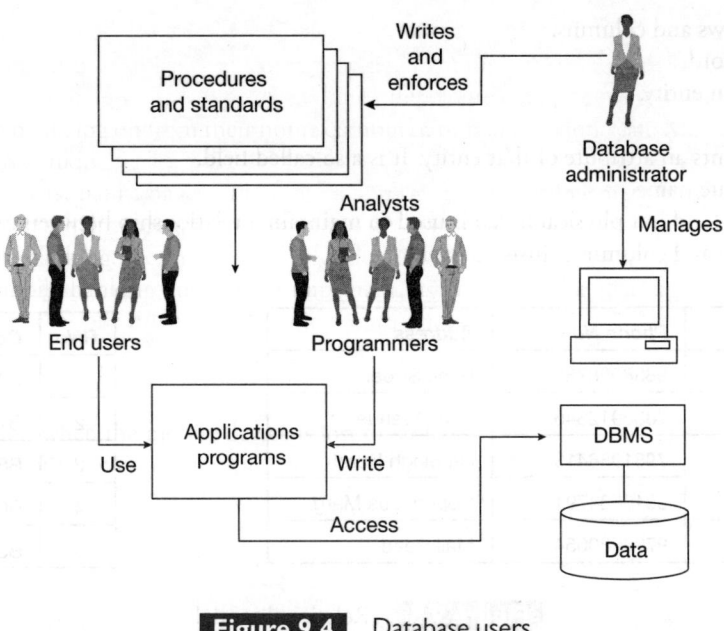

Figure 9.4 Database users

Application Programmers: An application programmer writes application programs to access, retrieve, update, delete or add new data to the database. These programs are written using a high-level language preferably SQL, which is a 4GL.

End-users: End-users are those users who use the application programs developed by the application developers. They need not know about the database design, working, access mechanism and other technical details of the database. Rather they just use the underlying database to get their work done. End-users may be further categorized in two groups.

Sophisticated end-users who write their own queries to access and process the data stored in the database.

Unsophisticated end-users who interact with the system through an already-written application program. They follow the instructions provided in the user interface to retrieve data from the database. For example, people working at railways reservation counters interact with the system through an already written application program. Another example of unsophisticated users is bank customers who use ATMs to draw money or check their balance.

Database Administrator (DBA): A DBA makes strategic and policy decisions regarding the data. He/she provides technical support for implementing these decisions and is responsible for overall control of the system at the technical level. He monitors as well as performs all activities related to database design, implementation, maintenance and security. Besides administering the database, he also trains employees in database management and use.

System Analyst: System analysts identify end-users' requirements, plan solutions and recommend hardware and software that best meets business goals. They conduct a technical and economic feasibility analysis of the identified requirements.

9.5 RELATIONAL DATABASES

Relational databases were developed by E F Codd in 1970. In a relational database, data and the relationship that exist between those data are represented using tables also known as **relations**. Therefore, a table is a collection of data records where each record contains the same fields but with a different value for the fields. The main features of relational data model are:

- A table consists of rows and columns.
- Each row stores a record.
- A record represents an entity.
- Each row is unique.
- Each column represents an attribute of that entity. It is also called field.
- Each field has a unique name
- A common attribute (and not physical links) is used to maintain a relationship between two tables.
- The sequence of rows and columns is insignificant.

RNo	Name	Phone No	Address
1	Anant	9838098789	Bank Street
2	Chaitanya	7838912345	Park Avenue
3	Deep	7981086413	Jai Singh Road
4	Fatima	9913534791	Copernicus Marg
5	Harpreet	9729980654	Mall Road

RNo	Course	Year
1	BTech	2020
2	BTech	2018
3	BSc	2019
4	BCA	2019
5	BSc	2020

Figure 9.5 Relational model

Look at Fig. 9.5, which shows the relational model and consists of two tables. The first table stores the roll number, name, address and phone number of the students. The second table stores the roll number, course and the year of admission. Note that these two tables have a common field – RNo. Now, if there is a query like in which course Fatima studies, then the first table will be searched to obtain the roll number of Fatima. This roll number will then be used to search for a particular record in the second table. In this way, we are joining two tables based on a common attribute. The result of this query would return – BCA.

9.5.1 Advantages of Relational Databases

- The data is organized in a way that makes it simple to understand and use.
- Data access is simpler than other models (like network and hierarchical).
- It is programmer friendly as it is easy to develop application programs for a relational database as compared to other databases.
- It provides flexible data organization.
- Future enhancements to the database like adding new table, row, field, etc. can be easily done.
- Relational model is close to the intuitive or logical model of real-life applications.

9.5.2 Disadvantages of Relational Databases

Not all types of data can be represented using relational data model. Some examples of such data include multimedia, temporal, spatial and unstructured data.

9.6 COMPONENTS OF DBMS

A database management system is a software that is used to manage an organization's data. **It enables users to create a database, define constraints, manipulate data, execute queries and generate reports**. Besides users, the database administrators use DBMS to administer, monitor, manage and take backup of the ever-growing database. The different components of a DBMS are shown in Fig. 9.6.

Data Management

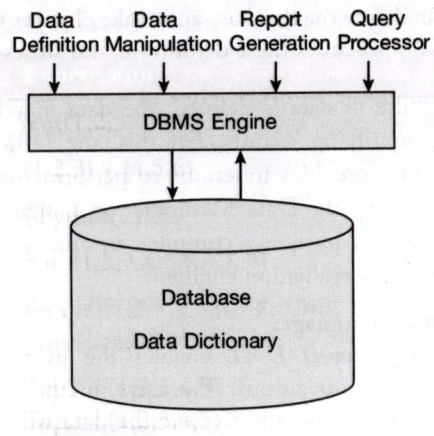

Figure 9.6 Components of DBMS

DBMS Engine: The DBMS engine is the core service for creating tables, storing, processing, and securing database data. It provides controlled access and fast processing to meet the time constraints of the most complex applications. Database Engine can be used to create relational databases for online transaction processing or online analytical processing of data. This includes creating tables for storing data, and database objects such as indexes, views, and stored procedures for viewing, managing, and securing data.

Data Dictionary: In every database, a certain amount of space is reserved for data dictionary. The data dictionary stores information about the data stored in the database. It stores information about different tables, schemas, views, indexes, functions, procedures, user permissions, user statistics, database design information, database growth and performance statistics, etc.

Query Processor: The query processor accepts user queries and transforms them into a series of instructions. For this, the query processor accesses the data dictionary to find the structure of relevant data and uses this information to restructure the query to optimally access the database. To hide all technical details from users, the query processor consists of three modules – DDL interpreter, DML compiler and a query evaluation engine

Report Writer: A report generator is a program that creates a report in the prescribed format. It is an essential part of the DBMS that utilizes the output of query execution to display it in an easy to understand format. Although results of queries are self-describing, users can also get the results in the form of pie charts, bar charts, and other diagrams.

In most of the DBMS available today, frequently used reports are already created and stored so that users can use them as and when required. Users can also create a new report if none of the available reports satisfy their requirements. In such a case, the newly created report can be stored in the list of available reports so that it can be used in future.

9.6.1 Other Important Modules of DBMS

A database management system is a complex software system. In addition to the components listed above, DBMS also has other very important modules for data definition and manipulation, data integrity, security, data recovery and concurrency control, and performance optimization. These modules can be explained as below:

Data Definition: The data definition module of DBMS provides functions to define the structure of the data. These functions are written using the data definition language (DDL). DDL enables the data administrators to define and modify the structure of the table, data type of fields, and integrity constraints to be satisfied before storing the data in each field.

> Every time a DDL statement is issued, the data dictionary gets modified.

Only the database administrator can define the database and make changes to its definition as and when required. The DDL compiler component of DBMS processes these definitions and stores them in the data dictionary.

Data Manipulation: After the structure of data is defined, the data may be manipulated by adding, deleting and modifying records. For this, the DBMS contains a data manipulation module that provides functions to perform these operations. These functions are written using the Data Manipulation Language (DML). The DML commands are compiled by query compiler, optimized by query optimizer and finally executed by query evaluation engine.

> The query optimizer refers the data dictionary to find information about the stored data.

There are two types of data manipulation language:

The ***non-procedural** (also called **high-level*****) DML** enables the users to easily and precisely specify complex database operations. The users just have to specify *what* data is required. They do not have to specify *how* the data will be retrieved. The most commonly used example of a non-procedural DML is the structured query language (or SQL).

The ***procedural** (also called **low-level*****) DML** requires users to write a step-by-step procedure to specify *what* data is required and *how* that data has to be accessed. The most commonly used example of procedural DML is relational algebra, which provides a set of operations like select, project, union, etc., to manipulate the data in the database.

> Query is the statement which is written to retrieve information. The part of the DML that retrieves the information is called a query language.

Data Security and Integrity: The data security and integrity module of the DBMS provides functions to handle security and integrity of data stored in the database. Data integrity ensures correctness, completeness and consistency of data.

Concurrency and Data Recovery: The concurrency and data recovery module of the DBMS provides functions to allow multiple users to access the database simultaneously. It also provides functions to recover data in case of system failure.

Performance Optimization: The performance optimization module provides a set of functions to optimize the performance of user queries. The module formulates and evaluates different execution plans of a given query and then selects the most efficient plan to be executed on the database.

> Some functions of the DBMS are supported by the operating system while others are built on top of it.

9.7 BASIC TERMINOLOGY OF RELATIONAL DATABASE SYSTEMS

In this section, we will learn about some terms that are frequently used when relational databases are used.

Relation: As discussed earlier, a relation is a table. In a table, data is arranged in rows and columns. Every relation exhibits some basic features such as,

- In any given column of a table, all the items are of the same type. Correspondingly, items in different columns may not be of the same type.
- Every row must have a single value for each column.
- Every row must have a unique value. That is, no two rows should have same value for all the fields.
- The ordering of rows in a relationship is insignificant.
- Every column must have a unique name.
- The order of columns is insignificant.

Tuple: The rows of tables are known as Tuples.

Attributes: The columns or fields of a table are called Attributes of the table.

Degree: The number of attributes in a relation determines the degree of relation. A table that has five columns has a relation of degree 5.

Cardinality: The number of tuples or rows in a relation is known as cardinality of the relation.

9.8 DATABASE KEYS

Real-world applications may have tables containing millions of records or rows and thousands of fields or columns. Just imagine how difficult it would be to uniquely identify each record of such a huge table.

In your school, there are thousands of students and each student is uniquely identified by his/her admission number. In our country, there are billions of people and each person is uniquely identified by his/her Adhaar Number. In a hospital, every patient has a unique Patient_ID. In a company every employee has a unique Employee_ID. Similarly, in a table – big or small, there must be some field or a combination of fields which should have only unique values. Such a field(s) is called a **database key or simply a key**.

Just think and answer: Can we use name of the student as a key? No. This is because names are not unique. Two or more students in the school may have the same name. So key is a field or a collection of fields that forms a unique combination.

A table can have different types of keys like candidate key, primary key, super key or alternate key. Let us know the difference between each of them.

Candidate Key

Candidate keys are those attributes or columns of a table, which have the properties of uniqueness and irreducibility. Here, ***uniqueness*** means that a relation (or table) must not have two different rows with the same value for that column (or attribute or field). ***Irreducibility*** means that no proper subset of the candidate key has the uniqueness property. In simple words, no individual attribute of the candidate key should be unique.

For example, **Roll Number** field of a Student table is a candidate key as every student has a unique roll number. But the combination of **Roll Number and Name** is not an example of appropriate candidate key as it does not satisfy the property of irreducibility which says that no subset of candidate key has uniqueness property. In our example, Roll Number has the uniqueness property.

However, if **Name and Class** combination of students are unique, then these two attributes can together form the candidate key. This is possible only when no two students in the same class have the same name.

Key points to remember

- Every relation has at least one candidate key.
- A candidate key should not have null value.
- There can be any number of candidate keys in a table.

Composite Key: When we create keys using more than one column then that key is known as composite key.

Super Key: A super key is a combination of two or more fields that satisfies the uniqueness property but not necessarily the irreducibility property. This means that a candidate key is a special case of a super key.

For example, if Roll Number of every student is unique then the set of attributes **(Roll Number, Name), or (Roll Number, Name, Class)** is a super key for the STUDENT table. This set of attributes is unique, but it does not satisfy the property of irreducibility because Roll Number, which is a subset of the composite key, is unique.

Primary Key: The primary key is an attribute or a set of attributes that uniquely identifies a specific record in the table. In case we have multiple candidate keys in a relation, any one of the candidate keys can be chosen as the primary key. Since a candidate key cannot have Null value, the primary key can also not contain any Null value because we cannot uniquely identify multiple Null values.

Every candidate key satisfies the properties of becoming the primary key. In our example, if we have two candidate keys- **Roll Number** and **(Name, Class)** then any one can be chosen as the primary key.

Key points to remember

To qualify as a primary key for an entity, an attribute must have the following properties:

1. The value of a primary key must *not change or should not become null*. For example, the admission number of a student can neither become null nor change throughout the time the student is in school.
2. The primary key must have *minimum number of attributes* that are sufficient enough to ensure uniqueness of the record. This also means that a super key should not be made the primary key. That is, if a combination of Name and Class are chosen as the primary key then Name, Class and Phone Number should not be set as the primary key.
3. The record must have a valid value for the primary key field when it is being entered in the table. Without primary key's existence, the record cannot be entered in the table.

Candidate keys, which are not chosen as the primary key, are known as *Alternate Keys*. Figure 9.7 shows different types of keys applicable to the STUDENT table

Foreign Key: Foreign key is an attribute or a combination of attributes which defines the relationship between two tables. Basically, a foreign key is a primary key in one table that appears as a field in another table.

For example, consider a table that has fields **Roll Number, Name, Class and Teacher ID** and another table that has fields **Teacher ID and Teacher Name** where Teacher ID is the primary key of Teacher's table. We see that the primary key, Teacher ID in Teacher's table is also a field in the Student's Table. Hence,

STUDENT_ID	NAME	PHONE NUMBER	COURSE_ID

Candidate Keys = STUDENT_ID and (NAME, PHONE NUMBER)
Primary Key = STUDENT_ID
Foreign Key = COURSE_ID
Alternate Key = (NAME, PHONENUMBER)
Composite Key = (NAME, PHONE NUMBER)

Figure 9.7 Keys in student database

Teacher ID acts as a foreign key that connects the two tables.

We can tell which teacher is teaching a student by seeing his/her Teacher ID and fetching teacher's name from the Teacher's table using the Teacher ID field. Thus, we see that foreign keys are used to link together two or more different tables which have some form of relationship or link with each other.

Uses of Foreign Key

1. A foreign key helps to maintain data integrity in the table (also known as referential integrity).
2. It is also used for navigating between different occurrences of an entity.

For the above two reasons, *foreign key values should always be matched by corresponding primary key values.* For example, in the above tables, if Teacher ID = 9 does not exist in Teacher's table and the user tries to enter Teacher ID as 9 in the Student's table, then it points to data incorrectness and violates data integrity.

So, we must first enter the Teacher Name and Teacher ID (= 9) in the Teacher's table and then use it in Student's table to maintain referential integrity. Look at Fig. 9.8. Can you tell details of student with roll number S04? Can you tell his/her name, course, fees, status, teacher and the course he/she is studying? Now do you realize the utility of foreign keys in real-world databases? Doesn't it keep our data better organized?

Roll_No	Name	Course ID	Teacher ID	Fees	Status
S01	Mehek	C07	T011	300000	Paid
S02	Chahat	C05	T024	500000	Not Paid
S03	Tamanna	C03	T007	100000	Paid
S04	Anushka	C01	T036	400000	Not Paid
S05	Anika	C08	T018	800000	Paid

Teacher ID	Teacher name	Course ID
T003	Jaya Sood	C03
T007	Mansi Jain	C01
T011	Shefali Garg	C08
T015	Divya Tripathi	C05
T018	Vaishnavi	C02
T022	Rahul	C10
T024	Manish Kumar	C07
T029	Krishna Aiyyar	C04
T035	Nagarajan	C06
T036	Sai Murthy	C09

Course ID	Course name
C01	IT
C02	CS
C03	Electronics
C04	Electrical Engineering
C05	Chemical Engineering
C06	Management
C07	Material Management
C09	Mathematics
C10	Operational Research
C11	Statistics

Figure 9.8 Use of foreign keys to access information from multiple tables

Artificial Keys

Sometimes the DBA has to create keys known as artificial keys in the table. This happens in two situations: when no attribute has all the primary key properties, or when the primary key is too large and complex to use.

For example, using the combination of **Name and Phone Number** fields as primary key is a little complicated. Therefore, if roll number of the student is not given then the DBA may add a ROW_ID column as primary key of the table. In such a scenario, the ROW_ID field is known as the Artificial Key.

9.8 RELATIONAL DATA INTEGRITY RULES

To maintain data integrity, certain rules must be enforced on tables in the database. These rules which are implemented as constraints or restrictions include:

Null or Unknown Value Constraint: Null represents a value for an attribute that is currently unknown or is not applicable for the row. Null values are used to denote incomplete or exceptional data. It is wrong to treat a Null value as equivalent to zero or a text string filled with spaces as they represent the absence of a value.

Entity Integrity rule: This rule states that value of primary key of a row cannot be Null. This is important as the primary key identifies a particular record and it must have a valid value.

Referential Integrity: Referential Integrity rule states that if a foreign key exists in a relation, then the foreign key value must match with the corresponding primary key value in the other table.

Enterprise Constraints: These are additional rules specified by the users or database administrators of a database. For example, while entering PHONE NUMBER in the Student's Table, a constraint can be added to check that the phone number must be of exactly 10 digits. When such a constraint is enforced on the table, it will not be possible to add a new student or update a record, whose phone number has less than or more than 10 digits.

Key Terms

Data atomicity: Feature that allows data to be restored to the correct state that existed prior to the failure.

Database: A collection of related data organized in a way that allows users to easily access, update and maintain the data.

Data dictionary or metadata: Repository that stores information about data stored data in the database.

Database Management System (DBMS): Software that interacts with users' application programs and database to insert, update, delete and retrieve data.

Database Administrator (DBA): The person responsible for making strategic and policy decisions regarding the data.

Table: A collection of data records where each record contains the same fields but with a different value for the fields.

Report generator: An essential part of the DBMS program that utilizes the output of query execution to create a report in the prescribed format.

Data Definition Language: Language that has modules and functions to define the structure of the data. This is useful for adding, deleting and modifying records.

Query: A DML statement that is written to retrieve information from the database.

Tuple: The rows of tables are known as Tuples.

Attributes: The columns or fields of a table are called Attributes of the table.

Degree: The number of attributes in a relation determines the degree of relation. A table that has five columns have a relation of degree 5.

Cardinality: The number of tuples or rows in a relation is known as cardinality of the relation.

Candidate key: Candidate keys are those attributes or columns of a table, which have the properties of uniqueness and irreducibility.

Composite key: When we create keys using more than one column then that key is known as composite key.

Primary key: The primary key is an attribute or a set of attributes that uniquely identifies a specific record in the table.

Alternate key: Candidate keys, which are not chosen as the primary key, are known as Alternate Keys.

Foreign key: An attribute or a combination of attributes which defines the relationship between two tables.

Null or Unknown Value Constraint: Null represents a value for an attribute that is currently unknown or is not applicable for the row.

Entity integrity rule: Integrity constraint which states that the value of primary key of a row cannot be null.

Referential integrity: Referential Integrity rule states that, if a foreign key exists in a relation, then the foreign key value must match with the corresponding primary key value in the other table.

Chapter Highlights

- Files do not respond to un-anticipatory queries or any kind of investigative or trend analysis.
- Database stores non-redundant data that can be shared by different application systems.
- Non-redundancy of data means that only a single copy of data exists in the entire system. Non-redundancy ensures data consistency.

- The hardware consists of the secondary storage devices on which data is stored; input and output devices for receiving/ giving data to users; and processor and main memory for processing the data in a fast and efficient manner.
- DBMS is responsible for maintaining the integrity and security of stored data, and for recovering information in case of system failure.
- An application programmer writes application programs to access, retrieve, update, delete or add new data to the database.
- System analysts identify end-users' requirements, plan solutions, recommend hardware and software and conduct a feasibility analysis of the identified requirements.
- In a relational database, data and the relationship that exist between the data are represented using tables also known as relations.
- In a table, each column represents an attribute of an entity. A common attribute in two tables is used to maintain a relationship between them.
- RDBMS organizes data in a way that is simple to understand and use. It also provides flexible data organization.
- The DBMS Engine is used to create tables, store, process and secure database data.
- The query processor accepts users' queries and transforms them into a series of instructions.
- DML commands are compiled by query compiler, optimized by query optimizer and finally executed by query evaluation engine.
- In a table, big or small, there must be some field or a combination of fields which should have only unique values. Such a field(s) is called a database key or simply a key.
- A super key is a combination of two or more fields that satisfies the uniqueness property but not necessarily the irreducibility property. This means that a candidate key is a special case of a super key.
- The primary key must have the minimum number of attributes that are sufficient enough to ensure uniqueness of the record.
- Sometimes DBA has to create artificial keys in the table. This happens in two situations: when no attribute has all the primary key properties, or when the primary key is too large and complex to use.

Review Questions

1. List some disadvantages of using files for storing data.
2. Define database. List some advantages of using a database.
3. How is a file different from a database?
4. What do you mean by data consistency?
5. List at least five applications of databases.
6. What is metadata? What information does it give?
7. What is DBMS?
8. Categorize different database users.
9. What do you understand by the term 'relation'?
10. Give the advantages of using a RDBMS.
11. Write a short note on Query processor.
12. Why do we add artificial keys in a table?
13. Define the different types of constraints on table.
14. Differentiate between data definition and data manipulation.
15. Explain the types of DML.
16. With the help of example, explain the concept of candidate keys, primary key, super key, alternate key and composite key.

17. What is ACID test?
18. Imagine that you have been assigned to design a database for storing student's name, class, section, activity of their interest (Cooking, Sports, Arts, Music, Dance or Dramatics) and date of joining the activity. Design the table(s). Specify the column(s) in the table(s). Demonstrate the design by inserting at least five records.

Fill in the Blanks

1. Redundancy means _____.
2. _____ means data is restored to the correct state that existed prior to the failure.
3. Non-redundancy ensures _____.
4. In a _____, only a single copy of data exists that is shared by all the applications running in every department.
5. _____ is a repository that stores information about data stored data in the database.
6. _____ maintains enormous amount of textual and multimedia data in databases.
7. _____ is the software that interacts with user application programs and database to insert, update, delete and retrieve data.
8. _____ identify end users' requirements and plan solutions.
9. A _____ is a collection of data records where each record contains the same fields but with a different value for the fields.
10. In a table, each _____ represents an attribute of an entity.
11. _____ consists of three modules – DDL interpreter, DML compiler and a query evaluation engine.
12. _____ utilizes the output of query execution to create a report in the prescribed format.
13. Every time DDL is executed, _____ gets modified.
14. Data type of fields can be changed and integrity constraints can be added using _____ language.
15. SQL is an example of _____ DML.
16. The rows of tables are known as _____.
17. The columns or fields of a table are called _____ of the table.
18. _____ means that a relation (or table) must not have two different rows with the same value for that column (or attribute or field).
19. _____ means that no proper subset of the candidate key has the uniqueness property.
20. When we create keys using more than one column then that key is known as _____ key.
21. _____ values are used denote incomplete or exceptional data.
22. _____ constraint states that the value of primary key of a row cannot be null.
23. _____ requires that concurrent transactions execute separately from each other.
24. _____ requires the ability to recover from an unexpected system failure or power outage to the last known state.
25. _____ requires that when a transaction has been committed, the data must conform to the database schema.

State True or False

1. Data can be retrieved conveniently and efficiently from files.
2. A DBMS is a collection of related data organized in a way that allows users to easily access, update and maintain the data.
3. Files store non-redundant data that can be shared by different application systems.

4. Non-redundancy means that only a single copy of data exists in the entire system.
5. Database administrator writes application programs to access, retrieve, update, delete or add new data to the database.
6. Unsophisticated end-users write their own queries to access and process the data stored in the database.
7. In a table, each row is unique.
8. Multimedia, temporal, spatial and unstructured data can be efficiently represented in relational databases.
9. Data Manipulation Language has modules and functions to define the structure of the data.
10. Only the database administrator can define the database and make changes to its definition as and when required.
11. Relational Algebra is an example of non-procedural DML.
12. The number of tuples or rows in a relation is known as cardinality of the relation.
13. No individual attribute of candidate key should be unique.
14. Every relation has only one candidate key.
15. A candidate key may have null value.
16. In case we have multiple candidate keys in a relation, any one of the candidate keys can be chosen as the primary key.
17. The primary key must have maximum number of attributes that are sufficient enough to ensure uniqueness of the record.
18. Files support data isolation.

Multiple Choice Questions

1. Files lack flexibility. This means that files do not support _____.
   a. un-anticipatory queries
   b. investigative analysis
   c. trend analysis
   d. All of these.
2. Advantages of a database do not include _____.
   a. data inconsistency
   b. data consistency
   c. data integrity
   d. data atomicity
3. _____ is responsible for maintaining the integrity and security of stored data, and for recovering information in case of system failure.
   a. Database
   b. DBMS
   c. Operating System
   d. MS Excel
4. Which of the following is not an example of DBMS?
   a. MS ACCESS
   b. SQL Server
   c. FoxPro
   d. None of these.
5. _____ need not know about the database design, working, access mechanism and other technical details of the database.
   a. Application programmers
   b. DBA
   c. End-users
   d. System analysts
6. A DBA does not _____.
   a. train users
   b. administer database
   c. ensure database security
   d. write queries to process data
7. _____ accepts users' queries and transforms them into a series of instructions.
   a. Query processor
   b. DBMS Engine
   c. Data Dictionary
   d. Report Writer
8. A DML cannot be used for _____.
   a. adding records
   b. deleting records
   c. adding integrity constraints
   d. modifying records
9. Which module of the DBMS provides functions to allow multiple users to access the database simultaneously?
   a. Data Security and Integrity
   b. Data Concurrency
   c. Performance Optimization
   d. Query Processor
10. The number of attributes in a relation determines the _____ of relation.
    a. Degree
    b. Cardinality
    c. Order
    d. Tuple

11. _____ key is a combination of two or more fields that satisfies the uniqueness property but not necessarily the irreducibility property.
    a. Candidate   b. Composite   c. Super   d. Primary
12. _____ key is an attribute or a combination of attributes, which defines relationship between two tables.
    a. Candidate   b. Foreign   c. Super   d. Primary
13. Which Integrity rule states that if a foreign key exists in a relation, then the foreign key value must match with the corresponding primary key value in the other table?
    a. Entity   b. Referential   c. Enterprise   d. Null value
14. _____ requires a transaction to execute completely or not at all.
    a. Atomicity   b. Consistency   c. Isolation   d. Durability

Answers

Fill in the Blanks

1. repetition
2. Data atomicity
3. data consistency
4. database
5. Data dictionary or metadata
6. world wide web
7. DBMS
8. System analysts
9. table
10. column
11. Query processor
12. Report generator
13. data dictionary
14. Data Definition
15. non-procedural
16. Tuples
17. attributes
18. Uniqueness
19. Irreducibility
20. composite
21. Null
22. Entity Integrity
23. Isolation
24. Durability
25. Consistency

State True or False

1. False
2. False
3. False
4. True
5. False
6. False
7. True
8. False
9. False
10. True
11. False
12. True
13. True
14. False
15. True
16. True
17. False
18. False

Multiple Choice Questions

1. d
2. a
3. b
4. d
5. c
6. d
7. a
8. c
9. b
10. a
11. c
12. b
13. b
14. a

Structured Query Language (SQL)

10

Chapter Objectives

In the last chapter, we discussed the basic concepts of database and DBMS. We shall now learn to practically implement a relational database and execute our queries on it. We have used MySQL software. You can download it freely from the Internet. Topics that we will be covering here include,

- Basic introduction about MySQL
- Understanding the Structured Query Language
- Data types, Arithmetic and Logical Operators in SQL
- Using the `Select` statement
- Applying functions on strings
- Creating and deleting database
- Creating, deleting, altering and updating tables
- Inserting values in a table
- Working with WHERE, WHERE IN, WHERE LIKE, WHERE BETWEEN, ORDER BY, DISTINCT, GROUP BY, HAVING clauses
- Using functions like min, max, avg, count
- Understanding referential integrity issues
- Handling NULL values
- Adding primary key and foreign key constraints
- SQL Joins

10.1 INTRODUCTION TO MYSQL

Before starting with SQL, we must first have a database. In this chapter, we have used the MySQL database because it is a fast, easy-to-use RDBMS that is widely used. MySQL is popular for the following reasons:

- MySQL is an open-source software, so users do not have to pay to use it.
- It is a very powerful program that can handle a large subset of the functionality of the most expensive and powerful database packages.
- MySQL uses SQL data language.
- It can be used on a number of operating systems.
- MySQL can be integrated with many languages including PHP, PERL, C, C++, JAVA, etc.
- It performs well with even large data sets having up to 50 million rows or more in a table. The default file size limit for a table is 4 GB. In fact, a database of even 8 million terabytes (TB) is not uncommon these days.
- MySQL can be customized as per user requirements.
- It satisfies ACID property.
- MySQL supports powerful techniques to ensure that only authorized users can access the database.

> MySQL is developed, marketed and supported by a Swedish company MySQL AB.

> The US tech company Sun Microsystems bought MySQL AB in 2008. Later, in 2010 Oracle acquired Sun Microsystems and MySQL has been practically owned by Oracle since then.

10.2 STRUCTURED QUERY LANGUAGE (SQL)

SQL, pronounced as S-Q-L or sometime See-Qwell, is a database query language. Many people think of it as a database but it is a language that helps users to access and manipulate data stored in a relational database. SQL queries (or statements) can be used to perform operations like retrieving, inserting, updating and deleting data. They can also be used to create tables or modify the structure of existing tables. However, to use SQL queries, you must first install a database like Oracle, MySQL, MongoDB, PostGres SQL, SQL Server, DB2, etc.

10.2.1 How MySQL Works

MySQL works on client-server model. Computers that install and run RDBMS software are called clients. Whenever they need to access data, they connect to the RDBMS server. That is the "client-server" part.

Figure 10.1 explains the basic client-server structure. One or more devices (clients) connect to a server to access data stored in the database server. Every client can make a request from the graphical user interface (GUI) on their screens, and the server responds with the desired output. The basic working of such a client-server model can be understood as,

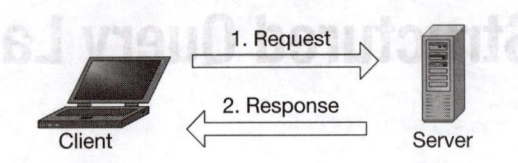

Figure 10.1 Client/server request/response model

1. MySQL creates a database for storing and manipulating data.
2. Clients request data using specific SQL statements that are executed on the MySQL.
3. The server application responds with the requested information that is then displayed on the client machine.

> MySQL is written in C and C++.

10.3 USES OF SQL

SQL allow users to create queries where a query is a request for data stored in one or more tables in the database. These queries are simple English-like statements. With the help of queries, users can **access, modify, insert and delete data** from table(s) stored in the database.

SQL can also be used to create metadata for describing the data. With SQL, users can **create and drop (delete) tables**.

Users can also **create procedures** and functions and set permission on them to restrict their usage.

Types of SQL Queries

The two types of SQL queries that we will be reading about in this chapter are DDL and DML. While DDL or the Data Definition Language is used to create or modify database objects (like tables, views, indexes, users, etc), the DML or the Data Manipulation Language, on the other hand, is used to manipulate data (like inserting, updating, deleting data).

10.4 SQL DATA TYPES

Before we actually start creating tables and inserting records into it using DDL and DML, we must first know the permitted data types in SQL. Each column in a table must have a valid name and a data type.

While creating a table, the SQL developer must specify what type of data will be stored in each column. In this chapter, we have used MySQL version 8.0. Some important data types used in MySQL are given in Table 10.1.

Table 10.1 Data types in SQL

Data type	Description
CHAR(SIZE)	A fixed-length string that may have alphabets, digits, and special characters. The size parameter specifies maximum number of characters. Its value may vary from 0 to 255. By default, its size is 1.
VARCHAR(SIZE)	A variable-length string that may have alphabets, digits, and special characters. The size parameter specifies maximum number of characters. Its value may vary from 0 to 65535. (Table 10.2 shows the difference between CHAR and VARCHAR).

Table 10.1 (*Continued*)

Structured Query Language (SQL)   319

Table 10.1   Continued

Data Type	Description
BOOL	Zero is considered as False, nonzero values are considered as true.
INT(SIZE)	It can be used to specify a signed or unsigned integer. A signed integer is in the range −2147483648 to 2147483647 and an unsigned integer is in the range 0 to 4294967295. The size parameter which can take any value from 0–255, specifies the maximum width for displaying the value.
FLOAT(P)	A floating-point number. MySQL uses the P value to determine whether to use FLOAT or DOUBLE for the resulting data type. If P is from 0 to 24, the data type becomes float and double when P varies from 25 to 53.

Table 10.2   Difference between CHAR and VARCHAR

CHAR Data Type	VARCHAR Data Type
It stands for Character.	It stands for a Variable Character.
Values are stored in fixed lengths and are padded with space characters to match the specified length.	Values are stored in variable length and are not padded with any characters
It can hold a maximum of 255 characters.	It can hold a maximum of 65,535 characters.
It uses static memory allocation.	It uses dynamic memory allocation.
Takes 1 byte per character for storage.	Takes 1 byte per character plus an additional 1 or 2 extra bytes for storing length information.
Used when the length of the variable is known.	Used only when the length of the variable is not known.
It only accepts characters.	It accepts both characters and numbers.
Performs faster than Varchar.	It is slower than Char.

10.4.1 Date and Time Types

The MySQL date and time datatypes are as follows:

Date: A date is stored in YYYY-MM-DD format, between 1000-01-01 and 9999-12-31. For example, September 30th, 2021 would be stored as 2021-09-30.

Datetime: A date and time combination in YYYY-MM-DD HH:MM:SS format, between 1000-01-01 00:00:00 and 9999-12-31 23:59:59. For example, 2:20 in the afternoon on September 30th, 2021 would be stored as 2021-09-30 14:20:00.

Timestamp: A timestamp between midnight, January 1st, 1970 and sometime in 2037. This looks like the previous DATETIME format, only without the hyphens between numbers; 2:20 in the afternoon on September 30th, 2021 would be stored as 20210930142000 (YYYYMMDDHHMMSS).

Time: Stores the time in HH:MM:SS format.

Year(M): Stores a year in a 2-digit or a 4-digit format. If the length is a 2-digit number then it can specify any year from 1970 to 2069 (70 to 69). If the length is a 4-digit number, then YEAR can be from 1901 to 2155. The default length of year is 4.

10.5 OPERATORS IN SQL

An operator is a reserved word or a character in SQL statement that is extensively used in WHERE clause of the query to perform arithmetic or comparison operations. These operators are used to specify conditions in an SQL statement. Just go through the arithmetic and logical operators given in Tables 10.3 and 10.4 and observe the result when a = 100 and b = 50.

Table 10.3 SQL arithmetic operators

Operator	Description	Example	Result
+	Adds values on either side of the operator	a + b	150
−	Subtracts right hand value from the left side value	a − b	100
*	Multiplies values on either side of the operand	a * b	5000
/	Divides left side value with the right side value	a / b	2
%	Divides left side value with the right side value and returns the remainder	a % b	0
>	Returns True if the left value is greater than the right and False otherwise.	a > b	True
>=	Returns True if the left value is either equal to or greater than the right and False otherwise.	a >= b	True
<	Returns True if the left value is less than the right and False otherwise.	a < b	False
<=	Returns True if the left value is either equal to or less than the right value and False otherwise.	a <= b	False
=	Returns True if the two values on either side are equal and False otherwise.	a = b	False
!= <>	Returns True if the two values on either side are not equal and False otherwise.	a != b a <> b	True True
!<	Returns True if the left value is not less than the right value and False otherwise.	a !< b	True
!>	Returns True if the left value is not greater than the right value and False otherwise.	a !> b	False

Table 10.4 SQL logical operators

Operator	Description
ALL	The ALL operator is used to compare a value to all values in another value set.
AND	The AND operator allows the existence of multiple conditions in an SQL statement's WHERE clause.
OR	The OR operator is used to combine multiple conditions in an SQL statement's WHERE clause.
ANY	Compares a value to any applicable values in the list as given in the condition.
BETWEEN	Searches for values that are within a set of values provided the minimum value and the maximum value are specified.

Table 10.4 (*Continued*)

Table 10.4   Continued

Operator	Description
IN	Checks for the presence of a value in the list of specified literal values.
LIKE	Searches for similar values using wildcard characters.
NOT	The NOT operator reverses the meaning of the logical operator with which it is used. Eg: NOT EXISTS, NOT BETWEEN, NOT IN, etc. This is a negate operator.
IS NULL	Checks if a given value is NULL.
UNIQUE	Ensures no duplicate values.

10.6 PERFORMING SIMPLE CALCULATIONS WITH SELECT STATEMENT

We can even use the SQL SELECT statement to perform mathematical calculations. In this special type of SELECT statement, no table is specified in the FROM clause. Examples of such SELECT statements are given below.

```
mysql> select 10 + 9;
+--------+
| 10 + 9 |
+--------+
|     19 |
+--------+
1 row in set (0.00 sec)
mysql> select 11*10;
+-------+
| 11*10 |
+-------+
|   110 |
+-------+
1 row in set (0.00 sec)
mysql> select 360/60;
+--------+
| 360/60 |
+--------+
| 6.0000 |
+--------+
1 row in set (0.00 sec)
mysql> select 100 > 50;
+----------+
| 100 > 50 |
+----------+
|        1 |
+----------+
1 row in set (0.00 sec)
mysql> select 90%4;
+------+
| 90%4 |
+------+
|    2 |
+------+
1 row in set (0.00 sec)
```

10.7 SQL NUMERIC FUNCTIONS

Numeric Functions are used to perform operations on numbers and return numbers. Some commonly used numeric functions used in SQL are discussed below.

ABS() returns the absolute value of a number.

```
mysql> SELECT ABS(-98.7);
+------------+
| ABS(-98.7) |
+------------+
|       98.7 |
+------------+
1 row in set (0.01 sec)
```

COS(), SIN(), TAN(), COT() functions return the cosine, sine, tangent and cotangent of the given number respectively.

```
mysql> SELECT TAN(45);
+--------------------+
| TAN(45)            |
+--------------------+
| 1.6197751905438615 |
+--------------------+
1 row in set (0.00 sec)
```

CEIL() returns the smallest integer value that is greater than or equal to a number.

```
mysql> SELECT CEIL(21.345);
+--------------+
| CEIL(21.345) |
+--------------+
|           22 |
+--------------+
1 row in set (0.00 sec)
```

DEGREES() converts a radian value into degrees.

```
mysql> SELECT DEGREES(1.02);
+-------------------+
| DEGREES(1.02)     |
+-------------------+
| 58.44169510334397 |
+-------------------+
1 row in set (0.00 sec)
```

DIV() is used for integer division.

```
mysql> SELECT 100 DIV 20;
+------------+
| 100 DIV 20 |
+------------+
|          5 |
+------------+
1 row in set (0.00 sec)
```

EXP() returns *e* raised to the power of the given number.

```
mysql> SELECT EXP(2);
+-------------------+
| EXP(2)            |
+-------------------+
| 7.38905609893065  |
+-------------------+
1 row in set (0.00 sec)
```

FLOOR() returns the largest integer value that is less than or equal to a number.

```
mysql> SELECT FLOOR(21.345);
+---------------+
| FLOOR(21.345) |
+---------------+
|            21 |
+---------------+
1 row in set (0.00 sec)
```

GREATEST() returns the greatest value in the given list.

```
mysql> SELECT GREATEST(-10,210,20,-20,30,-30,100,-100);
+------------------------------------------+
| GREATEST(-10,210,20,-20,30,-30,100,-100) |
+------------------------------------------+
|                                      210 |
+------------------------------------------+
1 row in set (0.00 sec)
```

LEAST() returns the smallest value in the given list.

```
mysql> SELECT LEAST(-10,210,20,-20,30,-30,100,-100);
+---------------------------------------+
| LEAST(-10,210,20,-20,30,-30,100,-100) |
+---------------------------------------+
|                                  -100 |
+---------------------------------------+
1 row in set (0.00 sec)
```

LN(), LOG10(), LOG2() returns the natural logarithm, base-10 logarithm and base-2 logarithm of a number respectively.

```
mysql> SELECT LOG10(100);
+------------+
| LOG10(100) |
+------------+
|          2 |
+------------+
1 row in set (0.01 sec)
```

MOD() returns the remainder of n divided by m.

```
mysql> SELECT 103 MOD 5;
+-----------+
| 103 MOD 5 |
+-----------+
|         3 |
+-----------+
1 row in set (0.00 sec)
```

PI() returns the value of Pi displayed to 6 decimal places.

```
mysql> SELECT PI();
+----------+
| PI()     |
+----------+
| 3.141593 |
+----------+
1 row in set (0.00 sec)
```

POW() returns m raised to the nth power.

```
mysql> SELECT POW(10,3);
+-----------+
| POW(10,3) |
+-----------+
|      1000 |
+-----------+
1 row in set (0.00 sec)
```

RADIANS() converts a value in degrees to radians.

```
mysql> SELECT RADIANS(360);
+-------------------+
| RADIANS(360)      |
+-------------------+
| 6.283185307179586 |
+-------------------+
1 row in set (0.00 sec)
```

RAND() returns a random number.

```
mysql> SELECT RAND();
+--------------------+
| RAND()             |
+--------------------+
| 0.8558367722256451 |
+--------------------+
1 row in set (0.00 sec)
```

ROUND() returns a number rounded to a certain number of decimal places.

```
mysql> SELECT ROUND(3.14156,2);
+------------------+
| ROUND(3.14156,2) |
+------------------+
|             3.14 |
+------------------+
1 row in set (0.00 sec)
```

SQRT() returns the square root of a number.

```
mysql> SELECT SQRT(144);
+-----------+
| SQRT(144) |
+-----------+
|        12 |
+-----------+
1 row in set (0.00 sec)
```

TRUNCATE() truncates the given number after the specified number of places right of the decimal point.

```
mysql> SELECT TRUNCATE(3.141567,3);
+----------------------+
| TRUNCATE(3.141567,3) |
+----------------------+
|                3.141 |
+----------------------+
1 row in set (0.00 sec)
```

10.8 STRING FUNCTIONS

The string functions in MySQL are used to manipulate textual data stored in tables. These functions can also be used along with update commands to change data values stored in tables. Some most frequently used string functions are discussed below.

ASCII() function is used to find the ASCII value of a character.

```
mysql> SELECT ASCII('R');
+------------+
| ASCII('R') |
+------------+
|         82 |
+------------+
1 row in set (0.02 sec)
```

CHAR_LENGTH() function is used to find the length of a string.

```
mysql> SELECT CHAR_LENGTH('GOOD
    MORNING');
+----------------------------+
| CHAR_LENGTH('GOOD MORNING') |
+----------------------------+
|                         12 |
+----------------------------+
1 row in set (0.02 sec)
```

CONCAT() function is used to add two words or strings.

```
mysql> SELECT CONCAT('GOOD','--
    ','MORNING');
+-----------------------------+
| CONCAT('GOOD','--','MORNING') |
+-----------------------------+
| GOOD--MORNING               |
+-----------------------------+
1 row in set (0.05 sec)
```

FIND_IN_SET() function is used to find a symbol from a set of symbols.

```
mysql> SELECT FIND_IN_
    SET('I','M,O,R,N,I,N,G');
+-------------------------------+
| FIND_IN_SET('I','M,O,R,N,I,N,G') |
+-------------------------------+
|                             5 |
+-------------------------------+
1 row in set (0.00 sec)
```

INSTR() function is used to find the occurrence of an alphabet.

```
mysql> SELECT INSTR('GOOD
    MORNING','R');
+---------------------------+
| INSTR('GOOD MORNING','R') |
+---------------------------+
|                         8 |
+---------------------------+
1 row in set (0.02 sec)
```

UCASE() function is used to convert the given string into upper case. You can even use the UPPER() function to do the same work.

```
mysql> SELECT UPPER('good
    morning');
+----------------------+
| UPPER('good morning')|
+----------------------+
| GOOD MORNING         |
+----------------------+
1 row in set (0.02 sec)
```

LPAD() function makes a string of specified size by adding the given symbol.

```
mysql> SELECT LPAD('GOOD
    MORNING',20,'*');
+----------------------------+
| LPAD('GOOD MORNING',20,'*')|
+----------------------------+
| ********GOOD MORNING       |
+----------------------------+
1 row in set (0.01 sec)
```

MID() function displays a sub-string of given length starting from the specified position. The SUBSTR() also performs the same task.

```
mysql> SELECT MID('GOOD MORNING
    WORLD',8,4);
+-------------------------------+
| MID('GOOD MORNING WORLD',8,4) |
+-------------------------------+
| RNIN                          |
+-------------------------------+
1 row in set (0.00 sec)
```

LCASE() function is used to convert the given string into lower case. You can even use the LOWER() function to do the same work.

```
mysql> SELECT LCASE('GOOD
    MORNING');
+----------------------+
| LCASE('GOOD MORNING')|
+----------------------+
| good morning         |
+----------------------+
1 row in set (0.05 sec)
```

LEFT() function is used to SELECT a sub-string from the left of given size or characters.

```
mysql> SELECT LEFT('GOOD
    MORNING',7);
+-----------------------+
| LEFT('GOOD MORNING',7)|
+-----------------------+
| GOOD MO               |
+-----------------------+
1 row in set (0.01 sec)
```

LTRIM() function removes leading white spaces from the given string.

```
mysql> SELECT LTRIM('      GOOD
    MORNING');
+---------------------------+
| LTRIM('      GOOD MORNING')|
+---------------------------+
| GOOD MORNING              |
+---------------------------+
1 row in set (0.00 sec)
```

REPEAT() function re-writes the given string, the specified number of times.

```
mysql> SELECT REPEAT('BYE',2);
+-----------------+
| REPEAT('BYE',2) |
+-----------------+
| BYEBYE          |
+-----------------+
1 row in set (0.01 sec)
```

REVERSE() function reverses a string.

```
mysql> SELECT REVERSE('GOOD
    MORNING');
+-------------------------+
| REVERSE('GOOD MORNING') |
+-------------------------+
| GNINROM DOOG            |
+-------------------------+
1 row in set (0.00 sec)
```

RIGHT() function selects a sub-string of given size from the right side of the string.

```
mysql> SELECT RIGHT('GOOD
    MORNING',10);
+-----------------------+
| RIGHT('GOOD MORNING',10) |
+-----------------------+
| OD MORNING            |
+-----------------------+
1 row in set (0.00 sec)
```

RPAD() function makes the given string as long as the given size by adding the given symbol on the right.

```
mysql> SELECT RPAD('GOOD
    MORNING',20,'*');
+----------------------------+
| RPAD('GOOD MORNING',20,'*') |
+----------------------------+
| GOOD MORNING********       |
+----------------------------+
1 row in set (0.01 sec)
```

RTRIM() function removes white spaces from the end of the given string.

```
mysql> SELECT RTRIM('GOOD MORNING
    ');
+--------------------------+
| RTRIM('GOOD MORNING    ') |
+--------------------------+
| GOOD MORNING             |
+--------------------------+
1 row in set (0.00 sec)
```

STRCMP() function compares two strings. If both the strings are equal, it returns 0. If the first string is smaller than the second, −1 is returned. Otherwise, the function will return 1.

```
mysql> SELECT STRCMP('GOOD MORNING','GOOD EVENING');
+---------------------------------------+
| STRCMP('GOOD MORNING','GOOD EVENING') |
+---------------------------------------+
|                                     1 |
+---------------------------------------+
1 row in set (0.00 sec)
```

TRIM() function removes leading and trailing white spaces from the given string.

```
mysql> SELECT TRIM('     GOOD MORNING     ');
+----------------------------------+
| TRIM('     GOOD MORNING     ')   |
+----------------------------------+
| GOOD MORNING                     |
+----------------------------------+
1 row in set (0.01 sec)
```

10.9 CREATING DATABASE

As mentioned before, a database is a collection of related tables. So, before we create any table, we must first create a database. This can be done using the CREATE DATABASE statement. The syntax of using this statement can be given as,

CREATE DATABASE database_name;

where database_name is a unique name or identifier for the database.

> **Example 10.1** Let us create a database named mydb.

```
mysql> create database myDB;
Query OK, 1 row affected (0.24 sec)
```

Once the database is created, we can use the **show databases;** statement to see a list of all the databases present in MySQL. Our newly created database must appear in this list.

```
mysql> show databases;
+--------------------+
| Database           |
+--------------------+
| information_schema |
| mydb               |
| mysql              |
| performance_schema |
| sys                |
+--------------------+
5 rows in set (0.33 sec)
```

Now, we need to select a particular database in which we would be working. Any table created will be added in the selected database. To select a particular database and start using it, we need the **use database** command as given below.

```
mysql> use mydb;
Database changed
```

10.10 REMOVING DATABASE

The DROP DATABASE statement is used to drop or remove an existing database. The syntax of this statement can be given as,

DROP DATABASE databasename;

However, before removing a database, always remember that when we delete a database, all the information stored in it is lost.

```
mysql> show databases;
+--------------------+
| Database           |
+--------------------+
| information_schema |
| mb                 |
| mydb               |
| mysql              |
| performance_schema |
| sys                |
+--------------------+
6 rows in set (0.00 sec)
mysql> drop database mb;
Query OK, 0 rows affected (0.11 sec)
```

```
mysql> show databases;
+--------------------+
| Database           |
+--------------------+
| information_schema |
| mydb               |
| mysql              |
| performance_schema |
| sys                |
+--------------------+
5 rows in set (0.00 sec)
```

10.11 CREATING TABLES

To create a table, we must specify the name of the table. We must also define its columns and each column's data type. In SQL, the **CREATE TABLE** statement is used to create a table. The basic syntax of this statement can be given as,

```
CREATE TABLE table_name(
    column1 datatype,
    column2 datatype,
    column3 datatype,
    .....
    columnN datatype,
    PRIMARY KEY(one or more columns )
);
```

In the above syntax,

CREATE TABLE is the keyword that specifies that you want to create a table in the database.
table_name is a unique name or identifier for the table. A round bracket is opened following the table_name. Within the opening and closing brackets, the list of columns and their corresponding data types are specified.

| Example 10.2 | Let us create a Student table with columns- Roll_Number, Name, Phone_Number, Marks and Class. Remember that NOT NULL is a constraint that means value for a particular field cannot be NULL. In the Student's table, we will explicitly specify that the Roll_Number, Name and Phone_Number cannot be NULL. We will also set Roll_Number as the primary key of the table. |

```
mysql>  CREATE TABLE STUDENT (
    -> ROLL_NUMBER INT NOT NULL,
    -> NAME VARCHAR(20) NOT NULL,
    -> PHONE_NUMBER CHAR(10) NOT NULL,
    -> AGE INT,
    -> MARKS INT,
    -> CLASS CHAR(10),
    -> PRIMARY KEY (ROLL_NUMBER)
    -> );
Query OK, 0 rows affected, 1 warning (1.32 sec)
```

Once the table is created, we can use the DESC command to see the description of the newly created table.

```
mysql> DESC STUDENT;
+--------------+-------------+------+-----+---------+-------+
| Field        | Type        | Null | Key | Default | Extra |
+--------------+-------------+------+-----+---------+-------+
| ROLL_NUMBER  | int(11)     | NO   | PRI | NULL    |       |
| NAME         | varchar(20) | NO   |     | NULL    |       |
| PHONE_NUMBER | char(10)    | NO   |     | NULL    |       |
| AGE          | int(11)     | YES  |     | NULL    |       |
| MARKS        | int(11)     | YES  |     | NULL    |       |
| CLASS        | char(10)    | YES  |     | NULL    |       |
+--------------+-------------+------+-----+---------+-------+
6 rows in set (0.04 sec)
```

The above results verify that the student table is created in our database with the specified fields and constraints.

10.12 DELETING TABLE

A table can be deleted using the **DROP TABLE** statement. When a table is deleted, all its definition, data, indexes, views, triggers, constraints and permission specifications are removed from the database. The syntax of DROP TABLE statement can be given as,

> You should be very careful while using the DROP TABLE command as once it is executed, the table is completely deleted along with all the information in it.

DROP TABLE table_name;

Example 10.3 Let us delete our table STUDENT.

```
mysql> drop table student;
Query OK, 0 rows affected (0.56 sec)
```

Note that 0 rows are affected as we have not inserted any row till now. To verify whether our table was deleted or not, let us again use the DESC statement and observe the result.

```
mysql> desc student;
ERROR 1146 (42S02): Table 'mydb.student' doesn't exist
```

Note that the error indicates that the student table in mydb database no longer exists.

10.13 INSERTING VALUES IN TABLE

To insert values in a table, it must first be created using the CREATE TABLE command. In the last section, we had deleted the STUDENT table but for executing other SQL statements, we have re-created the table using CREATE TABLE command.

In a table, values can be instead using the **INSERT INTO** statement. This statement is used to add new rows of data in a table that exists in the database.

There are two basic syntaxes of the INSERT INTO statement which are shown below.

INSERT INTO TABLE_NAME VALUES (value1,value2,value3,...valueN);

Example 10.4 Let us insert at least five rows in our student table.

```
mysql> INSERT INTO STUDENT VALUES(1,'RAHUL','9876543210',18, 89,'12-D');
Query OK, 1 row affected (0.26 sec)
mysql> INSERT INTO STUDENT VALUES(2,'SARFARAZ','9823416790',17, 97,'11-A');
Query OK, 1 row affected (0.07 sec)
mysql> INSERT INTO STUDENT VALUES(3,'RIA','7825516230',16,67,'10-C');
Query OK, 1 row affected (0.04 sec)
mysql> INSERT INTO STUDENT VALUES(4,'PALAK','9999123456',9,75,'9-B');
Query OK, 1 row affected (0.18 sec)
mysql> INSERT INTO STUDENT VALUES(5,'KRISH','9807126534',14,90,'8-D');
Query OK, 1 row affected (0.12 sec)
```

10.14 RETRIEVING DATA FROM TABLE

The **SELECT** statement in SQL is used to fetch or retrieve data from one or more tables in the database. The results of the SELECT statement is in the form of a table. This resultant table is known as the result-set. The syntax of the SELECT statement can be given as,

SELECT column1, column2, columnN FROM table_name;

Here, column1, column2... are fields of the table from which data has to be fetched. To fetch all fields from the table, the syntax is

SELECT * FROM table_name;

Example 10.5 Let us select the entire data from all fields in the student table. Also select only the Roll_Number and Marks fields from the student table.

```
mysql> SELECT * FROM STUDENT;
+-------------+----------+--------------+------+-------+-------+
| ROLL_NUMBER | NAME     | PHONE_NUMBER | AGE  | MARKS | CLASS |
+-------------+----------+--------------+------+-------+-------+
|           1 | RAHUL    | 9876543210   |   18 |    89 | 12-D  |
|           2 | SARFARAZ | 9823416790   |   17 |    97 | 11-A  |
|           3 | RIA      | 7825516230   |   16 |    67 | 10-C  |
|           4 | PALAK    | 9999123456   |    9 |    75 | 9-B   |
|           5 | KRISH    | 9807126534   |   14 |    90 | 8-D   |
+-------------+----------+--------------+------+-------+-------+
5 rows in set (0.00 sec)
mysql> SELECT ROLL_NUMBER, MARKS FROM STUDENT;
+-------------+-------+
| ROLL_NUMBER | MARKS |
+-------------+-------+
|           1 |    89 |
|           2 |    97 |
|           3 |    67 |
|           4 |    75 |
|           5 |    90 |
+-------------+-------+
5 rows in set (0.00 sec)
```

10.15 THE WHERE CLAUSE

The WHERE clause is used in the SELECT statement to specify a condition for retrieving data from one or more tables. We use the WHERE clause to filter the records in the table and fetch only those that meet the specified criteria.

In addition to the SELECT statement, the WHERE clause is also used with the UPDATE and DELETE statements. The basic syntax of the SELECT statement with the WHERE clause can be given as,

```
SELECT column1, column2, columnN
FROM table_name
WHERE [condition]
```

We can even use comparison and logical operators in the WHERE clause. Let us see a couple of queries to see how the SELECT statement with WHERE clause actually works.

Example 10.6 Display the name and class of the students who scored less than 90 marks.

```
mysql> SELECT NAME, CLASS FROM STUDENT WHERE MARKS < 90;
+--------+--------+
| NAME   | CLASS  |
+--------+--------+
| RAHUL  | 12-D   |
| RIA    | 10-C   |
| PALAK  | 9-B    |
+--------+--------+
3 rows in set (0.00 sec)
```

Example 10.7 Let us now select the phone number, marks and class of a student whose name is SARFARAZ.

```
mysql> SELECT PHONE_NUMBER, MARKS, CLASS FROM STUDENT WHERE NAME = 'SARFARAZ';
+--------------+-------+-------+
| PHONE_NUMBER | MARKS | CLASS |
+--------------+-------+-------+
| 9823416790   |    97 | 11-A  |
+--------------+-------+-------+
1 row in set (0.00 sec)
```

Observe that that all the character and strings should be specified within single quotes ('') but numeric values should be given without any quotes (as shown in the Example 10.5).

10.16 SQL AND AND OR OPERATORS

The SQL AND and OR operators are used for combining multiple conditions to specify a criterion for fetching data from a table. These two operators are called as the conjunctive operators.

As the name specifies, the AND operator allows the existence of multiple conditions in an SQL statement's WHERE clause. The basic syntax of using the AND operator can be given as,

```
SELECT column1, column2, columnN
FROM table_name
WHERE [condition1] AND [condition2]...AND [conditionN];
```

We can specify any number of conditions in the WHERE clause using the AND operator. For an action to be taken by the SQL statement, all conditions separated by the AND operator must be TRUE.

Example 10.8 Let us write a query to display the name and class of all the students having marks more than 90 and age >=15.

Note that we have inserted an additional row in the table.
```
mysql> SELECT NAME, CLASS FROM STUDENT WHERE MARKS < 90 AND AGE>=15;
+-------+-------+
| NAME  | CLASS |
+-------+-------+
| RAHUL | 12-D  |
| RIA   | 10-C  |
+-------+-------+
2 rows in set (0.00 sec)
```

The basic syntax of the OR operator with a WHERE clause can be given as,

```
SELECT column1, column2, columnN
FROM table_name
WHERE [condition1] OR [condition2]...OR [conditionN]
```

As per the syntax, *n* number of conditions can be tested using the OR operator. To execute the query, any one of the conditions separated by the OR operator must be TRUE.

Example 10.9 Display the name and class of students scoring more than 90 marks or having age = 18.

```
mysql> SELECT NAME, CLASS FROM STUDENT WHERE MARKS < 90 OR AGE = 18;
+-------+-------+
| NAME  | CLASS |
+-------+-------+
| RAHUL | 12-D  |
| RIA   | 10-C  |
| PALAK | 9-B   |
+-------+-------+
3 rows in set (0.00 sec)
```

Example 10.10 Display the name and class of students who have scored between 75 and 90 (boundaries inclusive).

```
mysql> SELECT NAME, CLASS FROM STUDENT
    -> WHERE MARKS >=75 AND MARKS <=90;
+-------+-------+
| NAME  | CLASS |
+-------+-------+
| RAHUL | 12-D  |
| PALAK | 9-B   |
| KRISH | 8-D   |
+-------+-------+
3 rows in set (0.00 sec)
```

10.17 THE WHERE BETWEEN CLAUSE

The WHERE BETWEEN clause returns values that fall within a given range. This clause is a shorthand for >= AND <=. Note that WHERE BETWEEN operator is inclusive of starting and ending values. The syntax of this clause can be given as,

```
SELECT column-names
FROM table-name
WHERE column-name BETWEEN value1 AND value2
```

Example 10.11 Display the Name, Class and Marks of students who scored between 75 and 90 (boundaries inclusive) using the WHERE BETWEEN clause.

```
mysql> SELECT NAME, CLASS, MARKS FROM STUDENT
    -> WHERE MARKS BETWEEN 75 AND 90;
+-------+-------+-------+
| NAME  | CLASS | MARKS |
+-------+-------+-------+
| RAHUL | 12-D  |   89  |
| PALAK | 9-B   |   75  |
| KRISH | 8-D   |   90  |
+-------+-------+-------+
3 rows in set (0.01 sec)
```

10.18 THE SQL WHERE IN CLAUSE

The WHERE IN clause returns values that match values in a list or a sub-query. This clause is a shorthand for multiple OR conditions. The general syntax of WHERE IN clause can be given as,

```
SELECT column-names
FROM table-name
WHERE column-name IN (values)
```

Example 10.12 Display the details of all the students who have got marks 89, 67 or 90.

```
mysql> SELECT * FROM STUDENT
    -> WHERE MARKS IN (89, 67, 90);
+-------------+-------+--------------+-----+-------+-------+
| ROLL_NUMBER | NAME  | PHONE_NUMBER | AGE | MARKS | CLASS |
+-------------+-------+--------------+-----+-------+-------+
|           1 | RAHUL | 9876543210   |  18 |    89 | 12-D  |
|           3 | RIA   | 7825516230   |  16 |    67 | 10-C  |
|           5 | KRISH | 9807126534   |  14 |    90 | 8-D   |
+-------------+-------+--------------+-----+-------+-------+
3 rows in set (0.00 sec)
```

10.19 THE SQL SELECT DISTINCT STATEMENT

The SELECT DISTINCT statement is used to return only distinct (different) values. In other words, this clause eliminates duplicate entries while displaying data from the table. The syntax of DISTINCT clause, when used with the SELECT statement, can be given as,

```
SELECT DISTINCT column1, column2,.....columnN
FROM table_name
WHERE [condition]
```

> The SQL DISTINCT keyword is used in conjunction with the SELECT statement to eliminate all duplicate records and fetch only unique records.

table_name specifies the name(s) of the table(s) from which data has to be retrieved. We can specify more than one table name also.
The WHERE condition is optional. If present, it specifies the conditions that must be satisfied before retrieving data.

Note that the DISTINCT clause does not ignore NULL values. So, if a table has null values, DISCTINCT clause will include them as well, in the result set.

Example 10.13 Consider the table given below.

```
mysql> SELECT * FROM ISSUE;
+--------+--------+-------------+-------+
| RollNO | Name   | Book_Issued | Class |
+--------+--------+-------------+-------+
|    121 | MAHEK  | LAB MANUAL  | XI-A  |
|    253 | NIYON  | PHYSICS     | IX-C  |
|    390 | GIRIJ  | SCIENCE     | X-B   |
|    404 | CHINUK | PHYSICS     | XII-B |
|    507 | fAIZAL | BIOLOGY     | X-D   |
|    611 | NASIMA | MATHS       | VI-A  |
|    729 | KIARA  | SCIENCE     | VII-C |
+--------+--------+-------------+-------+
7 rows in set (0.00 sec)
```

Let us select value for Book_Issued from the table without using the DISTINCT clause first.

```
mysql> SELECT Book_Issued FROM ISSUE;
+-------------+
| Book_Issued |
+-------------+
| LAB MANUAL  |
| PHYSICS     |
| SCIENCE     |
| PHYSICS     |
| BIOLOGY     |
| MATHS       |
| SCIENCE     |
+-------------+
7 rows in set (0.00 sec)
```

Now let us use the same query but with DISTICT clause to appreciate the results.

```
mysql> SELECT DISTINCT Book_Issued FROM ISSUE;
+-------------+
| Book_Issued |
+-------------+
| LAB MANUAL  |
| PHYSICS     |
| SCIENCE     |
| BIOLOGY     |
| MATHS       |
+-------------+
5 rows in set (0.00 sec)
```

Did you notice that the first select statement selected all values including duplicates from the Book_Issued column? The SELECT statement with DISTINCT clause, however, selected only non-duplicate values. To know how many distinct subjects books were issued, we can write

```
mysql> SELECT COUNT(DISTINCT Book_Issued) FROM ISSUE;
+-----------------------------+
| COUNT(DISTINCT Book_Issued) |
+-----------------------------+
|                           5 |
+-----------------------------+
1 row in set (0.00 sec)
```

10.20 ORDER BY CLAUSE

The ORDER BY statement in SQL is used to sort the retrieved data in either ascending or descending order. We can sort the values in the result-set by one or more columns using the ORDER BY clause.

By default, ORDER BY sorts the data in ascending order. To sort in descending order, we can use the keyword DESC. To specifically state ascending as the sorting order, the keyword ASC is used.

The syntax of all ways of using ORDER BY clause with the SELECT statement can be given as,

Sort according to one column: To sort in ascending or descending order we can use the keywords ASC or DESC respectively. The syntax for this can be given as,

```
SELECT expressions
FROM tables
[WHERE conditions]
ORDER BY expression [ ASC | DESC ]
```

where,

Expressions specifies the columns to be retrieved.
Tables is the table from which the records have to be retrieved. At least one table must be listed in the FROM clause.
WHERE condition is optional. If specified, the condition must be satisfied for the records to be selected.
ASC is optional as it is the default sorting order. ASC sorts the result-set in ascending order by *expression*.
DESC is optional. If present, it sorts the result-set in descending order by *expression*.
Sort according to multiple columns: To sort according to multiple columns, separate the names of columns by (,) operator. The syntax can be given as,

```
SELECT * FROM table_name ORDER BY column1 ASC|DESC , column2 ASC|DESC
```

Example 10.14 To sort records of Employee table in ascending order of their salaries, we can write,

```
mysql> SELECT EMPNO, SAL FROM EMPLOYEE ORDER BY SAL;
+-------+-------+
| EmpNo | SAL   |
+-------+-------+
|   456 |  NULL |
|   567 |  NULL |
|   678 |  NULL |
|   123 | 35000 |
|   234 | 50000 |
|   345 | 75000 |
+-------+-------+
6 rows in set (0.05 sec)
```

Correspondingly, to sort records based on ascending order of name and further on descending order of salary, if some employees have the same name, then we can write

```
mysql> SELECT * FROM EMPLOYEE ORDER BY NAME ASC, SAL DESC;
```

10.21 UPDATING THE TABLE

The SQL UPDATE statement is used to modify the existing data in a table. We can even use the WHERE clause with the UPDATE query to update only selected rows, so that not all the rows are affected. The basic syntax of the UPDATE query with a WHERE clause can be given as,

UPDATE table_name
SET column1 = value1, column2 = value2...., columnN = valueN
WHERE [condition];

Again, according to the syntax, any number of conditions can be specified using the AND or the OR operators in the WHERE clause.

Example 10.15 Update the STUDENT table to set age of the student in class 9-B to 15. Also show the records of the table to check whether the record was updated or not.

```
mysql> UPDATE STUDENT SET AGE = 15 WHERE CLASS = '9-B';
Query OK, 1 row affected (0.08 sec)
Rows matched: 1  Changed: 1  Warnings: 0
mysql> SELECT * FROM STUDENT;
+-------------+----------+--------------+------+-------+-------+
| ROLL_NUMBER | NAME     | PHONE_NUMBER | AGE  | MARKS | CLASS |
+-------------+----------+--------------+------+-------+-------+
|           1 | RAHUL    | 9876543210   |   18 |    89 | 12-D  |
|           2 | SARFARAZ | 9823416790   |   17 |    97 | 11-A  |
|           3 | RIA      | 7825516230   |   16 |    67 | 10-C  |
|           4 | PALAK    | 9999123456   |   15 |    75 | 9-B   |
|           5 | KRISH    | 9807126534   |   14 |    90 | 8-D   |
+-------------+----------+--------------+------+-------+-------+
5 rows in set (0.00 sec)
```

Example 10.16 Let us update the class of all the students to 6-A.

Note that in this case, we do not need the WHERE clause. We will simply write,
`mysql> UPDATE STUDENT SET CLASS = '6-A';`

10.22 DELETING ROWS FROM A TABLE

The DELETE query in SQL is used to delete existing record(s) from a table in the database. To delete only selected rows from the table, we can even use WHERE clause with DELETE query, otherwise all the records would be deleted. The basic syntax of the DELETE query, when used with WHERE clause, can be given as,

DELETE FROM table_name
WHERE [condition];

In the condition, any number of conditions can be specified using AND or OR operators.

Example 10.17 Let us delete the record of the student having roll number 6.

`mysql> DELETE FROM STUDENT WHERE ROLL_NUMBER = 6;`

Example 10.18 Let us delete all the records from the STUDENT table.

`mysql> DELETE FROM STUDENT;`

Now, the STUDENT table does not have any record.

10.23 THE WHERE LIKE CLAUSE IN SQL

The WHERE LIKE clause determines if a character string matches a pattern. It is usually used when only a fragment of a text value is known. That is, the SQL LIKE clause is used with the WHERE clause to compare a value to find similar values using wildcard characters. The two wildcard characters that are extensively used with the LIKE clause include % and _.

Here, % represents zero, one or multiple characters. And the underscore represents a single number or character. These two characters can also be used in combination. The basic syntax of LIKE clause can be given as,

```
SELECT FROM table_name
WHERE column LIKE 'XXXX%'
```

or

```
SELECT FROM table_name
WHERE column LIKE '%XXXX%'
```

or

```
SELECT FROM table_name
WHERE column LIKE 'XXXX_'
```

or

```
SELECT FROM table_name
WHERE column LIKE '_XXXX'
```

or

```
SELECT FROM table_name
WHERE column LIKE '_XXXX_'
```

Here, XXXX mean any numeric or string value.

Example 10.19 Let us select details of all the students whose name starts with 'R'.

```
mysql> SELECT * FROM STUDENT WHERE NAME LIKE 'R%';
+-------------+-------+--------------+------+-------+-------+
| ROLL_NUMBER | NAME  | PHONE_NUMBER | AGE  | MARKS | CLASS |
+-------------+-------+--------------+------+-------+-------+
|           1 | RAHUL | 9876543210   |   18 |    89 | 12-D  |
|           3 | RIA   | 7825516230   |   16 |    67 | 10-C  |
+-------------+-------+--------------+------+-------+-------+
2 rows in set (0.03 sec)
```

Example 10.20 Let us display details of all the students who study in the 'D' section.

```
mysql> SELECT * FROM STUDENT WHERE CLASS LIKE '%D';
+-------------+-------+--------------+------+-------+-------+
| ROLL_NUMBER | NAME  | PHONE_NUMBER | AGE  | MARKS | CLASS |
+-------------+-------+--------------+------+-------+-------+
|           1 | RAHUL | 9876543210   |   18 |    89 | 12-D  |
|           5 | KRISH | 9807126534   |   14 |    90 | 8-D   |
+-------------+-------+--------------+------+-------+-------+
2 rows in set (0.00 sec)
```

Example 10.21 Display the details of all the students whose phone number starts with a '9' and has a '7' in it.

```
mysql> SELECT * FROM STUDENT WHERE PHONE_NUMBER LIKE '9%7%';
+-------------+----------+--------------+------+-------+-------+
| ROLL_NUMBER | NAME     | PHONE_NUMBER | AGE  | MARKS | CLASS |
+-------------+----------+--------------+------+-------+-------+
|           1 | RAHUL    | 9876543210   |   18 |    89 | 12-D  |
|           2 | SARFARAZ | 9823416790   |   17 |    97 | 11-A  |
|           5 | KRISH    | 9807126534   |   14 |    90 | 8-D   |
+-------------+----------+--------------+------+-------+-------+
3 rows in set (0.00 sec)
```

Example 10.22 Select details of all the students who are not in class 10, 11 or 12.

```
mysql> SELECT * FROM STUDENT WHERE CLASS LIKE '_-_';
+-------------+-------+--------------+------+-------+-------+
| ROLL_NUMBER | NAME  | PHONE_NUMBER | AGE  | MARKS | CLASS |
+-------------+-------+--------------+------+-------+-------+
|           4 | PALAK | 9999123456   |   15 |    75 | 9-B   |
|           5 | KRISH | 9807126534   |   14 |    90 | 8-D   |
+-------------+-------+--------------+------+-------+-------+
2 rows in set (0.00 sec)
```

Note that here, we want a single digit only after '-'.

Example 10.23 Display details of all the students who are in class 10, 11 or 12.

```
mysql> SELECT * FROM STUDENT WHERE CLASS LIKE '__-%';
+-------------+----------+--------------+------+-------+-------+
| ROLL_NUMBER | NAME     | PHONE_NUMBER | AGE  | MARKS | CLASS |
+-------------+----------+--------------+------+-------+-------+
|           1 | RAHUL    | 9876543210   |   18 |    89 | 12-D  |
|           2 | SARFARAZ | 9823416790   |   17 |    97 | 11-A  |
|           3 | RIA      | 7825516230   |   16 |    67 | 10-C  |
+-------------+----------+--------------+------+-------+-------+
3 rows in set (0.00 sec)
```

Example 10.24 Display details of all the students whose name does not have an 'I'.

```
mysql> SELECT * FROM STUDENT
    -> WHERE NAME NOT LIKE '%I%';
+-------------+----------+--------------+------+-------+-------+
| ROLL_NUMBER | NAME     | PHONE_NUMBER | AGE  | MARKS | CLASS |
+-------------+----------+--------------+------+-------+-------+
|           1 | RAHUL    | 9876543210   |   18 |    89 | 12-D  |
|           2 | SARFARAZ | 9823416790   |   17 |    97 | 11-A  |
|           4 | PALAK    | 9999123456   |   15 |    75 | 9-B   |
+-------------+----------+--------------+------+-------+-------+
3 rows in set (0.01 sec)
```

10.24 SQL SELECT MIN, MAX STATEMENT

As the name suggests, the SELECT MIN statement in SQL returns the minimum value for a column. Correspondingly, the SELECT MAX statement returns the maximum value for a column.

The general MIN syntax is:

SELECT MIN(column-name)
FROM table-name

and the general MAX syntax can be given as,

SELECT MIN(column-name)
FROM table-name
```
mysql> SELECT MIN(MARKS) FROM STUDENT;
```

Example 10.25 Display the minimum marks obtained by a student.

```
+------------+
| MIN(MARKS) |
+------------+
|         67 |
+------------+
1 row in set (0.04 sec)
```

Example 10.26 Display the maximum marks obtained by a student.

```
mysql> SELECT MAX(MARKS) FROM STUDENT;
+------------+
| MAX(MARKS) |
+------------+
|         97 |
+------------+
1 row in set (0.04 sec)
```

Example 10.27 Display the details of students scoring maximum marks.

```
mysql> SELECT * FROM STUDENT
    -> WHERE MARKS = (SELECT MAX(MARKS) FROM STUDENT);
+-------------+----------+--------------+------+-------+-------+
| ROLL_NUMBER | NAME     | PHONE_NUMBER | AGE  | MARKS | CLASS |
+-------------+----------+--------------+------+-------+-------+
|           2 | SARFARAZ | 9823416790   |   17 |    97 | 11-A  |
+-------------+----------+--------------+------+-------+-------+
1 row in set (0.00 sec)
```

Example 10.28 Display the maximum marks obtained by students in classes 8 and 9.

```
mysql> SELECT MAX(MARKS) FROM STUDENT WHERE CLASS LIKE '_-_';
+------------+
| MAX(MARKS) |
+------------+
|         90 |
+------------+
1 row in set (0.00 sec)
```

Example 10.29 Display the maximum marks obtained by students in classes 10, 11 and 12.

```
mysql> SELECT MAX(MARKS) FROM STUDENT WHERE CLASS LIKE '_ _-_';
+------------+
| MAX(MARKS) |
+------------+
|         97 |
+------------+
1 row in set (0.00 sec)
```

Example 10.30 Display the maximum marks obtained by students having roll number greater than 3.

```
mysql> SELECT MAX(MARKS) FROM STUDENT WHERE ROLL_NUMBER >3;
+------------+
| MAX(MARKS) |
+------------+
|         90 |
+------------+
1 row in set (0.00 sec)
```

10.25 SELECT COUNT, SUM, AVG

The SELECT COUNT statement returns a count of the number of data values. The SELECT SUM returns the sum of the data values. And the SELECT AVG returns the average of the data values.

The general COUNT syntax is:

SELECT COUNT(column-name)
FROM table-name

Example 10.31 Let us find out number of rows in our STUDENT table.

```
mysql> SELECT COUNT(ROLL_NUMBER) FROM STUDENT;
+--------------------+
| COUNT(ROLL_NUMBER) |
+--------------------+
|                  5 |
+--------------------+
1 row in set (0.03 sec)
```

The general SUM syntax is:

SELECT SUM(column-name)
FROM table-name

Example 10.32 Let us display the total marks obtained by all the students in the STUDENT table where age is less than or equal to 15.

```
mysql> SELECT SUM(MARKS) FROM STUDENT
    -> WHERE AGE <= 15;
+------------+
| SUM(MARKS) |
+------------+
|        165 |
+------------+
1 row in set (0.03 sec)
```

The general AVG syntax is:

```
SELECT AVG(column-name)
FROM table-name
```

Example 10.33 Find out the average age of students scoring at least 90 marks.

```
mysql> SELECT AVG(AGE) FROM STUDENT
    -> WHERE MARKS >= 90;
+----------+
| AVG(AGE) |
+----------+
|  15.5000 |
+----------+
1 row in set (0.00 sec)
```

10.26 COLUMN ALIASES

By default, SELECT statement displays the column heading(s) in the result set as the name of that column in the table. However, we can use a column alias to change the name of the column heading in the result set. The syntax of creating a column alias is,

```
SELECT column_name AS column_alias
FROM table_name.
```

Consider the Employee table given below. Observe how the AS keyword can be used to create a column alias.

```
mysql> select * from Employee;      mysql> select EmpNo, Sal AS Salary from Employee;
+-------+-------+                   +-------+--------+
| EmpNo | Sal   |                   | EmpNo | Salary |
+-------+-------+                   +-------+--------+
|   123 | 35000 |                   |   123 |  35000 |
|   234 | 50000 |                   |   234 |  50000 |
|   345 | 75000 |                   |   345 |  75000 |
+-------+-------+                   +-------+--------+
3 rows in set (0.00 sec)
3   rows in set (0.00 sec)
```

Thus, we see that we can use column alias if the original column name does not meet our requirements or clearly define its purpose. In such a case, column alias can be used to define a meaningful name for the column.

We can also use column alias to give a name to a column that is dynamically created by applying an expression to an existing column in the table.

```
mysql> SELECT EmpNo, Sal, Sal + Sal * 0.10 As NEW_SAL FROM EMPLOYEE;
+-------+-------+---------+
| EmpNo | Sal   | NEW_SAL |
+-------+-------+---------+
|   123 | 35000 |   38500 |
|   234 | 50000 |   55000 |
|   345 | 75000 |   82500 |
+-------+-------+---------+
3 rows in set (0.00 sec)
```

> An alias only exists for the duration of the query.

From the above discussion, it can be seen that SQL aliases are used to give a table, or a column in a table, a temporary name. They are often used to make column names more readable.

10.27 THE SQL GROUP BY STATEMENT

The GROUP BY statement is used to create a summary of records. The statement groups rows that have the same values (in a column) to create summary rows. For example, we can find the number of students in each class (here we group by class), or average salary of employees in an IT department (here, we can group by department).

Therefore, the GROUP BY clause returns one row for each group, thereby reducing the number of rows in the result set.

The GROUP BY statement is often used with aggregate functions (COUNT, MAX, MIN, SUM, AVG) to group the result-set by one or more columns. The general syntax of GROUP BY statement can be given as,

```
SELECT column_name(s)
FROM table_name
WHERE condition
GROUP BY column_name(s)
ORDER BY column_name(s);
```

10.28 THE HAVING CLAUSE

We have learnt that WHERE clause is a powerful clause that is used for selective selection. But this clause cannot be used with aggregate functions. So, SQL has another clause – HAVING clause that can be used with aggregate functions.

Thus, the HAVING clause allows users to filter the values returned from a grouped query based on the results of aggregation functions. The syntax of HAVING clause can be given as,

```
SELECT expression1, expression2, ... expression_n, aggregate_function
(expression)
FROM tables
[WHERE conditions]
GROUP BY expression1, expression2, ... expression_n
HAVING condition;
```

Example 10.34 Consider the student table given below and print the number of students in each class.

```
mysql> SELECT * FROM STUDENT;
+-------------+----------+--------------+------+-------+-------+
| ROLL_NUMBER | NAME     | PHONE_NUMBER | AGE  | MARKS | CLASS |
+-------------+----------+--------------+------+-------+-------+
|           1 | RAHUL    | 9876543210   |   18 |    89 | 12-D  |
|           2 | SARFARAZ | 9823416790   |   17 |    97 | 11-A  |
|           3 | RIA      | 7825516230   |   16 |    67 | 10-C  |
|           4 | PALAK    | 9999123456   |    9 |    75 | 9-B   |
|           5 | KRISH    | 9807126534   |   14 |    90 | 8-D   |
|           6 | MANAN    | 8876101210   |   18 |    75 | 12-D  |
|           7 | TRISHA   | 823901790    |   17 |    69 | 11-A  |
|           8 | ROHIT    | 5509116230   |   16 |    87 | 10-C  |
|           9 | PAYAL    | 8289199450   |    9 |    55 | 9-B   |
+-------------+----------+--------------+------+-------+-------+
9 rows in set (0.00 sec)
mysql> SELECT COUNT(*) FROM STUDENT GROUP BY CLASS;
```

```
+----------+
| COUNT(*) |
+----------+
|        2 |
|        2 |
|        2 |
|        2 |
|        1 |
+----------+
4 rows in set (0.01 sec)
```

Example 10.35 Consider the student table and print the class in which total marks of students is greater than 150.

```
mysql> SELECT CLASS, SUM(MARKS) AS TOTAL_MARKS
    →  FROM STUDENT GROUP BY CLASS
    →  HAVING TOTAL_MARKS > 150;
+-------+-------------+
| CLASS | TOTAL_MARKS |
+-------+-------------+
| 12-D  |         164 |
| 11-A  |         166 |
| 10-C  |         154 |
+-------+-------------+
3 rows in set (0.00 sec)
```

10.29 HANDLING NULL VALUES

We now know how to retrieve data from a table using the SQL SELECT command along with the WHERE clause. But there is something more that has to be discussed. When we use a condition that compares a column value to NULL, it does not work properly. To handle such a situation, MySQL provides three operators,

IS NULL: which returns True if the column value is NULL. The basic syntax of using IS NULL operator is, column_name IS NULL.

IS NOT NULL: which returns True if the column value is not NULL. The basic syntax of using IS NOT NULL operator is, column_name IS NOT NULL.

<=> which compares values and gives true even for two NULL values.

Since conditions involving NULL values are special, we cannot use = NULL or != NULL to check for NULL values in columns. The code given below illustrates this concept.

```
mysql> SELECT * FROM EMPLOYEE;
+-------+-------+
| EmpNo | Sal   |
+-------+-------+
|   123 | 35000 |
|   234 | 50000 |
|   345 | 75000 |
|   456 |  NULL |
|   567 |  NULL |
|   678 |  NULL |
+-------+-------+
6 rows in set (0.00 sec)
mysql> SELECT * FROM EMPLOYEE WHERE Sal = NULL;
Empty set (0.00 sec)
```

We see that = does not work with NULL values. Therefore, we must re-write our SQL query as given below.

```
mysql> SELECT * FROM EMPLOYEE
    -> WHERE Sal IS NOT NULL;
+-------+-------+
| EmpNo | Sal   |
+-------+-------+
|   123 | 35000 |
|   234 | 50000 |
|   345 | 75000 |
+-------+-------+
3 rows in set (0.00 sec)
mysql> SELECT * FROM EMPLOYEE
    -> WHERE Sal IS NULL;
+-------+------+
| EmpNo | Sal  |
+-------+------+
|   456 | NULL |
|   567 | NULL |
|   678 | NULL |
+-------+------+
3 rows in set (0.00 sec)
```

From the above discussion, we can conclude that the SQL NULL is both a value as well as a keyword. In simple terms, NULL is a place holder for data that does not exist or whose value is not known.

Key points to remember

- NULL is not a data type in SQL.
- Arithmetic operations involving NULL always return NULL. For example, 10 + NULL = NULL.
- All aggregate functions affect only rows that do not have NULL values.
- Comparison operations can be used with NULL values. For example,

```
mysql> select 10 = NULL;
+-----------+
| 10 = NULL |
+-----------+
|      NULL |
+-----------+
1 row in set (0.00 sec)
mysql> SELECT NULL > NULL;
+-------------+
| NULL > NULL |
+-------------+
|        NULL |
+-------------+
1 row in set (0.00 sec)
mysql> SELECT NULL <=> NULL;
+---------------+
| NULL <=> NULL |
+---------------+
|             1 |
+---------------+
1 row in set (0.00 sec)
```

The `IFNULL()` Function: The `IFNULL()` function is used for replacing NULL values in MySQL. The function accepts two arguments. The first argument is returned only if it is not NULL. If it is NULL, then the second argument is returned instead. The code given below demonstrates the use of `IFNULL()` function.

```
mysql> SELECT * FROM EMPLOYEE;
+-------+-------+
| EmpNo | Sal   |
+-------+-------+
|   123 | 35000 |
|   234 | 50000 |
|   345 | 75000 |
|   456 |  NULL |
|   567 |  NULL |
|   678 |  NULL |
+-------+-------+
6 rows in set (0.00 sec)
mysql> SELECT EmpNo, IFNULL(Sal,0) FROM EMPLOYEE;
+-------+------------------+
| EmpNo | IFNULL(Sal,00000)|
+-------+------------------+
|   123 |            35000 |
|   234 |            50000 |
|   345 |            75000 |
|   456 |                0 |
|   567 |                0 |
|   678 |                0 |
+-------+------------------+
6 rows in set (0.00 sec)
```

The `IF()` Function: As an alternative to `IFNULL()` function, we can use the `IF()` function along with the IS NULL/IS NOT NULL operators. The operators check for NULL values, and the `IF()` function will take a suitable course of action depending on the outcome of the operators.

Example 10.36 Let us use the `IF()` function to replace NULL values with 0 in the salary column of the employee table.

```
mysql> SELECT EmpNo, IF(Sal IS NOT NULL, Sal, 0) FROM EMPLOYEE;
+-------+-----------------------------+
| EmpNo | IF(Sal IS NOT NULL, Sal, 0) |
+-------+-----------------------------+
|   123 |                       35000 |
|   234 |                       50000 |
|   345 |                       75000 |
|   456 |                           0 |
|   567 |                           0 |
|   678 |                           0 |
+-------+-----------------------------+
6 rows in set (0.00 sec)
```

10.30 SQL PRIMARY KEY CONSTRAINT

We know that the PRIMARY KEY constraint helps us to uniquely identify each record in the table. The primary key must contain UNIQUE values, and cannot have NULL values.

A table can have only one primary key and the primary key may consist of one or more fields. In this chapter, we have set the primary key by using the following syntax:

```
mysql>  CREATE TABLE STUDENT (
    -> ROLL_NUMBER INT NOT NULL,
    -> NAME VARCHAR(20) NOT NULL,
    -> PHONE_NUMBER CHAR(10) NOT NULL,
    -> AGE INT,
    -> MARKS INT,
    -> CLASS CHAR(10),
    -> PRIMARY KEY (ROLL_NUMBER)
    -> );
```

In the above statement, ROLL_NUMBER field has been set as the primary key. *To set more than one fields as the primary key*, we can write,

```
mysql> CREATE TABLE STUDENTS (
    -> ROLL_NUMBER INT NOT NULL,
    -> NAME VARCHAR(20) NOT NULL,
    -> PHONE_NUMBER CHAR(10) NOT NULL,
    -> AGE INT,
    -> MARKS INT,
    -> CLASS CHAR(10),
    -> CONSTRAINT STUDENTS PRIMARY KEY (NAME, PHONE_NUMBER)
    -> );
```

Query OK, 0 rows affected (0.38 sec)

Use the DESC statement to check the description of the newly created table.

```
mysql> DESC STUDENTS;
+--------------+-------------+------+-----+---------+-------+
| Field        | Type        | Null | Key | Default | Extra |
+--------------+-------------+------+-----+---------+-------+
| ROLL_NUMBER  | int(11)     | NO   |     | NULL    |       |
| NAME         | varchar(20) | NO   | PRI | NULL    |       |
| PHONE_NUMBER | char(10)    | NO   | PRI | NULL    |       |
| AGE          | int(11)     | YES  |     | NULL    |       |
| MARKS        | int(11)     | YES  |     | NULL    |       |
| CLASS        | char(10)    | YES  |     | NULL    |       |
+--------------+-------------+------+-----+---------+-------+
6 rows in set (0.01 sec)
```

The output shows that the fields NAME and PHONE_NUMBER are set as the primary keys of the table. To set PRIMARY KEY constraint on an already-created table, the ALTER TABLE command is used. However, before setting any field as the primary key, you must ensure that the field has been declared to not contain NULL values (using NOT NULL constraint). The syntax for ALTER TABLE command can be given as,

**ALTER TABLE table_name
ADD PRIMARY KEY (column_name);**

| Example 10.37 | Let us use the ALTER TABLE command to set ROLL_NUMBER as the primary key of an already existing table STUDENTS. |

```
mysql> ALTER TABLE STUDENTS
    -> ADD PRIMARY KEY (ROLL_NUMBER);
mysql> DESC STUDENTS;
+--------------+-------------+------+-----+---------+-------+
| Field        | Type        | Null | Key | Default | Extra |
+--------------+-------------+------+-----+---------+-------+
| ROLL_NUMBER  | int(11)     | NO   | PRI | NULL    |       |
| NAME         | varchar(20) | NO   |     | NULL    |       |
| PHONE_NUMBER | char(10)    | NO   |     | NULL    |       |
| AGE          | int(11)     | YES  |     | NULL    |       |
| MARKS        | int(11)     | YES  |     | NULL    |       |
| CLASS        | char(10)    | YES  |     | NULL    |       |
+--------------+-------------+------+-----+---------+-------+
6 rows in set (0.00 sec)
```

Correspondingly, to set primary key constraint on multiple columns, the syntax is,

ALTER TABLE table_name
ADD CONSTRAINT table_name PRIMARY KEY (column_name1, column_name2,..);

| Example 10.38 | Set the NAME and PHONE_NUMBER fields of an already existing STUDENTS table as the primary key. |

```
mysql> ALTER TABLE STUDENTS
    -> ADD CONSTRAINT STUDENTS PRIMARY KEY(NAME, PHONE_NUMBER);
```

10.31 DROP A PRIMARY KEY CONSTRAINT

To drop a PRIMARY KEY constraint, the DROP PRIMARY KEY statement is used with the ALTER TABLE statement. The general syntax can be given as,

ALTER TABLE table_name
DROP PRIMARY KEY;

| Example 10.39 | Let us remove the primary key constraint from an already-created table. |

```
mysql> ALTER TABLE STUDENTS
    -> DROP PRIMARY KEY;
mysql> DESC STUDENTS;
+--------------+-------------+------+-----+---------+-------+
| Field        | Type        | Null | Key | Default | Extra |
+--------------+-------------+------+-----+---------+-------+
| ROLL_NUMBER  | int(11)     | NO   |     | NULL    |       |
| NAME         | varchar(20) | NO   |     | NULL    |       |
| PHONE_NUMBER | char(10)    | NO   |     | NULL    |       |
| AGE          | int(11)     | YES  |     | NULL    |       |
| MARKS        | int(11)     | YES  |     | NULL    |       |
| CLASS        | char(10)    | YES  |     | NULL    |       |
+--------------+-------------+------+-----+---------+-------+
6 rows in set (0.01 sec)
```

From the output, it is clear that now no field is set as the primary key of the table.

10.32 ADDING FOREIGN KEY CONSTRAINT

In the last chapter, we read that a FOREIGN KEY is a key used to link two tables. FOREIGN KEY is basically a field (or collection of fields) in one table that refers to PRIMARY KEY in another table.

The FOREIGN KEY constraint prevents actions that would destroy links between tables. It also ensures that invalid data is not inserted into the foreign key column. Only the values given in the primary field column can be used as foreign key values. The general syntax of adding foreign key constraint can be given as,

```
CREATE TABLE table_name (
Column_1 data type,
Column_2 data type,
Column_J data type,
Column_N data type,
PRIMARY KEY (Column_I),
FOREIGN KEY (Column_J) REFERENCES Persons(Column_J)
);
```

Example 10.40 Create a table STUDENTS with Teacher_ID as foreign key.

Note that before creating table STUDENTS, we must create a table TEACHER.
```
mysql> CREATE TABLE TEACHER(
    -> TEACHER_ID INT NOT NULL,
    -> TEACHER_NAME VARCHAR(20),
    -> PRIMARY KEY(TEACHER_ID)
    -> );
Query OK, 0 rows affected (0.37 sec)
mysql> CREATE TABLE STUDENTS(
    -> ROLL_NO INT NOT NULL,
    -> SNAME VARCHAR(20),
    -> MARKS INT,
    -> TEACHER_ID INT,
    -> PRIMARY KEY(ROLL_NO),
    -> FOREIGN KEY (TEACHER_ID) REFERENCES TEACHER(TEACHER_ID)
    -> );
Query OK, 0 rows affected (0.40 sec)
```

To create a FOREIGN KEY constraint on an already existing table, we must use the ALTER TABLE command as given below:

```
ALTER TABLE STUDENTS
ADD FOREIGN KEY (TEACHER_ID) REFERENCES TEACHER(TEACHER_ID);
mysql> DESC STUDENTS;
+------------+-------------+------+-----+---------+-------+
| Field      | Type        | Null | Key | Default | Extra |
+------------+-------------+------+-----+---------+-------+
| ROLL_NO    | int(11)     | NO   | PRI | NULL    |       |
| SNAME      | varchar(20) | YES  |     | NULL    |       |
| MARKS      | int(11)     | YES  |     | NULL    |       |
| TEACHER_ID | int(11)     | YES  | MUL | NULL    |       |
+------------+-------------+------+-----+---------+-------+
4 rows in set (0.00 sec)
```

10.33 SQL JOIN

SQL Join statement is used to combine data or rows from two or more tables based on a common field between them. In this section, we will read about the different types of Joins that can be performed on tables. But before going into the details of these joins, let us consider two tables – STUDENT and STUDENT_COURSE as given below:

Student table

Roll_number	Name	Phone_number	Age	Marks
1	RAHUL	9876543210	18	89
2	SARFARAZ	9823416790	17	97
3	RIA	7825516230	16	67
4	PALAK	9999123456	9	75
5	KRISH	9807126534	14	90
6	NAVYA	9319012783	15	94

Student course table

Course id	Roll number
1	2
2	1
3	3
1	4
2	5
6	NULL

The two tables have a relation specified by primary and foreign key – ROLL_NUMBER. The extent of the overlapping between the two tables, if any, can be determined by how many records in first table match the records in the second table. Depending on what subset of data we would like to select from the two tables, we can use any of the four `join` types.

Inner Join to select all records from the two tables where the join condition is met.

Left Join to select all records from the first table with records from the second table for which the `join` condition is met (if at all).

Right Join to select all records from the second table with records from the first table for which the `join` condition is met (if at all).

Full Join to select all records from both the tables regardless of whether the `join` condition is met or not.

10.33.1 INNER JOIN

The INNER JOIN keyword selects all rows from both the tables if the condition is satisfied. Therefore, the result-set will be created by combining all rows from both the tables where the condition is satisfied or the value of the common field is same. The syntax for inner join is,

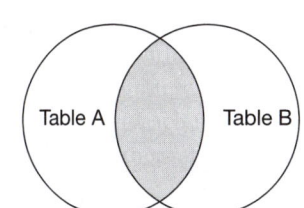

```
SELECT table1.column1,table1.column2,table2.column1,....
FROM table1
INNER JOIN table2
ON table1.matching_column = table2.matching_column;
```

Note that JOIN is same as INNER JOIN; so whether we write JOIN or INNER JOIN it would not make a difference.

Example 10.41 Write a query that shows the names, marks and course of students enrolled.

```
mysql> SELECT STUDENT.ROLL_NUMBER, STUDENT.NAME, STUDENT.MARKS, STUDENT_COURSE.COURSE_
    ID
    -> FROM STUDENT
    -> INNER JOIN STUDENT_COURSE
    -> ON STUDENT.ROLL_NUMBER = STUDENT_COURSE.ROLL_NUMBER;
+-------------+----------+-------+-----------+
| ROLL_NUMBER | NAME     | MARKS | COURSE_ID |
+-------------+----------+-------+-----------+
|           1 | RAHUL    |    89 |         2 |
|           2 | SARFARAZ |    97 |         1 |
|           3 | RIA      |    67 |         3 |
|           4 | PALAK    |    75 |         1 |
|           5 | KRISH    |    90 |         2 |
+-------------+----------+-------+-----------+
5 rows in set (0.01 sec)
```

10.33.2 LEFT JOIN

The LEFT JOIN returns all the rows of the table on the left side of the `join` and only the matching rows for the table on the right side of `join`. The rows in the table on the right side that do not match will contain *null in the resultant set. The basic syntax of* LEFT JOIN is given below.

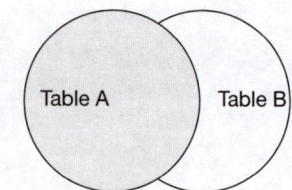

**SELECT table1.column1,table1.column2,table2.column1,....
FROM table1
LEFT JOIN table2
ON table1.matching_column = table2.matching_column;**

Example 10.42 Write a query that shows the names, marks and course of all students.

```
mysql> SELECT STUDENT.ROLL_NUMBER, STUDENT.NAME, STUDENT.MARKS, STUDENT_COURSE.COURSE_
    ID
    -> FROM STUDENT
    -> LEFT JOIN STUDENT_COURSE
    -> ON STUDENT.ROLL_NUMBER = STUDENT_COURSE.ROLL_NUMBER;
+-------------+----------+-------+-----------+
| ROLL_NUMBER | NAME     | MARKS | COURSE_ID |
+-------------+----------+-------+-----------+
|           1 | RAHUL    |    89 |         2 |
|           2 | SARFARAZ |    97 |         1 |
|           3 | RIA      |    67 |         3 |
|           4 | PALAK    |    75 |         1 |
|           5 | KRISH    |    90 |         2 |
|           6 | NAVYA    |    94 |      NULL |
+-------------+----------+-------+-----------+
6 rows in set (0.00 sec)
```

10.33.3 RIGHT JOIN

The RIGHT JOIN returns all the rows of the table on the right side of the `join` and only the matching rows for the table on the left side of `join`. The rows in the table on the left side that do not match will contain *null in the resultant set*. The basic syntax of RIGHT JOIN is given below.

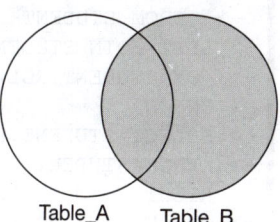

```
SELECT table1.column1,table1.column2,table2.
column1,....
FROM table1
RIGHT JOIN table2
ON table1.matching_column = table2.matching_column;
```

Example 10.43 Write a query that shows the names and marks of students enrolled in all the courses being offered.

```
mysql> SELECT STUDENT.ROLL_NUMBER, STUDENT.NAME, STUDENT.MARKS, STUDENT_COURSE.COURSE_
    ID
    -> FROM STUDENT
    -> RIGHT JOIN STUDENT_COURSE
    -> ON STUDENT.ROLL_NUMBER = STUDENT_COURSE.ROLL_NUMBER;
+-------------+----------+-------+-----------+
| ROLL_NUMBER | NAME     | MARKS | COURSE_ID |
+-------------+----------+-------+-----------+
|           2 | SARFARAZ |    97 |         1 |
|           1 | RAHUL    |    89 |         2 |
|           3 | RIA      |    67 |         3 |
|           4 | PALAK    |    75 |         1 |
|           5 | KRISH    |    90 |         2 |
|        NULL | NULL     |  NULL |         6 |
+-------------+----------+-------+-----------+
6 rows in set (0.00 sec)
```

10.33.4 FULL JOIN

FULL JOIN generates output by combining results of both LEFT JOIN and RIGHT JOIN. The result-set will contain all the rows from both the tables. In case of rows for which there is no matching, the result-set will contain *NULL* values. The general syntax for performing a full join can be given as,

```
SELECT table1.column1,table1.column2,table2.column1,....
FROM table1
FULL JOIN table2
ON table1.matching_column = table2.matching_
column;
```

> SELF JOIN is a join of a table to itself. Each row in a table is joined with itself. CROSS JOIN is a type of join in which a join clause is applied between each row of a table and every row of the other table.

Although MySQL does not support `full join` operation, we can still do it by doing a union of a `left join` with that of `right join` as given below.

```
SELECT STUDENT.ROLL_NUMBER, STUDENT.NAME, STUDENT.MARKS, STUDENT_COURSE.COURSE_ID
 ->   FROM STUDENT
 -> LEFT JOIN STUDENT_COURSE
 ->   ON STUDENT.ROLL_NUMBER = STUDENT_COURSE.ROLL_NUMBER
 -> UNION
 -> SELECT STUDENT.ROLL_NUMBER, STUDENT.NAME, STUDENT.MARKS, STUDENT_COURSE.COURSE_ID
 ->   FROM STUDENT
 -> RIGHT JOIN STUDENT_COURSE
 -> ON STUDENT.ROLL_NUMBER = STUDENT_COURSE.ROLL_NUMBER;
+-------------+---------+-------+-----------+
| ROLL_NUMBER | NAME    | MARKS | COURSE_ID |
+-------------+---------+-------+-----------+
|           1 | RAHUL   |    89 |         2 |
|           2 | SARFARAZ|    97 |         1 |
|           3 | RIA     |    67 |         3 |
|           4 | PALAK   |    75 |         1 |
|           5 | KRISH   |    90 |         2 |
|           6 | NAVYA   |    94 |      NULL |
|        NULL | NULL    |  NULL |         6 |
+-------------+---------+-------+-----------+
7   rows in set (0.00 sec)
```

Thus, we can conclude that

- JOINS allow us to combine data from more than one table to form the result set.
- JOINS enhance performance of queries.
- INNER JOINS only return rows that meet the given criteria. But OUTER JOINS like the Left Join and Right Join return rows where no matches have been found. The unmatched rows are returned with NULL values.
- The frequently used clause in JOIN operations is "ON". We can even use other clauses like USING, GROUP BY, WHERE, SUB QUERIES, AGGREGATE FUNCTIONS etc.

Key Terms

SQL: A database query language.
Clients: Computers that install and run RDBMS software are called clients.
Servers: To access data, clients connect to powerful machines called servers.
Metadata: Data describing data stored in database.
Data Definition Language (DDL): SQL statements used to create or modify database objects (like tables, views, indexes, users, etc).
Data Manipulation Language (DML): SQL statements used to manipulate data (like inserting, updating, deleting data).
Operator: A reserved word or a character in SQL statement that is extensively used in WHERE clause of the query to perform arithmetic or comparison operations.
Database: A collection of related tables.
Conjunctive operators: The SQL AND and OR operators that are used to combine multiple conditions to specify a criterion for fetching data from a table are called as the conjunctive operators.
Foreign key: A field (or collection of fields) in one table that refers to PRIMARY KEY in another table.

Chapter Highlights

- MySQL is an open-source software; so users do not have to pay to use it.
- SQL queries (or statements) can be used to perform operations like retrieving, inserting, updating and deleting data. They can be also used to create tables or modify the structure of existing tables. However, to use SQL queries, you must first install a database, like Oracle, MySQL, MongoDB, PostGres SQL, SQL Server, DB2, etc.
- In MySQL, every client can make a request to a server, which then responds with the desired output.
- We can use the SQL SELECT statement to perform mathematical calculations.
- Numeric Functions are used to perform operations on numbers and return numbers.
- The string functions in MySQL are used to manipulate textual data stored in tables.
- A database is created using the CREATE DATABASE statement.
- To select a particular database and start using it, we need to use the database command.
- In SQL, the CREATE TABLE statement is used to create a table.
- A table can be deleted using the DROP TABLE statement. When a table is deleted, all its definition, data, indexes, views, triggers, constraints and permission specifications are removed from the database.
- INSERT INTO statement is used to add new rows of data in a table that exists in the database
- The SELECT statement in SQL is used to fetch or retrieve data from one or more tables in the database.
- SELECT DISTINCT statement eliminates duplicate entries while displaying data from the table.
- The WHERE clause is used in the SELECT statement to specify a condition for retrieving data from one or more tables.
- The ORDER BY statement in SQL is used to sort the retrieved data in either ascending or descending order.
- The SQL UPDATE statement is used to modify the existing data in a table.
- The DELETE query in SQL is used to delete existing record(s) from a table in the database.
- Column alias are used to change the name of the column heading in the result set.
- The SQL NULL is both a value as well as a keyword. In simple terms, NULL is a place holder for data that does not exist or whose value is not known.
- PRIMARY KEY constraint helps us to uniquely identify each record in the table. The primary key must contain UNIQUE values and cannot have NULL values.
- A table can have only one primary key which, in turn, may consist of one or more fields.
- To set PRIMARY KEY constraint on an already-created table, the ALTER TABLE command is used.

Review Questions

1. What is SQL? Why is it used?
2. MySQL and SQL are the same. Comment on this statement.
3. Explain the working of MySQL.
4. Differentiate between DDL and DML.
5. Why do we need to specify data type? List some data types used in SQL.
6. Differentiate between `char` and `varchar`.
7. How can we create a database in SQL?
8. Write the SQL statements that you will use for the following:
   a. Create a database
   b. View a list of all the databases present in MySQL
   c. Change to another database
   d. Delete a database
   e. Create table

f. To return values that match values in a list or a sub-query
g. To sort the retrieved data in either ascending or descending order
h. To remove records from a table
i. To return the maximum value for a column
j. To return the minimum value for a column
k. To return a count of the number of data values
l. To return the sum of the data values
m. To return the average of the data values
n. To set PRIMARY KEY constraint on an already-created table
o. To drop a PRIMARY KEY constraint.

9. Differentiate between DROP TABLE and DROP DATABASE statements.
10. Explain the syntax of the SELECT statement.
11. What are conjunctive operators? Explain with the help of an example.
12. With the help of an example, explain how you will use the ORDER BY clause to sort data based on multiple columns.
13. What are column aliases?
14. Explain some operators that are used to handle NULL values in SQL.
15. What does primary key constraint state? How can we enforce such a constraint in SQL?
16. Write the instructions for the following:
    a. The SQL statement creates an index named "idx_lastname" on the "LastName" column in the "Persons" table.
    b. Write the instruction for creating an index on the site_name column of websites table.
    c. Write the instruction for creating a unique index on the site_name column of websites table.
    d. Write the instruction for creating an index on the site_name and server columns of websites table.
17. Consider the tables given below and write instructions for the following:

CID	First_name	Last_name	Email	Address	City	State	Zipcode
1	Girish	Patel	gpatel@gmail.com	3200 Kirti Nagar	Merrut	UP	22121
2	John	Samuel	John.s@gmail.com	1250 Windsor	Lansdowne	UK	02169
3	Tina	Bhargava	Bhargava.tina@gmail.com	931 Thomas Jefferson Road	Trichy	TN	22902
4	Jamat	Ali	Alij786@gmail.com	11350 Indira Nagar	Bangalore	KA	22960
5	Nick	Jones	nickjones@gmail.com	2050 Jammu Highway	Katra	JK	22902

Order_id	Order_rate	Amount	CID
1	07/04/1776	234.56	1
2	03/14/1760	78.50	3
3	05/23/1784	124.00	2
4	09/03/1790	65.50	3
5	07/21/1795	25.50	10
6	11/27/1787	14.40	9

a. Get a list of those customers who placed an order and the details of the order they placed.
b. Append information about orders to customers table, regardless of whether a customer placed an order or not.
   Hint: Use a `left join`.
c. Append Orders Information with Customer Information.
d. Get a list of all orders for which we failed to record information about the customers who placed them.
e. A list of all records from both tables, on which we can use a `full join`.

18. Consider the tables and write a query to list all orders with product names, quantities, and prices.

Product
ID
ProductName
SupplierId
UnitPrice
Package
IsDiscontinued

Order Item
ID
OrderId
ProductId
UnitPrice
Quantity

19. Consider the table given below and write the following queries.
    a. Select the name and age of Students.
    b. Fetch data for students with age more than 17.
    c. Student with information of male students, of age more than 17.

ID	Name	Subject	Age
100	Ashish	Maths	19
200	Rahul	Science	20
300	Naina	Physics	20
400	Sameer	Chemistry	21

20. Explain the queries:
    a. σ `topic = "Database" (Tutorials)`
    b. σ `topic = "Database" and author = "guru99"( Tutorials)`
    c. σ `sales > 50000 (Customers)`
    d. σ`teacher = "database"(Names)`
    e. Π`staffNo, fName, lName, salary(Staff)`
    f. σ`subject = "database"(Books)`
    g. σ`subject = "database" and price = "450"(Books)`
    h. σ`subject = "database" and price = "450" or year > "2010"(Books)`
    i. Π`subject, author (Books)`
    j. Π `author (Books)` $\cup$ Π `author (Articles)`
    k. Π `author (Books)` $-$ Π `author (Articles)`
    l. σ`author = 'tutorialspoint'(Books X Articles)`

Programming Exercises

1. Create a database having two tables with the specified fields, to computerize a library system of a Delhi University College.
   LibraryBooks (Accession number, Title, Author, Department, PurchaseDate, Price)
   IssuedBooks (Accession number, Borrower)
   a) Identify the primary and foreign keys. Create the tables and insert at least 5 records in each table.
   b) Delete the record of Book titled "Database System Concepts".

c) Change the Department of the book titled "Discrete Maths" to "CS".
d) List all books that belong to "CS" department.
e) List all books that belong to "CS" department and are written by author "Navathe".
f) List all computer (Department="CS") that have been issued.
g) List all books which have a price less than 500 or purchased between "01/01/1999" and "01/01/2004".

2. Create a database having three tables to store the details of students of Computer Department in your college.
Personal information about Student (College roll number, Name of student, Date of birth, Address, Marks(rounded off to whole number) in percentage at 10 + 2, Phone number)
Paper Details (Paper code, Name of the Paper)
Student's Academic and Attendance details (College roll number, Paper code, Attendance, Marks in home examination).
   a) Identify primary and foreign keys. Create the tables and insert at least 5 records in each table.
   b) Design a query that will return the records (from the second table)along with the name of student from the first table, of students who have more than 75% attendance and more than 60% marks in Paper 2.
   c) List all students who live in "Delhi" and have marks greater than 60 in Paper 1.
   d) Find the total attendance and total marks obtained by each student.
   e) List the name of student who has got the highest marks in Paper 2.

3. Create the following tables and answer the queries given below:
Customer (CustID, email, Name, Phone, ReferrerID)
Bicycle (BicycleID, DatePurchased, Color, CustID, ModelNo)
BicycleModel (ModelNo, Manufacturer, Style)
Service (StartDate, BicycleID, EndDate)
   a) Identify primary and foreign keys. Create the tables and insert at least 5 records in each table.
   b) List all the customers who have the bicycles manufactured by manufacturer "Honda".
   c) List the bicycles purchased by the customers who have been referred by customer "C1".
   d) List the manufacturer of red colored bicycles. e)List the models of the bicycles given for service.

4. Create the following tables, enter at least 5 records in each table and answer the queries given below.
EMPLOYEE (Person_Name, Street, City)
WORKS (Person_Name, Company_Name, Salary)
COMPANY (Company_Name, City)
MANAGERS (Person_Name, Manager_Name)
   a) Identify primary and foreign keys.
   b) Alter table employee, add a column "email" of type `varchar(20)`.
   c) Find the name of all managers who work for both Samba Bank and NCB Bank.
   d) Find the names, street address and cities of residence and salary of all employees who work for "Samba Bank" and earn more than $10,000.
   e) Find the names of all employees who live in the same city as the company for which they work.
   f) Find the highest salary, lowest salary and average salary paid by each company.
   g) Find the sum of salary and number of employees in each company.
   h) Find the name of the company that pays highest salary.

5. Create the following tables, enter at least 5 records in each table and answer the queries given below.
Suppliers (SNo, Sname, Status, SCity)
Parts (PNo, Pname, Colour, Weight, City)
Project (JNo, Jname, Jcity)
Shipment (Sno, Pno, Jno, Qunatity)
   a) Identify primary and foreign keys.
   b) Get supplier numbers for suppliers in Paris with status>20.
   c) Get suppliers details for suppliers who supply part P2. Display the supplier list in increasing order of supplier numbers.
   d) Get suppliers names for suppliers who do not supply part P2.
   e) For each shipment get full shipment details, including total shipment weights.
   f) Get all the shipments where the quantity is in the range 300 to 750 inclusive.
   g) Get part nos. for parts that either weigh more than 16 pounds or are supplied by suppliers S2, or both.
   h) Get the names of cities that store more than five red parts.

i) Get full details of parts supplied by a supplier in Delhi.
j) Get part numbers for part supplied by a supplier in Allahabad to a project in Chennai.
k) Get the total number of project supplied by a supplier (say, S1).
l) Get the total quantity of a part (say, P1) supplied by a supplier (say, S1).

Fill in the Blanks

1. MySQL works on _____ model.
2. _____ describes data stored in database.
3. _____ Language is used to create or modify database objects (like tables, views, indexes, users, etc).
4. Data type _____ is used to define fixed length strings.
5. _____ is a reserved word or a character in SQL statement that is extensively used to perform arithmetic or comparison operations.
6. _____ keyword ensures no duplicate values.
7. _____ function displays a sub-string of given length starting from the specified position.
8. _____ statement is used to see a list of all the databases present in MySQL.
9. The DROP DATABASE statement is used to _____ an existing database.
10. In SQL, the _____ statement is used to create a table.
11. Once the table is created, we can use the _____ command to see the description of the newly created table.
12. _____ statement is used to add new rows of data in a table that exists in the database.
13. The _____ statement in SQL is used to fetch or retrieve data from one or more tables in the database.
14. _____ statement eliminates duplicate entries while displaying data from the table.
15. The _____ clause returns values that fall within a given range.
16. The _____ keyword can be used to create a column alias.
17. _____ operator returns true, if the column value is NULL.
18. _____ KEY is a key used to link two tables.
19. The _____ constraint ensures that invalid data is not inserted into the foreign key column.

State True or False

1. MySQL is a proprietary software.
2. MySQL satisfies ACID property.
3. MySQL is a database query language.
4. The server application responds with the requested information that is displayed on the client machine.
5. DDL is used to manipulate data.
6. `char` performs faster than `varchar`.
7. The ALL keyword is used to compare any applicable value in the list.
8. The `strcmp()` function returns 1, if the first string is smaller than the second.
9. When we delete a database, all the information stored in it is lost.
10. The WHERE clause can be used retrieve data only from a single table.
11. The WHEREIN clause returns values that matches values in a list or a sub-query.
12. The ORDER BY clause can be used to sort data according to multiple columns.
13. An underscore represents zero, one or multiple characters.
14. A column alias permanently changes the heading of the column.
15. Equality operator does not work with NULL values.

16. NULL is a data type in SQL.
17. All aggregate functions affect only rows that do not have NULL values.
18. Comparison operations cannot be performed on NULL values.
19. The primary key must contain NULL values.
20. A table can have only one primary key and the primary key may consist of one or more fields.

Multiple Choice Questions

1. We cannot _____ data using SQL statements.
   a. delete   b. update   c. retrieve   d. None of these.
2. Which of the following is not an example of a database?
   a. MySQL   b. SQL   c. PostGres SQL   d. SQL Server
3. Which function returns the smallest integer value that is greater than or equal to a number?
   a. Ceil()   b. floor()   c. round()   d. abs()
4. Which function is used to remove leading and trailing white spaces from the given string?
   a. TRIM()   b. LTRIM()   c. RTRIM()   d. RPAD()
5. Which clause is used with SELECT statement to filter the records in the table and fetch only those that meet the specified criteria?
   a. ORDER BY   b. WHERE   c. DISTINCT   d. UPDATE
6. Which SQL statement is used to modify the existing data in a table?
   a. ORDER BY   b. WHERE   c. INSERT INTO   d. UPDATE
7. Which clause is used with the WHERE clause to compare a value to find similar values using wildcard characters?
   a. IN   b. BETWEEN   c. LIKE   d. DISTINCT
8. Which operator compares values and gives True even for two NULL values?
   a. IS NULL   b. IS NOT NULL   c. <=>   d. All of these.
9. The SQL NULL is a _____.
   a. value   b. keyword   c. Both of these. d. None of these.
10. Which function is used for replacing NULL values in MySQL?
    a. IS NULL   b. IFNULL()   c. IS NOT NULL   d. <= >
11. Which command is used to create a FOREIGN KEY constraint on an already existing table?
    a. ALTER TABLE   b. CREATE TABLE
    c. INSERT INTO   d. UPDATE TABLE

Give the Output

1. SELECT 20 + 5 - 10 * 3
2. SELECT 100/20 *2 + 8 -4;
3. SELECT (50 > 10) AND (50 <= 100);
4. SELECT POW(CEIL(ABS(-12.34)),2);
5. SELECT LOG10(MOD(110,FLOOR(100.89)));
6. SELECT CHAR_LENGTH(CONCAT('PYTHON','PROGRAMMING'));
7. SELECT LCASE(RIGHT('PYTHON PROGRAMMING',10));
8. SELECT LPAD(LTRIM('   PYTHON PROGRAMMING'),25,'#');
9. SELECT REPEAT(MID('PYTHON PROGRAMMING',7,7),3);
10. SELECT RPAD(REVERSE('PYTHON'),15,'@');

11. Consider the tables given below.

    Employee table

EmpID	EmpFname	EmpLname	Age	EmailID	PhoneNo	Address
1	Vinay	Lal	22	Vinay12@gmail.com	9976673229	Delhi
2	Hemant	Sharma	32	sharmahemant@gmail.com	9827554567	Mumbai
3	Ayush	Prasad	24	Payush@gmail.com	9134555511	Kolkata
4	Hiten	Mishra	25	Hiten_mishra@gmail.com	9899087612	Bengaluru
5	Anitha	Kumar	26	Kumar_a@gmail.com	9512983405	Hyderabad

    Project table

ProjectID	EmpID	ClientID	ProjectName	ProjectStartDate
101	1	5	Project1	2021-01-21
102	2	1	Project2	2020-09-12
103	3	2	Project3	2021-02-10
104	3	4	Project4	2020-04-30
105	5	2	Project5	2020-02-23
106	9	3	Project6	2021-01-19
107	7	1	Project7	2021-02-25
108	8	3	Project8	2020-08-29

    Client table

ClientID	ClientFname	ClientLname	Age	ClientEmailID	PhoneNo	Address	EmpID
1	Kriti	Juneja	30	kjuneja@gmail.com	9465611739	Kolkata	2
2	Alice	John	27	ajohn@gmail.com	9175546568	Kolkata	3
3	Danish	Ali	22	Ali.danish@gmail.com	9577638511	Delhi	9
4	Zubin	Junjunwala	40	Zubin45@gmail.com	9955123422	Hyderabad	3
5	BV	Reddy	32	bvreddy@gmail.com	9643463239	Mumbai	1

    Give the output of the following queries.

    a. `SELECT Employee.EmpID, Employee.EmpFname, Employee.EmpLname, Projects.ProjectID, Projects.ProjectName`
    `FROM Employee`
    `INNER JOIN Projects ON Employee.EmpID=Projects.EmpID;`
    b. `SELECT Employee.EmpFname, Employee.EmpLname, Projects.ProjectID`
    `FROM Employee`
    `FULL JOIN Projects`
    `ON Employee.EmpID = Projects.EmpID;`

c. SELECT   Employee.EmpFname,   Employee.EmpLname,   Projects.ProjectID,
   Projects.ProjectName
   FROM Employee
   LEFT JOIN
   ON Employee.EmpID = Projects.EmpID ;
d. SELECT   Employee.EmpFname,   Employee.EmpLname,   Projects.ProjectID,
   Projects.ProjectName
   FROM Employee
   RIGHT JOIN
   ON Employee.EmpID = Projects.EmpID;

12. Consider the Tables A and B and give the output of:
    a. A Union B
    b. A – B

Table A		Table B	
column 1	column 2	column 1	column 2
1	1	1	1
1	2	1	3

Answers

Fill in the Blanks

1. client-server
2. Metadata
3. Data Definition
4. char
5. Operator
6. UNIQUE
7. MID()
8. show databases.
9. remove
10. CREATE TABLE
11. DESC
12. INSERT INTO
13. SELECT
14. SELECT DISTINCT
15. WHERE BETWEEN
16. AS
17. IS NULL
18. FOREIGN
19. FOREIGN KEY

State True or False

1. False
2. False
3. False
4. True
5. False
6. True
7. False
8. False
9. True
10. False
11. True
12. True
13. False
14. False
15. True
16. False
17. True
18. False
19. False
20. True

Multiple Choice Questions

1. d
2. b
3. a
4. a
5. b
6. d
7. c
8. c
9. c
10. b
11. a

Give the Output

1. -5
2. 14
3. 1
4. 169
5. 1
6. 17
7. rogramming
8. #######PYTHON PROGRAMMING
9. PROGRA PROGRA PROGRA
10. NOHTYP@@@@@@@@
11. Refer solutions manual
12. Refer solutions manual

Interfacing Python With MySQL

11

Chapter Objectives

Now that we have studied the basic concepts of databases and DBMS, and also covered SQL through MySQL database, let us move a step ahead and see how we can work with our MySQL tables and manipulate data stored in it using scripts (or programs) written in Python. However, before starting to code, let us first quickly look at the important topics that will be discussed in the chapter.

- Connecting to the database through Python code
- Create an object for the database
- Creating tables, inserting values, setting primary key, modifying existing data through Python interface
- Execute SQL query on the database through Python
- Fetch records from the result
- Update data in the database
- ACID Property of databases

11.1 INTERFACING PYTHON WITH MYSQL

To work with MySQL database through our Python program, we need to first connect with MySQL. Only then will it be possible to execute our SQL queries to create tables, insert data into it, retrieve data, update or delete the data and execute all other queries that we have already studied in the previous chapter.

To connect MySQL database with Python programs, we must follow the steps given below.

Step 1: Connect to the database.

Step 2: Create an object for the database.

Step 3: Execute the SQL query.

Step 4: Fetch records from the result.

Step 5: Save the database in case any changes were made in any of the tables.

All these steps are elaborated in Fig. 11.1. However, make sure that you have installed the mysql-connector-python package before starting. In Windows, this can be done by executing the pip install mysql-connector-python command in the Command Prompt.

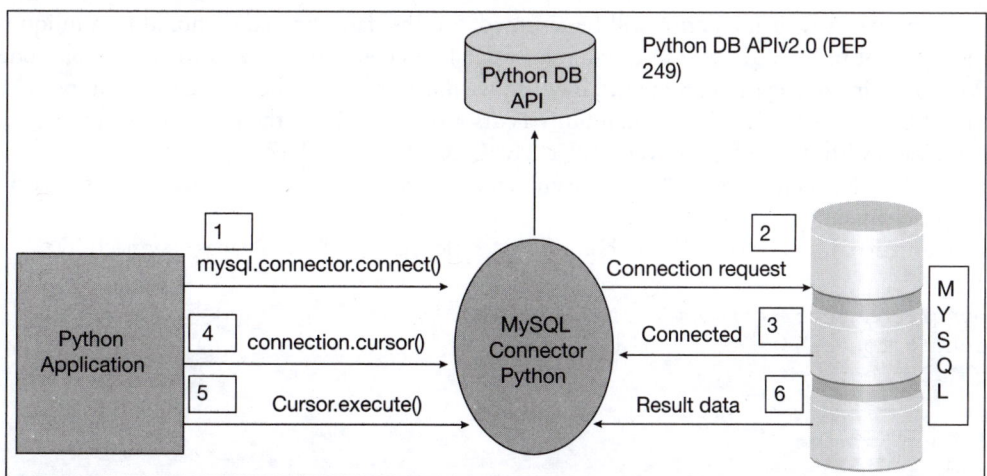

Figure 11.1 MySQL database connection in Python

Step 1: Connect to Database

The `connect()` method is used to establish a connection between MySQL database and Python program (Fig. 11.1). Once a connection is established, MySQLConnection object is returned. This object is then used to perform various operations on the MySQL Database.

However, the `connect()` method throws an exception if the connection could not be established as for example, if one of the required parameters (like user name, password) is wrong. In our programs, we have obtained the connection object in variable db.

> `is_connected()` is the method of the MySQLConnection class through which we can verify if our Python application is connected to MySQL.

We can connect to the database using username and password of MySQL. If you don't remember these details then you can also create a new user with the specified password using the create user command having syntax,

```
CREATE USER  user_name
IDENTIFIED BY 'password';
```

Here, user_name is the name of the user and password is the chosen password. You can use any value for these two parameters.

```python
import mysql.connector as mysql
## connecting to the database using 'connect()' method
## it takes 3 required parameters 'host', 'user', 'passwd'
db = mysql.connect(
    host = "localhost",
    user = "reema",
    passwd = "********"
)
print(db)
```

OUTPUT

```
<mysql.connector.connection.MySQLConnection object at 0x036B2580>
```

Step 2: Creating Databases

We have studied that before creating a table, we must first create a database. In MySQL, a database is created using the create database command. The syntax of this command is,

```
CREATE DATABASE database_name
```

If the database already exists, then an error will be returned. So, the database_name should be a unique one. To see all the databases present in MySQL, we can use the show databases command. Let us write a simple code to create a database in MySQL using our Python program. However, we must first learn about some more important functions.

The `connection.cursor()` method returns a cursor object which is then used to execute SQL queries. The cursor object interacts with the MySQL server using a MySQLConnection object.

`cursor.close()` method is used to close the cursor object. Once the cursor object is closed, we cannot execute any SQL statement.

Similarly, `connection.close()` method is used to close the MySQL database connection.

```python
import mysql.connector as mysql
## connecting to the database using 'connect()' method
db = mysql.connect(
    host = "localhost",
    user = "reema",
    passwd = "********"
)
```

```
cursor = db.cursor()
## executing the statement using 'execute()' method
cursor.execute("SHOW DATABASES")
## 'fetchall()' method fetches all the rows from the last executed statement
databases = cursor.fetchall() ## it returns a list of all databases present
## printing the list of databases
print(databases)
## showing one by one database
for database in databases:
    print(database)
```

OUTPUT
```
[('information_schema',), ('mydb',), ('mysql',), ('performance_schema',), ('sys',)]
('information_schema',)
('mydb',)
('mysql',)
('performance_schema',)
('sys',)
```

Here,

Username is the username that you use to work with MySQL on your computer. The default username for the MySQL database is **root**.

Password is specified by the user at the time of installing the MySQL database. The User working as **root** does not need a password.

Host Name is the server name or IP address on which MySQL is running. You can specify it as localhost or 127.0.0.0, if you are running MySQL on your own computer.

Database Name is the name of the database to which you want to connect. Here we are using database mydb.

Step 3: Execute the Query

The `cursor.execute()` method is used to run or execute an SQL query through a python program. Another method, cursor.executemany(operation, seq_of_parameters) is used to prepare a database query and execute it against all parameter sequences found in the sequence `seq_of_params`. That is, the `executemany()` method iterates through the sequence of parameters, each time passing the current parameters to the `execute()` method.

11.2 CREATING TABLES

A database can have one or more tables. Our data is stored in these tables. However, before creating a table, first select the database in which it has to be created.

In MySQL, a table is created using the **CREATE TABLE table_name**. Again, the name of the table should be unique. To see the table_name, we can use the `show tables` command.

The basic syntax of this statement can be given as,

```
CREATE TABLE table_name(
    column1 datatype,
    column2 datatype,
    column3 datatype,
    .....
    columnN datatype,
    PRIMARY KEY(one or more columns )
);
```

Within the opening and closing brackets, the list of columns and their corresponding data types are specified.

11.3 SETTING PRIMARY KEY

We have studied that the primary key helps us to uniquely identify each record in the table. While creating the table, we can set one or more columns as the primary key. However, we should remember that the primary key must contain UNIQUE values and cannot have NULL values.

The code given below creates a table STUDENT in mydb database.

Example 11.1

```
import mysql.connector as mysql
## connecting to the database using 'connect()' method
db = mysql.connect(
    host = "localhost",
    user = "reema",
    passwd = "********",
    database = "mydb"
)
cursor = db.cursor()
## creating a table called 'STUDENT' in the 'mydb' database
cursor.execute("CREATE TABLE STUDENT (ROLLNO INT(11) NOT
    NULL PRIMARY KEY, NAME VARCHAR(30), MARKS INT)")
## 'DESC table_name' is used to get all columns information
cursor.execute("DESC STUDENT")
## it will print all the columns as 'tuples' in a list
print(cursor.fetchall())
```

> A table can be deleted using the DROP TABLE statement. The syntax of DROP TABLE statement is,
> DROP TABLE table_name;

OUTPUT

```
[('ROLLNO', 'int', 'NO', 'PRI', None, 'auto_increment'), ('NAME', 'varchar(30)',
    'YES', '', None, ''), ('MARKS', 'int', 'YES', '', None, '')]
```

Now to make sure that our table is created, we have used the SHOW TABLES command in the code given below.

Example 11.2

```
import mysql.connector as mysql
## connecting to the database using 'connect()' method
db = mysql.connect(
    host = "localhost",
    user = "reema",
    passwd = "********",
    database = "mydb"
)
cursor = db.cursor()
## getting all the tables which are present in 'mydb' database
cursor.execute("SHOW TABLES")
tables = cursor.fetchall() ## returns list of tables present in database
for table in tables:   ## showing all the tables one by one
    print(table)
```

OUTPUT

('student',)

In case you forget to add the primary key constraint while creating the table, you can still make one or more columns as the primary key by using the ALTER TABLE command. The syntax for ALTER TABLE command can be given as,

```
ALTER TABLE table_name
ADD PRIMARY KEY (column_name);
```

Example 11.3

```
import mysql.connector as mysql
## connecting to the database using 'connect()' method
db = mysql.connect(
    host = "localhost",
    user = "reema",
    passwd = "********",
    database = "mydb"
)
cursor = db.cursor()
cursor.execute("ALTER TABLE STUDENT ADD COLUMN ROLLNO INT(11) NOT NULL PRIMARY KEY")
cursor.execute("DESC STUDENT")
print(cursor.fetchall())
```

OUTPUT

```
[('ROLLNO', 'int', 'NO', 'PRI', None, ''), ('NAME', 'varchar(30)', 'YES', '', None,
    ''), ('MARKS', 'int', 'YES', '', None, '')]
```

11.4 DROPPING PRIMARY KEY

If we wish to remove the primary key constraint from our table, then we can use the DROP PRIMARY KEY command that is used with the ALTER TABLE statement. The general syntax of this command can be given as,

```
ALTER TABLE table_name
DROP PRIMARY KEY;
```

Look at the code give below and carefully observe the output. ROLLNO is no longer the primary key of the table STUDENT.

Example 11.4

```
import mysql.connector as mysql
## connecting to the database using 'connect()' method
db = mysql.connect(
    host = "localhost",
    user = "reema",
    passwd = "********",
    database = "mydb"
)
cursor = db.cursor()
cursor.execute("ALTER TABLE STUDENT DROP ROLLNO")
cursor.execute("DESC STUDENT")
print(cursor.fetchall())
```

OUTPUT

```
None
[('NAME', 'varchar(30)', 'YES', '', None, ''), ('MARKS', 'int', 'YES', '', None, '')]
```

11.5 INSERTING DATA

Before inserting values in a table, it must first be created using the CREATE TABLE command. We use the **INSERT INTO** statement to add new rows of data in an existing table. Syntax of INSERT INTO statement can be given as,

```
INSERT INTO TABLE_NAME VALUES (value1,value2,value3,...valueN);
```

The code given below inserts a row in the table STUDENT that we created in mydb database.

Example 11.5

```
import mysql.connector as mysql
## connecting to the database using 'connect()' method
db = mysql.connect(
    host = "localhost",
    user = "reema",
    passwd = "******",
    database = "mydb"
)
cursor = db.cursor()
query = r'INSERT INTO STUDENT VALUES(1,"PARAS",54)'
## executing the query with values
cursor.execute(query)
## to make final output we have to run the 'commit()' method of the database object
db.commit()
print(cursor.rowcount, "records inserted")
```

OUTPUT

```
1 records inserted
```

11.5.1 Inserting Multiple Rows

To insert multiple rows into the table, `executemany()` method is used. The method takes a query as the first argument and a list of tuples containing the data as a second parameter. The code given below illustrates inserting multiple rows in a table.

Example 11.6

```
import mysql.connector as mysql
## connecting to the database using 'connect()' method
db = mysql.connect(
    host = "localhost",
    user = "reema",
    passwd = "********",
    database = "mydb"
)
cursor = db.cursor()
query = "INSERT INTO STUDENT (ROLLNO, NAME, MARKS) VALUES (%s,%s, %s)"
## storing values in a variable
values = [
    (1,"PARAS",56), (2,"NEON",68), (3,"MEERA", 99), (4,"SHIV", 89) ]
## executing the query with values
cursor.executemany(query, values)
## to make final output we have to run the 'commit()' method of the database object
db.commit()
print(cursor.rowcount, "records inserted")
4 records inserted
```

11.6 RETRIEVE OR SELECT DATA

The **SELECT** statement in SQL is used to fetch or retrieve data from one or more tables in the database. The results of the SELECT statement is in the form of a table. This resultant table is known as the result-set. The syntax of the SELECT statement can be given as,

```
SELECT column1, column2, columnN FROM table_name;
```

Here, column1, column2... are the fields of the table from which data has to be fetched. To fetch all the fields from the table, the syntax is

```
SELECT * FROM table_name;
Before
```

Step 4: Fetch Records from the Result

To read data from a table, we need to fetch records stored in the database. After database connection is established, we can execute an appropriate query (using the SELECT statement). The results of this query can then be accessed using either `fetchone()` method to fetch single record or `fetchall()` method to fetch multiple values from a database table.

fetchone(): This method fetches the next row of a query result set. Note that a result set is an object that is returned when a cursor object is used to query a table.

fetchall(): It fetches all the rows in a result set.

rowcount: It is a read-only attribute and returns the number of rows that were affected by an `execute()` method.

Example 11.7

```
import mysql.connector as mysql
## connecting to the database using 'connect()' method
db = mysql.connect(
    host = "localhost",
    user = "reema",
    passwd = "********",
    database = "mydb"
)
cursor = db.cursor()
query = "SELECT * FROM STUDENT"
## getting records from the table
cursor.execute(query)
## fetching all records from the 'cursor' object
records = cursor.fetchall()
## Showing the data
for record in records:
    print(record)
```

OUTPUT

```
(1, 'PARAS', 54)
(2, 'HEENA', 68)
(3, 'MANAB', 75)
(4, 'ZYAN', 81)
```

11.6.1 Getting Some Columns

To select some columns from the table, mention column name after the SELECT in the statement. Let us retrieve the username column from the STUDENT table.

Example 11.8

```
import mysql.connector as mysql
## connecting to the database using 'connect()' method
db = mysql.connect(
    host = "localhost",
    user = "reema",
    passwd = "********",
    database = "mydb"
)
```

```
cursor = db.cursor()
## defining the Query
query = "SELECT NAME, MARKS FROM STUDENT"
## getting 'NAME', 'MARKS' columns from the table
cursor.execute(query)
## fetching all records from the 'cursor' object
data = cursor.fetchall()
## Showing the data
for pair in data:
    print(pair)
```

OUTPUT

```
('PARAS', 56)
('NEON', 68)
('MEERA', 99)
('SHIV', 89)
```

11.6.2 WHERE Clause

The WHERE clause is used in the SELECT statement to specify a condition for retrieving data from one or more tables. We use the WHERE clause to filter the records in the table and fetch only those that meet the specified criteria.

In addition to the SELECT statement, the WHERE clause is also used with the UPDATE and DELETE statements. The basic syntax of the SELECT statement with the WHERE clause can be given as,

```
SELECT column1, column2, columnN
FROM table_name
WHERE [condition]
```

We can even use comparison and logical operators in the WHERE clause. Let us examine a couple of queries to see how the SELECT statement with WHERE clause actually works.

Example 11.9

```
import mysql.connector as mysql
## connecting to the database using 'connect()' method
db = mysql.connect(
    host = "localhost",
    user = "reema",
    passwd = "********",
    database = "mydb"
)
cursor = db.cursor()
## defining the Query
query = "SELECT * FROM STUDENT WHERE MARKS > 75"
## getting 'NAME', 'MARKS' columns from the table
cursor.execute(query)
## fetching all records from the 'cursor' object
data = cursor.fetchall()
## Showing the data
for pair in data:
    print(pair)
```

OUTPUT

```
(3, 'MEERA', 99)
(4, 'SHIV', 89)
```

11.7 ORDER BY CLAUSE

The ORDER BY statement in SQL is used to sort the retrieved data in either ascending or descending order. We can sort the values in the result-set by one or more columns using the ORDER BY clause.

By default, ORDER BY sorts the data in ascending order. To sort in descending order, we can use the keyword DESC. To specifically state ascending as the sorting order, the keyword ASC is used.

The syntax of all ways of using ORDER BY clause with the SELECT statement can be given as,

Sort according to one column: To sort in ascending or descending order, we can use the keywords ASC or DESC respectively. The syntax for this can be given as,

```
SELECT expressions
FROM tables
[WHERE conditions]
ORDER BY expression [ ASC | DESC ]
```

where,

expressions specifies the columns to be retrieved.

tables is the table from which the records have to be retrieved. At least one table must be listed in the FROM clause.

WHERE condition is optional. If specified, the condition must be satisfied for the records to be selected.

ASC is optional as it is the default sorting order. ASC sorts the result set in ascending order by *expression*.

DESC is optional. If present, it sorts the result set in descending order by *expression*.

Sort according to multiple columns: To sort according to multiple columns, separate the names of columns by (,) operator. The syntax can be given as,

```
SELECT * FROM table_name ORDER BY column1 ASC|DESC , column2 ASC|DESC
```

Example 11.10

```
import mysql.connector as mysql
## connecting to the database using 'connect()' method
db = mysql.connect(
    host = "localhost",
    user = "reema",
    passwd = "*******",
    database = "mydb"
)
cursor = db.cursor()
## defining the Query
query = "SELECT * FROM STUDENT ORDER BY MARKS DESC"
## getting 'NAME', 'MARKS' columns from the table
cursor.execute(query)
## fetching all records from the 'cursor' object
data = cursor.fetchall()
for record in data:
    print(record)
```

OUTPUT

```
(3, 'MEERA', 99)
(4, 'SHIV', 89)
(2, 'NEON', 68)
(1, 'PARAS', 56)
```

Step 5: Saving Records

All database operations must ensure data consistency. For this, every operation must satisfy the following four properties that are also known as ACID properties:

Atomicity: Either an operation executes completely or it is not executed at all.

Consistency: Every operation must leave data in the database in a consistent state (where data is correct).

Isolation: Intermediate results of query execution are not visible outside the current transaction.

Durability: Once an operation changing database values has executed completely, then the operation is committed and changes made by it are persistent, even after a system failure. Python provides two methods to either *commit* or *rollback* a transaction.

Commit Operation: The `commit()` function is used to finalize changes in the database. After this operation, changes cannot be reverted. To use the `commit()` method, we can write `db.commit()`.

Rollback Operation: To undo or to revert the changes made to the database, `rollback()` method is used. To use the `rollback()` method, we can write db.rollback().

11.8 UPDATING THE TABLE

The SQL UPDATE statement is used to modify the existing data in a table. We can even use the WHERE clause with the UPDATE query to update only selected rows, so that not all the rows are affected. The basic syntax of the UPDATE query with a WHERE clause can be given as,

UPDATE table_name
SET column1 = value1, column2 = value2...., columnN = valueN
WHERE [condition];

Again, according to the syntax, any number of conditions can be specified using the AND or the OR operators in the WHERE clause.

Example 11.11

```
import mysql.connector as mysql
## connecting to the database using 'connect()' method
db = mysql.connect(
    host = "localhost",
    user = "reema",
    passwd = "********",
    database = "mydb"
)
cursor = db.cursor()
## defining the Query
query = "UPDATE STUDENT SET NAME = 'KARAN' WHERE ROLLNO = 3"
## executing the query
cursor.execute(query)
## final step to tell the database that we have changed the table data
db.commit()
## defining the Query
query = "SELECT * FROM STUDENT"
## executing the query
cursor.execute(query)
data = cursor.fetchall()
for record in data:
    print(record)
```

OUTPUT

```
1, 'PARAS', 56)
(2, 'NEON', 68)
(3, 'KARAN', 99)
(4, 'SHIV', 89)
```

11.9 AGGREGATE FUNCTIONS

An aggregate function is one that performs a calculation on multiple values and returns a single value. For example, we can use the `avg()` aggregate function that takes multiple numbers and returns the average value of the numbers. The general syntax of an aggregate function is, function_name(DISTINCT | ALL expression)

where,
func_name can be any name from the table.
DISTINCT is used to perform calculations based on distinct values.
expression can be a column or expression. It can include column names and arithmetic operators.

Table 11.1   Aggregate functions in SQL

Aggregate Function	Description
AVG()	Returns the average of non-NULL values.
BIT_AND()	Returns bitwise AND.
BIT_OR()	Returns bitwise OR.
BIT_XOR()	Returns bitwise XOR.
COUNT()	Returns the number of rows in a group, including rows with NULL values.
GROUP_CONCAT()	Returns a concatenated string.
MAX()	Returns the highest value (maximum) in a set of non-NULL values.
MIN()	Returns the lowest value (minimum) in a set of non-NULL values.
STDEV()	Returns the population standard deviation.
SUM()	Returns the summation of all non-NULL values in a set.
VARIANCE()	Returns the population standard variance.

Example 11.12

```
import mysql.connector as mysql
## connecting to the database using 'connect()' method
db = mysql.connect(
    host = "localhost",
    user = "reema",
    passwd= "*******"
    database ="mydb"
)
cursor = db.cursor()
## defining the Query
query = "SELECT COUNT(*) FROM STUDENT GROUP BY CLASS"
## executing the query
cursor.execute(query)
data = cursor.fetchall()
for record in data:
    print(record)
## defining the Query
query = "SELECT MAX(MARKS) FROM STUDENT GROUP BY CLASS"
## executing the query
cursor.execute(query)
data = cursor.fetchall()
for record in data:
    print(record)
```

OUTPUT
(3,)
(3,)
(2,)
(2,)
(89,)
(97,)
(79,)
(84,)

Key Terms

SQL: A database query language.
Clients: Computers that install and run RDBMS software are called clients.
Servers: To access data, clients connect to powerful machines called servers.
Metadata: Data describing data stored in database.
Data Definition Language (DDL): SQL statements used to create or modify database objects (like tables, views, indexes, users, etc).
Data Manipulation Language (DML): SQL statements used to manipulate data (like inserting, updating, deleting data).
Database: A collection of related tables.
Aggregate function: Function that performs a calculation on multiple values and returns a single value.

Chapter Highlights

- PRIMARY KEY constraint helps us to uniquely identify each record in the table. The primary key must contain UNIQUE values, and cannot have NULL values.
- A table can have only one primary key and the primary key may consist of one or more fields.
- To set PRIMARY KEY constraint on an already created table, the ALTER TABLE command is used.
- The `cursor.execute()` method is used to run or execute an SQL query through a python program. Another method, `cursor.executemany(operation, seq_of_parameters)` is used to prepare a database query and executes it against all parameter sequences found in the sequence `seq_of_params`.
- The results of this query can then be accessed using either `fetchone()` method to fetch single record or `fetchall()` method to fetch multiple values from a database table.
- The GROUP BY statement is used to create a summary of records. The statement groups rows that have the same values (in a column) to create summary rows.

Review Questions

1. List the steps for interfacing Python with MySQL.
2. How can we create a database in SQL?
3. Explain the syntax of the SELECT statement.
4. With the help of an example explain how you will use the ORDER BY clause to sort data based on multiple columns
5. What does primary key constraint state? How can we enforce such a constraint in SQL?
6. Differentiate between `execute` and `executemany()`.
7. How is `fetchone()` different from `fetchall()` function?
8. How is durability ensured while working with MySQL?
9. With the help of an example, explain the significance of GROUP BY and HAVING clause.
10. Write the SQL statements that you will use to filter the values returned from a grouped query based on the results of aggregation functions.
11. Consider the given table and write a query that returns the number of orders in each status.
12. Consider the orders and orderdetails table. Write a query to get the total amount of all orders by status. (**Hint:** Join the orders table with the orderdetails table). Also write the query that returns the order numbers and the total amount of each order.

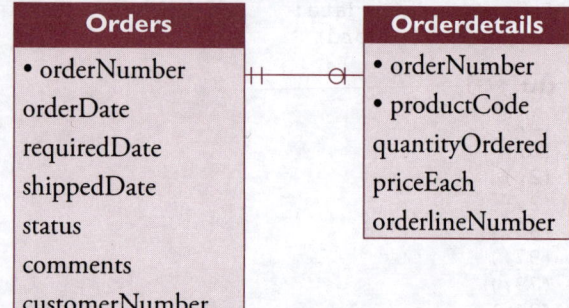

13. Explain the given queries.
    a. ```
    SELECT YEAR(orderDate) AS year, SUM(quantityOrdered * priceEach) AS total
    FROM orders
    INNER JOIN orderdetails
        USING (orderNumber)
    WHERE status = 'Shipped'
    GROUP BY   year
    HAVING year > 2003;
    ```
    b. ```
    import mysql.connector
    connection = mysql.connector.connect(host='localhost',
                                         database='Electronics',
                                         user='pynative',
                                         password='pynative@#29')
    mySql_Create_Table_Query = """CREATE TABLE Laptop (
         Id int(11) NOT NULL, Name varchar(250) NOT NULL,
         Price float NOT NULL, Purchase_date Date NOT NULL,
         PRIMARY KEY (Id)) """
    cursor = connection.cursor()
    result = cursor.execute(mySql_Create_Table_Query)
    print("Laptop Table created successfully ")
    if (connection.is_connected()):
       cursor.close()
       connection.close()
       print("MySQL connection is closed")
    ```
    c. ```
    select bst.start_station_name, count(*) as num_trips
    from modeanalytics.sf_bike_share_trip bst
    group by bst.start_station_name
    ```
    d. ```
    select bst.start_station_name, count(*) as num_trips, avg(bst.duration)
    as avg_duration_seconds, min(bst.duration) as min_duration_seconds,
      max(bst.duration) as max_duration_seconds
    from modeanalytics.sf_bike_share_trip bst
    group by bst.start_station_name
    ```
    e. ```
    select bst.start_station_name, bst.end_station_name, count(*) as num_trips,
       avg(bst.duration) as avg_duration_seconds, min(bst.duration) as
    min_duration_seconds, max(bst.duration) as max_duration_seconds
    from modeanalytics.sf_bike_share_trip bst
    group by bst.start_station_name,bst.end_station_name
    ```
    f. ```
    select bst.start_station_name, bst.end_station_name, count(1) as num_trips,  avg(duration) as  avg_duration_seconds,min(duration)  as  min_duration_seconds, max(duration) as max_duration_seconds
    from modeanalytics.sf_bike_share_trip bst
    group by 1,2
    having count(1) > 1000
    ```
    g. ```
    import MySQLdb
    db = MySQLdb.connect("localhost","testuser","test123","TESTDB")
    cursor = db.cursor()
    cursor.execute("SELECT VERSION()")
    data = cursor.fetchone()
    print "Database version : %s " % data
    db.close()
    ```
    h. ```
    import MySQLdb
    db = MySQLdb.connect("localhost","testuser","test123","TESTDB" )
    cursor = db.cursor()
    cursor.execute("DROP TABLE IF EXISTS EMPLOYEE")
    ```

Programming Exercises

1. Write a program that creates a table Employee with attributes FIRST_NAME, LAST_NAME, AGE, SEX, and INCOME.
   a) Insert at least 10 rows in the table.
   b) Display all the records from EMPLOYEE table having salary more than 1000
   c) Increase AGE of all the males by one year.
   d) Delete all the records from EMPLOYEE where AGE is more than 20

2. Write a Python code to create a database having two tables with the specified fields, to computerize a library system of a Delhi University College:
   LibraryBooks (Accession number, Title, Author, Department, PurchaseDate, Price)
   IssuedBooks (Accession number, Borrower)
   a) Identify the primary and foreign keys. Create the tables and insert at least 5 records in each table.
   b) Delete the record of book titled "Database System Concepts".
   c) Change the Department of the book titled "Discrete Maths" to "CS".
   d) List all books that belong to "CS" department.
   e) List all books that belong to "CS" department and are written by author "Navathe".
   f) List all computer (Department="CS") that have been issued.
   g) List all books which have a price less than 500 or purchased between "01/01/1999" and "01/01/2004".

3. Write a Python code to create a database having three tables to store the details of students of Computer Department in your college.
   Personal information about Student (College roll number, Name of student, Date of birth, Address,
   Marks(rounded off to whole number) in percentage at 10 + 2, Phone number)
   Paper Details (Paper code, Name of the Paper)
   Student's Academic and Attendance details (College roll number, Paper code, Attendance, Marks in home examination).
   a) Identify primary and foreign keys. Create the tables and insert at least 5 records in each table.
   b) Design a query that will return the records (from the second table) along with the name of student from the first table, of students who have more than 75% attendance and more than 60% marks in Paper 2.
   c) List all students who live in "Delhi" and have marks greater than 60 in Paper 1.
   d) Find the total attendance and total marks obtained by each student.
   e) List the name of student who has got the highest marks in Paper 2.

4. Write a Python code to create the following tables and answer the queries given below:
   Customer (CustID, email, Name, Phone, ReferrerID)
   Bicycle (BicycleID, DatePurchased, Color, CustID, ModelNo)
   BicycleModel (ModelNo, Manufacturer, Style)
   Service (StartDate, BicycleID, EndDate)
   a) Identify primary and foreign keys. Create the tables and insert at least 5 records in each table.
   b) List all the customers who have the bicycles manufactured by manufacturer "Honda".
   c) List the bicycles purchased by the customers who have been referred by customer "C1".
   d) List the manufacturer of red colored bicycles. e) List the models of the bicycles given for service.

5. Write a Python code to create the following tables, enter at least 5 records in each table and answer the queries given below.
   EMPLOYEE (Person_Name, Street, City)
   WORKS (Person_Name, Company_Name, Salary)
   COMPANY (Company_Name, City)
   MANAGERS (Person_Name, Manager_Name)
   a) Identify primary and foreign keys.
   b) Alter table employee, add a column "email" of type `varchar(20)`.
   c) Find the name of all managers who work for both Samba Bank and NCB Bank.
   d) Find the names, street address and cities of residence and salary of all employees who work for "Samba Bank" and earn more than $10,000.
   e) Find the names of all employees who live in the same city as the company for which they work.
   f) Find the highest salary, lowest salary and average salary paid by each company.

g) Find the sum of salary and number of employees in each company.
h) Find the name of the company that pays highest salary.

6. Write a Python code to create the following tables, enter at least 5 records in each table and answer the queries given below.

Suppliers (SNo, Sname, Status, SCity)
Parts (PNo, Pname, Colour, Weight, City)
Project (JNo, Jname, Jcity)
Shipment (Sno, Pno, Jno, Qunatity)

a) Identify primary and foreign keys.
b) Get supplier numbers for suppliers in Paris with status>20.
c) Get suppliers details for suppliers who supply part P2. Display the supplier list in increasing order of supplier numbers.
d) Get suppliers names for suppliers who do not supply part P2.
e) For each shipment get full shipment details, including total shipment weights.
f) Get all the shipments where the quantity is in the range 300 to 750 inclusive.
g) Get part nos. for parts that either weigh more than 16 pounds or are supplied by suppliers S2, or both.
h) Get the names of cities that store more than five red parts.
i) Get full details of parts supplied by a supplier in Delhi.
j) Get part numbers for part supplied by a supplier in Allahabad to a project in Chennai.
k) Get the total number of project supplied by a supplier (say, S1).
l) Get the total quantity of a part (say, P1) supplied by a supplier (say, S1)

Fill in the Blanks

1. _____ is a database query language.
2. _____ Language is used to create or modify database objects (like tables, views, indexes, users, etc).
3. Data type _____ is used to define fixed length strings.
4. _____ statement is used to see a list of all the databases present in MySQL.
5. In SQL, the _____ statement is used to create a table.
6. Once the table is created, we can use the _____ command to see the description of the newly created table.
7. _____ statement is used to add new rows of data in a table that exists in the database.
8. The _____ statement in SQL is used to fetch or retrieve data from one or more tables in the database.
9. _____ statement eliminates duplicate entries while displaying data from the table.
10. The _____ method returns a cursor object which is then used to execute SQL queries.
11. The default username for the MySQL database is _____.
12. To insert multiple rows into the table, _____ method is used.
13. _____ is a read-only attribute and returns the number of rows that were affected by an execute() method.
14. _____ function is used to finalize changes in the database.
15. The GROUP BY statement is often used with _____ functions.

State True or False

1. MySQL is a proprietary software.
2. MySQL can be used only on Windows.
3. MySQL satisfies ACID property.
4. MySQL is a database query language.
5. The server application responds with the requested information that is displayed on the client machine.
6. DDL is used to manipulate data.
7. Char performs faster than varchar.
8. The ALL keyword is used to compare any applicable value in the list.
9. The WHERE clause can be used to retrieve data only from a single table.

10. The ORDER BY clause can be used to sort data according to multiple columns.
11. The primary key must contain NULL values.
12. A table can have only one primary key and the primary key may consist of one or more fields.
13. We can execute a query even after the cursor object is closed.
14. User working as root does not need a password.
15. `fetchone()` method fetches all the rows in a result set.
16. `commit()` method is used to revert the changes made to the database.

Multiple Choice Questions

1. Which data type uses dynamic memory allocation?
   a. `char` b. `varchar` c. `int` d. `float`
2. We cannot _____ data using SQL statements.
   a. delete b. update c. retrieve d. None of these.
3. Which of the following is not an example of a database?
   a. MySQL b. SQL c. PostGres SQL d. SQL Server
4. Which clause is used with SELECT statement to filter the records in the table and fetch only those that meet the specified criteria?
   a. ORDER BY b. WHERE c. DISTINCT d. UPDATE
5. Which SQL statement is used to modify the existing data in a table?
   a. ORDER BY b. WHERE c. INSERT INTO d. UPDATE
6. Which method is used to establish a connection between MySQL database and Python program?
   a. `connect()` b. `cursor()` c. `close()` d. `interface()`
7. Which method is used to close the MySQL database connection?
   a. `connect.close()` b. `connection.close()`
   c. `cursor.close()` d. `db.close()`
8. _____ is the server name or IP address on which MySQL runs.
   a. User name b. Connection name c. Host name d. Database name
9. Which method fetches the next row of a query result set?
   a. `fetch()` b. `fetchone()` c. `fetchnext()` d. `fetchall()`

Answers

Fill in the Blanks

1. SQL
2. Data Definition
3. `char`
4. `show databases;`
5. CREATE TABLE
6. DESC
7. INSERT INTO
8. SELECT
9. SELECT DISTINCT
10. `connection.cursor()`
11. root.
12. `executemany()`
13. rowcount
14. `commit()`
15. aggregate

State True or False

1. False
2. False
3. False
4. False
5. True
6. False
7. True
8. False
9. False
10. True
11. False
12. True
13. False
14. True
15. False
16. False

Multiple Choice Questions

1. b
2. d
3. b
4. b
5. d
6. a
7. b
8. c
9. b